# Athletic Training for Student Assistants

Lorin A. Cartwright, MS, ATC, EMT
*Ann Arbor Pioneer High School*

William A. Pitney, MS, ATC
*Northern Illinois University*

**Human Kinetics**

**Library of Congress Cataloging-in-Publication Data**

Cartwright, Lorin, 1956-
  Athletic training for student assistants / Lorin A. Cartwright,
William A. Pitney.
      p.  cm.
  Includes bibliographical references (p.    ) and index.
  ISBN 0-7360-3622-9
  1. Athletic trainers.   2. Physical education and training.
  I. Pitney, William A., 1965-      II. Title.
  RC1210.C36   1999
  617.1'027--dc21                                      99-21226
                                                         CIP
ISBN: 0-7360-3622-9

**Acquisitions Editor:** Loarn D. Robertson, PhD; **Developmental Editor:** Elaine Mustain; **Assistant Editor:** Melissa Feld; **Copyeditor:** Judy Peterson; **Proofreader:** Sarah Wiseman; **Indexer:** Pilar Wyman; **Graphic Designer:** Nancy Rasmus; **Graphic Artist:** Yvonne Griffith; **Photo Editor:** Clark Brooks; **Cover Designer:** Jack Davis; **Photographer (cover):** Tom Roberts; **Photographer (interior):** Tom Roberts, except where otherwise noted; **Illustrators:** Argosy (computer illustrations), Beth Young (anatomical drawings, except figures 1.2, 1.3, and 11.4 by Katherine Galasyn-Wright), Keith Blomberg (line drawings, except figures 22.4a, 22.4c, 22.4h by Michael Richardson); **Printer:** United Graphics

Printed in the United States of America   10  9  8  7  6  5


**Human Kinetics**
Web site: www.HumanKinetics.com

*United States:* Human Kinetics, P.O. Box 5076, Champaign, IL 61825-5076
800-747-4457
e-mail: humank@hkusa.com

*Canada:* Human Kinetics, 475 Devonshire Road, Unit 100, Windsor, ON N8Y 2L5
800-465-7301 (in Canada only)
e-mail: orders@hkcanada.com

*Europe:* Human Kinetics, 107 Bradford Road, Stanningley
Leeds LS28 6AT, United Kingdom
+44 (0) 113 255 5665
e-mail: hk@hkeurope.com

*Australia:* Human Kinetics, 57A Price Avenue, Lower Mitcham, South Australia 5062
08 8277 1555
e-mail: liahka@senet.com.au

*New Zealand:* Human Kinetics, P.O. Box 105-231, Auckland Central
09-523-3462
e-mail: hkp@ihug.co.nz

To the educators of high school student assistants. You are expanding the knowledge and horizons of future certified athletic trainers.

# Contents

List of Anatomical Drawings     ix

Acknowledgments     x

Introduction     xi

## Unit I    Basics of Human Anatomy and Physiology    1

### Chapter 1    Introduction to Anatomy    3

Objectives • The Anatomical Position • Common Medical Terms of Location • Body Tissues • Classification of Joints • Movement • Summary • Key Terms • Questions for Review • Activities for Reinforcement • Above and Beyond

### Chapter 2    Basics of Tissue Injury    13

Objectives • Soft Tissue Injuries • Bone Injuries • Summary • Key Terms • Questions for Review • Activities for Reinforcement • Above and Beyond

## Unit II    First Aid    21

### Chapter 3    The Crisis Plan    23

Objectives • The Crisis Plan • Summary • Key Terms • Questions for Review • Activities for Reinforcement • Above and Beyond

### Chapter 4    First Aid    29

Objectives • Emergency Procedures and Assessment • Primary Assessment • Breathing Emergencies • Cardiopulmonary Emergencies • Hemorrhage • Communicable Disease Transmission • Summary • Key Terms • Questions for Review • Activities for Reinforcement • Above and Beyond

### Chapter 5    Secondary Procedures    39

Objectives • HIT • Specific Conditions • PRICE • Summary • Key Terms • Questions for Review • Activities for Reinforcement • Above and Beyond

### Chapter 6    First Aid for Environmental Injuries    51

Objectives • Heat-Related Problems • Cold-Related Problems • Severe Weather • Bites and Stings • Summary • Key Terms • Questions for Review • Activities for Reinforcement • Above and Beyond

### Chapter 7   Extrication                                                   59

Objectives • Equipment Removal • Lifting and Moving an Athlete • Summary • Key Terms • Questions for Review • Activities for Reinforcement • Above and Beyond

## Unit III   Understanding Athletics-Related Injuries to the Lower Quarter                                          69

### Chapter 8   Foot, Ankle, and Lower Leg Injuries                           71

Objectives • Anatomy of the Foot, Ankle, and Lower Leg • Preventing Foot, Ankle, and Lower Leg Injuries • Treating Foot, Ankle, and Lower Leg Injuries and Conditions • Summary • Key Terms • Questions for Review • Activities for Reinforcement • Above and Beyond

### Chapter 9   Knee Injuries                                                 79

Objectives • Anatomy of the Knee • Preventing Knee Injuries • Treating Knee Injuries and Conditions • Summary • Key Terms • Questions for Review • Activities for Reinforcement • Above and Beyond

### Chapter 10   Hip, Pelvis, and Thigh Injuries                             87

Objectives • Anatomy of the Hip, Pelvis, and Thigh • Preventing Hip Injuries • Treating Hip, Pelvis, and Thigh Injuries and Conditions • Summary • Key Terms • Questions for Review • Activities for Reinforcement • Above and Beyond

## Unit IV   Understanding Athletics-Related Injuries to the Axial Region                                            93

### Chapter 11   Spinal Injuries                                             95

Objectives • Anatomy of the Spine • Postural Considerations • Preventing Spinal Injuries • Treating Lumbar Spine Injuries and Conditions • Treating Cervical Spine Injuries and Conditions • Summary • Key Terms • Questions for Review • Activities for Reinforcement • Above and Beyond

### Chapter 12   Abdominal Injuries                                          105

Objectives • Anatomy of the Abdomen • Preventing Abdominal Injuries • Treating Abdominal Injuries and Conditions • Summary • Key Terms • Questions for Review • Activities for Reinforcement • Above and Beyond

### Chapter 13   Throat and Thorax Injuries                                  111

Objectives • Anatomy of the Throat • Anatomy of the Thorax • Preventing Throat and Thorax Injuries • Treating Throat Injuries and Conditions • Specific Conditions and Treatment Considerations for the Thorax • Summary • Key Terms • Questions for Review • Activities for Reinforcement • Above and Beyond

### Chapter 14  Head Injuries                                                121

Objectives • Anatomy of the Head • Preventing Head Injuries • Head Injury Mechanisms • Treating Head Injuries • Summary • Key Terms • Questions for Review • Activities for Reinforcement • Above and Beyond

### Chapter 15 Facial Injuries     129

Objectives • Anatomy of the Facial Region • Preventing Facial Injuries • Treating Eye Injuries • Treating Ear Injuries • Treating Nose Injuries • Treating Mouth Injuries • Summary • Key Terms • Questions for Review • Activities for Reinforcement • Above and Beyond

## Unit V   Understanding Athletics-Related Injuries to the Upper Quarter     141

### Chapter 16 Shoulder Injuries     143

Objectives • Anatomy of the Shoulder • Preventing Shoulder Injuries • Treating Shoulder Injuries • Summary • Key Terms • Questions for Review • Activities for Reinforcement • Above and Beyond

### Chapter 17 Elbow Injuries     151

Objectives • Anatomy of the Elbow • Preventing Elbow Injuries • Treating Elbow Injuries and Conditions • Summary • Key Terms • Questions for Review • Activities for Reinforcement • Above and Beyond

### Chapter 18 Wrist and Hand Injuries     159

Objectives • Anatomy of the Wrist and Hand • Preventing Wrist and Hand Injuries • Treating Wrist and Hand Injuries and Conditions • Summary • Key Terms • Questions for Review • Activities for Reinforcement • Above and Beyond

## Unit VI   Preventing Athletics-Related Injuries     165

### Chapter 19 Protective Taping and Wrapping     167

Objectives • Principles of Taping Procedures • Taping Techniques • Elastic Wrapping Techniques • Summary • Key Terms • Questions for Review • Activities for Reinforcement • Above and Beyond

### Chapter 20 Protective Equipment Used in Athletics     181

Objectives • Basic Principles of Protective Equipment • Protective Equipment for the Head and Face • Protective Equipment for the Upper Body • Protective Equipment for the Lower Body • Summary • Key Terms • Questions for Review • Activities for Reinforcement • Above and Beyond

## Unit VII   Rehabilitation and Reconditioning of Athletics-Related Injuries     191

### Chapter 21 Concepts of Rehabilitation     193

Objectives • Assessing the Athlete and Documenting the Findings • Phases of Treatment • Proper Progression • Therapeutic Modalities • Summary • Key Terms • Questions for Review • Activities for Reinforcement • Above and Beyond

### Chapter 22 Reconditioning Programs     209

Objectives • Strength and Conditioning Principles • Types of Movements • Muscular Development Programs • Joint Flexibility • Exercises for Reconditioning Muscles • Cardiovascular Conditioning • A Word on Safety • Summary • Key Terms • Questions for Review • Activities for Reinforcement • Above and Beyond

**Chapter 23  Psychology and Athletic Training**                    **225**

Objectives • Psychology and Athletics • Dealing With the Death of an Athlete • When an Athlete Is Injured • Practical Suggestions • Summary • Key Terms • Questions for Review • Activities for Reinforcement • Above and Beyond

## Unit VIII  Other Athletic Conditions and Concerns          231

**Chapter 24  Conditions and Illnesses**                            **233**

Objectives • Conditions of the Respiratory Tract • Conditions of the Gastrointestinal Tract • Diabetes • Conditions of the Blood and Vascular System • Neurological Conditions • Summary • Key Terms • Questions for Review • Activities for Reinforcement • Above and Beyond

**Chapter 25  Communicable Diseases**                               **241**

Objectives • Defending Against Microorganisms • The Most Common Communicable Diseases • Blood-Borne Conditions • Summary • Key Terms • Questions for Review • Activities for Reinforcement • Above and Beyond

**Chapter 26  Common Drugs Used in Athletics**                      **249**

Objectives • What Is a Drug? • Therapeutic Drugs in Sport • Recreational Drugs • Performance-Enhancing Drugs • Drug Abuse • Drug Testing • Summary • Key Terms • Questions for Review • Activities for Reinforcement • Above and Beyond

**Chapter 27  Nutrition and Weight Control**                        **257**

Objectives • Major Nutrients • Balanced Diet and Portions • Eating Disorders • Athletic Nutrition • Popular Nutritional Supplements • Summary • Key Terms • Questions for Review • Activities for Reinforcement • Above and Beyond

## Unit IX  Professional and Administrative Aspects of Athletic Training          269

**Chapter 28  Athletic Training as a Profession**                   **271**

Objectives • Roles of the Athletic Trainer • Sports Medicine and the Sports Medicine Team • Becoming a Certified Athletic Trainer • Athletic Training Careers • Summary • Key Terms • Questions for Review • Activities for Reinforcement • Above and Beyond

**Chapter 29  Aspects of Administration and Professional Development**          **279**

Objectives • Legal Issues • Avoiding Legal Problems • Preventing Athletic Injuries • Administrative Issues and Documentation • Professional Development • The PREMIER Model for Becoming a Professional • Summary • Key Terms • Questions for Review • Activities for Reinforcement • Above and Beyond

Glossary                                                             293

Resources Used for This Book                                         303

Index                                                                306

About the Authors                                                    316

# Anatomical Drawings

Anatomical planes .............................. 4

General bony anatomy, anterior
view ..................................................... 5

General bony anatomy, posterior
view ..................................................... 6

General superficial muscular
anatomy, anterior view ...................... 8

General superficial muscular
anatomy, posterior view ..................... 9

Bones of the foot ............................... 72

Arches of the foot .............................. 72

Major muscles of the lower leg ......... 73

Ligaments of the foot ........................ 73

Knee, lateral and posterior view ...... 80

Major ligaments of the knee ............. 80

The quadriceps muscles ................... 81

The hamstring muscles ..................... 81

Hip and pelvis, lateral view .............. 88

Hip muscles ........................................ 88

Spine, lateral view ............................ 96

Normal vertebra ................................ 96

Disk cross section ............................. 97

Abdominal quadrants ...................... 106

Anatomy of the throat
and thorax ......................................... 112

Interior of the heart ......................... 113

Major arteries ................................... 113

Bones of the skull ............................ 122

Brain areas and function ................. 122

Facial bones ...................................... 130

Sinuses ............................................... 130

Anatomy of the eye .......................... 130

The ear ............................................... 131

Tooth cross section .......................... 132

Bones, joints, and ligaments of the
shoulder ............................................. 144

Rotator cuff muscles ....................... 144

Elbow, anterior view ........................ 152

Elbow, lateral view .......................... 152

Elbow and wrist musculature ........ 152

# Acknowledgments

- To Stretch and Mary Lou, for your pride in my accomplishments and the encouragement to keep going. You have provided great comfort over the years.
- Rhonda DeLong, Mary Beth Grisdale, Cindy Nordlinger, John Nordlinger, and Anne Solari for reading, and making sense of the things on the original pages.
- Bruce Cartwright, Barb Hansen, and Kathy Kyle for your assistance in typing and references.
- Renee Revis Shingles and Frank Walters for your expertise and encouragement.
- Anne Solari, Chris Moore, and Ann Arbor Pioneer High School students for being preliminary photo models.
- Thanks to Linda Cartwright, Madeline Cartwright, Marieka Cartwright, and Barb Hansen for patience, support, and love throughout the project. You make it easy to come home.

*Lorin A. Cartwright*


- Craig Voll and Phil Voorhis for critiquing and giving suggestions to early portions of this project; Melinda Long for artistic assistance in the early aspects of the project.
- Clayton Corless, Greg Ehlers, Andrea Hein, Gretchen Schlabach, and Phil Voorhis for your uncompromising sense of mission toward athletic training education. The pleasure has been all mine.
- My students at NIU . . . you have taught me more than you will ever know . . . well done, grasshoppers!
- My best friend, my soul mate, my everything—Lisa, for her love and devotion . . . did I ever tell you you're awesome?

*William A. Pitney*


- To our editors at HK: Elaine Mustain, Loarn Robertson, and Melissa Feld for their professionalism and expertise.

*Lorin A. Cartwright and William A. Pitney*

# Introduction

Athletic training is an exciting field of study and a fast-growing profession. Increasingly, high schools are recognizing the advantages of having someone on staff who is highly trained and skilled to deliver health care to athletes. This has prompted many high school students to volunteer to work in the training rooms and learn from athletic trainers by assisting in injury care and prevention, administrative duties, and rehabilitation in closely supervised situations. As a result of their experience, some of these students seriously consider athletic training or another health care field as a profession. This textbook is for the student who needs further training for volunteering in a school's athletic training program or the student who is thinking of going into the area as his or her lifelong work. *Athletic Training for Student Assistants* provides a broad overview of the areas that you can investigate as a volunteer and as a potential professional.

Your most important role is to learn as much as possible. Although you cannot perform many of the tasks of a certified athletic trainer, this text is designed to give you an understanding of what you will observe during your experience in the training room or in a medical profession. In this book, we have addressed the concepts, injuries, and illnesses that we, as certified athletic trainers, have dealt with at the high school level.

The book is divided into nine units:

- Unit I explains basic anatomy and how injured tissue heals.
- Unit II covers first aid, the athletic injury assessments that you will observe on a daily basis, and the emergency procedures that an athletic trainer performs.
- Units III, IV, and V cover the types of injuries that affect athletes.
- The sixth unit discusses injury prevention and focuses on taping and wrapping and protective equipment.
- Unit VII explains how to get an athlete back into action after an injury and discusses psychological considerations that apply to rehabilitation and athletic participation.
- Unit VIII covers many other aspects of athletic training such as drugs, nutrition, conditions and illnesses, and communicable diseases.
- Finally, unit IX gives an overview of athletic training by discussing preparation for professional and administrative aspects of athletic training.

*Athletic Training for Student Assistants* includes several features that will help you throughout the course. We state the objectives for each chapter, at the outset, to help you understand the focus of learning. We have included real-life stories of athletic injuries to illustrate how concepts are applied and to give you a taste of the wide variety of experiences you will have if you become a certified athletic trainer. Each chapter contains a section that asks, "what would you do if . . . ?" These segments are designed to make you consider the factors involved in making a medical decision and may be used to spur class discussions. FYIs (for your information) are used within the chapter to explain information that is necessary for understanding, but that you will not be required to define for exams.

At the end of each chapter are four sections: Key Terms, Questions for Review, Activities for Reinforcement, and Above and Beyond. The key terms are bolded within the text where they are defined and are also listed at the conclusion of each chapter. The questions for review reflect major topics and objectives. Defining the key terms and answering the questions for review will help you check how well you are learning and serve as a review for chapter tests. Activities for reinforcement are just that: recommended hands-on experiences that will enable you to apply the theory in the chapter in practical ways. These activities will both clarify and reinforce the facts and techniques presented in the text. We challenge the student who wants to dig deeper with suggested projects in the Above and Beyond sections.

Using all of these features of the text will help you master the material presented. You will find that not only are you a better assistant for the school's certified athletic trainer, you'll also enjoy your work more. And—who knows?—you may discover your lifelong calling in the process!

# Unit I

# Basics of Human Anatomy and Physiology

# Introduction to Anatomy

## OBJECTIVES

Upon completing this chapter the student will be able to do the following:
- Define the anatomical planes and describe the anatomical position.
- Label general muscular and bony anatomy.
- Describe the functions of skin, bone, muscle, ligament, tendon, and cartilage.
- Describe the types of bones and give examples.
- Describe the classification of joints and explain the types of motion produced.

An understanding of human anatomy is the foundation of many health care professions, including that of the certified athletic trainer, or ATC. An ATC must have an excellent understanding of anatomy in order to determine what structures have been injured; he or she must understand what constitutes normal movements in order to design appropriate rehabilitation and strength and conditioning programs.

## The Anatomical Position

To improve communication between health care professionals and to facilitate a better understanding of human movement, medical professionals have accepted a particular alignment of the body as standard. Called the **anatomical position**, it refers to an erect stance, arms at the sides and palms facing forward. The body moves in relation to three planes: **frontal**, **sagittal**, and **transverse**. These can be seen in figure 1.1 on the next page.

## Common Medical Terms of Location

You will need to know several common medical terms that help health care providers explain to one another where an injury is located on the body. There are many different terms, and it is beyond our scope to offer all of them here. Instead, we will present the

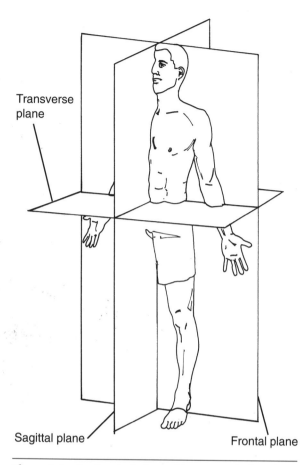

Transverse plane

Sagittal plane

Frontal plane

**Figure 1.1** Anatomical planes. The anatomical position refers to a standing alignment with the arms at the sides and the palms of the hands facing forward. Note the planes that slice through the body.

most common ones that an ATC would use in the training room. For instance, you will hear the terms *anterior, posterior, medial, lateral, proximal,* and *distal.* These terms are all used in reference to the anatomical position.

- **Anterior** refers to the front of the body. When you face an athlete, you are looking at the athlete's anterior aspect. If you were to read an injury report stating that an athlete was hit at the anterior aspect of the lower leg, you would know that the front of the leg was injured.

- **Posterior** refers to the back of the body. When you watch an athlete walk away from you, you are looking at his posterior aspect. If an athlete indicates that the back of her knee hurts, the ATC would report that the posterior aspect of the knee was injured.

- The terms **medial** and **lateral** are defined in relation to the sagittal plane, shown in figure 1.1. This imaginary line that divides the body into left and right halves is also called the midline of the body. If a body part faces the midline it is said to be medial, and if it is closer to the midline than a different body part, it is said to be more medial. Thus, when you look at the side of an athlete's calf that faces the other leg, you are looking at the medial aspect. On the other hand, if a body part is located away from the midline it is said to be lateral, and if it is farther from the midline than another part, it is more lateral. Thus, when you look at the side of an athlete's calf that faces out, you are looking at the lateral aspect; your left ear is lateral to your left eye.

- **Proximal** means towards an attachment, such as where a limb attaches to the trunk of the body. Thus, the shoulder is proximal to the elbow, and the hip is proximal to the knee.

- **Distal** means away from an attachment. The knee is distal to the hip. A fingertip joint is distal; one at the base is proximal.

## Body Tissues

Athletics-related injuries typically involve injuries to the skin, bones, cartilage, muscles, tendons, and ligaments. Before we can understand the specific injuries that occur to these tissues, we must first understand the basic function of these structures.

## Skin

Skin is the outermost surface of the body. It is the first line of defense against external forces such as insects, air, dirt, bacteria, and blows. The skin keeps bodily fluids in, it picks up sensations, and it secretes an oily substance. The skin is made up of several layers; skin cells do not divide rapidly, so several layers are helpful for continuation of proper body function. If one layer is scraped off, the next layer becomes the exterior. A break in the skin is a wound.

Skin has the ability to expand, for example, skin expands to accommodate an increase in muscle **girth** (the distance around a body part) from weightlifting. Stretch marks are lines on the skin where it was stretched excessively until elastic fibers ruptured. If the athlete loses girth, the skin will recover to a small extent.

## Bones

Bones have three primary functions.

1. They protect vital organs and structures from trauma. Consider the brain. It is packaged in a hard shell (the skull) filled with fluid (cerebral spinal fluid), which helps to help absorb shock and protect the brain. Similarly, the lungs and heart are surrounded by the rib cage, which supports and protects them.

2. Bones are the stiff structures that are acted on by muscles to create movement.

3. Bones are metabolically active; that is, they produce blood cells and store minerals such as calcium and phosphorus.

Bones also protect the nerves and blood vessels that travel alongside them.

The human body has approximately 206 bones and an astounding number of muscles. The skeleton is categorized into the **axial skeleton**, which includes the bones of the spine, thorax, and skull, and the **appendicular skeleton**, which includes the bones of the extremities. While we will discuss specific bones in more detail in later chapters, here we present a general discussion of bony anatomy, bone types, and joint classification. See figure 1.2, a-b for a look at the bones of the body.

Bones come in several shapes and sizes, including long (like the femur), short (like the

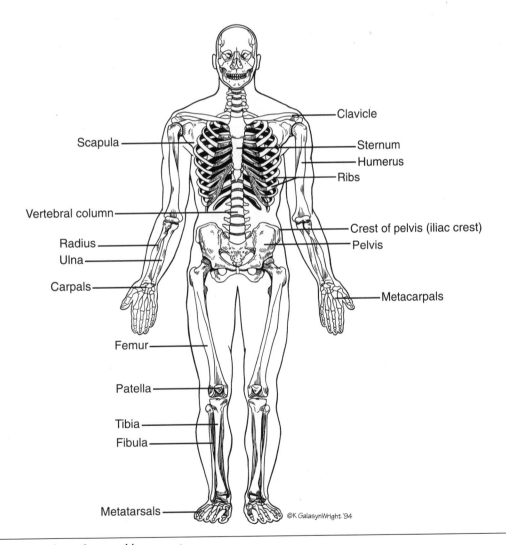

Scapula

Clavicle

Sternum

Humerus

Ribs

Vertebral column

Crest of pelvis (iliac crest)

Pelvis

Radius

Ulna

Carpals

Metacarpals

Femur

Patella

Tibia

Fibula

Metatarsals

©K GalasynWright '94

**Figure 1.2a**   Anterior view of general bony anatomy.

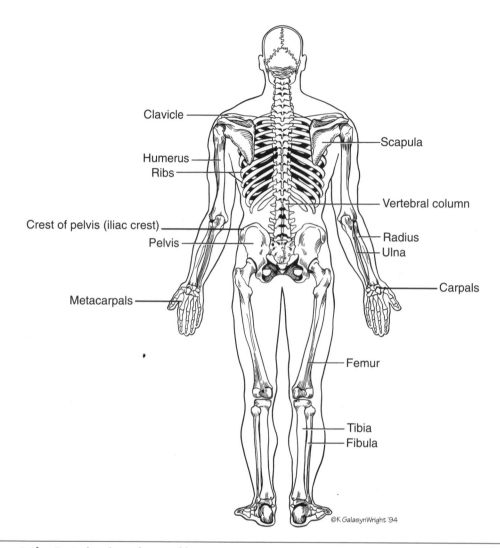

Clavicle

Scapula

Humerus
Ribs

Vertebral column

Crest of pelvis (iliac crest)
Pelvis

Radius
Ulna

Carpals

Metacarpals

Femur

Tibia
Fibula

©K GalasynWright '94

**Figure 1.2b** Posterior view of general bony anatomy.

metacarpal), flat (like the scapula) and irregular (like the vertebra). Long bones possess an interesting feature. At the end of each long bone is an area where growth primarily takes place; this area is called an **epiphysis,** or growth plate. The area is somewhat spongy during adolescence and can be problematic for the adolescent athlete. The ATC working in a high school setting should know that these growth plates are vulnerable to injury—a bone will often fracture at the growth plate.

## Cartilage

Cartilage covers the ends of long bones and can be found between bones. While there are differ-ent types of cartilage, it typically functions to join structures (for example, the ribs and sternum), absorb shock, and permit smooth bone movement.

## Muscles, Tendons, and Ligaments

Muscle contractions allow the body to accelerate, decelerate, stop movement, and help to maintain normal postural alignment. Moreover, they produce heat. Ligaments and tendons are both composed of connective tissue. **Tendons** attach muscle to bone and transmit the force that a muscle exerts. **Ligaments** connect bones together and help to form joints.

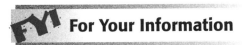

# Classification of Joints

There are three classifications of joints:

- Diarthrodial
- Amphiarthrodial
- Synarthrodial

**Diarthrodial joints** are also known as synovial joints. They have fantastic mobility and consist of a **joint capsule** (a sleevelike ligament that surrounds the entire joint), a **synovial membrane** (a slick lining on the inside of the capsule), **hyaline cartilage** (a thin layer of cushioning at the ends of the bones), and ligaments. Diarthrodial joints are divided into several types, including hinge and multiaxial joints. Examples of **hinge joints** are the elbow and knee; they move back and forth like a hinge on a door. Examples of **multiaxial joints** are the hip and shoulder. These joints can be moved in multiple directions (along many axes). The shoulder and hip joints are also commonly referred to as **ball-and-socket joints**; that is, the end of the long bone is rounded like a ball and is set into a cuplike socket of the other bone. Generally, these joints have a great deal of mobility as compared to other joints.

**Amphiarthrodial joints** are those that have cartilage attaching two bones together. They are also known as cartilaginous joints. An example of an amphiarthrodial joint is found where the ribs join the sternum. **Synarthrodial joints** are also called **fibrous joints**. These joints are held together by tough connective tissue, and the joints are basically immovable. This type of joint joins the bones of the skull and the tibia and fibula in the lower leg.

# Movement

Without muscles, the body could not move. An understanding of general muscular anatomy is essential for proper assessment of an athletic injury and proper rehabilitation following an injury. Therefore, an ATC must learn where muscles are located and what actions they perform. Figure 1.3, a-b illustrate the muscles located just underneath the skin. We will talk more about specific muscles in later chapters.

As muscles contract and produce movement, bony segments are moved in specific directions. Movement results from the angle at which the muscle pulls on the segment and the type of joint that joins the bones. Directional terms most commonly used by ATCs and other medical professionals are *flexion* and *extension*, *abduction* and *adduction*, *pronation* and *supination*, *inversion* and *eversion*, *protraction* and *retraction*, *rotation*, and *circumduction* (figure 1.4 on page 10 illustrates all of these movements). They are discussed below:

- **Flexion** of a hinge joint is the bending of the joint. The anatomical position (elbows and knees straight) shows those joints in **extension**. However, hinge joints like the knee, elbow, fingers, and toes are not the only ones capable of flexing and extending. The shoulder, neck, trunk, hip, and wrist also flex and extend.

- Movement of a body segment away from the midline (the line of the sagittal plane) is termed **abduction**. For example, moving one leg outward from the anatomical position is abduction of the hip. Subsequently returning it toward the midline is termed **adduction**.

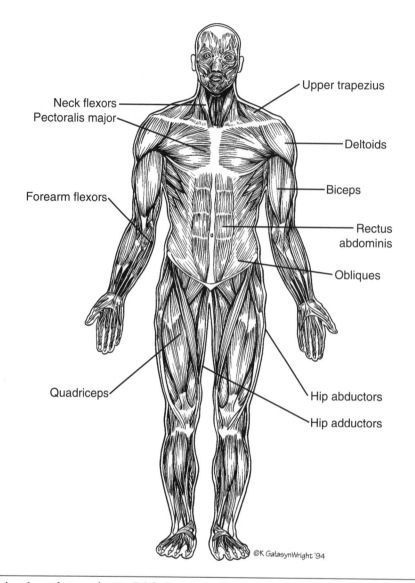

**Figure 1.3a** Anterior view of general superficial muscular anatomy.

• **Pronation** and **supination** occur at the wrist and ankle. At the wrist, for example, if you turned your palm toward the sky as though you were going to hold a bowl of soup, you would be supinating your wrist (soup-n-ation!). Conversely, turning your wrist so the palm faces the ground, as if you were pouring out the bowl of soup, would be pronation. In the anatomical position the wrist is supinated.

• **Inversion** and **eversion** of the ankle can be seen in figure 1.4. Inversion occurs when the sole of the foot is turned inward, and eversion is when the sole of the foot is turned outward.

• **Protraction** occurs when a segment glides forward, as when the lower jaw pushes outward until the chin sticks out. **Retraction** is gliding a segment backward, as when the scapulae squeeze together.

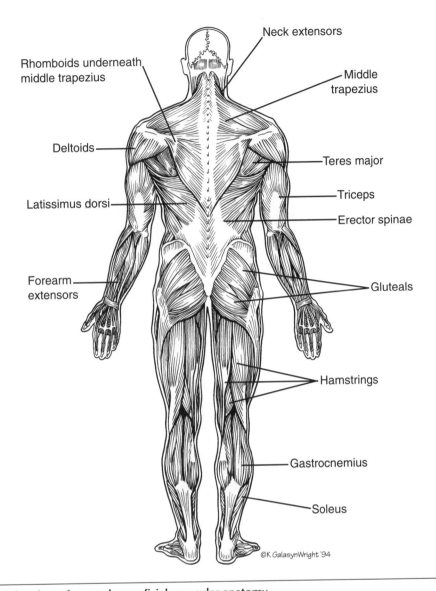

Neck extensors

Rhomboids underneath
middle trapezius

Middle
trapezius

Deltoids

Teres major

Triceps

Latissimus dorsi

Erector spinae

Forearm
extensors

Gluteals

Hamstrings

Gastrocnemius

Soleus

©K GalasynWright '94

**Figure 1.3b**   Posterior view of general superficial muscular anatomy.

• **Rotation** occurs when a bony segment (or series of segments) spins or turns on an axis. An example of rotation is turning your head to look over your shoulder.

• **Circumduction** occurs when a ball-and-socket joint, such as the shoulder or hip, encompasses several directions with one movement. In so doing, the joint is moved in a circular fashion around its axis.

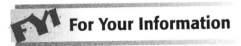 **For Your Information**

### Axis

An axis is an imaginary line around which a segment such as an arm or leg will rotate. For example, if you flex your hip (bring your knee toward your chest), you can say that the axis of motion is where the thigh (femur) joins the hip (pelvis).

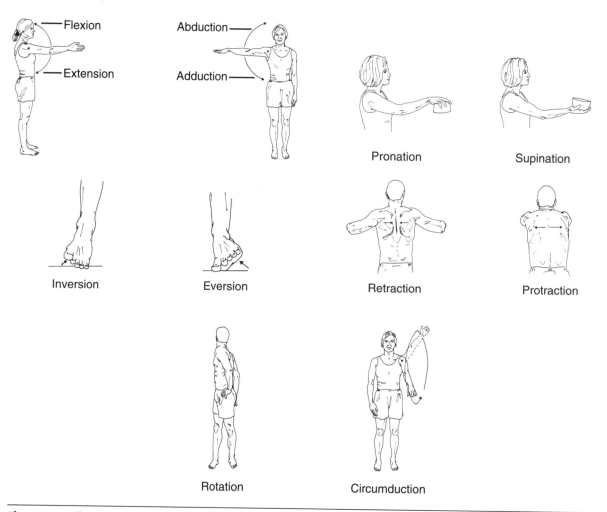

**Figure 1.4** Illustrations of directional terms most commonly used by ATCs.

## 🌐 The Real World

As an athletic trainer, I have had the opportunity to work with a great number of physicians who come regularly to our school to evaluate injured athletes. I will typically examine the athlete before the physician arrives in order to give the doctor some good information about how the athlete was injured and to brief him or her on the problem. One afternoon I told our team physician that an athlete was having pain at the 4th lumbar vertebra in his low back. After his examination, the team physician felt we should get an X ray of the spine to make sure there wasn't a fracture. The physician thought, however, that the pain was at the 3d lumbar vertebra. I found it odd that we disagreed about which vertebra was injured. After receiving the X rays, we found two interesting facts—the athlete did not have a fracture, but he did have a rare, extra vertebra in his spine. Given the circumstances, we agreed that we were both right about which vertebra was involved!

Anonymous

## Summary

Understanding basic human anatomy is essential for understanding athletic injuries. The ATC will use precise medical terminology when talking of a body area, and the student assistant should be familiar with this terminology in order to understand exactly what the ATC is discussing. The body is made up of several tissue types: skin, cartilage, bone, ligaments, tendons, and muscle. Bones come in a variety of shapes and sizes. A joint is a point of contact between bones, and joint structure determines the type of movement possible. Muscles move the bones through the planes of the body. The ligaments, cartilage, and tendons help hold the joints together and produce smooth movement.

## Key Terms

Define the following terms found in this chapter:

| | | |
|---|---|---|
| abduction | extension | posterior |
| adduction | fibrous joints | pronation |
| amphiarthrodial joint | flexion | protraction |
| anatomical position | frontal plane | proximal |
| anterior | girth | retraction |
| appendicular skeleton | hinge joint | rotation |
| axial skeleton | hyaline cartilage | sagittal plane |
| ball-and-socket joint | inversion | supination |
| circumduction | joint capsule | synarthrodial joints |
| diarthrodial joints | lateral | synovial membrane |
| distal | ligaments | tendons |
| epiphysis | medial | transverse plane |
| eversion | multiaxial joint | |

## Questions for Review

1. What are the three anatomical planes of the body? pp. 3-4
2. How does the function of a ligament differ from that of a tendon? p. 6
3. Give two examples each of a long bone, an irregular bone, and a flat bone in the body. pp. 5-6
4. Describe a synovial joint and give two examples. p. 7

## Activities for Reinforcement

1. Working with a partner, move each joint through its various positions, and give the proper term for each movement.
2. Point to a body part, and have your partner name it. Include muscle groups and bones.
3. Working with a partner, point to a body part and have the other person describe its location using medical terminology. For example, when you point to the

forearm, your partner might state that the location is proximal to the wrist and distal to the elbow.

4. Using an anatomical chart, identify each of the major bones of the body.

## Above and Beyond

Those students who are interested in learning more detailed anatomy can investigate the readings suggested below:

Anthony, C.P., and G.A. Thibodeau. 1983. *Textbook of anatomy and physiology.* St. Louis: Mosby.

Seeley, R.R., T.D. Stephens, and P. Tate. 1992. *Anatomy and physiology.* 2d ed. St. Louis: Mosby Year Book.

Templin, J.M. 1992. *Anatomy and physiology laboratory manual.* 2d ed. St. Louis: Mosby Year Book.

# Basics of Tissue Injury

## OBJECTIVES

Upon completing this chapter the student will be able to do the following:
- Explain the various types of soft tissue injuries.
- Explain tissue repair and healing.
- Explain the various bone injuries.
- Explain bone repair and healing.

The body is made up of a variety of different tissues, each of which has unique characteristics and functions. In this chapter we discuss the various body tissues, in both healthy and injured states.

## Soft Tissue Injuries

Soft tissue injuries, often called wounds, are commonplace in athletics. When a tissue is injured it may bleed, become inflamed, or produce extra fluid. The chart on page 14 describes different types of wounds.

**Sprains** and **strains** are wounds that bleed internally, which may cause a fluid buildup. Sprains are injuries to ligaments—the strong pieces of tissue that hold adjoining bones together. A strain is an injury to a muscle or tendon. A tendon attaches a muscle to a bone and transmits the force that a muscle exerts.

Sprains and strains are categorized in order of severity as first-, second-, or third-degree injuries. If there is no loss of motion in the injured body part, the sprain or strain is first degree. If there is some loss of motion, the injury is second degree. If the athlete cannot move the body part, the injury is third degree.

Another soft tissue that can be injured is a nerve. Nerve tissue connects the brain and spinal cord with all of the parts of the body. Nerves transmit the sensations of touch, pain, hot, and cold; they relay messages from the brain to signal a muscle to contract or relax. Therefore, when a nerve is injured the athlete may experience a lack of sensation and even of movement. A stretched nerve can send a message of extreme pain. An injury to a nerve takes a long time to heal, and if the damage is severe, it will not heal.

## Incision

An incision is an open wound made by a cutting object such as a scalpel. It is rarely seen in athletics.

## Abrasion

An abrasion results from scraping off a layer of skin. It may or may not bleed, depending on its depth. A base runner in softball or baseball may acquire an abrasion when sliding into a base.

## Contusion

A contusion is a closed wound, commonly called a bruise. It bleeds under the skin, which can cause swelling and discoloration. An athlete receives a contusion from running into something, for example, when an athlete's eye runs into another person's elbow.

## Laceration

A laceration is a jagged, irregular open wound created by a noncutting object such as a steel pole or a wall. For example, a lacrosse player who runs into the goalpost may receive a laceration.

## Avulsion

An avulsion is a partial tearing away of a body part. An avulsion of a finger may occur if one catches a ring on the basketball hoop when dunking a basketball.

## Amputation

An amputation is an open wound in which a part is completely cut away from the body. Cutting off a finger with an ice skate is an example of an amputation.

## Puncture

A puncture wound occurs when a pointed object enters the body—stepping on a nail, for example. Puncture wounds do not bleed much, so they are more likely to become infected than freely bleeding wounds.

## Contrecoup

A contrecoup injury occurs on the opposite side of the initial injury. This usually occurs in the brain when the head hits against an unyielding object or surface. The impact to the back of the head, for example, forces the brain against the anterior part of the skull resulting in a contrecoup injury.

## Stages of Soft Tissue Healing

When soft tissue is injured, it progresses through three stages of healing: acute inflammatory, repair, and remodeling. We will describe each stage in the following sections.

• **Stage I: Acute inflammatory**. When a body part is injured, cells within the area die, not only from being ripped apart, but also from being cut off from their food and oxygen supply. In the acute inflammatory stage, an increased flow of blood to the injured area brings cells and chemicals to begin the healing process. **Phagocytes** are specialized cells that engulf and eat up the dead cells. **Leukocytes** are infection-fighting white blood cells. **Platelets** carry blood-clotting materials. The acute stage lasts for about two days after the initial injury.

• **Stage II: Repair.** The injured area has now been filled with the blood, cells, and chemicals to rebuild the area to as near normal as possible. The **fibroblasts** (fiber-building cells) begin building fibers across the area of injury. Fibroblasts form the scar, which takes from six weeks to as long as three months, depending on the extent of the injury.

• **Stage III: Remodeling.** Remodeling takes up to a year or more to accomplish. It is the body's way of building tissue strength in the tendons, ligaments, and muscles to withstand the stress applied to the body during activity.

## Healing Time

In general, the greater the injury to the tissue, the longer the healing time—it depends on the degree of the injury, the location of and blood supply to the injury, and the age of the athlete. If blood supply to an area is poor, such as in the eyeball, the healing process will take longer. Other factors that will significantly slow the healing process are poor nutrition, illnesses like diabetes, medications (like corticosteroids), and infections. Some athletes believe that eating certain foods will hasten healing, but no research supports this.

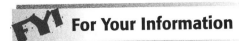 **For Your Information**

### Corticosteroids

Corticosteroids are chemicals made in the body that help reduce inflammation. When an injury occurs, a synthetic corticosteroid may be used as a medication to help reduce inflammation, but it can also increase the healing time.

### Skin closures

A skin closure is a thin, tough piece of material that can bring together the edges of the wound and close a deep wound effectively. A skin closure may also be called a butterfly.

One complication of healing is scar tissue, if more tissue is laid down than is necessary to repair the wound. Excessive scar tissue can delay healing time. Some scar tissue forms deep within joints, and it may have to be surgically removed so that proper movement can occur.

Large wounds, whose edges are far apart, take longer to heal. Keeping the wounds closed with stitches or skin closures will help the healing.

If activity is resumed too soon after an injury, healing time will be longer because the early activity can cause more cellular injury. Although athletes are always anxious to get back to playing, the ATC must use good judgment early in the healing process to insure proper healing of the injury.

# Bone Injuries

Athletic trainers must be familiar with the types of bone injuries and their stages of healing.

## Types of Bone Injuries

Dislocations and fractures are common athletic injuries. Why do bones break? How much force must be applied before a bone will break? The answers to these questions vary depending upon the athlete, where the force is applied, the bone type, the body position, and so forth.

### Dislocation

When bones come together at a joint they are said to **articulate**. A **dislocation** occurs when a significant force displaces bone so that the two bone ends in the same joint no longer line up. A dislocation can also cause avulsion fractures (see chart), strains, sprains, disruption of blood flow, and disruption of nerve conduction. Dislocations present with deformity and pain and are not easily moved. Dislocations are cared for by the team physician and are not put back in place by the ATC.

### Fractures

The amount of energy required to cause a **fracture**—a broken bone—is called the **failure point**. Failure points vary with the athlete, age, and bone structure. For example, an athlete with osteoporosis will have a lower failure point than an athlete with healthy bones.

Fractures are named according to the type of impact and how failure of the bone occurs; for example, we say a bone has been broken, cracked, or chipped, or we may say it has a hairline fracture. All of these terms mean that the bone has been compromised and weakened. With any fracture injury the athlete will be in a splint or cast for six to eight weeks, which is the amount of time required for proper healing. However, some fractures can be splinted, and the athlete can resume participation immediately. A student assistant should be familiar with the types of fractures described in the following chart.

## Types of Fractures

### Avulsion

An avulsion occurs when a ligament or tendon pulls so hard at its bony attachment that a portion of the bone is torn away. Avulsion fractures are common with sprains, strains, and dislocations.

### Stress

A stress fracture, also known as a fatigue fracture, occurs in a bone that has been subjected to a repetitive stress. The athlete will complain of a persistent sore spot over the bone. Stress fractures are microscopic and cannot be viewed on an X ray.

### Spiral

A torsional force along the length of a bone causes a spiral fracture. Imagine that you are in-line skating and you are not very good—if your foot moves to the right while the rest of your body goes to the left, the stress may cause a spiral fracture. On an X ray, the spiral fracture looks like the stripe on a candy cane.

### Longitudinal

A longitudinal fracture runs the length of a bone; it is usually caused by an impact. A pole-vaulter who misses the mat and lands on her feet is likely to suffer a longitudinal fracture.

### Compression

A compression fracture occurs when opposing forces are applied to a bone from both ends at the same time. Compression fractures often occur in the spine. For example, a compression fracture may result when an athlete lands on his feet or buttocks from a height. The impact from the ground is one force, and the weight of the falling body is the other. The opposing forces cause the compression fracture in the vertebrae.

## Oblique

Imagine a diagonal line across a bone from one side to another. You have just visualized an oblique fracture. An oblique fracture in a weight-bearing bone, such as a leg bone, takes longer to heal because the diagonal angle of the bone ends makes it easy for the bones to move out of alignment, even in a cast.

## Comminuted

When a bone is crushed into smaller pieces, we say that it is comminuted—think of a baseball catcher whose bare hand is hit by a bat.

## Greenstick

Adolescents' and children's bones are soft; that is, their bones still have some of the properties of cartilage. These bones tend to bend and fracture only partway through—this is known as a greenstick fracture.

## Transverse

A fracture that travels across a bone, perpendicular to that bone, is called transverse. Transverse fractures occur from impacts perpendicular to that bone. A lacrosse player who comes down with his stick across another player's forearms can cause a transverse fracture.

## Depressed

A depressed fracture usually occurs from a direct impact to the skull, which, naturally rounded, indents. This indentation is called a depression.

## Blowout

A blowout fracture occurs when an eye is pushed hard backwards and down into the eye socket. The small bones under the eye are crushed and embedded into the muscles of the eye. A blowout can occur when a hard object like a baseball strikes the eye.

## Pathological

A disease process like a bone tumor can weaken the bones so that a little stress will cause a fracture. Improper nutrition and eating disorders are the most common causes of pathologic fractures among teenage athletes. The bones weaken because minerals are taken from them to support vital functions.

## Epiphyseal

The area of a bone where bone growth occurs, the epiphysis, is susceptible to fracture because the bony tissue is stronger than the epiphysis. In adolescents and children many epiphyseal fractures occur, especially in the long bones. Adults do not get epiphyseal fractures because their growth areas are closed; that is, they do not have active growth centers. An X ray will not reveal a fracture of the epiphysis because epiphyses are clear on film.

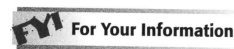

## For Your Information

### Deformity

Deformity refers to a misalignment of a body part.

### Team physician

The team physician is the medical authority of the sports medicine team. The doctor's role is to work with the athletic trainer to oversee the entire sports medicine team.

### Osteoporosis

Osteoporosis is a condition in which bones are porous and fragile, caused in a young person by lack of calcium in the diet or by the body's inability to absorb minerals, especially calcium.

### Osteogenesis

The process of laying down new bone, which provides a thickening of the bony structure, is known as osteogenesis. Bone cells are called osteocytes: a bone-forming cell is an osteoblast; a cell involved in bone resorption is called an osteoclast. As an athlete grows, osteoblasts replace cartilage and form bone tissue by laying down a new layer on the outside of bones. Osteoclasts "eat" at the interior layer of the bone. This normal process allows bone growth, it removes older bone cells, and it helps control the weight of a bony structure.

### Cartilage

Cartilage is a tissue found at the ends of long bones and between bones that absorbs shock and permits smooth bone movement at joints.

## Bone Fracture Healing

Like soft tissue injuries, bone fractures go through the acute, repair, and remodeling stages of healing.

• **Stage I: Acute.** An injury to the bone causes the bone to break, and bleeding occurs in the area. Osteoclasts begin to "eat" the debris or resorb it into the body. Osteoblasts begin to add new layers to the outside of the bone tissue. This continues for about four days.

• **Stage II: Repair.** During the repair stage osteoclasts and osteoblasts continue to regenerate the bone. A bony splint, called a fibrous **callus**, forms. The fibrous callus, which extends both internally and externally to hold the bone ends together, is transformed into a sleeve of hard callus bone. The process of transforming callus to bone begins at about week three and continues for three months. In most cases, after six weeks in a cast the fracture is strong enough to allow participation with protection, and the athlete is able to return to competition. However, the athlete must remember that the healing process is far from complete.

• **Stage III: Remodeling.** Stage III takes several years to complete. During this phase the callus is reabsorbed and replaced with a fibrous cord of bone that is formed around the fracture site. Growth of this fibrous cord of bone can be stimulated through surgically implanted electrodes when the bones are not healing. Bones contain minerals that have an electrical charge, and adding electrical stimulation increases the layering of the bone. If a bone never heals, it is referred to as a **nonunion** fracture. A nonunion fracture in a weight-bearing bone, such as a leg, means that the athlete will not walk. A common nonunion fracture of the wrist occurs in the scaphoid bone. Such a fracture is painful and may lead to arthritis and inability to move the wrist.

## What Would You Do If...

An athlete who has had a contusion under his toenail notices that the nail is pulling away from the nail bed. He says the nail is getting stuck on his sock. He has heard that pulling the nail off will make the new nail grow faster. He hands you a pair of pliers and asks you to pull it off.

## The Real World

While working in a physician's clinic, I had an opportunity to work with diabetic patients. A common symptom exhibited by diabetics is that it takes longer for their wounds to heal than it does for people without diabetes. One physician with whom I worked found that applying low amounts of electrical current to diabetics' wounds helped them heal faster. For example, one of his patients had an open wound (an ulcer) on her foot. He ran a controlled amount of current into the patient's foot and would take a picture after each session in order to document the healing process. He found that the healing time was much faster when he used the electrical current than when he used more traditional forms of treatment.

John Robinson, ATC

## Summary

The body can get injured and, being a miraculous thing, repair itself. Indications of an injury to soft or bony tissue most commonly include pain, swelling, and bleeding. A soft tissue injury may keep an athlete sidelined for longer than it takes a broken bone to heal. Healing a fractured bone requires making new bone and fibers and reabsorbing the injured bone tissue. Healing time depends upon the athlete's health at the time of injury and the care given during the healing process.

## Key Terms

Define the following terms found in this chapter:

| | | | |
|---|---|---|---|
| articulate | failure point | leukocytes | platelets |
| callus | fibroblasts | nonunion | sprain |
| dislocation | fracture | phagocytes | strain |

## Questions for Review

1. Make a list of the various types of fractures and determine who is most likely to suffer from each (i.e., adolescent, adult, male, or female), and why. pp. 16-17
2. What is the difference between a sprain and a strain? p. 13
3. How is a first-, second-, or third-degree sprain or strain defined? p. 13
4. Name the stages of soft tissue healing and describe what happens in each one. p. 15
5. Name the stages of bone healing and describe what occurs during each one. p. 18
6. What is the typical healing time for a fracture? pp. 16, 18

## Activities for Reinforcement

1. Gather pictures of various wounds.
2. Have a physician demonstrate closing wounds with stitches and butterflies.
3. Make a picture showing how tissue repair and healing occur.
4. Make a picture showing how bone repair and healing occur.

## Above and Beyond

1. Using the following materials, write a report about the healing process and some of the procedures that may enhance it.

   Arnheim, D.D. 1989. *Modern principles of athletic training.* St. Louis: Times Mirror/Mosby.

   McCulloch, J.M., L.C. Kloth, and J.A. Feedar. 1995. *Wound healing: Alternatives in management.* 2d ed. Philadelphia: Davis.

2. Interview a local physician. Determine when and why he or she uses certain materials to cast different fractures.

# Unit II
# First Aid

# The Crisis Plan

**CHAPTER**

**3**

## OBJECTIVES

Upon completing this chapter the student will be able to do the following:
- Design a basic crisis plan.
- Understand the role of the student assistant during a crisis.

There will be times when you, as a student assistant, have to help a coach or athletic trainer care for a seriously injured athlete. To be sure that the sports medicine team and coaches will perform to the best of their ability, it is necessary to have a crisis plan before the emergency happens. In this chapter we focus on what should be planned for in the event of an emergency and how a student can help.

## The Crisis Plan

The **crisis plan** will enable the central **sports medicine team** to cope with emergency situations. It should be shared with all school personnel and the emergency medical responders (athletic trainers, team physician, coaches, school nurse, and all emergency medical services). Practice this plan in all facilities and parts of the building on a regular basis and anticipate possible problems that can arise with different circumstances and personnel.

Most often the athletic trainer deals with a controlled situation and the crisis plan is very simple. The plan becomes intricate when there are serious injuries. The sports medicine team, prior to any emergency, should answer the following questions:

1. **Who is in charge of assessing an injury and beginning first aid until the proper help arrives?** In order, the person in charge is (1) the team physician, (2) the athletic trainer, (3) the coach, and (4) the person with the most training in first aid and CPR. Do not delay rendering care while waiting for the athletic trainer to arrive. A student assistant who is certified in first aid and cardiopulmonary resuscitation can begin giving care until a better-trained person takes over. Once the team physician or athletic trainer arrives the initial person at the scene should give a full account of what has been done, and then be ready to perform other duties as assigned.

2. **Are both an emergency phone number and money for a pay phone, available?** Emergency phone numbers change when the team travels to away games. It is important

to confirm the numbers before the start of a game—do not wait until something happens. Some athletic trainers tape the money for an emergency phone call inside their training kits. If the trainer uses a cellular phone, the battery must be charged and the bill must be paid on time. If the telephone service is cut off, how will help get to the injured athlete? It is also important to have home and work phone contacts for all parents.

3. **Who will call for an ambulance?** It is best to have someone who is not directly responsible for giving care or getting supplies call the ambulance. To ensure that the caller does not panic and gives the right information, copy the "Emergency Telephone Contacts" form on page 25, and keep the list readily available for that person to use. The ideal order of people who should call for an ambulance goes as follows: coach, student assistant, and athletic director.

4. **Who will control the crowd?** It is best to have someone who is not directly responsible for giving care or getting supplies control the crowd. It is very difficult for those giving care if people are hovering over them. The noncaregivers need to be moved away. On the field, the team captains must take charge and move the team away. If possible, the team should practice or play on another field while care is being given, so they will not, in their concern for their friend, get in the way of the caregivers. A coach, student, game supervisor, or athletic director usually is available to control the crowd. Parents should be allowed to talk with their injured son or daughter, and someone should be prepared to give them support, drive them to the hospital, or remove them from the scene if necessary.

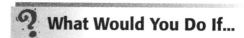

## ? What Would You Do If...

A football player has suffered a head injury. At the scene, you are asked to locate the parent. Upon arriving at the sideline the parent becomes argumentative saying, "There is nothing wrong. I came all this way to watch the game, put the boy back in!" Then the parent says to the son, "Why did you let that player do that to you? Are you drunk?"

## ? What Would You Do If...

At a gymnastics meet an athlete loses control, flies off the high bar, and lands on his back. The athletic trainer does an assessment and determines he could have a spinal cord injury. You are instructed to call 911. A person comes out of the crowd and stops you, saying, "There is nothing wrong with the athlete." Would you call? Would you wait? Would you try to facilitate dialogue?

5. **Who will bring supplies and equipment, and what supplies are needed?** Be sure that the supplies in the training kits, golf carts, splint bags, and so forth are always stocked and the equipment is in proper working order. If the athletic trainer or coach receives a report of an injured athlete while she is in the training room, before leaving for the accident site, she should grab the things most likely to be needed—most often a walkie-talkie or cellular phone, training kit, ice, and crutches. If the mishap has taken place on a field, having a student assistant who can read the universal signals that tell what equipment to bring out to the injured athlete can save valuable time (figure 3.1). If the trainer discovers on her arrival at the accident scene that she needs more equipment than she has brought, she can simply signal that assistant, who is stationed within sight but as close to the training room as possible, to bring whatever is necessary.

6. **Who will transport or assist the athlete from the field of play?** Sometimes an athlete is too severely injured to move. We will discuss these situations in chapter 7. But most often the injured athlete can be moved, and the athletic trainer can assist him from the field, perhaps with a golf cart, stretcher, or crutches. If the athlete is too tall or too heavy for the athletic trainer to assist alone, the trainer can recruit a couple of athletes and direct them in how to get their injured teammate to the sideline. If the injured athlete is taken to the hospital, someone from the school must travel with him. This person can be the athletic director, a coach, or an athletic trainer. If the injured athlete in need of the ambulance is from an opposing team, the

## Emergency Telephone Contacts

| Agency | Information |
|---|---|
| **Ambulance** | 1. Give your name and title.<br>2. Give the address and exact location of the injured.<br>3. Give the nature of the injury and what you need.<br>4. Tell them what is being done for the injured and the qualifications of the person giving care.<br>5. Give the telephone number from which you are calling.<br>6. Give the nearest crossroads.<br>7. Tell them how many athletes are injured.<br>8. Do not hang up first. |

After the call is completed, be sure to have someone waiting at the door to escort the emergency medical technician to the athlete. Document the time of the telephone call.

| | |
|---|---|
| **Hospital emergency room** | 1. Give your name and title.<br>2. Give the reason for your call (be specific about the injury).<br>3. Estimate the time of arrival of the injured. |
| **Parents** | 1. Give your name and title.<br>2. Document the name of the parent you spoke to and the time.<br>3. Use the athlete's name and tell the parents what the athlete was doing when she was injured.<br>4. Tell them what body part was injured and how it is being treated.<br>5. Give the exact location of the athlete and directions to that location so her parents can find her.<br>6. Tell the parents what you think is needed.<br>7. Ask which physician or hospital should be involved.<br>8. Ask how to transport the injured athlete.<br>9. Give them the training room phone number in case they need to call. |

*Source:* American National Red Cross (1973, 1987), American Red Cross (1988, 1993), and Campbell (1988).

visiting coach is responsible for contacting the athlete's parents. Be sure that both the athletic director and principal of the school know who has been sent to what hospital, because they will get phone calls from people who are concerned about the athlete.

7. **What is the safest and easiest access to the area of the injured athlete for the emergency services to use?** The area around the injured athlete should be clear of materials, cars, and so forth, and any locks barring access to the area should be unlocked.

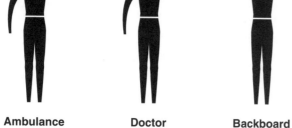

Ambulance    Doctor    Backboard

Neck injury    Training kit    Splints

**Figure 3.1** Sideline signals. The athletic trainer can use sideline signals so that prompt care of the athlete can occur. The student athletic assistant will read the signals of the athletic trainer and jump into action, getting equipment, the team physician, or calling for help.

8. **Who will direct the emergency services to the injured athlete?** A coach, student, or athletic director usually is available to direct an ambulance to the area. A person should be stationed at every possible point where the ambulance might approach the scene, and each of these people should be instructed in the proper technique for signaling and guiding the emergency vehicle.

9. **Who will notify the parents that their daughter has been injured?** It is always best to

## Items Needed in an Emergency

Walkie-talkie or cellular phone
Training kit
Ice
Crutches

let the athlete herself call and tell her parents that she has been injured. If she is in no condition to call, it is best to have the athletic trainer, coach, or team physician do so, as long as the athlete's care is not compromised. Ask the athlete who is best to talk with in the family (the person who will remain calm and be able to make medical decisions). The caller will tell that person what happened, what is being done, and who is caring for the athlete. He will find out which hospital is preferred by the family and will tell the parents where to meet emergency personnel. The ATC should see to it that an emergency card, which gives emergency personnel permission to treat each athlete, is with every athletic team at all times.

10. **If more than one athlete is injured, what area will be used to sort the severity of injuries, and how will athletes get to this facility?** Most often the area where decisions are made about which injuries must be treated first (also known as the "triage area") is the training room or nurse's office. There may be times when the normal **triage** facilities are not available (fire, locked doors), so an alternative must be set up and its location communicated. Communication is essential. Make sure everyone on the emergency team has a walkie-talkie with charged batteries. Getting people who are hurt to the triage site may not be an easy task, especially if the injuries have occurred in an area that is difficult to reach because of locked doors and no keys, multiple stairways, or remoteness. Plan ahead of time for the best way to move the injured: wheelchairs, crutches, a backboard, stretcher, an executive chair with wheels, or whatever is available.

11. **What personnel are available in the event of a mass casualty?** How many faculty members, coaches, or students have been trained in first aid and CPR? Who can assist? If they are not on campus can they be reached to help? At the beginning of the school year a seminar should be held to train all faculty in first aid and CPR techniques. Get a list of those faculty members who want to be a part of the emergency medical responders team. Decide who will be responsible for first aid kits, flashlights (in the event electricity goes out), the crisis plan, and first aid care for each area of the building. It is important to have people in charge of the section of the building where they normally work. There may

be times when there will be no outside access to parts of the building, for example, in the case of an explosion; therefore, you will need people inside that know what to do.

12. **Who will make out an accident report form and get statements from other witnesses?** It is best to have someone document what is being done as it is going on.

13. **How will the emergency medical response team work around known obstacles?** Try to anticipate obstacles that will be fairly common in an emergency situation: cars obstructing a driveway, stairways, pools, a poisonous gas, locked doors, smoke, no lights, no phone, foul weather, equipment failure, communication problems, lots of injuries and no help, and so forth. Deal with each of these obstacles and any others you can think of, in the plan. If the plan is to remove an athlete from the field by a golf cart, and it is snowing and the golf cart will not go, be prepared with an alternative plan. Make sure all the people in the response team have keys to the areas they will be responsible for. Everyone should have access to a walkie-talkie and a lantern.

14. **How will the crisis plan change for each facility (pool, gym, outdoors, games vs. practice, ski hill, ice arena)?** Make sure there are people who are capable of performing the crisis plan in each facility for which the response team is responsible.

15. **How will the various facilities be evacuated?** An evacuation is a difficult situation because there are generally spectators who know nothing about the facility. Within the building, evacuation instructions should be posted in every room. The outdoors must be evacuated when lightning storms, tornadoes, or hurricanes are headed into the area. The evacuation plan should include the site where each team should go for protection and accounting purposes. Have practice evacuations so that everyone becomes familiar with the procedures.

16. **What should be done if someone forgets what to do?** The crisis plan should be made available to all members of the emergency medical response team and coaching staff. Since all of the members on the team have walkie-talkies, if someone forgets what to do another member can read the plan page by page and assist in getting through the plan.

 **The Real World**

One of the rules in cross-country is never touch a runner, even if she appears hurt, unless it is absolutely clear that she will not be able to finish the race anyway; otherwise you will disqualify her. We had spent a long day working a cross-country meet. The last race of the day was a combined boys and girls middle school race. I was responsible for an area on an uphill slope. As a young girl approached the hill, she began to cry. I encouraged her to keep going. Instead, she lay down on the grass and kept crying. I again encouraged her to get up and finish the race. She just lay there. Suddenly she stopped crying and appeared to have fallen to sleep. I stood next to her and tried to elicit a response by talking to her. She did not respond. At this point I had to touch her. I checked her breathing and heartbeat, and everything was normal. I radioed to our central location to try to get more information. Her coach didn't know if the girl had any illness that would put her in this condition. The coach was on her way to us, when the girl's grandmother arrived. The grandmother stated that she was a nurse, and the girl would be fine with more air. Suddenly the anxious woman slapped her grandchild across the face so hard her head rocked. Then she began giving the girl mouth-to-mouth breathing. I radioed for help, but before anyone else arrived, the girl became conscious and walked away with her grandmother. I never saw her again. To this day I wish I had had the authority to intervene, and I still wonder if the girl was ill or if she just hated running.

Anonymous

17. **Who should talk to the press?** The school system normally designates who will give information to the press and to the members of the faculty and student body. Let the information person give the facts to the press. An in-school fact sheet can be given to all staff members, to keep rumors to a minimum.

18. **Who will give counseling to those who need it?** School counselors are usually designated to help with counseling. Most situations do not require counseling, but often it is helpful to talk over a situation and review what happened.

## Summary

To be the best athletic trainer, coach, or student assistant, it is important to have a crisis plan, good evaluation skills, and good treatment skills. The crisis plan has 18 parts, which, when complete, will make caregivers more effective. Once the plan is designed, it is critical to practice it. Practice will prepare the caregivers and help them foresee many problems. The student assistant can help by being trained to fill a role in the crisis team and by obtaining first aid and cardiopulmonary resuscitation training.

## Key Terms

Define the following terms found in this chapter:

crisis plan          sports medicine team          triage

## Questions for Review

1. Why is a crisis plan important? p. 23
2. Who should be included in a crisis plan? p. 23
3. What types of things can a student do in the event of a crisis? pp. 23-27

## Activities for Reinforcement

1. With another student, design a crisis plan for an athletic facility on the day of an event.
2. Design a crisis plan and go through a practice drill.
3. Make a list of the people on the athletic training team. Determine who will do each of the following: give first aid, call the ambulance, get first aid supplies, keep the crowd back, direct the ambulance, and call the parent or guardian.

## Above and Beyond

1. Using the following textbook, design a crisis plan for a large arena.
   American Red Cross. 1996. *Responding to emergencies.* 2d ed. St. Louis: Mosby-Lifeline.

# First Aid

## OBJECTIVES

Upon completing this chapter the student will be able to do the following:
- Explain the difference between primary and secondary assessment.
- Explain the difference between signs and symptoms.
- Explain the ABC's of a life-threatening emergency.
- Define the procedure used to restart breathing once it has stopped.
- Explain the types of illnesses or injuries that cause breathing and the heart to stop.
- Explain when cardiopulmonary resuscitation is used.
- Explain how external bleeding is controlled.
- Explain what precautions can be taken to prevent the exchange of bodily fluids.

Athletes who become injured or ill trust the ATC, coach, team physician, and student assistant to render appropriate care, which is called first aid. In this chapter, we discuss first aid for life-threatening injuries. In subsequent chapters we will cover many of the routine athletic injuries and their care.

## Emergency Procedures and Assessment

An athletic trainer can begin emergency procedures only after determining the problem. Taking care of an athlete who is injured or ill is like putting together the pieces of a puzzle. The athletic trainer takes all of the pieces of information gathered during an assessment—the mechanism of injury, a history, primary assessment, secondary assessment, and vital signs—and completes the puzzle to determine what is going on with the athlete.

In the unusual case that the athletic trainer is working with unfamiliar athletes, he should begin with an introduction. Next, it is important to ask permission to treat an athlete, although, in most cases, the athletes are teenagers and cannot refuse treatment because of the policies that many school districts and states have about who can refuse treatment. In addition, it is customary for parents to sign waivers to allow treatment in their absence. However, if a parent of an injured teenager has refused to give permission to treat, then no treatment should be given. In that case it is important for the athletic trainer to document the refusal of permission to treat by having the athlete sign the

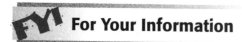

## For Your Information

### Secondary Assessment

The secondary assessment is an evaluation of injuries that are not life threatening.

### Unconscious

An athlete who does not respond to touch or to voice commands is considered to be unconscious. An athlete who is unconscious will lose the ability to move and speak, but she may still be able to hear and to think.

---

refusal in front of a witness. A refusal for treatment is rare but must be followed.

When investigating an athlete's injuries, the athletic trainer will ask her questions and observe her for signs and symptoms. A **sign** is objective evidence that a rescuer can measure or sense, like sweating, breath odor, temperature, blood pressure, breathing rate, or heart rate. A **symptom** cannot be seen, smelled, or heard; it is subjective evidence of what the athlete feels. Examples of symptoms are pain, nausea, and anxiety. The ATC must talk to the athlete throughout the assessment process, as a way of reassuring the athlete; and she may be less anxious if someone is talking to her. The last sense to be impaired by unconsciousness is hearing, so the ATC will continue talking to the athlete at all times. Even if the athlete is unconscious, talking to her is helpful.

## Primary Assessment

The assessment of each injury is divided into two categories, primary and secondary. The **primary assessment** deals with those injuries that are life threatening, injuries involving the ABC's—**A**irway, **B**reathing, and **C**irculation. The secondary assessment involves all non–life-threatening injuries. Luckily, most athletic injuries are not life threatening.

The order in which the assessment is done is crucial to ensuring that the injuries that are life threatening will be cared for first. The primary assessment is done in the following order: (1) assess responsiveness by lightly tapping or shaking (not so hard that the neck gets twisted or jostled) and talking to the athlete, (2) open the

## Life-Threatening Injuries

1. Respiratory arrest (breathing has stopped)
2. Cardiac arrest (heart has stopped)
3. Internal bleeding
4. Shock
5. Burns
6. Heat-related illness
7. Cold-related illness
8. Asthma attack
9. Diabetic emergency
10. Drowning
11. Electrocution
12. Falls from heights
13. Poisoning
14. Severe bleeding
15. Anything else that causes breathing or cardiac impairment

*Sources:* American Academy of Orthopedic Surgeons (1991), American Red Cross (1993), Anderson and Hall (1995).

---

airway, (3) assess breathing, (4) check the pulse, and (5) check for severe bleeding. The student assistant should become certified in first aid and CPR so that when an emergency happens, she will be better prepared to help.

## Determining Responsiveness

The first step is to determine whether an athlete is conscious and able to respond. To check responsiveness, the athletic trainer will gently talk to and tap the athlete.

An unconscious athlete may be able to hear the athletic trainer or first aider and may be able to respond to a voice, if he does not have a severe head injury. The response may be no more than a squeeze of a hand, but even such a feeble sign is an indication that the athlete is hearing and reacting. No one near the athlete should talk harmfully about the athlete when he is unconscious because he may be able to hear. Reasons for unconsciousness include poisoning, respiratory arrest, cardiac arrest, hemorrhaging, diabetic illness, heat-related illness, cold-related illness, and head injury.

**For Your Information**

### Conscious

A conscious athlete is one who quickly responds to outside stimuli such as talking, tapping, or shouting and is aware of his environment.

### Respiratory Arrest

An athlete in respiratory arrest has stopped breathing.

### Diabetic Illness

Diabetic illness is a disease of the body in which sugar is not metabolized properly. The chemical, insulin, which helps break down sugar, may be lacking, or the tissues may have a resistance to the insulin that is present.

If an athlete is able to respond clearly and logically to the responsiveness check, the ATC will know that there is airway, breathing, and circulation. At that point in the primary assessment the athletic trainer can skip the ABC's (numbers 2–4 in the primary assessment) and proceed to check for severe bleeding.

## The ABC's

The **ABC's** are critical in determining if the respiratory and the circulatory systems are functioning normally. If either system is impaired, the athlete's life is in danger, and the ATC must respond quickly to give the athlete the best chance for survival.

• **Airway.** The first priority is to make sure the airway is open. To do so, the athletic trainer will place one hand on the athlete's forehead

 **What Would You Do If...**

You are a spectator at a soccer game. The temperature is cool. A parent who is videotaping the game is pale and sweating. The man's wife, who knows that you are a student assistant, asks you to take a look at her husband. You check his pulse. It's so rapid you cannot count that fast. The man insists there is nothing wrong with him. The athletic trainer is on the sideline, watching the game.

and two fingers of the other hand under the athlete's chin. Simultaneously lifting the chin upward while controlling the head will open the airway by pulling the tongue away from the back of the throat.

• **Breathing.** To check breathing, we use a technique called look, listen, and feel. The athletic trainer will *look* at the chest and watch for the chest to rise and fall, *listen* for breathing by placing an ear close to the mouth, and *feel* for "hot" breath on his cheek. It is easy to overreact in an emergency situation, and the athletic trainer must take his time and be sure of what he can see, feel, and hear. If the athlete is able to breathe, the ATC will determine the number of breaths per minute.

• **Circulation.** The ATC will determine the status of circulation by taking a pulse. A pulse is an indication that the heart is beating. The pulse is best checked in the carotid artery, which is located next to the Adam's apple in the groove toward the side of the neck. He will check the pulse for at least ten seconds to make sure of what he is feeling. This initial check is to determine the presence of a pulse, not the rate. If there is no pulse, the heart has stopped; and the athlete needs cardiopulmonary resuscitation. (The student assistant may notice blood spurting, a steady heavy flow of blood, or blood pooling. This type of bleeding is considered severe and is an emergency that requires immediate attention from the athletic trainer or first aider.)

## Breathing Emergencies

Any situation in which breathing has stopped or is compromised is considered life threatening. Breathing emergencies can involve any part of the respiratory system, and the compromise of any part of the respiratory system can cause death. Direct traumas, such as rupture of the diaphragm or punctured lungs, anaphylaxis, or an illness like asthma can cause a breathing emergency. Drowning, suffocation, or an airway obstruction can cause an athlete to stop breathing. If the brain does not receive oxygen, cells begin to die. The longer the brain is without oxygen, the greater the number of cells that die; then whole portions of the brain die, eventually causing the death of the athlete. As little as four

 **For Your Information**

### Diaphragm

The diaphragm is the muscle that separates the chest and abdominal cavities and assists in breathing.

### Asthma

Asthma is a condition in which the air passages narrow in response to an allergy. The allergen can be pollen, dust, or mold; exercise may also trigger an attack. The air passage may close entirely.

### Anaphylaxis

Anaphylaxis is an allergic reaction in which the air passages narrow in response to a foreign protein, such as bee venom, or to a drug, such as medication to which the person has been sensitized.

### Blood Pressure

Blood pressure is the pressure exerted against the walls of the vessels by the blood as it moves through them. The blood pressure of an average teenager is 110-120 systolic (when the heart beats) and 65-80 diastolic (when the heart is relaxed, between beats).

### Hyperventilation

Hyperventilation is rapid and deep breathing consisting of 24 breaths or more per minute.

## Signs and Symptoms That Require the Emergency Medical System (911)

1. Athlete is unconscious at any time (this athlete is placed on his side)
2. Athlete is having trouble breathing, or breathing has stopped
3. Athlete is dizzy or light-headed
4. Athlete has bleeding that will not stop
5. Athlete has pain or pressure in the abdomen
6. Athlete vomits, passes, or coughs blood
7. Athlete has fallen from a height
8. Athlete has possible head, neck, or back injuries
9. Athlete has lost sensation or cannot move extremities
10. Athlete has seizures, regardless of history
11. Athlete has been poisoned
12. Athlete has chest pain or heartbeat has stopped
13. The amount of care necessary is beyond the ATC's ability
14. Athlete has broken bones, false movement, or crepitus (see page 44)
15. Athlete has slurred speech
16. Athlete has difficulty remembering things
17. Athlete has loss of pulse in an extremity

*Sources:* American Academy of Orthopedic Surgeons (1991), American Red Cross (1993), Anderson and Hall (1995).

minutes without oxygen can cause permanent brain damage. The sooner lifesaving efforts can begin, the better the chances are that the athlete will survive without brain injury. Most often the emergency medical system (EMS) will have a response team to the location within four to ten minutes. If proper care begins immediately, the chances of survival are 98 percent. If proper care is delayed by four minutes after breathing has stopped, the chances of survival are significantly reduced.

## Mouth-to-Mouth Breathing

In mouth-to-mouth breathing, which is also known as rescue breathing, the ATC places his mouth over the injured athlete's mouth and exhales into the athlete's lungs. After giving a breath the ATC will always turn his head and look at the athlete's chest. This not only helps the ATC see if the athlete has begun to breathe but also slows him down so that he does not hyperventilate. Placing one's mouth on another's mouth or nose can transmit some diseases, and several devices are available that act as a barrier between the athletic trainer and the injured person. At least one of these devices should be a part of every emergency kit.

## Obstructed Airway

An athlete's airway can become obstructed in a number of ways, but the tongue is the number one airway obstructer. In an unconscious athlete, especially one lying on her back, the tongue likely will relax and obstruct the air passage. Other possible obstructions are food, gum, mouth guards, broken teeth, blood, vomit, and

## ❓ What Would You Do If...

In the cafeteria a student tells a joke and another begins to cough forcefully just after laughing. The student continues to cough, her face is turning red, and tears are rolling down her cheeks. The athletes next to you say, "She is choking. Do something!"

chewing tobacco. (To prevent airway obstruction, we recommend barring food, gum, and chewing tobacco from practices and games.) A conscious athlete with an obstructed airway will grab at his throat. If the athlete is unconscious, the athletic trainer will have to open his airway, check his breathing, and actually begin giving breaths before discovering that there is an airway obstruction. An airway obstruction may be partial or total.

### Partial Airway Obstruction

A **partial airway obstruction** occurs when an object covers the air passage but does allow some air to flow in and out of the lungs. The athlete will grab for his throat—the **universal choking sign**—as an indication that he has an air passage problem (see figure 4.1). To determine if this obstruction is partial or total, the ATC will ask him if he can speak, cough, or breathe. If he can, he has a partial airway obstruction. An athlete who has a high-pitched whistling noise coming from his throat has a total airway obstruction.

### Total Airway Obstruction

A **total airway obstruction** occurs when an object blocks the entire air passage and does not allow enough air to flow into the lungs for the athlete to take a breath. Under such conditions, the athlete may have a high-pitched whistling noise coming from his throat, which comes from a small amount of air, but not enough to sustain life, pushing past the object in his throat. A conscious athlete will demonstrate the universal choking sign. He will show redness of the face and tearing.

## Other Breathing Emergencies

Illnesses such as asthma that cause a breathing emergency can most often be dealt with by elevating the athlete's head and, when appro-

**Figure 4.1** The universal choking sign. Placing the hands upon the throat is an indication of choking.

priate, helping the athlete take her medication. A punctured lung must be cared for in a different manner, which we will cover later in the textbook.

## Cardiopulmonary Emergencies

There are two cardiopulmonary emergencies that concern the athletic trainer: heart attack and cardiac arrest. Both are life-threatening emergencies that must be dealt with immediately.

## Heart Attack

A **heart attack** occurs when the heart muscle is damaged by blockage of a vessel to the heart, a clot, stress over a period of time, or an injury to the heart muscle itself. A student assistant may think, "I am going to work with healthy young athletes, so I will probably not have to know much about heart attacks." However, we urge those students to consider the people in the stands and the athlete who was not properly diagnosed and who may have heart problems.

## What Would You Do If...

The star female track athlete is doing some pre-season sprints to get into shape. She suddenly drops to the ground and is not moving. When you arrive, you see she is not breathing, and you cannot find a heartbeat. Your friends say you must be mistaken. The athlete is only 15 years old. You check again—no breathing and no heartbeat.

The student assistant may be the one called upon to help a heart attack victim.

Signs of a heart attack are breathing difficulty, shortness of breath, breathing faster than normal, a pulse rate that is faster or slower than normal or irregular, skin that is pale or bluish, profuse sweating, vomiting, sudden unexplained fainting (**syncope**), and elevated blood pressure. Symptoms of a heart attack include nausea, persistent chest pain or discomfort that is not relieved by rest or by changing positions, anxiety, a general feeling of weakness, and light-headedness.

The victim often describes a feeling of someone standing on or tightening a belt around his chest. This crushing chest pain is medically named **angina pectoris**. It is common for people to be embarrassed by a chest pain if it turns out there is nothing wrong. Many people having heart attacks die because they do not go to the hospital, thinking they have nothing more than an upset stomach. It is better to go to the hospital, and let the experts rule out a heart attack, than it is to die or have irreparable heart damage.

The treatment of a heart attack begins with recognizing that a heart attack is occurring. The athletic trainer must assess the athlete quickly and get help.

## Cardiac Arrest

A **cardiac arrest** occurs when the damage to the heart muscle is so severe that the heart stops beating. If the damage is too severe, lifesaving measures will not start the heart again. This, however, is a determination that an athletic trainer cannot make—he must treat the cardiac arrest whether he thinks the damage is severe or not.

If an athlete is in cardiac arrest, the athletic trainer must begin treatment immediately to save the athlete's life. He will place the athlete on a hard flat surface and begin giving CPR (see figure 4.2). An ambulance must be called because professional medical care is critical for the survival of the athlete.

Unfortunately, an ATC can rarely restart the heart by performing CPR; it will probably be necessary to stimulate the heart by electrical shock or injected medication. Nonetheless, the ATC must start CPR to circulate the athlete's blood and provide oxygen to his brain.

# Hemorrhage

A hemorrhage is a discharge of blood, externally or internally, that may be severe enough to cause death. The average adult has 6 quarts of

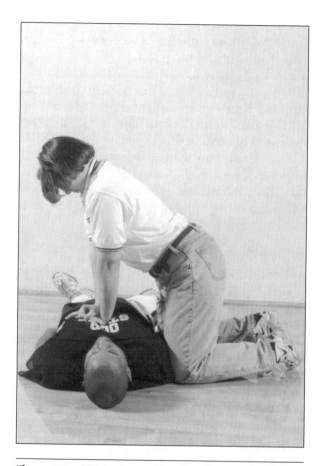

**Figure 4.2** CPR is given to a person who is not breathing and who has no heartbeat. The ATC will administer 15 compressions and two breaths. For effective compressions, the shoulders of the ATC must be over the sternum of the victim.

## The Real World

I was sitting in the training room doing some paper work with a senior student assistant. I looked up to see a football player being helped into the doorway. He was staggering, and he was a bloody mess—he had fallen into a glass door. I immediately dialed 911, and I told him to lie down and elevate his legs because I could see that he was showing signs of shock and hysteria. He was holding his wrists—each had a deep cut, down to the tendons. He had a third severe laceration—about a two-and-a-half-inch gash across his forehead. I put on gloves and grabbed a pole of gauze. I applied direct pressure on the forehead and to the worst of the two wrist lacerations.

Then things got complicated. I literally had my hands full, so my student assistant (a first responder) gloved up to help me. I thought, "This will be a great experience for her." As she was standing next to me putting on her gloves, she said, "I'm going to faint." Before I could tell her to sit down, she did faint, striking her head on the floor. She had a petit mal seizure caused by the bump. I could see she was breathing, so I kept my pressure on the wounds, kept an eye on her, and basically waited for the police and paramedics to arrive. It was quite the scene. The other athletes in the area were kind of freaked out. Everything turned out okay, though. We got the bloody football player bandaged and off to the emergency room where they stitched him up. My embarrassed assistant just ended up icing the large lump on the back of her head.

Steve Marti, ATC

## For Your Information

**Elevate**

Elevate means to lift up.

**Bandage**

A bandage is a strip of cloth used to hold gauze in place.

and chest, have a greater blood supply than other areas and therefore may bleed profusely. A large pool of blood indicates that the athlete has suffered a severe blood loss. The ATC must act immediately, or the athlete could die.

To control bleeding, the athletic trainer will following the procedures below in order:

1. Apply **direct pressure** to the wound, using a hand to squeeze the area tightly.

2. Elevate the body part—but only if no fractures are present and direct pressure has not slowed the bleeding.

3. Apply a pressure bandage when bleeding is controlled or if another injured athlete needs care.

4. Apply pressure to a **pressure point**. This will slow blood flow to the extremity but will not stop it entirely. Use this measure only if all the other measures fail.

Internal bleeding must be dealt with by a physician. The ATC will call for the ambulance. We will discuss the signs and symptoms of internal bleeding in the next chapter.

# Communicable Disease Transmission

When dealing with bleeding wounds, the ATC must protect herself and the athlete from infection. We tend to assume that athletes are free from communicable diseases because they look and act healthy, but this is not necessarily true.

## Why Take Precautions?

An athlete may hide certain medical conditions to avoid discrimination. If an athlete chooses to reveal such a condition, it should be noted on the physical.

blood, and the loss of 10 percent of that can result in death.

## External Bleeding

External bleeding occurs when a person suffers a laceration, incision, amputation, avulsion, puncture, or abrasion (see page 14). If the blood is spurting from a wound, an artery has been cut. Blood that is flowing rapidly, but not spurting, is most likely from a vein.

## Control of Bleeding

The body's blood-clotting mechanism easily controls most bleeding. However, some areas of the body, such as the head, abdomen, thighs,

Communicable diseases are transmitted, either directly or indirectly, by contact with an infected person. Although most viruses and bacteria cannot live long in the absence of a host, the ATC and the athletes should take sensible precautions against possible infections. They should make it a habit not to share drinking glasses or towels, and they should avoid "sneezers" as much as possible. Some viruses, namely HIV and HBV (the viruses that cause AIDS and hepatitis B, respectively), may be present in bodily fluids from oozing wounds or fluids removed by a needle. Thus, the athletic training team should take precautions when handling any body fluids or when handling cloth, paper, or surfaces that have been soaked with body fluids (i.e., blood, urine).

## What Precautions Are Needed?

Special precautions must be taken against the spread of HIV and HBV, which may be present in blood or other bodily fluids. Every staff member of the school, not only the athletic staff, should be trained in **universal precautions** to prevent the spread of the blood-borne diseases. A person with HIV or hepatitis B may show no signs or symptoms of the disease and may not even know she has the disease, yet the disease may be transmitted through contact with her blood. Therefore, universal precautions must be used every time blood is present. To take universal precautions, five simple rules must be observed: (1) Carefully wash your hands after any and all contact with an injured athlete. (2) Use rubber gloves to create a barrier between you and the athlete. Figure 4.3 illustrates how to properly remove gloves. (3) Thoroughly clean any tables, counters, or playing surfaces in an athletic training room or court with a disinfectant such as a 1:10 bleach and water solution. (4) Deposit in a red biohazard bag any material, including clothes, gloves, or gauze pads, that is contaminated to the point where bodily fluids drip when the item is squeezed. (5) Dispose of any needles or syringes used by a team physician in a specially made sharps container.

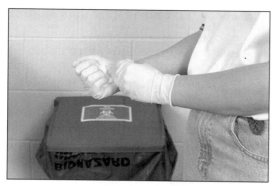

a

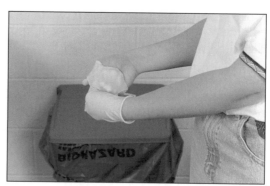

b

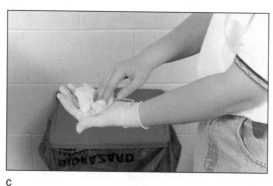

c

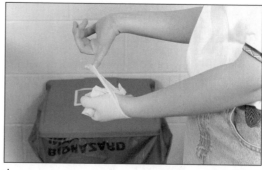

d

**Figure 4.3** Glove removal. When removing latex gloves (a) place all waste in one hand and with the opposite pinch the latex near the wrist, (b) pull the first glove off with the waste inside the glove, (c) place the first glove into the second hand, (d) slide a finger under the inside edge of the second glove and pull the glove off. Discard the gloves into a biohazard container.

Athletes should observe other standard precautions, which, for example, will help to prevent the spread of common cold and flu viruses. The ATC should not allow players to dip their cups into a team cooler to get water; this practice allows saliva to be mixed into the cooler. Every athlete should drink from his or her own glass or squeeze bottle. Athletes should avoid tasting each other's food, borrowing utensils, and sharing drinking glasses. They should also avoid sharing personal items such as combs, towels, and clothes, and they should shower after each practice.

## Summary

An injured athlete must be assessed immediately so that prudent care can begin. The ATC will assess the athlete for life-threatening injuries first: he will check the ABC's, the athlete's airway, breathing, and circulation. An athlete who has no ABC's needs immediate care and emergency medical services. Everyone, including the ATC, coach, and student assistant, needs to observe universal precautions when working with the bodily fluids of an athlete.

## Key Terms

Define the following terms found in this chapter:

| | | |
|---|---|---|
| ABC's | heart attack | symptom |
| angina pectoris | partial airway obstruction | syncope |
| cardiac arrest | pressure point | total airway obstruction |
| CPR | primary assessment | universal choking sign |
| direct pressure | sign | universal precautions |

## Questions for Review

1. What are the ABC's? pp. 30-31
2. What is the most common airway obstruction? p. 32
3. How can an athletic trainer prevent the exchange of bodily fluids between the athlete and herself? p. 36
4. What medical conditions or illnesses would cause the heart to stop beating? p. 33
5. What method(s) are used to provide oxygen to the body of an athlete who is not breathing? pp. 32, 34

## Activities for Reinforcement

1. Take a class in first aid and cardiopulmonary resuscitation and become certified.
2. Invite the local emergency medical service to demonstrate CPR and electrical monitoring of the heart.

## Above and Beyond

1. Read the appropriate sections in the following textbooks, and give a presentation on the person who is most likely to suffer a heart attack and how one could be prevented.

American Red Cross. 1996. *Responding to emergencies.* 2d ed. St. Louis: Mosby-Lifeline.

American Red Cross. 1993. *Community first aid & safety*. St. Louis: Mosby-Lifeline.

American Red Cross. 1993. *CPR for the professional rescuer.* St. Louis: Mosby-Lifeline.

2. Determine which cardiac and pulmonary conditions cannot be helped by using CPR. What are the reasons for the failure of CPR in each instance?

# Secondary Procedures

CHAPTER

5

## OBJECTIVES

Upon completing this chapter the student will be able to do the following:
- Ask the basic questions for obtaining the history of an injury or illness.
- List the common vital signs, and explain how they help identify an injury or illness.
- Determine whether an injury can cause shock.
- Describe the procedures that the athletic trainer uses when testing an athlete's injury.

The athletic trainer performs a secondary assessment after she has completed the primary survey and taken care of any life-threatening injuries. In the secondary assessment she will check, in the following order, history, head, vital signs, both arms, chest, abdomen, hips, and both legs. If at any time during the secondary assessment the airway, breathing, or circulation changes, the ATC will immediately give care and abandon the secondary assessment.

## HIT

Most of the time an athletic trainer is dealing with a specific complaint like "my thumb hurts." When he is doing an assessment on a specific body area he uses the **HIT** technique (see figure 5.1). HIT stands for **H**istory, **I**nspection, and **T**esting. The trainer takes a history to gather information about the situation and the injury. Inspection is a visual examination of the body part. Testing includes touching, specific evaluations, checking the range of motion, and neurological testing. We will use the HIT technique throughout this text.

### History

Taking a history includes both asking questions and checking vital signs.

**H** History—Take a history by asking questions and checking vital signs.

**I** Inspection—Observe the surroundings and injured body part.

**T** Testing—Do specific testing to determine the severity of injury.

**Figure 5.1** Athletic injury assessment follows a predictable sequence: taking a **H**istory, **I**nspecting the area, and **T**esting.

## Questions

In taking a **history**, the athletic trainer will obtain information about what is happening and information about the athlete's previous injuries and illnesses because they may play a role in the present problem (see "Questions for History of Injury"). If the athlete is unconscious, reviewing her physical and talking to other athletes who may have seen the injury may be helpful.

The ATC will check the athlete for a medical alert tag and the physical for information that may help determine the cause of the current condition. The same questions can be used to take a history for any injury and illness. We will refer to the "Questions for History of Injury" in the following chapters, so the student should copy the list and keep it handy. Questions that apply to a specific body area will be listed in the appropriate chapter.

## Vital Signs

The **vital signs** checked in the secondary assessment are body temperature, skin color, breathing rate, heart rate, response to pain, pupillary reaction, ability to move, and capillary refill. The ATC can also assess breath sounds and blood pressure if a stethoscope and blood pressure cuff are available.

### Heart Rate

**Heart rate** is measured at **pulse points**, where an artery lies close to the skin. The pulse points of the carotid artery and the radial artery are used most often. The carotid artery can be found by placing two fingers on the Adam's apple and then sliding them toward the shoulder until the fingers go into a depression in the neck. The radial artery is located on the volar

---

## Questions for History of Injury

The following questions should be asked as a part of the history:

1. What happened?
2. When did it happen?
3. Has this happened before?
4. Where was the pain initially?
5. Did you hear or feel a pop, snap, crack, slip, or give?
6. Were you able to continue participating?
7. How soon did it swell?
8. Does it feel unstable?
9. What relieves the pain?
10. How severe is the pain?
11. What does the pain feel like?
12. What treatment was applied immediately? Later?
13. Have you had a previous injury to this body part?

If the problem relates to an illness rather than an injury, ask the following questions:

1. Are you allergic to any medications?
2. What have you eaten today?
3. Are you allergic to anything?
4. Have you had anything to drink today?
5. What events led to this situation?

---

aspect (palm side), thumb side of the wrist. Once the pulse is found, the ATC will count the number of times the heart beats in a minute—the pulse rate. The normal **pulse rate** for an average teenager or adult is between 60 and 80 beats per minute. A highly trained athlete, however, may have a pulse rate as low as 40 beats per minute and be perfectly healthy. A person may also have a pulse rate below the norm because of medication (legal or illegal) she is taking, heart abnormalities, or internal injuries. Rapid pulse rates may be due to shock, hyperventilation, medication (legal or illegal), anxiety, or recent physical activity.

### Breathing Rate

**Breathing rate** is determined by counting the number of times the chest rises and falls in a

## What Would You Do If...

The athletic trainer is doing an evaluation. For every body part the ATC touches the athlete responds by saying, "That hurts!" The ATC tells you to get a backboard and call 911.

minute. The normal breathing rate for a teenager or adult is between 12 and 20 breaths per minute. Breathing rates can be slower than normal due to a head injury, lung injury, medication (legal or illegal), shock, diabetes, and hyperventilation. Breathing rates that are rapid may be the result of shock, medication (legal or illegal), anxiety, heat-related illnesses, or recent physical activity. Athletes may also have **dyspnea,** which is difficulty breathing—common among athletes with asthma, cystic fibrosis, shock, pneumonia, lung injuries, allergic reactions, airway obstructions, and upper respiratory illnesses (colds or flu). When the ATC checks an athlete's breathing rate she will not tell him, because it is often hard for a person to breathe naturally if he knows he is being watched. He may hold his breath or breathe faster, invalidating the count. The ATC will check the pulse and, while pretending to be taking the athlete's pulse, count the breathing

## For Your Information

### Breath Sounds

Breath sounds are heard through the chest wall with a stethoscope. No breath sounds mean that the athlete is not breathing or the lung is seriously injured.

### Cystic Fibrosis

Cystic fibrosis, a disease that affects the pancreas and lungs, is inherited.

### Shock

Shock is a condition in which inadequate oxygen is getting into the tissues of the body due to lack of blood flow.

### Pneumonia

Pneumonia is an inflammation of the lungs caused by an infection or irritant.

rate. **Apnea** is the temporary stopping of breathing—it is a serious symptom in an athlete because it may indicate a head injury. An athlete who has an unusual or out-of-the-ordinary breath odor should be checked for possible poisoning, intoxication, or diabetes.

When the athletic trainer uses a stethoscope to listen to the lungs, she will listen to each side of the chest for one cycle of breathing and compare them. Then she will listen to the lower lung portions for one cycle to insure that there are no immediate problems with the lungs.

### Blood Pressure

The heart pumps the blood to move blood cells, nutrients, and oxygen throughout the body. Blood pressure is the pressure that is exerted by the blood on the walls of the blood vessels, especially the arteries. The **systolic pressure** is the pressure when the heart is contracting. The **diastolic pressure** is the pressure when the heart is relaxed, between beats. The **pulse pressure** is the difference between the diastolic and systolic pressures. The blood pressure of a normal teenager is 110 mm Hg (mercury) systolic and 65-80 mm Hg diastolic. The blood pressure can increase due to a head injury, recent activity, medication (legal or illegal), and illnesses. Blood pressure will drop due to heart failure, hemorrhage, shock, and certain medications (legal or illegal) and illnesses.

A person measures blood pressure with a stethoscope and a blood pressure cuff, which is sized in proportion to the athlete's arm (see figure 5.2). The cuff is placed on the upper arm and pressurized until no blood can flow through the superficial arteries. As the pressure in the cuff is slowly released, the person listens through the stethoscope, which has been placed on the inside of the elbow, and watches the dial on the cuff. The first time a sound is heard, the person reads the dial; that is the systolic pressure. When the sounds stop, the dial is read again; that is the diastolic pressure. If a stethoscope is not available, the systolic blood pressure can be taken by feeling (palpating) for a radial pulse, although this method is less accurate. As the blood pressure cuff is released, the person reads the dial when he feels the radial pulse; that will be the systolic pressure. When taking a blood pressure reading, bear in mind that an athlete who has just finished exercising will have a

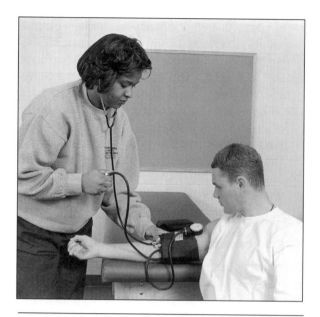

**Figure 5.2** Place the stethoscope over the artery and listen as the pressure is released from the blood pressure cuff. The systolic pressure is read from the dial when the first pumping sound is heard. The diastolic pressure is read when the last pumping sound is heard.

higher-than-normal blood pressure and so will an athlete who is upset. If the ATC is having trouble getting a blood pressure, he will check the athlete for the following:

- A heart beat
- Shock
- Placement of the stethoscope
- Blockage of the artery

### Body Temperature

Normal **body temperature** is 98.6 degrees Fahrenheit (36.6 degrees Celsius). An athlete's body temperature can rise if he has an infection or heat stroke, or drop if he is in shock or exposed to cold. Electronic temperature-measuring de-

### ? What Would You Do If...

At a soccer game two athletes collide. After a brief evaluation both players are able to continue play. At the start of the second half you notice that one of the players is on the ground. After talking with him you notice that his wrists are flexing, and he says he has a headache.

vices, which are quick and accurate, are now available. The temperature can be taken with an oral thermometer, which is left in place for three minutes. It is also possible, although unreliable, to take a temperature by placing a thermometer in the armpit, for 10 minutes. It is not possible to measure a person's temperature, or even tell if she has a fever, by feeling her forehead, but the ATC may feel an athlete's forehead to determine if the athlete is hot, cold, sweaty, or dry.

### Skin Color

Skin color can give information about what illness or injury may have occurred. Four skin-color changes are significant: a cherry red is an indication of heat stroke or carbon monoxide poisoning, a bluish tinge is an indication of poor oxygen supply, yellow is an indication of liver illness, and a lack of color or a paleness of the nail beds and lips is an indication of shock or lack of circulation. The athletic trainer will also check for color changes in the whites of the eyes (sclera), the inside of the lip, and the fingernail and toenail beds—especially if the athlete has a dark complexion.

### Capillary Refill

**Capillary refill** is an indication that blood is flowing to the fingertips and toes (see figure 5.3). It is determined by pressing on the nail and

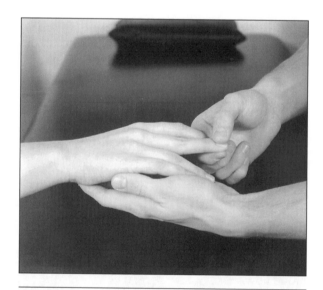

**Figure 5.3** How quickly blood returns to the tip of a finger after you press on the nail bed and then release pressure is a measure of the blood supply to the finger. Poor capillary refill can mean restricted blood vessels or poor blood supply.

measuring how long it takes the color to return to normal (approximately one second). When the athletic trainer is checking capillary refill, he will check both arms or both legs at the same time. That way he can tell if there is a difference between them, which may indicate a fracture or a blood clot in one of the body parts.

### Pupil Response

The pupils of the eyes change size in response to light. When light shines into the eye the pupils **constrict,** or get smaller, to decrease the amount of light entering the eye. In the dark the pupils enlarge, or **dilate,** to allow more light into the eye. When the eyes do not respond normally to changes in light, a serious problem is indicated. If his pupils dilate when light shines into them, the athlete may have been poisoned or medicated, or he may even be dead. Pupils that constrict when there is darkness are an indication of heatstroke or poisoning. If the pupils are unequal in size (one is large and one is small) the ATC will suspect a head injury, although a small percentage of people normally have unequal pupils. People who are blind may or may not have pupillary response, depending on the origin of the blindness. Figure 5.4 illustrates pupil responses.

### Ability to Move

It is important to find out if the athlete can still move. This will help to determine what injury may have occurred and how to treat the athlete. **Paralysis,** the inability to move, is caused by an injury to the brain or spinal cord. The inability of an athlete to move one side of the body is known as **hemiplegia**, which is an indication of a head injury on the side opposite to the paralyzed side of the body. The extent of the paralysis depends on the location of the injury—the higher in the spine the injury occurs, the greater the extent of limb impairment. The inability to move the legs is called **paraplegia**. The inability to move arms and legs is called **quadriplegia**. Paralysis may be temporary, but physicians must care for the athlete.

### Response to Pain

People respond differently to being injured. Pain cannot be used to determine the severity of an

 **The Real World**

One day I arrived at work just as a fellow employee pulled into the parking lot, so we walked together across the street to the hospital. We saw a casually dressed man lying in the grass between the curb and the sidewalk, apparently unconscious. As we approached him to check his breathing, he opened his eyes and said loudly, "Please don't call an ambulance, just let me lie here." I wondered why we shouldn't call for help, but we couldn't just leave him there—I stayed with the man while my colleague went to the emergency room, just inside the nearest building, to report the problem. The man's skin felt cool and clammy to the touch, and when I checked his pulse, I noticed an alert tag on his wrist, which said the wearer had epilepsy. He must have had a seizure and fallen on the grass. He said he was very tired, and his speech was slurred. The EMS arrived in only a few minutes and took him to the emergency room. When I went to check on him later that morning, the man had been released to his family's care. What a way to start the morning! It just goes to show that you must be prepared for anything at all times.

Bill Pitney, MS, ATC

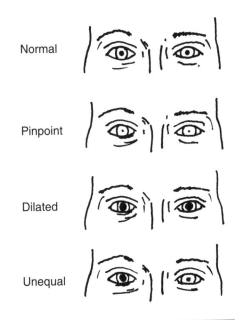

**Figure 5.4** In response to light, the pupils normally get smaller. Pupils that dilate in response to light indicate a serious head injury or medication, or the athlete may be dead. Pinpoint pupils are an indication of medication. Unequal pupils indicate a head injury on the same side as the enlarged pupil.

injury, because people have different tolerances for pain and will respond to the pain of an injury in different ways. Paralysis, medication, and shock can also disguise pain reactions.

## Inspection

The athletic trainer will observe the athlete's body and her surroundings for clues as to what may have happened, which will suggest treatment options. If a chair has been tipped over, it is possible that the athlete fell out of it. Think about the injuries that could occur from a fall while sitting on a chair. Now think about the injuries that could occur if the athlete fell while standing on the chair. Are they the same?

An empty bottle should raise red flags. Is this a poisoning, or was the athlete taking medication to care for an illness? An arm that bends where it never did before means what? The questions that are the hardest to answer are the ones on which the ATC will concentrate. An even greater problem will be trying to get other athletes to talk about how the injury occurred. Some athletes will not want to help because they do not want to be involved, they fear lawsuits, or they just do not care.

## Testing

Most often an athletic trainer will do the primary survey quickly, and during the history portion of the assessment the athlete will indicate what happened. At that point the athletic trainer can assess the body part involved. She can do specific tests to determine the severity of injury before swelling and muscular contractions oc-

cur, which will cause the body part to become immobile and make it difficult to determine the extent of the injury. The tests will also help determine how the athlete should be moved, if he should be splinted, or if medical help is immediately necessary. Testing should be stopped if the swelling is exceedingly rapid, crepitus is felt, there is deformity, or excessive pain.

### Palpation

During **palpation** the athletic trainer will examine the athlete by touch, feeling for depressions, fluid leakage, bumps, crepitus, and things that are not symmetrical. He will look for signs of pain on the athlete's face, decreased strength, decreased sensation, and false movement. Crepitus and excessive pain are reasons to stop palpation and splint the body part before moving the athlete. The palpation examination of the body is done in the following order:

1. Head
2. Chest and thorax
3. Abdomen
4. Upper extremities
5. Lower extremities
6. Special tests

### Listening to the Heart

Listening to the heart and obtaining any useful information requires a lot of practice. For most athletic trainers listening to the heart will be limited to establishing that there is a heartbeat and determining a heart rate.

### Range of Motion Testing

The range of motion (ROM) must be tested at the injured segment as well as at the joints

above and below the injury. The testing should be performed both actively and passively. That is, the injured athlete should move the injured segment if he is able (active), or the athletic trainer will attempt to move it (passive).

An athlete with a suspected broken bone, a bone with deformity, or a spinal cord injury should not be put through any ROM testing. Suspected broken bones should be splinted before an injured athlete is moved.

Range of motion should be measured from the anatomical position. When documenting ROM test results, the ATC should be sure to note the position the athlete was in when she took the measurements. For example, the report should state that the athlete was supine (lying on her back), or the athlete was prone (on her stomach). By doing this, follow-up measurements can be taken with the athlete in the same position, thus making them more consistent. It is vital that the range of motion of a limb be compared to that of the opposite "good" limb.

### Strength Testing

Performing resistive range of motion testing helps to measure the strength of an area of the body. Muscular strength testing is often done with a technique called manual muscle testing (MMT), which is an objective way to determine the level of an individual's strength. It is based on the following grading system of "zero" to "normal." A grade of "zero" indicates an inability to even twitch a muscle. "Trace" means an ability to perform a muscle twitch. A grade of "poor" indicates that an athlete can move a segment through a full range of motion only if gravity is eliminated. "Fair" means the athlete can move a segment through a full range of motion against gravity but with no other resistance. "Good" means that the athlete can move the segment through a full range of motion, against gravity, and with some resistance applied by the athletic trainer. A grade of "normal" indicates that the athlete can move the segment through a full range of motion, against gravity, and with full resistance from the athletic trainer. Some ATCs use MMT without grading by simply comparing the resistive range of motion of an extremity to the one on the opposite side. The MMT strength-grading system allows athletic trainers and other health care providers to document strength

consistently, and thus communicate the condition of an athlete efficiently and effectively. The MMT strength-grading system can be found in table 5.1.

### Testing to Rule Out Neurological Problems

Once strength and ROM have been assessed, the injured athlete can be evaluated for neurological problems, which might include an inability to feel or move a body part. Each nerve that exits the spinal column is responsible for sensation and movement at a particular area of the body. By exposing these specific areas to a light touch or pricking stimulus and by asking the athlete to try to move the area, an athletic trainer can determine if a specific nerve may be involved in the injury. If a spinal cord injury is suspected the athlete must be backboarded before moving him.

# Specific Conditions

Specific conditions that must be considered during a secondary assessment include shock and fractures. Here we discuss the common signs and symptoms and the necessary care of each.

## Recognizing Shock

Shock is a condition in which inadequate blood and oxygen are supplied to vital organs. The body has five organs that must always receive an adequate blood supply to maintain life. These organs are the brain, heart, lungs, liver, and kidneys. When an athlete becomes seriously injured the body tries to protect the vital organs by increasing blood flow to these organs while decreasing blood flow to the arms and legs. There are three main reasons why a body goes into shock:

1. The blood vessels in the head, chest, and abdomen enlarge, getting ready to carry more blood. If the blood vessels in the arms and legs constrict and do not move blood into the vessels of the head, chest, and abdomen, blood pressure in these vessels decreases because the vessels have enlarged while the volume of blood has not increased. This means that the supply of oxygen to the vital organs is reduced.

## Table 5.1  Manual Muscle Testing to Determine an Athlete's Strength Level

| Strength classifications (number or grade) | | Description |
|---|---|---|
| 5 | Normal | The athlete can move the joint through a full range of motion against gravity and against full resistance from the athletic trainer. |
| 4+ | Good plus | The athlete can move the joint through a full range of motion against gravity and against a significant amount of resistance from the athletic trainer. |
| 4 | Good | The athlete can move the joint though a full range of motion against gravity and against some amount of resistance from the athletic trainer. |
| 3+ | Fair plus | The athlete can move the joint through a full range of motion against gravity and against very minimal resistance from the athletic trainer. |
| 3 | Fair | The athlete can move the joint through a full range of motion against gravity with no applied resistance from the athletic trainer. If any resistance is applied, full range of motion is not achieved. |
| 2 | Poor | The athlete can only move the joint through full range of motion if gravity is eliminated or against gravity with assistance from the athletic trainer. |
| 1 | Trace | When asked to move the joint, the athlete will not be able to do so. However, a muscle contraction should be observable. |
| 0 | Zero | When asked to move the joint, the athlete will not be able to do so. Moreover, a muscle contraction will not be visible. |

Data obtained from Kendall, McCreary, and Provance (1993), Konin (1997), Starkey and Ryan (1996), and Magee (1992).

2. The body will go into shock if the heart stops. Obviously, if the heart stops no blood is flowing to the vital organs. When this happens, restarting the heart, not shock, is the first concern.

3. The body goes into shock if there is a significant loss of blood. If blood is leaking from the vessels, there is a smaller amount of blood to pump. If too much blood is lost, the organs will not get enough oxygen and nutrients to sustain life, the organs will shut down, and the athlete will die.

If shock is not recognized early and treated rapidly, shock, and not the initial injury, can cause death. Signs of shock include agitation (usually the first sign), rapid weak pulse, decreased blood pressure—100 mm Hg or lower, cold clammy skin, sweating, cyanosis, increasing unconsciousness, and pale skin tone. Symptoms are nausea, thirst, anxiety, and dizziness.

Table 5.2 describes the kinds of shock and what causes each.

## Treating Shock

Treatment of shock includes all of the following procedures: treat the original injury; keep the athlete warm; if the arms and legs are not broken, elevate them 10 to 12 inches above the heart; measure breathing and pulse rate every five minutes; do not give anything to eat or drink; if vomiting occurs, turn victim on side and clear the airway; and get her to the hospital as soon as possible.

If the athlete has head or neck injuries and is in shock, she must be placed on a backboard and sent to the hospital for care. She can be covered with a blanket to maintain her body heat, but keep her lying flat. An athlete with respiratory injury can have her head elevated if there are no head or neck injuries. That will

## Table 5.2 Types and Description of Shock

| Type of shock | Characteristic |
|---|---|
| Psychogenic | Temporary loss of nervous function causing blood vessels to dilate (fainting). |
| Septic | General infection causing circulatory failure. |
| Neurological | Loss of control over the nervous system causing blood vessels to dilate (spinal cord injury). |
| Cardiogenic | Heart stops (cardiac arrest). |
| Hemorrhagic or hypovolemic | Loss of blood (internal bleeding). |
| Metabolic | Loss of fluids via vomiting, diarrhea, or urination (diabetics). |
| Respiratory | Breathing stops, causing a change in oxygen supply in the blood. This change causes organs to shut down because of loss of oxygen. |
| Anaphylactic | Toxin in the system causes breathing to stop. This changes the oxygen supply within the body and causes the organs to shut down (asthma, bee sting). |

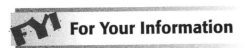 For Your Information

### Cyanosis

Cyanosis is a blue coloration of the skin caused by lack of oxygen.

### Backboard

Backboards are platforms that extend from the head to the toes. An athlete is secured to a backboard ("backboarded") when a spinal cord injury is suspected.

make it easier for her to breathe. Table 5.3 shows which measures are appropriate for treating each kind of shock.

## Assessing and Managing a Fracture

When assessing an athlete with a possible fracture, the athletic trainer must check capillary refill, the pulse rate in that extremity, and sensation of the body part. The athlete should never be asked to use the body part because this could cause further injury. If the trainer finds poor circulation, lack of sensation, or decreased capillary refill, the athlete may have seriously injured the nerve or vessels to that body part, and he requires immediate attention by the team physician. If the trainer cannot tell

for sure whether the part is fractured, he should splint the area to be safe.

### Types of Splints

Several types of splints can be used to manage fractures. A traction splint is used when the femur has been fractured, because the muscles in the thigh are so strong that, without proper splinting, they can cause the limb to shorten. The traction splint pulls the bone ends apart and into alignment, which causes muscle tissue to relax, thus decreasing the pain.

A rigid splint, which is made of a stiff material, is applied to either the side, front, or back of an extremity. The splint must be padded and bandaged securely to the limb to hold the fracture in position. Examples of rigid splints are box splints, boards, and aluminum splints.

A semi-rigid splint is a moldable splint that hardens in place to hold a fracture—an example is a vacuum splint. Soft splints remain soft after the splint is applied to a fracture; examples include pillows, slings and swathes, and air splints. The trainer must check his supply of air splints regularly—they get holes and may not be usable when needed in an emergency. Figure 5.5 illustrates different types of splints.

### Moving After Splinting

Once a body part is splinted, the athlete can be moved (assuming he has no other major problems), and body parts can be elevated

## Table 5.3  Shock Care

| Type of shock | Elevate feet? | Elevate head? | Do secondary assessment? | Position of patient for transportation |
|---|---|---|---|---|
| Psychogenic | Yes | No | Yes | Supine |
| Septic | Yes | No | No | Supine |
| Neurological | No | No | Yes | Supine |
| Cardiogenic | No | Yes | Yes | Head up |
| Hemorrhagic or hypovolemic | Yes | No | Yes | Supine |
| Metabolic | Yes | No | No | Supine |
| Respiratory | No | Yes | Yes | Head up |
| Anaphylactic | No | No | No | Supine |

Data obtained from American Academy of Orthopedic Surgeons (1987), Bergeron and Greene (1989), and American Red Cross (1993).

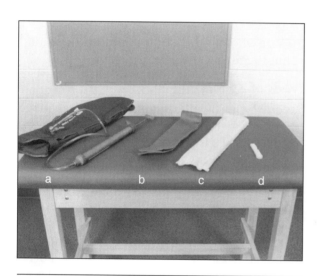

**Figure 5.5** A vacuum splint (a) is applied and then air is withdrawn from it to mold it to a suspected fracture. Aluminum splints (b) are padded and molded for a specific body part. Economical board splints (c) are also padded. Finger splints (d) are made of various types of materials and are small enough to splint a finger.

appropriately for shock. On the way to the hospital, the athletic trainer must make sure the athlete is as comfortable as possible and prevent the splinted fracture from bouncing around in the transport vehicle. A fractured arm can be placed in a sling with a pillow between the arm and the athlete's lap. A fractured leg can be wrapped in blankets, which act as a comfort barrier, and strapped to the other leg.

## PRICE

Most sprains, strains, and splinted fractures can be cared for with the **PRICE** method—**P**rotection, **R**est, **I**ce, **C**ompression, and **E**levation. The body part must be protected from further injury. Rest allows the body part to heal. Ice, compression, and elevation reduce the swelling.

Ice is applied for no longer than 20 minutes at a time because longer applications can cause frostbite. There should be at least one hour between icings. A body part should be iced no more than three times a day. The ice can be applied in a bag or by a solid chunk in an ice cup. When applying ice to a body part, the athlete may experience pain and the sensation of extra pressure before the body part becomes numb. Compression is pressure applied to the injured body part that does not allow swelling to build. It is achieved with pads and snug application of elastic wraps or tape. Before elevating the body part, the student assistant or ATC should arrange sufficient blankets, towels, or padding to lift the body part 10 to 12 inches above the heart. The body part can then be gently lifted, while the support is slid under it.

## Summary

When determining the nature and severity of an injury, the athletic trainer will do a complete assessment of the athlete. The secondary assessment begins with HIT. Some injuries may cause the athlete to go into shock, which may be fatal. Treatment for shock depends upon its cause. Sprains, strains, and splinted fractures are usually treated with PRICE.

## Key Terms

Define the following terms found in this chapter:

| | | | |
|---|---|---|---|
| apnea | dilate | palpation | pulse pressure |
| body temperature | dyspnea | paralysis | pulse rate |
| breathing rate | heart rate | paraplegia | quadriplegia |
| capillary refill | hemiplegia | PRICE | systolic pressure |
| constrict | history | pulse points | vital signs |
| diastolic pressure | HIT | | |

## Questions for Review

1. Explain how a secondary assessment is performed. pp. 39-45
2. Make a list of all the questions you can think of to ask during the history portion of an injury assessment. Compare your list with your partner's list. Did you forget any questions? p. 40
3. List three reasons why an athlete may go into shock. pp. 45-46
4. What injuries can be determined from assessing an athlete's vital signs? pp. 40-44
5. Explain the HIT principle. p. 39
6. Under what circumstances is testing (touching, specific evaluations, checking the range of motion, and neurological testing) of a body part to be avoided? p. 44
7. What injuries are treated with PRICE? p. 48

## Activities for Reinforcement

1. List the vital signs, and explain what each of them can tell you about an injured athlete.
2. Make a list of items that could be used to splint a fracture, if regular splints were not available.
3. Practice taking someone else's blood pressure reading.

## Above and Beyond

1. Review the following textbooks, and write a brief report on the various types of shock.

   American Red Cross. 1996. *Responding to emergencies.* 2d ed. St. Louis: Mosby-Lifeline.

American Red Cross. 1993. *Community first aid & safety*. St. Louis: Mosby-Lifeline.

American Red Cross. 1993. *CPR for the professional rescuer.* St. Louis: Mosby-Lifeline.

Flegel, M.J. 1992. *Sport first aid*. Champaign, IL: Human Kinetics.

Kendall, F.P., E.K. McCreary, and P.G. Provance. 1993. *Muscles, testing and function.* 4th ed. Baltimore: Williams & Wilkins.

Steele, V., and J. White. 1986. Injury prediction in female gymnasts. *British Journal of Sports Medicine* 120(1): 31–33.

# First Aid for Environmental Injuries

## OBJECTIVES

Upon completing this chapter the student will be able to do the following:
- Explain how to care for heat-related illnesses.
- Describe how the body gets rid of excessive heat.
- Explain how heat-related illnesses can be prevented.
- Describe the person who is more prone to cold- and heat-related injuries.
- Explain the treatment of cold- and heat-related injuries.
- Explain how to prevent insect bites.

We live in a changing environment. Some days are rainy, and others are clear and sunny. Athletes like to practice in the same environment in which they will perform on game day. Some days, however, surprise the body with weather it is not accustomed to—like a day in October with uncommonly high temperatures, which may cause problems for heat-sensitive athletes. In addition, for some athletes, an insect bite can lead to a life-threatening illness. In this chapter, we discuss the first aid necessary to care for an athlete who becomes ill because of something in the environment.

## Heat-Related Problems

**Hyperthermia** is an exceptional rise in body temperature. Body temperature rises when the athlete is exercising, the temperature in the environment is excessive, the athlete has an infection, or the body's temperature-regulation system has failed. The body regulates temperature via the hypothalamus gland, which is located in the brain. As blood flows through the hypothalamus, heat receptors indicate a need to increase or decrease body temperature to maintain the body's core temperature at a constant 98.6 degrees

Fahrenheit (36.6 degrees Celsius), which is the temperature at which the body's systems normally function. Through the hypothalamus, the body maintains a delicate balance in temperature, attempting to cool the body if heat production causes the body temperature to rise or trying to conserve body heat if the body temperature is decreasing. If body cooling exceeds heat production, the blood vessels in the arms and legs constrict, which reduces the flow of blood passing close to the surface where it would lose heat more rapidly. If body temperature begins to rise, in an attempt to rid the body of excess heat the blood vessels in the extremities dilate so that more blood flows close to the surface.

## Types of Heat-Related Illnesses

Heat-related illnesses range from mild heat cramps to severe heatstroke, which is considered a medical emergency. Heat exhaustion is considered a moderate illness.

### Heat Cramps

**Heat cramps** are involuntary muscle contractions caused by dehydration and a loss of sodium as a result of profuse sweating. A poor daily diet may also contribute to the problem. The calf and abdominal muscles are those most likely to be involved. Heat cramps should be treated by having the athlete drink water, stretch the involved muscle, and apply ice to the muscle to alleviate pain.

### Heat Exhaustion

**Heat exhaustion** is caused by prolonged exercise in a hot, humid environment to the point of severe dehydration. Symptoms of heat exhaustion include fatigue, dizziness, nausea, headache, muscle cramps, shortness of breath, and distorted vision. Signs of heat exhaustion are excessive sweating, rapid weak pulse, decreased blood pressure, skin that is cold and pale, and a normal body temperature. To treat heat exhaustion, cool the athlete by removing him from the hot environment (get him into the shade), place a fan on him, and apply cold wet towels. Encourage him to sip water if he can. If he loses consciousness or his case is severe, refer him to a physician—if prompt medical attention is not given, the athlete's condition may progress to heatstroke.

### Heatstroke

**Heatstroke** is a dangerously high core body temperature that is caused by the shutdown of the hypothalamus. Hypothalamus dysfunction can result from exercising in a hot, humid environment, severe dehydration, excessive weight loss, obesity, or untreated heat exhaustion. Symptoms of impending heatstroke are feeling extremely hot, confusion, headache, and dizziness. Signs of heatstroke are little or no sweating, hot, dry skin, a fever of 105 degrees Fahrenheit (40.1 degrees Celsius) or more, low blood pressure, rapid weak pulse, rapid breathing rate, dilated pupils, and unconsciousness. If the ATC suspects heatstroke, he will call 911 for emergency assistance. He will begin cooling the body as quickly as possible, being sure to apply cold wet towels to the neck, armpits, feet, and groin region. Elevating the legs will help prevent shock. If the athlete is not treated immediately, death or irreversible brain damage will occur.

## Heat Loss and the Environment

The amount of body heat lost to the environment depends on the air temperature, humidity, radiation, body surface exposure, air currents, clothing, and equipment. Evaporation is the process that causes the cooling of the body. When sweat evaporates, the amount of heat energy necessary to change liquid water (or sweat) to gas is removed from the skin, which cools the body. Thus, factors that affect the rate of evaporation also affect the body's ability to cool itself—air temperature, humidity, air movement, and radiation factors. If the humidity is low, that is, if the air is dry, it can pick up and hold additional moisture, so sweat from a hot athlete will evaporate quickly and cool her effectively. If the humidity is high, that is, if the air is moist, as the athlete's core temperature rises and she sweats, the moist air cannot hold much additional moisture so the sweat does not evaporate. Air movement is helpful because a breeze tends to move moist air away and bring drier air to the skin, which aids sweat evaporation.

A plot of air temperature and humidity is referred to as the **heat index**. The heat index predicts the body's ability to dissipate heat and indicates how safe it is to participate in activities on a given day. For example, if the humidity is 90 percent and the temperature is 75 degrees, it is safe to practice. However, if the humidity is 90 percent and the temperature is 90 degrees, practice should be canceled (see figure 6.1).

# Preventing Heat-Related Illness

When preparing for athletic competition in hot weather, athletes must remember that the body needs time to get used to temperature extremes. In "Preventing Heat-Related Illnesses" on page 54 we present a number of suggestions that will help an athlete cope with heat. Rushing into athletic competition without proper conditioning and training can cause a heat-related injury.

## *Adjusting Clothing and Equipment*

Clothing affects heat dissipation in several ways. Dark colors absorb heat, so light-colored clothes should be selected to reflect the sun. A layer of air between the clothing and the skin helps the process of evaporation, which subsequently cools the body. Air flowing through the clothing can improve evaporation, so jersey material in a loose weave is often desirable. Cotton material

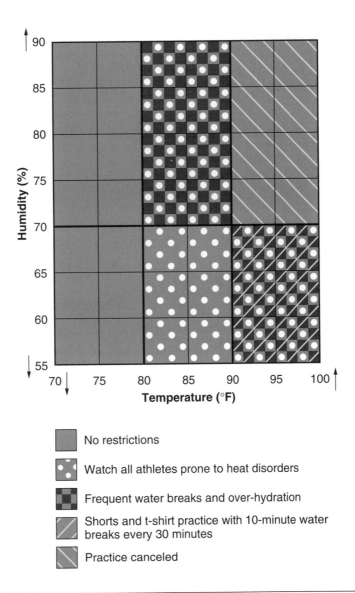

**Figure 6.1**  Heat index training training standards.

will help absorb sweat, but athletes should avoid heavy clothing, long sleeves, long socks, and additional taping or wraps. Rubber suits, such as those sometimes worn by high school wrestlers, are dangerous because they prevent cooling through evaporation and lock the heat around the body.

Equipment such as helmets, padding, and uniforms reduces the amount of body surface exposure, and this limits the body's ability to evaporate moisture. Moreover, the athlete must work harder with the added weight of the equipment, which is an increased energy expenditure that generates more heat. Coaches should modify practices so that some equipment does not have to be worn when there is a high heat index. During extremely hot and humid days, for example, if the football players avoid contact, they can practice without shoulder pads and wear shorts instead of pants.

### Other Preventive Measures

Heat-related illnesses can be prevented if the athletes gradually acclimatize to the heat and humidity for a period of ten days, drink plenty of water, and take rest breaks as needed to keep cool. Ideally, if an athlete is physically fit and not overweight, is well nourished, and drinks plenty of fluids before, during, and after activity, he will be better able to prevent heat-related illnesses. Unfortunately, almost no one drinks enough fluids during activity to replace the water lost during participation. In fact, most athletes drink enough to replace only about one-half of the fluids they loose during activity. The ATC can encourage the athletes to drink more fluids—before and during an activity they should drink 20 ounces of water every fifteen minutes if they can, until a full feeling is reached. They will be able to drink more if the water temperature is

## Preventing Heat-Related Illnesses

Acclimatize.

Wear lightweight uniforms.

Take frequent water breaks.

Change into dry clothing.

Weigh in before and after practice.

Check the humidity and temperature daily during practice.

Avoid staying in saunas and hot tubs for extended periods.

Eat properly.

Get plenty of rest.

Drink fluids after practice to replace fluid lost during practice.

about 40 degrees Fahrenheit (4.4 degrees Celsius). We do not recommend fluids containing high amounts of sugar because they are absorbed more slowly than those without sugar. Drinking fluids with high salt content is usually unnecessary because most people get enough salt with a well-balanced diet. The athletes should weigh themselves before and after practice—at least two cups of water should be consumed for every pound of weight lost. Workouts and practices should be scheduled in the morning or evening, if possible, to avoid the hottest times of the day.

## Cold-Related Problems

In a cold environment, the body must conserve or generate more heat to maintain its normal core temperature. As we mentioned earlier, in response to signals from the hypothalamus the size of blood vessels in the extremities is reduced to keep most of the blood at the chest, head, and abdomen. In addition, the body will metabolize some of its stores of fat and carbohydrates—think of it as burning fuel to generate heat. Thus, people with low energy supplies (little stored fat and carbohydrates) are more prone to cold-related injury.

To help retain body heat the athlete must dress appropriately by wearing layered clothing, gloves, a hat, and warm footwear (see "Preventing Cold-Related Injuries" for additional

### ? What Would You Do If...

After a rainy field hockey game, the coach tells you that one of the players is missing. You go back out to the field and find the player huddled in the corner next to the storage shed. He is cold and wet. His lips are blue, his skin is pale, and he is shivering uncontrollably. The athlete is unable to walk.

ideas). Several light layers of clothing maintain more warmth for the body because warmed air is retained between each layer of clothing. However, the athlete should avoid wearing so many layers that he begins to sweat because then he will lose heat by evaporation. As he warms up, he may be able to remove a layer or two so he can stay comfortable and dry. Clothing that is wind resistant prevents heat loss because it does not allow a flow of air over the body, which promotes evaporation.

Shivering is another mechanism the body uses to try and create heat. Shivering is uncontrolled muscular contractions—when muscles contract, they generate heat. If she starts to shiver, however, the athlete should be moved to a warm area. She can progress from a simple cold injury such as frostnip to hypothermia or death if care is not taken in extreme cold. If the extremities do not get enough blood flow from the body to stay warm, the athlete will begin to get frostbite. If she gets so cold that her core body temperature begins to drop, she has **hypothermia**.

## Hypothermia

Hypothermia results from prolonged exposure to damp cold. The athlete's body temperature begins to drop—at 95 degrees Fahrenheit (34.6 degrees Celsius), the first signs and symptoms of hypothermia occur. Symptoms include headache, a feeling of cold, numbness, dizziness, and slowed breathing and heart rates. Signs of hypothermia are pale skin, shivering, swelling, patches of discolored skin, decreased heart rate, change in consciousness, and low body temperature. One of the first signs of hypothermia is shivering—should it occur, send the athlete to a warm place. An athlete may be vulnerable to cold exposure if she has cardiovascular disease, alcoholism, or asthma, has had previous bouts of hypothermia, has poor nutrition, is exposed to water or rain, has inadequate protective clothing, or is fatigued. An athlete who is not treated for hypothermia is at risk of death.

Hypothermia is treated by getting the athlete near a heat source—placing her in a warm room and removing any wet clothing, for instance. Warm the athlete with a dry blanket. Be careful not to place her too close to an open flame or a heater—this may cause the blood vessels to dilate rapidly, which causes ruptures. Remember that another person is a source of heat, so getting into a sleeping bag or a blanket with the chilled athlete will help to warm her up. The ATC will call 911—the athlete must be seen by a physician.

## Frostbite

Frostbite is caused from exposure to cold for a long period of time. The exposure causes the body part (usually nose, ears, fingers, toes, or penis) to freeze. The people most likely to get frostbite are those who fail to wear proper clothing, those who drink alcohol before or while outdoors, diabetics, or those who have a heart condition. Symptoms of frostbite include numbness and a prickling sensation. Early signs of frostbite are redness of skin and swelling; with continued exposure, the skin becomes pale, and eventually the tissue hardens.

Frostbite should be treated by gradually rewarming the effected body part in water heated to 102 degrees Fahrenheit (38.5 degrees Celsius). Once the part is pink, gently dry it and wrap it in dry sterile dressings. Do not massage the affected body parts or ask the athlete to walk on frozen feet. Do not rub snow on the body part or apply any lotions or creams. The athlete must be referred to a physician.

## Preventing Cold-Related Injuries

Wear dry nonrestrictive clothing.

Acclimatize.

Wear layers of lightweight clothing.

Stay indoors during extremely cold weather.

Cover head, mouth, and extremities.

Avoid use of alcohol or smoking.

Avoid getting wet.

Avoid sitting on cold objects (ice, aluminum benches).

If predisposed to being cold, stay indoors in cold weather.

Wear wind-resistant clothing, such as wool and windbreakers.

# Severe Weather

Severe-weather conditions increase the risk of injury to those people who get caught outdoors. Thankfully, many cities support an early warning weather system. When a severe storm is about to pounce on an area, a television and radio warning goes out, which may include a storm watch, storm warning, tornado watch, or tornado warning. The term "watch" indicates that conditions are right for severe weather or a tornado. A "warning" means that a storm or tornado has been sighted. In many communities, a tornado warning will activate sirens, telling people to take cover. During the severe-weather season, the athletic trainer should have a battery-operated radio ready to operate so that weather reports can be heard. The early warning storm system will indicate when the storm has passed. Remember, "Don't mess with Mother Nature." Take cover, she can be fierce!

## Tornadoes

In the event of a tornado warning, athletes must move to safety immediately. The safest area during a tornado is a low, reinforced area such as a basement. If protection indoors is not available, the athletes should find a ditch or low-lying area and lie as flat as possible, which will allow the tornado to pass over and protect them from flying debris. People should not seek shelter in a car or bus, because, although they appear to be safe, they are easily shifted and moved by a tornado.

## Thunder and Lightning

When there is thunder or lightning, it is time to take cover inside. Many people either are not aware of the danger or do not want to appear to their friends to be afraid, and so they stay outside in severe weather, sometimes with tragic consequences. Several years ago a group of people were walking to a high school football game in Michigan when they felt their hair stand on end, which is a sign that lightning is about to strike. They were hit and knocked to the ground—several had no heartbeat. Luckily, some ATCs were attending the game and administered CPR—all of the injured survived. In another incident, three adult recreational soc-

cer players were waiting a storm out under a tree hoping to resume a game. A bolt of lightning hit and traveled down the tree, knocking them to the ground. One of the soccer players died when he could not be revived. These incidents are not that unusual, so the best policy regarding thunder and lightning is to take cover indoors immediately. A team can proceed with competition after thunder and lightning have not been heard or seen for a period of 15 to 30 minutes.

In the event a team is caught by a sudden storm, the following hints may be helpful:

- Go inside.
- Stay away from all metal objects.
- Avoid any electrical devices, including telephones.
- Do not stand under a tree.
- Do not stand on a hilltop.
- Remove all metal objects from your body (cleats, chains, money clips).
- Assume the lightning-safe position (crouching with legs and arms together).

If an athlete has been struck by lightning, the ATC must be prepared to give CPR. An electrical charge may cause the heart to stop.

# Bites and Stings

We share our environment with an enormous number and variety of insects. Their bites may contain harmful venom or bacteria.

For most people, being stung by a bee or being bitten by some other insect is painful but not life threatening. However, a few people are so sensitive to the insect venom that, for them, bites or stings can result in shock and death. To treat an insect sting the first thing an ATC must do is remove the stinger. Many people try to

## 🌐 The Real World

Most of us dislike bugs because they bite and sting, but they can cause unusual problems as well. I treated an athlete who reported having ear pain for a few days. We referred him to a physician who was extremely surprised when he looked in the young man's ear with an otoscope and found a dead cockroach that had begun to decompose.

Phil Voorhis, MSEd, ATC

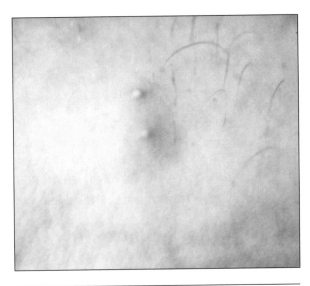

**Figure 6.2** Not all stings involve stingers. The fire ant stings shown above are a result of the ant biting and then injecting venom. No need to scrape out a stinger from this wound: just apply ice.
Photo courtesy of Dr. Jerome Goddard. From: *Physician's Guide to Arthropods of Medical Importance,* 2nd edition, copyright 1996 by CRC Press, Inc.

remove the stinger by probing it with a needle or grasping it with tweezers. Any time the stinger is squeezed it injects more poison into the athlete, so this should be avoided. It is best to use an object such as a knife or the edge of a credit card to scrape off the stinger. The ATC can apply ice, which will reduce the blood flow to and from the area and help control the pain and swelling (see figure 6.2).

The athlete's breathing and heart rate should be monitored for an allergic reaction. If there are signs of breathing difficulty, wheezing, excessive swelling, or rapid heart rate, he should be taken by ambulance to the hospital. Athletes who have had previous severe reactions can be given medication to use in the event of a bite. The medication is already in a syringe, sometimes called an "Epi-pen," and the athlete just has to insert the needle and give himself the injection. The athletic trainer needs to be aware of athletes with this condition.

Insects are attracted to the sugar found on discarded candy wrappers and in empty pop cans. Keeping garbage cans emptied around playing fields will help reduce the numbers of insects present there.

## Summary

Many environmental athletic injuries can be prevented by following a few common-sense procedures—drink plenty of fluids, wear appropriate clothing, take cover from storms, and keep the trash cans emptied. All of these measures increase athletes' safety. The role the athletic trainer takes in preventing injuries is just as important as the part he plays in the evaluation and care of injuries. Athletes who are particularly sensitive to insect bites should be prepared to treat themselves for an allergic reaction in case they get bitten or stung, and the ATC should be prepared to deal with an allergic reaction, too.

## Key Terms

Define the following terms found in this chapter:

| | | |
|---|---|---|
| heat cramps | heat index | hyperthermia |
| heat exhaustion | heatstroke | hypothermia |

## Questions for Review

1. What is the difference between heatstroke and heat exhaustion? How are heat illnesses treated? p. 52
2. What is the difference between frostbite and frostnip? p. 55
3. How can heat- and cold-related injuries be prevented? pp. 53-55
4. How does the body get overheated or too cold? How does the body rid itself of heat and warm itself if cold? pp. 51-52, 53, 54-55
5. How are the various cold-related injuries treated? p. 55
6. What can the athlete do to prevent being bitten by insects? p. 57

## Activities for Reinforcement

1. Design a policy for preventing heat-related injuries.
2. Design a policy for preventing cold-related injuries.

## Above and Beyond

1. Interview someone who has been struck by lightning, write an article, and print the story in the school newspaper.
2. Working with a local meteorologist, determine the number of days in the last year that could have caused a heat- or cold-related injury.
3. Design a severe-weather drill for athletes and coaches.

# Extrication

Upon completing this chapter the student will be able to do the following:
- Understand why equipment is removed.
- Explain how to remove an athlete from the field.
- Explain when a backboard is necessary.
- Explain when an athlete should walk or use an aid to get off the field.

**Extrication** is removing an injured athlete from a playing field or court or dangerous situation to get them care without causing additional harm—a tackler is carried off the field, an out-of-bounds skier is dug out of an avalanche and removed from the slope, or a diver is taken from the pool.

Prior to extrication, once the athlete is accessible and out of immediate danger, and provided that the scene is safe to approach without risk of injury to rescuers, the athlete's injuries should be briefly assessed and primary or secondary care should be given. For example, a severe joint injury or fracture should be splinted before moving the victim. Sometimes the athlete's equipment must be removed to properly treat the injury.

## Equipment Removal

The team physician and the local emergency medical services may be comfortable treating a fully equipped injured athlete. The athletic trainer should check with them—in some cases, the athlete's equipment will not need to be removed. If there are too few trained personnel to help remove equipment, it should be left in place unless it is life threatening. A face mask must be removed in all breathing emergencies, and shoulder pads and face mask must be removed for cardiac emergencies.

### Face Mask

An athletic trainer must remove a face mask to gain access to an athlete's airway. If the athlete has breathing problems, the trainer should always suspect a head or neck injury, and therefore, while he removes the face mask, a second person must hold the player's head and neck in line to prevent excessive movement.

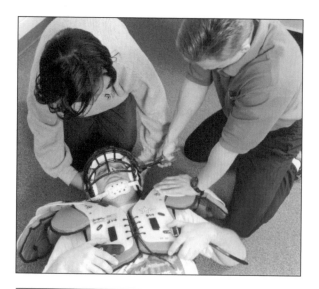

**Figure 7.1** Football face mask removal. To remove a football face mask cut the plastic retaining pieces located on each side of the helmet. Swinging the face mask upward gives the rescuer access to the athlete's face.

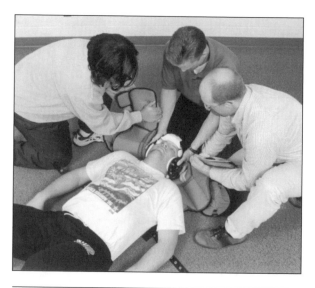

**Figure 7.2** When an athlete is supine and the shoulder pads must be removed, cut the strings in the front and unhook the chest straps. Spread the shoulder pads apart and pull over the athlete's head.

A cutter tool is required to remove a face mask. To remove a football face mask, the athletic trainer cuts the two side mounting loops and flips the face mask up (see figure 7.1). This gives access to the athlete's face and mouth. Any time an athlete is to be transported to medical care, his face mask and mouth guard should be removed, but his chin strap should be left in place because it holds the head and neck securely.

To remove a hockey player's face mask, the ATC unsnaps the straps on each side of the mask and flips the mask up. A baseball helmet has a face mask that is held in place either by screws or loops similar to those on a football mask. If the face mask is secured with screws, they must be removed with a screwdriver, and the face mask can be lifted off. When loops are present, the two side loops are cut and the face mask will flip away.

## Jerseys and Shoulder Pads

Shoulder pads can stay in place in most situations. When evaluating a shoulder, the athletic trainer can reach the injured area by sliding a hand up the sleeve or through the neck opening. If shoulder pads must be removed, however, first remove the jersey—it may need to be cut off

to avoid excessive movement. The jersey can be cut at the seams if it is desired to keep it for possible repair and reuse, or it should be cut up the middle and up each sleeve to the neck. If the athlete is lying supine, next unhook the chest straps and unlace or cut the laces in the front of the chest (or at the back of the pads if the athlete is lying prone). While someone holds the athlete's head and neck in line, a second person pulls the shoulder pads over the athlete's head, bends the pads backward around the first person's arms, and the pads are removed (see figure 7.2).

To remove shoulder pads from an athlete who is lying on his side, remove the jersey, unhook the chest straps, and unlace or cut the laces or straps in the front and back of the pads. Someone must maintain the position of the head and neck while another person pulls the shoulder pads sideways and off. The shoulder pads on the side that is lying on the ground can be removed easily as the athlete is being placed on the backboard.

## Neck Roll

Removing the **neck roll** will depend on what type it is. If the neck roll is attached by string to the shoulder pads, the athletic trainer can cut the string. If the neck roll is attached by screws to the shoulder pads, the ATC may decide to remove the shoulder pads with the neck roll still attached. When removing a neck roll that is screwed to the pads, someone must hold the athlete's head and neck in position while another person unscrews the neck roll.

A third type of neck roll is put on before the shoulder pads and is held in place by the downward pressure of the jersey. To remove this type of neck roll, the jersey and shoulder pads must be removed, then the laces on the front are cut, and the neck roll will come off.

## Helmet

A helmet should be left in place at all times unless it interferes with the ability of the ATC to give proper care. If a helmet is removed, the shoulder pads and neck roll must also be removed, or the athlete's neck will be placed in extension, which can aggravate head or neck injuries and may cause further harm. If he must

remove a football helmet, the athletic trainer should enlist at least one trained first aider and proceed as follows:

1. The ATC will control the head and keep it in line (figure 7.3a).
2. The first aider will remove the cheek pads (figure 7.3b).
3. The first aider will control the head from inside the helmet (figure 7.3c).
4. The ATC unsnaps the chin strap.
5. The ATC pulls the helmet up over the head while pulling the helmet opening apart (figure 7.3d).
7. The ATC fills the gap between the head and the ground with towels or other conforming cloth to keep the head and neck in line with the back (figure 7.4b).
8. The ATC again takes control of the head as shown in figure 7.3a.

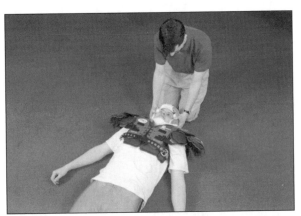
a
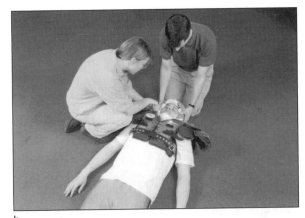
b
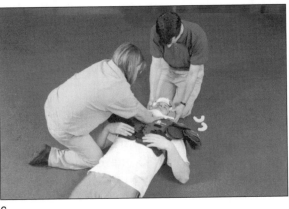
c
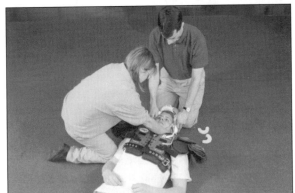
d

**Figure 7.3** Football helmet removal. *(a)* The ATC holds the exterior of the helmet, and *(b)* the cheek pads are loosened and removed. *(c)* The second rescuer controls the athlete's head from inside the helmet, and *(d)* from the top of the athlete's head, the ATC grabs the helmet by the ear holes, widens the helmet as much as possible, and pulls it superiorly off.

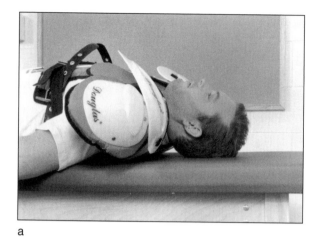
a

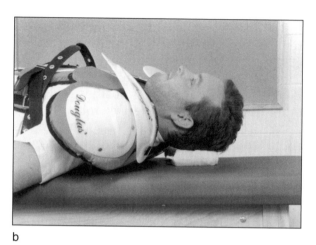
b

**Figure 7.4** *(a)* If the helmet is removed and the shoulder pads are still on, the head will tip back to the floor at an angle. *(b)* Placing padding under the head or removing the shoulder pads maintains the proper alignment of the head and neck to the body.

## Uniforms and Padding

If the athletic trainer needs to assess a non-serious injury, the athlete can remove his own uniform if he can do it without further harm to himself. If the injured part is a limb, it is generally best to first remove the uniform from the noninjured extremity. This will allow more room to manipulate the uniform around the injured body part. A sock can be removed from an injured leg or foot by widening the diameter of the sock while removing it. If that creates pain, cut the sock off.

Padding around an injured body part should be cut off—cautiously—to keep the injured body part from moving and causing unnecessary pain. Padding on the rest of the body can be removed in the normal fashion.

## Lifting and Moving an Athlete

Once an athlete has been assessed, the athletic trainer will decide how he should be removed from the field. If the injury is minor, the athlete may be able to walk off on his own or with minimal help. However, if the injury is more serious, the ATC can use various devices such as straps, stretchers, and backboards to move the athlete from one location to another. When lifting an athlete, or when lifting any heavy weight, the athletic trainer must have a good base of support, keep his feet shoulder-width apart, and always look upward

before and during the lifting. Once the athlete has been secured to a stretcher or backboard, he should be moved feetfirst rather than sideways so that he is less likely to become nauseous.

In normal circumstances injured athletes are splinted and cared for before they are moved. However, in extreme emergencies an athlete may have to be moved before she can be splinted. If, for example, a wall is about to fall on her, to prevent her death the athletic trainer must move her. If she is not splinted, move her lengthwise to keep her bones aligned (see figure 7.5).

## Backboarding

After an injured athlete receives an assessment and care, backboard him

- for any spinal or back injury,
- when the extent of injuries cannot be determined, or
- when there is not enough time to splint obvious fractures, and the injury is serious.

Backboarding an athlete requires several trained emergency personnel and athletic trainers. One person will be in charge and direct the others. Backboard an athlete according to the following procedure, with the person in charge controlling the head throughout the operation:

1. Control the head.
2. Call 911.

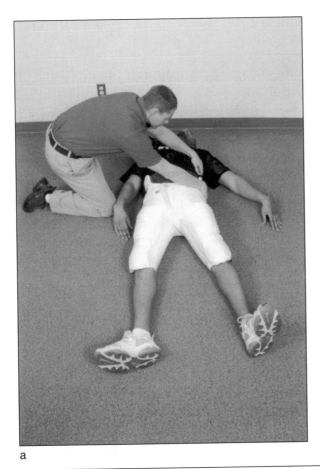

a

b

**Figure 7.5** Emergency movement. *(a)* Moving an athlete sideways causes the extremities to move away from the direction of force. *(b)* Lengthwise movement is less likely to further injure the athlete. The athletic trainer must always keep looking upward to prevent personal back injury while lifting.

3. Place a cervical collar on the injured athlete.

4. Prepare the backboard:

   a. Make sure all the straps are in place.

   b. Match the straps, buckle and clip (usually these are color coded to avoid confusion).

   c. Remove the head block (or sandbags or rolled blanket) and ready it to be placed.

5. Under the direction of the person in control of the head, roll the athlete onto the backboard so that his head is at the top and he is centered on the board.

6. Place both cross-chest straps on over the collarbones and tighten.

7. Put head block (or sandbags or rolled blanket) in place.

8. Tape the head to the board, one strip over the forehead and another over the chin. (Local EMS may or may not require a chin strap.)

9. Place a hip strap.

10. Place a foot strap.

At least four people are needed to carry the backboard—one on each end and two in the middle.

## Short Boarding

Short boarding is done when an athlete reports spinal pain, but is in a seated position. Short

### ❓ What Would You Do If...

At the football game, a player has injured his knee and has been splinted. The athletic trainer indicates they need the golf cart to carry the injured player from the field. You try several times, but the golf cart will not start.

## 🌐 The Real World

One of the basic rules in football is "keep your head up." When the athlete has his head up it is easier to see and it places his neck in a position where an impact is less likely to be harmful.

The running back was handed the ball; he dipped his head and was immediately hit by several opposing team players. He didn't get up at the end of the play. The athletic trainer assessed the player and asked him questions. His evaluation revealed that the injured player had a tingling sensation in both arms and legs. The ATC decided not to move the player, and he called the emergency medical service. The paramedics evaluated the athlete and determined that he had suffered a life-threatening cervical spine injury. They called for a helicopter evacuation.

It was a scary, sobering moment when the helicopter landed in the middle of the football field and evacuated the player to a local hospital.

Thankfully, the young man had suffered only muscle strains on both sides of his neck. He was kept overnight for observation, then sent home. His doctor ordered him to wear a neck brace and strengthen his neck muscles to rehabilitate the muscle strains, before returning to football the following season—there were only two games remaining in the current season. His injury actually changed the behavior of every player on the team—they all paid more attention to their posture after that.

Anonymous

---

boarding should be done only by highly trained emergency personnel and athletic trainers. Short board (figure 7.6) an athlete according to the following procedure, with the person in charge controlling the head and neck of the injured person:

1. Control the head from behind.
2. Call 911.
3. Place a cervical collar on the injured athlete.
4. Prepare the short board:
   a. Make sure all the straps are in place.
   b. Match the straps, buckle and clip (usually these are color coded to avoid confusion).
5. With the person in charge holding tension on the head and neck, wedge the short board between the athlete and the chair.
6. Put the chest straps in place.
7. Control the head from the front, and strap the head to the board.
8. Strap the legs, hips flexed.
9. Place a long backboard perpendicular to the athlete's chair.
10. Rotate the athlete onto the long backboard, keeping the athlete's knees drawn up toward the chest.
11. Release the leg straps so the legs can lie flat on the backboard.
12. Place strap across the chest, but not over the heart area.
13. Place a hip strap.
14. Place a foot strap.

## Ambulatory Movement of Athlete

Ideally, an athlete will be able to walk from the field without support; we can then say he is **ambulatory**. However, an athlete should not be allowed to get up and walk around before the athletic trainer or team physician has made a decision about the extent of an injury. A serious injury should be immobilized before extrication, and an athlete with a suspected serious lower-extremity injury should not be allowed to walk without support. If two students are giving ambulatory aid, the athlete can place one arm over each assistant's shoulders and they can grasp the athlete's back or pants to give support. The

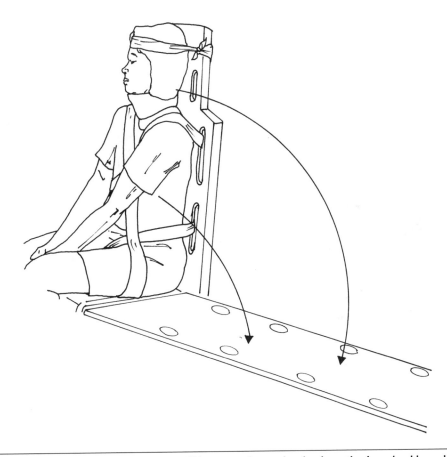

**Figure 7.6** Short boarding. The injured person will be rotated onto her back on the long backboard.

## ❓ What Would You Do If...

After successfully backboarding a wrestler, it is discovered that two of the straps are crossed and are not buckled to themselves, but to another strap. The straps are then switched and buckled correctly. The athletic trainer directs you to make sure that the buckles and the clips need to be easily identified when backboarding.

athlete should not be allowed to apply pressure on the injured body part. If only one assistant is available to give aid, the assistant should be on the same side as the injury with the athlete's arm over the assistant's shoulder while he holds the athlete's hip or pants (see figure 7.7).

An athlete who is not seriously injured and can be cooperative may also be removed from the field using a seated carry. To perform the removal, two student assistants face each other

and lock their arms together as illustrated in figure 7.8. The athlete sits on one set of the locked arms while the other set supports his upper back. He places his arms around the shoulders of the student assistants. The athlete is carried off in the direction he is facing (see figure 7.9).

## Other Methods of Moving an Athlete

Previously in this chapter we discussed the more traditional methods of removing an injured athlete. In this section, we explain two additional methods for removing an athlete.

### Stretcher

What is the difference between a stretcher and a backboard? A backboard is rigid and inflexible and is used to immobilize spinal injuries. A stretcher is made of canvas and is used to transport an athlete without spinal injuries.

**Figure 7.7** A one-person carry is used if the athlete is ill and needs support or when an injured lower extremity can support limited pressure. The injured lower extremity must be next to the rescuer.

## ⁇ What Would You Do If...

An athlete goes down on the field. The ATC has asked you to run out with her whenever that happens today. You are wearing clogs.

A stretcher is used appropriately for an athlete suffering from a knee injury, an asthma attack, dizziness, a diabetic crisis, and so forth. After assessing the athlete and caring for all injuries, logroll the athlete onto the stretcher and secure her in place with three straps, one each at the chest, hips, and feet. The athlete may be able to just slide onto the stretcher, which is fine as long as no pressure is placed upon the injured body part.

As with a backboard, it takes at least four people to carry the stretcher—one on each end and two in the middle—and the athlete should be moved feetfirst or headfirst.

**Figure 7.8** The arm lock is performed with the hand of one rescuer grasping the forearm of another. If the hand slips off the forearm there still is a hand to grasp, whereas if a hand-to-hand grip slips, only air is left.

**Figure 7.9** The two-person carry is used when the injured athlete cannot get off the field without help and should not apply pressure to the injured body part. All splinting should be done before moving the athlete.

### Scoop Stretcher

The scoop stretcher is made of metal and can be separated into two parts. One part provides a thin metal structure that slides underneath the athlete, and then the two parts are reattached at the head and feet (see figure 7.10). Presto, the athlete is on the stretcher and she has not been rolled or lifted. Athletes have one complaint about the scoop stretcher—on a cool night, the metal is cold to the touch.

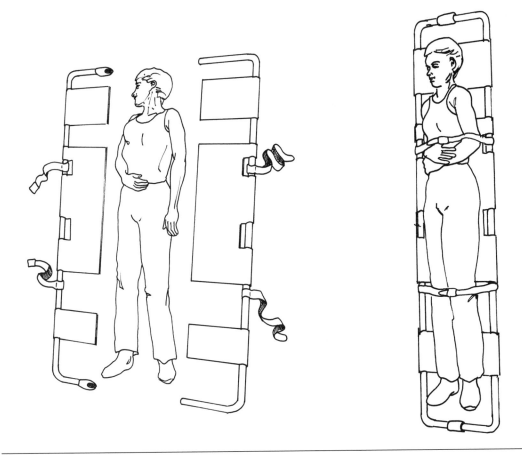

**Figure 7.10**  Scoop stretcher.

## Summary

When an injured athlete must be examined or removed from the field, it is crucial that the injured body part be disturbed as little as possible. Movement of the body part causes pain and aggravation, and it may cause further injury. Athletes who are ambulatory may still need assistance. The athletic trainer must not be rushed into moving an athlete off the field before he is properly splinted or backboarded.

## Key Terms

Define the following terms found in this chapter:

ambulatory          extrication          neck roll

## Questions for Review

1. When is it necessary to remove the equipment and uniform from an athlete? p. 59
2. When should an athlete walk off the field without support? pp. 62, 64-65
3. An athlete who is standing indicates that he has neck pain and tingling sensations. What is the best way to remove him from the field? p. 62
4. List the ways a student assistant can help when the athletic trainer needs to backboard an athlete. pp. 62-63
5. If an athlete has a suspected serious knee injury, list the ways she might be removed from the field. p. 64-67
6. Why is an injured athlete moved feetfirst when she is on a stretcher or a backboard? p. 62

## Activities for Reinforcement

1. Make a list of the various types of splints and other equipment necessary for removing an athlete from a game.
2. With the supervision of an ATC, practice removing an athlete in the various ways discussed in this chapter.
3. Prepare a checklist of items that are necessary to remove game equipment. Look for the equipment before two home games. Is it where it is supposed to be?

## Above and Beyond

1. Using various tools, practice removing a helmet. Make a chart of any problems encountered with each tool. Determine which tool is the easiest to use. The following article can be helpful in identifying the tools.

   Knowx, K.E., and D.M. Kleiner. 1997. Efficiency of tools used to retract a football helmet face mask. *Journal of Athletic Training* 32(3): 211–15.

2. Interview the local EMS personnel. Determine the protocols used to remove an athlete by basic-level ambulance, advanced-level ambulance, and helicopter.

# Unit III

# Understanding Athletics-Related Injuries to the Lower Quarter

# Foot, Ankle, and Lower Leg Injuries

## OBJECTIVES

Upon completing this chapter the student will be able to do the following:
- Understand the basic anatomy of the foot, ankle, and lower leg.
- Describe the various injuries that occur in the foot, ankle, and lower leg.

The foot, ankle, and lower leg support the weight and transfer force as a person walks and runs. The feet and lower legs work to maintain balance and adapt to various surfaces.

Ankle injuries are among the most common injuries seen by team physicians and athletic trainers—in fact, the ankle may be the most frequently injured joint.

## Anatomy of the Foot, Ankle, and Lower Leg

The lower leg, foot, and ankle play a critical role in balance, shock absorption, and movement—the bones provide structure and protection, while the muscles and tendons produce movement.

### Bones and Joints

There are 28 bones in the foot (see figure 8.1). The bones in the toes are called **phalanges**. The toes are numbered one to five, the great toe being number one, and each toe, except the great toe, has three bones: the distal, middle, and proximal phalanges. The great toe has only distal and proximal phalanges. The toe joints are referred to as interphalangeal joints. Under the great toe are two small bones, the sesamoids, which assist with flexion of the toe. The **metatarsals** are the long bones of the foot—like the toes, they are numbered one to five. The joints between the phalanges and the metatarsals are the metatarsophalangeal joints. The midfoot, which lies between the metatarsals and the **talus** and **calcaneus**, contains several small bones that articulate (join together at a joint) with one another, producing some very subtle movements. The ankle is the joint between the talus and calcaneus of the foot and the fibula and tibia of the lower leg. The calcaneus, also known as the heel bone, is below the talus. The posterior portion of the calcaneus is the attachment point of the Achilles tendon.

## For Your Information

### Sesamoids

Sesamoids are bones or cartilage located within a tendon, especially at a joint, that ease muscular movement over a bony surface.

The tibia and fibula articulate at both distal and proximal ends, while between the bones are muscles and ligaments that hold the two bones together from one end to the other. The **medial malleolus** is the end of the tibia on the medial

side and the end of the fibula at the lateral aspect is known as the **lateral malleolus**. The ankle, which is the joint between the foot and the lower leg, is held together by ligaments. The fibula extends past the ankle joint and will stop severe eversion movement (see figure 8.1).

## ❓ What Would You Do If...

A hockey player with an ankle sprain has been instructed to apply ice for 20 minutes when she gets home. She "logically" tells you that if 20 minutes is good then 40 minutes should be great.

## Arches of the Foot

There are three arches on the **plantar** (bottom) **surface** of the foot that function as shock absorbers—the transverse, longitudinal, and metatarsal arches (see figure 8.2). The transverse arch is located in front of the heel and goes from

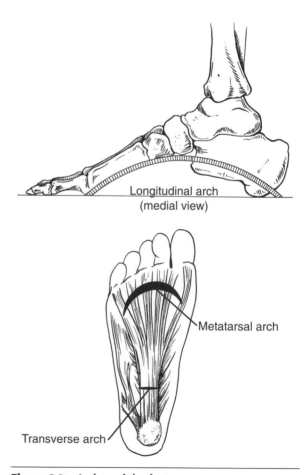

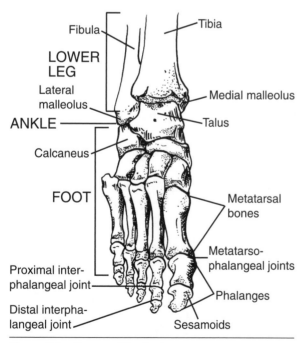

**Figure 8.1** Bones of the foot.

**Figure 8.2** Arches of the foot.

the fifth metatarsal to the navicular bone of the foot. The longitudinal arch runs from the calcaneus to the metatarsal heads. The metatarsal arch runs along the metatarsal heads.

## Muscles

The muscles of the lower leg and ankle control movement of the foot and leg (see figure 8.3). The peroneal muscles, including the peroneus brevis and peroneus longus, attach to the lateral aspect of the lower leg and run a course to the lateral aspect and underside of the foot. As you can imagine, this muscle group helps stabilize the lateral aspect of the ankle. The **gastrocnemius** is a powerful muscle in the calf, which attaches by the Achilles tendon at the posterior aspect of the lower leg—it allows athletes to propel themselves when running.

## Ligaments

There are strong ligaments of the foot located laterally, medially, and on the plantar surface. Many of the names of the ligaments give the attachment points, making it easier to identify their locations. The lateral aspect of the ankle has numerous ligaments including the anterior

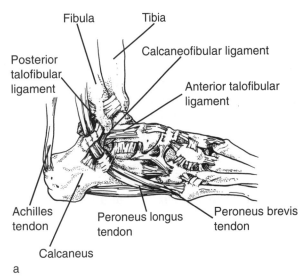

a

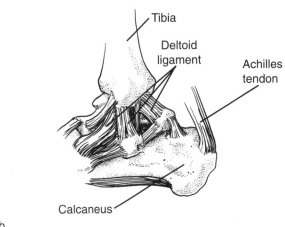

b

**Figure 8.4** Ligaments of the foot (*a*) lateral view, (*b*) medial view.

talofibular, posterior talofibular, and calcaneofibular ligaments (see figure 8.4a). The lateral ligaments hold the bony structures together on the lateral side but are not as strong as the medial ligament. The medial ligament is called the deltoid (see figure 8.4b). The deltoid covers the entire surface of the medial side of the ankle and maintains stability, especially during eversion. The deltoid ligament is stronger than all of the lateral ligaments combined.

## Preventing Foot, Ankle, and Lower Leg Injuries

Taking care of the foot, ankle, and lower leg is essential to injury prevention and continuous athletic participation. Many athletes take protective measures such as wearing shoes that

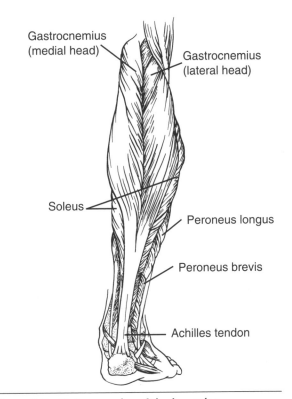

**Figure 8.3** Major muscles of the lower leg.

provide ankle and arch support, using supportive ankle taping (to prevent ankle inversion), and wearing shin guards (to prevent contusions of the lower leg). Strengthening and conditioning programs can also help to prevent injuries. If the team physician finds a weakness in the athlete's foot, ankle, or lower leg, the athlete should be placed on a rehabilitation program that emphasizes strengthening. In some instances, muscles that are very tight will need to be stretched. Proper conditioning, under the guidance of a coach, may prevent stress fractures.

# Treating Foot, Ankle, and Lower Leg Injuries and Conditions

The feet and legs form the foundation on which an athlete walks and runs. Injuries to ligaments, muscles, tendons, and bones in this area are disabling.

## Ligament Injuries

A sprain is a stretching or tearing of ligaments and usually occurs as a result of trauma to a joint that is forced to an extreme of its range of movement. In this region of the body, sprains commonly occur at the great toe, arch, lateral ankle joint, and medial ankle joint.

### Great Toe Sprain

The great toe helps an athlete kick a ball, push off when walking or running, and maintain balance. When excessive force is applied to the great toe, such as forced flexion or extension, the ligaments can be sprained. Some sports medicine specialists believe that artificial turf causes more great toe sprains than real grass. Regardless of the cause, the athlete will experience pain, swelling, discoloration, and the inability to walk or run normally. The athletic trainer will recommend PRICE (see chapter 5). When the athlete returns to action, the great toe can be taped and padded to provide support and decrease pain.

### Arch Sprain (Transverse and Longitudinal)

An arch sprain can be caused by running on a hard surface, improper footwear, or repetitive stress. The athlete will report significant pain over the involved arch and will experience difficulty walking or running. During the assessment the athletic trainer will notice swelling and possibly some discoloration over the plantar surface. PRICE is the best way to handle the arch sprain. The application of an arch pad may relieve some of the pain, because the foot flattens somewhat during walking or running. The athlete should strengthen the arch by exercising the muscles of the foot and by stretching the Achilles tendon.

### Lateral and Medial Ankle Sprains

One of the enemies of athletic participation is an ankle sprain. About 85 percent of ankle sprains occur due to excessive inversion. Only about 15 percent of ankle sprains occur because the ankle is excessively everted. The reason for this difference is twofold—first, the deltoid ligament is very strong compared to the lateral ligaments, and second, the fibula prevents severe eversion.

When the ankle inverts, the lateral ligaments are injured—the severity of the injury will depend upon the amount of force, the amount of taping, the type of shoe, and the strength of the muscles. During an excessive eversion, the deltoid ligament will be injured.

The athlete with an ankle injury must be evaluated to determine its severity. Therefore, the shoe must be removed, and the sock must be cut off or removed by the athlete. Upon examination of the ankle the athletic trainer may observe swelling and discoloration—he will determine the severity of injury based on the athlete's ability to move the ankle. If there is no decreased range of motion or strength, the athlete may be allowed to play with the ankle protected by a special brace or tape. Any decrease in range of motion will be treated with PRICE. A referral to the team physician is necessary when there is crepitus, rapid swelling, or bony deformity—a fracture is likely in any of those instances.

### Ankle Dislocation

An ankle dislocation can occur either anteriorly or posteriorly. An anterior dislocation occurs when the heel of the foot strikes the ground forcefully. A posterior dislocation occurs with a blow to the anterior aspect of the leg while the ankle is in plantar flexion. The athlete will be in

## What Would You Do If...

The athletic trainer has been caring for an athlete who has lower-leg pain. In gym class you note that this athlete plays without shoes. He constantly limps during class and at practices.

obvious pain and will refuse to move, or allow touching of, the foot. There will be deformity and the inability to use the foot. Swelling will rapidly appear. It is important to act quickly in the case of an ankle dislocation. The athletic trainer should call 911, splint the lower leg and ankle, ice, and remove the athlete from the field. In addition to damaging the ligaments, nerves and blood vessels can be injured; therefore the team physician must put the bones back in place.

## Muscle and Tendon Injuries

Strains occur as a result of overstretching or putting a muscle or tendon under excessive tension. **Tendinitis**, which is the inflammation of a tendon, typically occurs as a result of a repetitive stress such as running or jumping. Common tendon injuries and strains in this region involve the Achilles tendon.

### Achilles Tendinitis

The **Achilles tendon** is the strong tendon joining the gastrocnemius muscle in the calf to the heel. Any sport involving repeated running, jumping, and landing may cause cells in the tendon to break down prematurely—this irritation or inflammation is referred to as tendinitis. During an evaluation the athletic trainer will note swelling and tenderness and an expression of pain on the athlete's face when he palpates the Achilles tendon, especially with dorsiflexion and crepitus. The athlete will also be weak when plantar flexion is resisted. She must rest the tendon and apply ice, and she may need to be referred to a physician for medication. As healing progresses, gentle stretching and strengthening exercises are helpful. If the athlete does not follow instructions or resumes activity too soon, the tendon may thicken, which is the body's protective response. Unfortunately, a thickened tendon will limit her range of motion and decrease her running and jumping

ability. With severe damage the athletic trainer will feel crepitus over the tendon, and in the worse case the tendon may completely rupture.

### Achilles Tendon Rupture

An athlete falls to the court or field clutching his leg in pain, and he reports that he feels as if someone shot him in the back of the lower leg— a typical symptom of an Achilles tendon rupture. The rupture occurs when there is forced dorsiflexion of the foot, a blow over the Achilles tendon, or a sudden forceful contraction of the gastrocnemius muscle. The athlete will feel the tearing, and he will have difficulty walking. Weakness or complete loss of plantar flexion will be noticed. The ATC will observe swelling and an obvious depression where the Achilles tendon used to be attached. The athlete will be in obvious pain and should be referred to the team physician immediately after he has been placed in a splint, iced, and given crutches. The Achilles tendon must be repaired surgically by reattaching it to the calcaneus.

## Bone Injuries

Direct impacts to an area and repetitive use can cause fractures. Common symptoms include pain, pressure, and an inability to move the body part. The athletic trainer will discover crepitus, swelling, and possible bone displacement. After splinting, the athlete must be referred to a physician for X rays and a cast. The base of the fifth metatarsal and the epiphyses of the distal tibia and fibula are common fracture sites. Stress fractures, which are caused by repetitive use, are often seen in several areas around the foot, ankle, and lower leg.

### Fifth Metatarsal Avulsion Fracture (Jones Fracture)

The most common avulsion fracture is of the fifth metatarsal—a **Jones fracture** (figure 8.5). When an ankle is forced into inversion, the muscles contract so forcefully to stabilize the lateral aspect of the ankle that the peroneus brevis tendon pulls part of the bone away at its attachment. The athletic trainer will treat the injury initially using the PRICE technique and refer the athlete to the team physician. Many physicians will cast the ankle to allow the bone to heal.

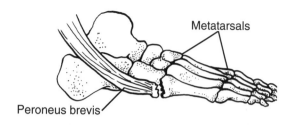

Metatarsals

Peroneus brevis

**Figure 8.5**  Jones fracture.

### *Epiphyseal Injury of Distal Tibia and Fibula*

The distal tibia and fibula epiphyses, or growth plates, can become injured when the ankle is forced into plantar flexion and inversion. The athlete will experience pain and swelling over the epiphysis, and she will have difficulty walking or running because of pain. The athletic trainer will splint the injury and refer her to a physician for X rays. This is a potentially serious injury because it is possible for the epiphysis to close prematurely, which will stunt bone growth at that site.

### *Stress Fractures*

Stress fractures of the lower leg and foot most commonly occur to the tibia, fibula, and metatarsals, and repetitive stress due to running is usually the cause. The athlete will present with pain that becomes more intense at night and following activity. Pain and swelling will be located over the bone. Some physicians believe that a stress fracture can be distinguished by using a tuning fork—the vibrations from the tuning fork vibrate the bone but they do not irritate muscles. The edge of one tine of the fork is struck against the assessor's knee, and the base of the tuning fork is placed on the injured site. If the athlete indicates pain, she most likely has a fracture. A bone scan can be used to verify the diagnosis of a stress fracture. An X ray will not show a stress fracture until two weeks after the initial injury when a callus begins to form at the site. Stress fractures require four to six weeks of rest, and the athlete should be referred to the team physician. Although stress fractures are rarely casted, the athlete will be issued crutches to eliminate pressure on the limb. If the injury is not detected early or the athlete fails to report it, a complete fracture

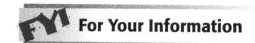

## For Your Information

### Bone scan

A bone scan is a diagnostic test performed with a radioactive substance that allows physicians to see very small disruptions in the bone.

may result, which could create serious complications for the athlete.

## Other Common Injuries

The weight-bearing lower extremities are prone to other injuries, including shinsplints, anterior compartment syndrome, and contusions.

### *Shinsplints, or Medial Tibial Stress Syndrome*

**Shinsplints** is a common term used for pain in the lower leg. Some people call a muscle strain, stress fracture, and even tendinitis, shinsplints. However, to doctors, shinsplints are known as medial tibial stress syndrome. The muscle fibers on the medial side of the tibia become torn and irritated. The athlete will complain of pain and inability to run or walk properly. The pain will be located over the distal, medial side of the tibia, although there may be swelling on the lateral side as well. The athlete will generally have tight calf muscles, older shoes, and be out of shape for the running she is currently doing. There are several successful methods of relieving shinsplints—PRICE is first and foremost. If the athlete limps she must stop running and rest or at least change her training to biking instead of running, for example. When she has permission to return to participation, the athletic trainer may wrap the medial side of the leg, pulling the soft tissue toward the bone, and recommend new shoes, stretching, and arch supports.

### *Anterior Compartment Syndrome*

Anterior compartment syndrome is sometimes mistaken for shinsplints, but as its name implies, it is an anterior compartment injury. The muscles to the anterior aspect of the tibia are enclosed in connective tissue. If, due to overuse or a severe impact, the tissue in the compartment swells, it increases the pressure on the connective tissue, which causes severe pain that increases with activity and does not subside when there is no activity or a period of rest. The athletic trainer will note hot, red skin, loss of foot motion, and hardness of the area. An inability to move the foot and severe pain are critical indicators of this problem. The athlete must be seen by a physician immediately to prevent nerve damage caused by the pressure—the physician will make an incision in the leg to relieve the pressure, and the athlete can return to activity while wearing a supportive brace or bandage.

### Contusions

Soccer and field hockey players are prone to contusions of the lower leg—thus the invention of the shin guard, to prevent these contusions. The impact of a ball, stick, or foot on the shin will cause swelling, pain, and discoloration. The athlete may limp and have limited range of motion. The ATC will recommend ice and rest until full range of motion is restored. The athlete will need additional padding, such as a donut, to protect the area from further impacts.

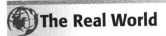 **The Real World**

A football player complained of feeling a pop in his right lower leg during the first half of a football game. We examined him—he had full range of motion and strength of the right lower extremity—and then he completed the game. In the training room after the game we examined him again. He complained of pain in the lateral calf, and again he had full range of motion and strength in the leg with pain over the proximal and distal fibula. We placed him on crutches with instructions not to put any weight on the leg and told him to call if the pain increased. He called that evening, saying he was in the greatest pain that he had ever had. We told him to go to the emergency room. His X rays were negative for a fracture, but he had increased pressure in the anterior and lateral compartments of his lower leg. He had surgery that night to relieve the pressure in each compartment. The anterior release was without complications, but when the lateral release was performed, the doctors found a major complication—a tear in a muscle, specifically the peroneus longus.

Phil Voorhis, MSEd, ATC

## Summary

In addition to fractures, sprains, and strains, injuries due to stress and overuse are common in the lower leg, foot, and ankle area. The bones, ligaments, and tendons must be aligned to prevent injury and for the joints to function properly. PRICE is used to care for injuries of the lower extremity.

## Key Terms

Define the following terms found in this chapter:

| | | | |
|---|---|---|---|
| Achilles tendon | Jones fracture | metatarsals | shinsplints |
| calcaneus | lateral malleolus | phalanges | talus |
| gastrocnemius | medial malleolus | plantar surface | tendinitis |

## Questions for Review

1. On an anatomical picture of the foot, label the anatomical structures discussed in this chapter. pp. 71-73
2. What area of the ankle is vulnerable to sprain and strain injuries? pp. 74-75
3. List all of the injuries that can happen as a result of an inversion of the ankle. pp. 74, 75

4. Make a list of ways to care for the feet that are critical in prevention of injury. pp. 73-74
5. Why are there more lateral than medial ankle sprains? pp. 73-74
6. Crepitus over the Achilles tendon is a sign of what injury? p. 75
7. What causes medial tibial stress syndrome? p. 76

## Activities for Reinforcement

1. Volunteer to work in a local podiatrist's office for an afternoon. What types of athletic injuries does the podiatrist regularly treat?
2. Spray the bottom of your foot with water and make an imprint on a paper towel. What type of plantar arch do you have? Is it the same as others in the class?

## Above and Beyond

1. Do a report on one of the following subjects, including the prevention, cause, treatment, and rehabilitation of the condition:
   - plantar fasciitis
   - Athlete's foot
   - anterior compartment syndrome
2. Using the textbooks listed in item 3, do a report on one of the following topics:
   - orthotics and their uses
   - walking and running gaits
3. Using a text dedicated to athletic injury assessment, create a checklist describing how to assess foot, ankle, or lower leg injuries.

   Anderson, M., and S. Hall. 1995. *Sports injury management.* Baltimore: Williams & Wilkins.

   Anthony, C.P., and N.J. Kolthoff. 1975. *Textbook of anatomy and physiology.* St. Louis: Mosby.

   Arnheim, D.D. 1989. *Modern principles of athletic training.* St. Louis: Times Mirror/Mosby.

# Knee Injuries

The knee is vulnerable to ligament sprains, tendon strains, and cartilage damage. In this chapter we describe basic anatomy of the knee and injuries common to athletes.

## Anatomy of the Knee

The knee is a hinge joint at the articulation, or point of contact, of three bones. The joint is stabilized by four major ligaments, cartilage, and strong musculature. The knee is also able to rotate.

### Bones

The bones that form the knee joint are the femur, tibia, and patella (see figure 9.1). The primary movement of the knee occurs at the articulation of the tibia and femur, which is called the tibiofemoral joint. The patella is a sesamoid, or floating bone, which is embedded in the patellar tendon that attaches the quadriceps muscles to the front of the tibia and protects the front of the joint. As the knee flexes and extends, the patella glides up and down on the front of the femur. This is called the patella femoral joint.

### Cartilage

The ends of the tibia and the femur are covered and cushioned by pieces of tough cartilage tissue called the **menisci**. Without the menisci, the tibia and femur would rub against each other, which would cause the bone to wear down quickly. The menisci also

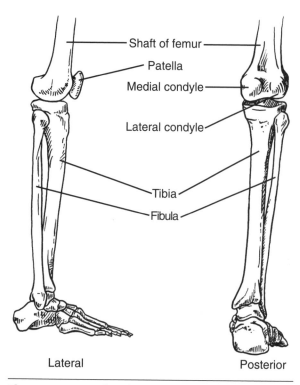

**Figure 9.1** Lateral and posterior views of the knee.

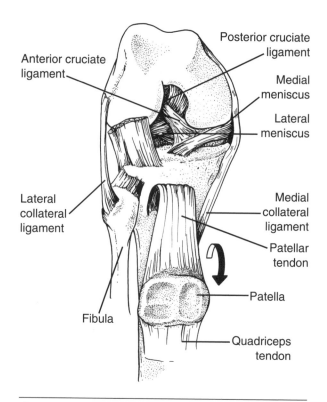

**Figure 9.2** Major ligaments of the knee. Knee ligaments include the medial collateral, lateral collateral, anterior cruciate, and posterior cruciate ligaments. Note how the cruciate ligaments cross in the center of the knee.

help to stabilize the knee joint. The top of the tibia is flat, like a tabletop. The end of the femur, specifically the condyles, is rounded like an orange. Without something to stabilize the joint, the femur would move a lot on the tibia—in other words, the orange would roll around on the tabletop. The menisci are thicker on the sides and thinner in the middle, forming a dish-shaped hollow. They are also attached to the top of the tibia, which provides a seat for the femoral condyles to sit in on top of the tibia—like putting the orange in a bowl on the table. The femur can move, but it will not roll off of the tibia.

## Ligaments

There are four primary knee ligaments (see figure 9.2). The medial collateral ligament helps to provide stability to the inside or medial aspect of the knee. The lateral collateral ligament helps to stabilize the outside or lateral aspect of the knee. The **anterior cruciate ligament (ACL)** keeps the tibia from moving forward on the femur, and the posterior cruciate ligament prevents the tibia from moving backward on the femur. The anterior and posterior cruciate ligaments pass through the middle of the knee joint

and cross each other, hence the name cruciate, which means "cross-shaped."

## Muscles

The muscles of the knee provide both movement and stability. The primary muscles spanning the knee include the quadriceps group and the hamstring group. Knee extension is primarily performed by the four quadriceps muscles: the vastus medialis, vastus lateralis, vastus intermedius, and rectus femoris (see figure 9.3).

Flexion of the knee is predominantly the result of contracting the hamstring muscles. The term **hamstrings** refers collectively to the biceps femoris, semimembranosus, and the semitendinosus muscles (see figure 9.4). The three hamstring muscles attach on the posterior aspect of the lower pelvis, run down the back of the thigh, and across the knee to their attachment on the tibia—by the location of their attachments, they help prevent forward movement of the tibia on the femur.

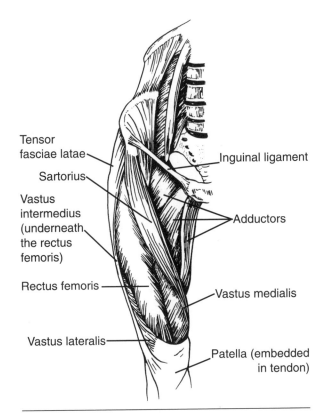

Tensor fasciae latae

Sartorius

Vastus intermedius (underneath the rectus femoris)

Rectus femoris

Vastus lateralis

Inguinal ligament

Adductors

Vastus medialis

Patella (embedded in tendon)

**Figure 9.3** The quadriceps muscles.

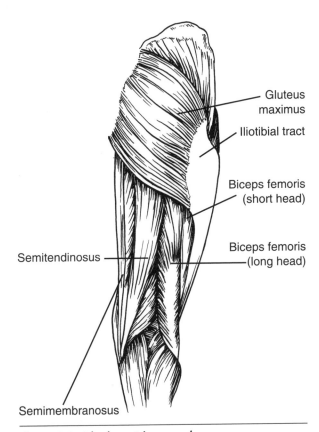

Gluteus maximus

Iliotibial tract

Biceps femoris (short head)

Biceps femoris (long head)

Semitendinosus

Semimembranosus

**Figure 9.4** The hamstring muscles.

# Preventing Knee Injuries

Ligament sprains are among the most common injuries seen at the knee. Remembering that the muscles provide stability to the knee and help resist abnormal bony movement, athletes should develop strength in the muscles in the area—the quadriceps and hamstrings as well as the gastrocnemius (calf), and the hip abductors and adductor muscles. Heel raises are a good way to strengthen the gastrocnemius, which is located at the back of the lower leg and helps to point the toes. We will discuss the hip abductor and adductor muscles in chapter 10. Some ATCs and athletes use preventive knee braces that are designed to protect the medial collateral ligament (see figure 9.5).

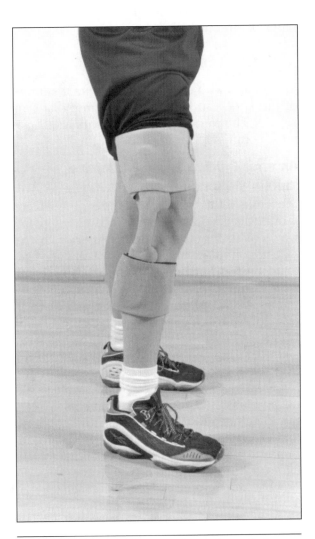

**Figure 9.5** A protective knee brace is applied to an athlete's knee to prevent tearing of the medial collateral ligament, which can result from a blow to the lateral side.

An athlete has been treated in the athletic training room for jumper's knee. While you are getting the water coolers set up for practice you notice that this athlete is starting to play one-on-one with a teammate before warming up and stretching.

# Treating Knee Injuries and Conditions

The knee is exposed to many forces. This makes it vulnerable to injuries, especially to the ligaments, but tendon and bone injuries also occur. The patella and menisci are subject to unique types of athletics-related injuries.

## Ligament Injuries

In common with other joints, ligament sprains of the knee can be either mild, moderate, or severe. The four primary ligaments are those most commonly sprained.

### Anterior Cruciate Ligament Injuries

The ACL keeps the tibia from moving forward on the femur. If this ligament is injured, the athlete is often disabled, complaining of the knee giving way, collapsing, and popping. Injuries to the ACL are often the most serious of all knee ligament injuries, and the ACL is the ligament that is most frequently surgically reconstructed.

The ACL is often injured as the athlete is attempting to change directions quickly and twists the lower leg—he may hear a popping sound during the twisting mechanism. However, it can also be injured because of excessive hyperextension. A torn ACL causes rapid swelling and loss of knee function. Immediate treatment includes PRICE, and a knee immobilizer and crutches provide additional knee protection. Follow-up with an orthopedist is necessary if a torn ACL is suspected.

An athlete rarely can continue a high level of function with a torn ACL, and these injuries often need to be surgically reconstructed. This, however, is a determination that must be made by the athlete, the surgeon, and the athlete's family. The decision may depend on the amount of instability that exists, the level of function desired by the athlete, and the age of the athlete.

Rehabilitation of an ACL injury focuses on strengthening the hamstrings to help stabilize the tibia as well as to regain full function. Even with an aggressive ACL rehabilitation program, it may be six months before the athlete can return to participation.

### Posterior Cruciate Ligament Injuries

The **posterior cruciate ligament (PCL)** prevents posterior tibial movement on the femur. The PCL is frequently injured when an athlete falls and a bent knee bears his full weight, when the knee is forcefully hyperflexed, or a blow is delivered to the front of the tibia.

The ATC may suspect a PCL injury, after determining the mechanism of the injury, if the athlete reports having heard a pop. Surprisingly, there is often little swelling with PCL injuries. Initial treatment should include PRICE and referral to a physician. A rehabilitation program for mild or moderate PCL sprains will focus on strengthening the quadriceps and regaining full function. Although some physicians disagree about whether or not surgery should be performed on a severe PCL injury, even complete PCL tears can be rehabilitated without surgical intervention—many athletes can become functional again after the initial pain and swelling are controlled and the knee is strengthened.

### Medial Collateral Ligament Sprains

The medial collateral ligament (MCL) is frequently injured when an athlete receives a blow to the outside of the knee. This causes the knee to bend inward (valgus stress) and stresses the MCL. A *mild* MCL sprain will usually result in medial joint line pain, little if any swelling, no joint laxity when stressed by the ATC, and full knee flexion and extension. A *moderate* MCL sprain will often result in mild swelling, discomfort, and some joint laxity when stressed by the ATC during the injury assessment. A moderate or severe amount of swelling, loss of function, and a great deal of joint laxity often characterize a *severe* MCL injury.

Regardless of the severity of the injury, the athlete's knee should be treated with PRICE. A mild injury may only need an elastic wrap for compression and support. However, with a moderate or severe MCL injury, the knee should be put in an immobilizer. Rehabilitation considerations include focusing on strengthening the muscles that cross the medial aspect of the knee. If the knee has moderate or severe MCL damage, the ATC should consider the possibility of damage to the menisci or an ACL injury.

### Lateral Collateral Ligament Injuries

Lateral collateral ligament (LCL) injuries occur less frequently than MCL injuries—the signs and symptoms are similar except, of course, the discomfort is at the lateral aspect of the knee. Treatment for a LCL injury is the same as for a MCL injury. In terms of regaining joint stability, strengthening exercises should focus on the lateral thigh muscles and hamstrings.

## Muscle and Tendon Injuries

Patellar tendinitis is an overuse disorder characterized by quadriceps weakness and tenderness over the patellar tendon, with minimal swelling. The condition is also called jumper's knee because athletes who perform a lot of jumping (e.g., basketball and volleyball players) often get this condition. In the early stages, the athlete typically has pain after activity. The ATC treating an athlete with this condition will attempt to control inflammation by applying ice and modifying her activity level, usually restricting running and jumping. The rehabilitation program should address any flexibility problems or weakness of the leg.

## Bone Injuries

Although the patella is not immune to fracture, other bone injuries are more common, such as chondromalacia and patellar dislocations.

### Patellar Femoral Syndrome

Patellar femoral syndrome is a fancy name for a set of symptoms that include pain and discomfort around the patella—often caused by patellar tracking problems. As the knee bends, instead of riding smoothly the patella is grated across the femur, causing the cartilage on the back of the patella to soften or wear away. This is known as **chondromalacia,** which is characterized by achiness around the patella, especially with prolonged sitting in the same position. The athlete will often report a grinding sensation with flexion and extension. In fact, if the ATC places her hand over the patella as the athlete flexes and extends his knee, the grinding can even be felt. The treatment plan for chondromalacia involves correcting any patellar tracking problems that exist, strengthening the vastus medialis muscle, and developing better flexibility of the quadriceps and hamstring muscles. Bent leg activities should be avoided because they tend to aggravate the condition.

### Patella Dislocation

Occasionally an athlete's patella will be forced to the lateral aspect of the knee. This often occurs while the knee is bent and forced to twist inward.

## The Real World

As an athletic trainer at a large high school, I was summoned to the track and field area because an athlete had reportedly fallen over the hurdles. When I arrived at the track, the athlete was in obvious pain and moaning that his knees were injured. I gently pulled up his pant legs to see what was wrong. There were obvious deformities at the anterior aspects of both knees. Where the patellae should have been were two large depressions. The patellae themselves were sitting several inches above his knee joints, where his quadriceps had pulled them. We called EMS immediately. I acted very calm and reassuring, knowing that if the young man panicked, things would only get worse. We immobilized his legs and treated him for shock. Once he was at the hospital, the surgeons determined that he had ruptured one patellar tendon and fractured his other patella in half. Although future contact with this athlete was limited, his recovery looked positive because he received quick advanced care by physicians, and he was in good health.

Lisa V. Pitney, MSEd, ATC

This deformity is hard to overlook. The athlete is often in distress, and the EMS must be called unless the team physician is present. Only a physician should reduce a dislocated patella; otherwise complications may result and the posterior aspect of the patella may be injured further.

Treatment involves immobilizing the knee for a short time, and then the athlete should begin exercising to regain mobility and strength around the knee joint. Sometimes athletes are advised to wear a knee sleeve with a patellar hole to help keep the patella in place during activity.

# Other Common Injuries

Each large piece of fibrous cartilage in the knee joint is referred to as a meniscus—its function is shock absorption and stability. Unfortunately, the menisci are vulnerable to significant injury, specifically tears.

## Meniscal Injuries

The most common injury to the meniscus is a tear, which can be on the outer edge, middle, or inside edge of the meniscus, or on the ends (horns) of the meniscus. Tears of the meniscus typically happen with a twisting movement of the knee, or with hyperflexion and hyperextension injuries. An athlete with a torn meniscus will often complain of pain at the joint line; have problems putting weight on the limb; complain of clicking, catching, or locking; and walk with a limp. He is also unable to fully extend and flex the knee and may have some swelling.

Tears of the meniscus used to be treated by surgically removing the entire meniscus (called a **meniscectomy**). Now, due in part to the prevalence of **arthroscopic surgery** where very small surgical instruments are put into the knee through tiny holes, treatment of a torn meniscus often involves taking out only the small piece of tissue that has been torn. Depending upon where the meniscus is torn, sometimes surgeons are able to suture (sew) it back together.

During rehabilitation after an injury or surgery on the meniscus, an athlete will use exercises initially that do not involve placing any weight on the injured leg—aquatic therapy programs are ideal for helping to reestablish range of motion and strength. Then she will progress slowly to more weight-bearing exercises as tolerated.

## Osgood-Schlatter Disorder

Younger athletes who perform a great deal of running and jumping sometimes develop an irritation at the site of the patellar tendon attachment to the front of the tibia, which is called the tibial tuberosity. The bones of an adolescent are still somewhat soft, and repeated stressful activity can sometimes cause the patellar tendon to partially pull away from the bone, an injury called **Osgood-Schlatter disorder**, or Osgood-Schlatter disease. It typically causes discomfort of the knee, swelling, tenderness, and pain during activity. Athletes with this condition should restrict their activity until it is resolved. This, however, does not mean they should stop all activity. For example, although a basketball player should stop aggressive running and jumping, an alternative activity that may not irritate the injury is stationary bicycling. She can maintain her fitness level, without causing additional problems. As a general rule of thumb, pain should be used as a guide; that is, activity should be modified based on the pain level reported by the athlete. If she does not modify her activity appropriately, she may experience prolonged periods of pain. Ice applications before and after activity are also helpful. A special pad may need to be made to fit over the front of the tibia because this area becomes extremely tender. Osgood-Schlatter disorder often improves by age 16 or 17, but a bony growth may develop at the top of the tibia. Unfortunately, the bump remains even after the symptoms of the condition have disappeared.

## Summary

The knee is the joint between the femur, tibia, and patella. The cartilage, or menisci, of the knee provides a cushion between the tibia and femur. Four primary ligaments aid in the stability of the knee—the medial collateral, lateral collateral, anterior cruciate, and posterior cruciate ligaments. A complete tear to the anterior cruciate ligament needs to be surgically repaired by an orthopedic surgeon. The quadriceps and the hamstrings help to extend and flex the knee, respectively.

## Key Terms

Define the following terms found in this chapter:

| | |
|---|---|
| anterior cruciate ligament (ACL) | meniscectomy |
| arthroscopic surgery | menisci (meniscus) |
| chondromalacia | Osgood-Schlatter disorder |
| hamstrings | posterior cruciate ligament (PCL) |

## Questions for Review

1. Name the three bones that comprise the knee joint. p. 79
2. Identify the four primary ligaments that give the knee stability. p. 80
3. Find the names of the four muscles of the quadriceps. p. 80
4. What three muscles comprise the hamstrings? What movements can they produce? p. 80
5. If an injury caused the tibia to move forward on the femur, what ligament would most likely become overstretched or torn? p. 82
6. Name the ligament that would be likely to become stretched or torn if an athlete had an opponent fall into the outside of her knee and it was bent inward. p. 82
7. Describe how an ATC should care for a grade two, or moderate, medial collateral ligament sprain. pp. 82-83

## Activities for Reinforcement

1. Invite an ATC to class to demonstrate how she evaluates a knee injury.
2. Invite an orthopedic surgeon to class to discuss common knee surgeries.

# Above and Beyond

1. Find a text dedicated to athletic injury assessment and develop a checklist of how to assess a knee injury. Following are some references to consider:

   Booher, J.M., and G.A. Thibodeau. 1989. *Athletic injury assessment*. 2d ed. St. Louis: Times Mirror/Mosby.

   Hartley, A. 1991. *Practical joint assessment*. St. Louis: Mosby.

2. Select an article from the list below, and do a report on knee injuries among athletes.

   Beck, J.L., and B.P. Wildermuth. 1985. The female athlete's knee. *Clinics in Sports Medicine* 4: 345–66.

   Gray, J.J., D. Taunton, D. McKenzie, J. Clement, J. McConkey, and R. Davidson. 1985. A survey of injuries to the anterior ligament of the knee in female basketball players. *International Journal of Sports Medicine* 6: 314–16.

   Pritchett, J. 1988. A claims-made study of knee injuries due to football in high school athletes. *Journal of Pediatric Orthopedics* 8(5): 551–53.

# Hip, Pelvis, and Thigh Injuries

The hip, pelvis, and thigh contain some of the strongest muscles in the body; but the area is also subjected to tremendous demands. Thus, they are vulnerable to injuries that can sideline a player for long periods of time. Both their importance in sports and their vulnerability make it particularly important to know how to prevent and treat injuries to these areas.

## Anatomy of the Hip, Pelvis, and Thigh

The hip joint, which is a synovial ball-and-socket joint, is the articulation between the femur and the pelvis—the head of the femur fits into the cup-shaped acetabulum. The **acetabulum** is also called the hip socket; it is very deep and covered by thick ligamentous structures, which provide stability. Figure 10.1 shows the lateral view of the hip and pelvis.

The pelvis and femur, which is the longest bone in the body, are connected with thick, strong ligaments. Two of the muscle groups of the femur are the quadriceps and hamstrings.

The hip muscles include the most powerful muscles in the body. The hip flexor group flexes the thigh, and the hamstrings and gluteus maximus extend the thigh (see figure 10.2). Abduction of the hip is predominantly the result of contracting the lateral muscles, which include the gluteus medius and minimus and the tensor fascia latae. Adduction of the hip is performed primarily by contracting the groin muscles, which originate and mesh into the symphysis pubis region and run a course down the medial aspect of the femur.

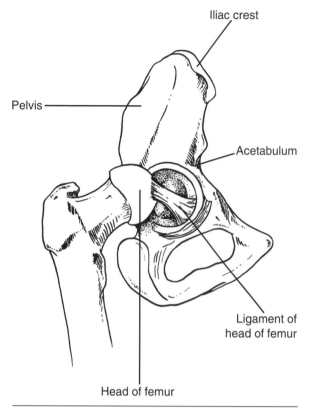

**Figure 10.1** Lateral view of hip and pelvis.

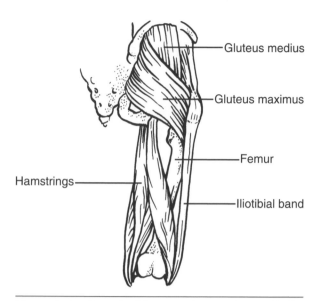

**Figure 10.2** Posterior hip musculature. Along with the hamstrings, the gluteus maximus and gluteus medius help extend the thigh.

# Preventing Hip Injuries

Because the hip is a very stable joint, the athletic trainer will not see many sprained ligaments or dislocations in this area. He will, however, see many muscular strain-related injuries. Therefore, proper flexibility training and stretching prior to vigorous exercise or activity is warranted. Moreover, because many sports expose the thigh to contact, the athletes must wear proper equipment—for example, in football, athletes should wear a secure thigh pad that covers a significant portion of the quadriceps. Contact-type injuries also can occur at the iliac crest (the point of the hip), because this area has little natural protection. In sports such as football the players are required to wear a hip pad to cover this area. Proper strength training for any portion of the body can never be too strongly emphasized, and the muscles around the hip and lower torso region are considered the "core" region—proper strength in these muscles is necessary for normal balance and stability.

# Treating Hip, Pelvis, and Thigh Injuries and Conditions

Most injuries to the hip, pelvis, and thigh are strains and contusions. However, the area is not exempt from other injuries, such as fractures and dislocations.

## Ligament Injuries

The hip is a ball-and-socket joint that is extremely stable—mostly because the head of the femur sits so deeply in the pelvis. Very thick ligamentous structures and strong muscles also surround the hip.

## Muscle and Tendon Injuries

Thigh strains are common athletic injuries, especially to the hip flexor, extensor, and groin musculature. Many muscles in the leg cross two joints—for example, the hamstrings cross the back of the hip joint to help with extension and the knee joint to help flex the knee—and some people see this as the cause of the strains in the region. Another theory is that when a strength imbalance occurs, the stronger muscle group puts excessive tension on the opposing muscle group; for example, if an athlete has a great deal of strength in her quadriceps, but her hamstrings are weak, the hamstrings are prone to being strained.

Strains should initially be treated with PRICE and wrapped with a supportive elastic bandage. Moderate and severe strains may need to be referred to a physician. Rehabilitation will focus on regaining strength and range of motion and enhancing flexibility prior to returning to play.

## Bone Injuries

Although pelvic fractures are not common, they can occur when excessive stress is placed on the bone tissue. Athletic-related fractures of the hip, pelvis, and femur often occur as a result of an avulsion (the tendon pulling away the bone), disruption of the epiphysis (damage to the growth plate), stress, or trauma to the femur.

### Avulsions

Avulsion fractures occur as a result of forceful muscle contractions that literally pull the bone away at the site where the tendon attaches. This may happen, for example, when a football player continues to run aggressively forward while a defender is holding his leg. The hip flexor may forcefully contract, causing a fracture.

### Growth Plate Fractures

Epiphyseal fractures occur at the growth plates of bones, especially at the **capital femoral epiphysis**, which is where the neck of the femur joins the head. According to some experts, this injury is the most common hip disorder in active children between the ages of 10–15. The head of the femur slips off of the neck. This problem causes pain in the groin, hip, and knee. When an ATC suspects this condition, the athlete should be referred to a physician because the treatment includes stopping the slippage and helping to close the growth plate with a surgical procedure.

### Stress Fractures

Although uncommon, femoral stress fractures do occur in running-oriented athletes. Stress fractures are caused by repetitive stress, typically as a result of the force of the pounding of the lower extremity while running. This pounding can cause the femur to bend slightly. Just like bending a pencil, one side of the bone is com-

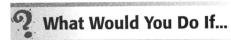

## What Would You Do If...

While at football practice, the ATC and a student assistant are helping an injured player off the field. You see that another athlete seems to have injured his leg during a play—it appears to be externally rotated, and he is in a lot of pain. As you approach the athlete, another player starts to grab his teammate's injured leg saying that it needs to be straightened out.

pressed while the other side is stretched. When bone tissue is repeatedly stretched, small hairline fractures can develop causing a great deal of pain and discomfort. Rest and an alternative activity such as aquatic therapy are indicated to reduce the stress to the fracture site so it can heal.

### Femur Fractures

Because the femur is the largest bone in the body, the stress required to fracture it is often extreme. A femur fracture is characterized by severe pain and loss of function as well as internal bleeding, swelling, or tearing of muscles, tendons, nerves, and arteries. Typically, the athlete is unable to move the leg. A femur fracture often causes the leg to externally rotate. Initial treatment for a femur fracture includes immobilization and transportation to the hospital by EMS personnel. They will often use a traction splint that gently pulls the femur, which helps reduce leg pain and spasm.

### Hip Dislocations

Extreme stress can cause a dislocation. Most hip dislocations occur posteriorly and usually accompany other trauma such as a fracture. Severe damage can occur in this area because of the nerve and vascular structures. An athlete with a dislocated hip is likely to be in extreme pain, and his leg is often internally rotated (see figure 10.3). With such an injury, the ambulance should be called immediately, and he should be transported to the hospital as soon as possible. Only a physician should reduce a hip dislocation. Significant follow-up treatment is required before the athlete can return to activity. Rehabilitation for a hip dislocation often begins with establishing normal range of motion and

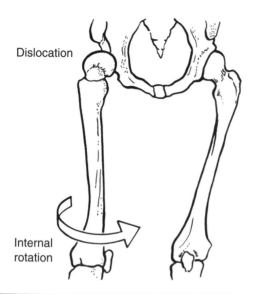

**Figure 10.3**  A hip dislocation. Note that the leg is internally rotated.

strength. Gait training, or relearning how to walk normally, will be necessary. As you can imagine, this is a long process.

## Other Common Injuries

A common injury in contact sports such as football is thigh contusion. Another injury that an ATC must always keep in mind, especially with a younger population of athletes, is a condition known as Legg-Calvé-Perthes disease.

### Hip and Thigh Muscle Contusions

Deep thigh contusions are common, especially in collision sports. While many bruises suffered in athletics are minor, thigh contusions can cause disability. The more severe contusions can actually cause tissue tearing and extensive bleeding. If not managed appropriately, serious thigh contusions can cause a condition known as **myositis ossificans,** which is the formation of bone tissue within the muscle. Because bone tissue is not as extensible as muscle tissue, disability and loss of function is a typical consequence.

When treating a thigh contusion it is important to proceed with the PRICE technique, but the knee should be flexed during the ice application. In fact, an ATC may put an athlete with this

## The Real World

I always look forward to the first football scrimmage of the year in anticipation of the season. I was watching as a defensive back came up near the sideline to make a play on the wide receiver, just as a blocker for the wide receiver hit the defensive back in the hip with his shoulder pad in an attempt to block. The defensive back did the splits while being blocked and tackling the receiver. He was in severe pain, supine with hip and knee flexion, unable to get up. After I assessed him, I determined he had dislocated his hip and called for emergency medical assistance. We placed him on a backboard with padding beneath his knee to maintain flexion. At the hospital his hip was relocated. Unfortunately, a dislocated hip needs several months of rest and rehabilitation for proper healing—he never played in a game that year.

Lorin Cartwright, MS, ATC, EMT

type of injury in a hinged knee immobilizer with it locked into flexion. This limits the total loss of flexibility due to the injury. With a moderate to severe contusion, the athlete should be placed on crutches to minimize stress to the area and be referred to the team physician. Active rest and the use of ice and gentle stretching routines are effective in restoring mobility. Ultrasound (discussed in chapter 21, pages 200-202) is often used to help resolve the blood that collects internally and to break up the bony tissue deposits. The ATC must make certain that a protective pad is placed over the contusion to prevent repeated contusions to the area as this too can create myositis ossificans.

### Legg-Calvé-Perthes Disease

In some children and teens who are still growing, a disruption of blood flow to the head of the femur causes the tissue at the head of the femur to die, a condition known as **Legg-Calvé-Perthes** disease. Typical signs and symptoms of this problem include groin or knee pain and walking with a limp. If this condition is suspected, the athlete should be referred to a physician immediately.

## Summary

The hip is a very stable joint not only because of its bony structure but also because it has strong muscles and ligaments surrounding it. The thigh has very strong musculature but can receive deep contusions, especially to the quadriceps, if not properly protected. These injuries can be debilitating for the athlete and require immediate care. The ATC must be aware that an adolescent athlete may develop Legg-Calvé-Perthes disease or growth plate fractures at the capital femoral epiphysis. He should take care to get a thorough history and observe the athlete's hip for joint position because this can often help detect a fracture of the growth areas around the hip. Rehabilitation of the hip often involves reestablishing proper flexibility and muscle strength around the joint.

## Key Terms

Define the following terms found in this chapter:

acetabulum        Legg-Calvé-Perthes disease        myositis ossificans

capital femoral epiphysis

## Questions for Review

1. What aspects of its anatomy make the hip an extremely stable joint? p. 87
2. What injuries discussed in this chapter typically are received by younger athletes? pp. 89-90
3. How should an ATC treat an athlete who has received a severe thigh contusion? p. 90
4. Describe how an ATC might treat a strain to the thigh musculature. p. 89
5. Why is the thigh musculature vulnerable to muscle strains? pp. 88-89

## Activities for Reinforcement

1. Have an ATC review injury assessment techniques for the hip, thigh, and pelvis.
2. Have an ATC demonstrate common exercises used in hip rehabilitation.

## Above and Beyond

Read one of the following articles and explain common signs, symptoms, and treatment of the conditions described.

Casterline, M., S. Osowski, and G. Ulrich. 1996. Femoral stress fractures. *Journal of Athletic Training* 31(1): 53–56.

Johnson, B.C., and L.A. Klabunde. 1995. The elusive slipped capital femoral epiphysis. *Journal of Athletic Training* 30(2): 124–27.

# Unit IV

# Understanding Athletics-Related Injuries to the Axial Region

# Spinal Injuries

The joints in the spine, like the other joints in the body, consist of articulated bones supported by muscles and ligaments. However, the spinal column is more complex than many joints and includes other structures such as disks and nerves. Because it protects our spinal cord, injuries to the spine can be life threatening and need careful attention by the ATC. Because most spinal cord injuries are in the lumbar and cervical regions, we will only consider injuries to those areas.

## Anatomy of the Spine

The spine is a complex structure of bones with four segments—the **sacrum** (tailbone area), **lumbar** (lower spine), **thoracic** (middle spine), and **cervical** (upper spine) regions (figure 11.1). Normal anatomical alignment and muscular strength keep the spinal segments aligned properly. An individual's spine should have normal curvature at each of these areas. Normal alignment is termed a **neutral spine**—this means that the spinal curves of the lumbar, thoracic, and cervical region are curved neither too much nor too little, and the spine is "comfortable." Such a position is anatomically the strongest.

### Bones

The bones in the spine are separated by disks and held together by ligaments. The muscles of the spine and trunk permit many movements and also help to stabilize the spine.

The bones of the spine are called vertebrae—there are 7 cervical, 12 thoracic, 5 lumbar, and 5 sacral (which are fused together) vertebrae. While there are differences among the vertebrae of each region, they also share many similarities. Each vertebra has

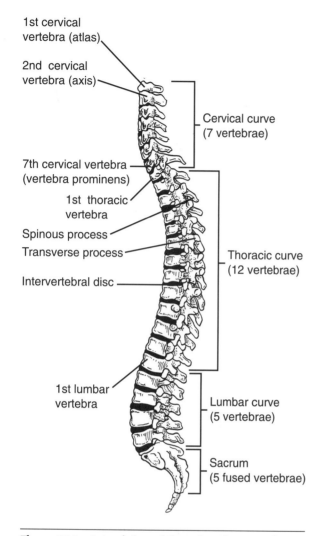

Figure 11.1 labels:
1st cervical vertebra (atlas)
2nd cervical vertebra (axis)
Cervical curve (7 vertebrae)
7th cervical vertebra (vertebra prominens)
1st thoracic vertebra
Spinous process
Transverse process
Intervertebral disc
Thoracic curve (12 vertebrae)
1st lumbar vertebra
Lumbar curve (5 vertebrae)
Sacrum (5 fused vertebrae)

**Figure 11.1** Lateral view of the spine. The natural anterior and posterior curves of the spine allow it to absorb shock. Note also the differences in size of the cervical, thoracic, and lumbar vertebrae.

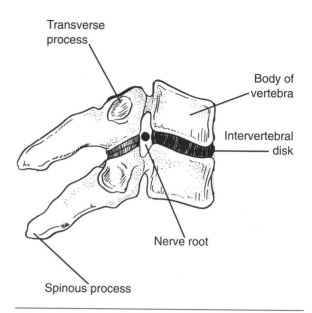

Figure 11.2 labels:
Transverse process
Body of vertebra
Intervertebral disk
Nerve root
Spinous process

**Figure 11.2** A normal vertebra. Each vertebra consists of a body, a transverse process, and a spinous process. An **intervertebral disk** lies between each pair of vertebrae to absorb shock.

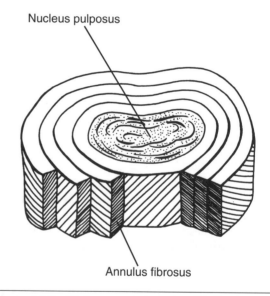

Figure 11.3 labels:
Nucleus pulposus
Annulus fibrosus

**Figure 11.3** Disk cross section. The disk lies between the vertebral bodies. The nucleus pulposus, located at the center of the disk, is a jellylike substance.

a body, a transverse process, and a spinous process (see figure 11.2). The bony spinal column has several functions: protecting the spinal cord, holding the body upright for walking, and serving as a site for muscular attachments.

## Disks

The disks that lie between the vertebrae absorb shock and resist compression during activity. They keep the vertebrae separated, which allows movement and flexibility, and provide space for nerves to exit the spinal cord to the rest of the body. Figure 11.3 shows a disk cross section.

A disk has two distinct parts: a jellylike core called the **nucleus pulposus**, surround by several layers of cartilage called the **annulus fibrosus**. Unfortunately, the disks of the spine do not receive any blood supply, and so they do not have the same healing potential as some of the body's other tissues. The disks are compressible—a person is slightly taller first thing in the morning than she will be later in the day after gravity has been compressing the disks—and in old age we become shorter.

## Muscles

The muscles of the trunk and neck attach to the spine and provide both a wide range of movement and some much needed stability. Two highly respected physical therapists, James Porterfield and Carl DeRosa, suggest thinking of the spine as a mast on a ship. A mast has many cables attached to it at various points that extend to different places on the ship. These cables keep the mast stable as the wind catches its sail. Likewise, the spine has many muscles attached to it at various points that extend to different places on the pelvis, legs, and arms. These muscles keep the spine stable as the body performs tasks such as throwing, catching, and kicking. If the ship has a mast that bends and folds, the sail will not catch the wind effectively. Similarly, if the body has a spine that bends and gives because of a lack of stability, it will not perform athletic-related tasks effectively.

The abdominal muscles are extremely important for supporting trunk movement—especially the rectus abdominis and the internal and external obliques (see figure 1.3). The spinal extensors run the entire length of the spine posteriorly and attach to various structures including the pelvis, ribs, and vertebrae. These muscles work together to keep the body upright.

The upper trapezius extends the cervical spine (see figure 1.3). It attaches to the occipital bone (back of head) and fans out to each side of the neck and attaches to the acromion process of the scapula (see figure 1.2).

Cervical flexion is accomplished by the scalenius muscles, which attach to the cervical vertebrae and run down to the first and second ribs—there are three muscles in all, each of which has a different attachment point. These muscles also help with the breathing process. Cervical side bending and rotation are accomplished by the sternocleidomastoid muscle, which is attached to the top of the sternum and runs up the neck, attaching to the mastoid process just behind the ear. The sternocleidomastoid rotates the head to the direction opposite the attachment and side-bends the head to the same side; for example, if the left sternocleidomastoid contracts, it rotates the head to the right.

## Postural Considerations

Take a look at a friend's posture. How do you know if the posture is normal? In order to understand postural problems, you must first understand normal postural alignment.

### Normal Posture

The athletic trainer can determine if a person has normal posture by viewing him from the side (see figure 11.4). Picture a straight line dropping

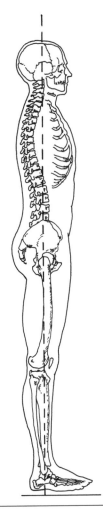

**Figure 11.4**   Normal posture. Note how the plumb line runs just behind the ear, through the shoulder, past the hip, through the knee to just in front of the lateral malleolus.

from the ceiling. If an athlete were standing with proper posture beside the line, specific body segments could be observed in alignment. The line would pass just behind the ear, through the center of the shoulder, down through the middle of the greater trochanter of the hip, just behind the patella, and down to just in front of the lateral malleolus.

## Abnormal Posture

Imagine a plumb line in reference to an athlete you are viewing from the side—you may identify several postural faults. For example, if his ear were projected in front of the line, he would have a **forward head posture**. This puts a great deal of stress at the back of the neck. If the line passed through the back of his shoulders instead of the middle, he would have rounded shoulders. The thoracic spine should be somewhat curved, but excessive roundedness is undesirable and is called **kyphosis**. Likewise, at the lumbar spine, too much forward curve is called **lordosis**. If the spine is correctly aligned, the normal cervical, thoracic, and lumbar curves are ideal for flexibility and absorbing shock. When the athlete cannot maintain proper posture, the ability of the spine to absorb shock is diminished, which will eventually result in injury.

Not only can the spine be too rounded at the thoracic region and too curved forward at the lumbar region, it can also bend from side to side. When observed from behind, the spine may be crooked rather than running straight from the skull to the sacrum. This is called **scoliosis**. Some people have this condition in mild forms. However, on occasion, ATCs will find an athlete with a very prominent deviation. While doctors often screen for this during a preparticipation physical examination, it is sometimes difficult to see. If a previously undetected deviation is suspected, the athlete should be referred to an orthopedic surgeon for an assessment.

As a student you can do things to prevent poor postural habits. Try to imagine balloons attached to your head pulling you up straight. You can also alternate carrying your book bag or gym bag on opposite shoulders. Putting a heavy book bag on one shoulder every day throughout your high school and college career can take its toll on the spine. You can stay fit and exercise regularly, too. Your body is made to move—being a slug will cause stiffness. Be kind to your spine, and use proper posture whenever possible.

## Preventing Spinal Injuries

Preventing injury to the cervical and lumbar regions of the spine is an active process—the athlete should participate in exercise and flexibility programs, maintain proper posture, learn to lift properly, and perhaps use back supports when lifting.

Proper exercise and flexibility programs are necessary for the muscles surrounding and supporting the spine, especially the abdominal muscles. A strong abdomen can help decrease stress on the lumbar spine. The muscles around the hip should also be strengthened because the hip directly influences the spine. If the hip is tilted forward, the spine will move into extension, and conversely, if the hip is tilted backward, the spine will move into flexion. Therefore, the hip musculature should be both flexible and strong to allow proper movement and positioning in the lumbar region.

Proper lifting procedures reduce the risk of injury (see figure 11.5). Business people understand that if an employee improperly lifts a weight she can injure her back. To prevent that, businesses have begun sending employees to "back school." Back schools are short-term instructional programs that teach people proper posture and lifting techniques. Proper lifting technique is maintaining a slight curve in the lumbar spine while lifting with the knees and the hips rather than the spine. It also involves keeping the head up when lifting. A lifting posture in which the spine is too rounded or flexed may cause a strain or disk injury.

Back supports have become very popular. Go to any home repair store, lumberyard, and even some grocery stores, and you will see many of the workers wearing these belts. The back sup-

**Figure 11.5** Proper lifting entails keeping the head up, the feet in a wide stance, and the spine in a neutral position. Also, keeping the load close to the body reduces stress on the back.

ports can increase the pressure around the spine and decrease the amount of stress to the vertebrae. A back support, however, should not be used to take the place of other means of injury prevention—the use of the brace alone cannot prevent all injuries.

## Treating Lumbar Spine Injuries and Conditions

Like other parts of the body, the spine is susceptible to ligament, muscle and tendon, and bone injuries. In addition, the disks that lie between the bodies of the vertebrae cause unique problems.

### Ligament Injuries

Sprains at the lumbar joints commonly occur when athletes are forced into excessive trunk flexion or attempt to flex the spine and rotate at the same time. An example of this mechanism is when a football player is tackled and forced

forward. When the trunk flexion is combined with some rotation, the posterior aspect of the vertebral joints can separate and stretch over the ligaments. Characteristics of a lumbar sprain include pain to one side of the spine and limited movement due to pain and muscle spasm. An ATC who takes a thorough history of the injury and performs special spinal tests can determine if the ligaments are involved; although, sometimes, it can be difficult to differentiate from a muscle strain. During an assessment, an ATC might gently perform a stress test that pushes each of the vertebrae anteriorly. This will usually be painful if the joint is sprained, but should not be painful if a strain is present—unless the strain is severe. Of course, such a test would not be done by an ATC if signs or symptoms of a fracture (as discussed earlier) were present.

When a sprain initially occurs, the ATC should treat it like any other acute injury; that is, PRICE should be performed. Many individuals believe that heat should always be used for spine injuries. With an acute injury, however, this may do more harm than good because heat tends to increase swelling and pain. After 48 hours postinjury it is typically all right to use heat. While rest is recommended, complete bed rest is no longer the accepted norm. Rather, the athlete should engage in active rest, whereby she maintains a comfortable neutral spine position and gently performs strengthening exercises to stabilize the spine. (Strengthening exercises are discussed in chapter 22.) As the initial inflammation subsides, the ATC can have the athlete begin some flexibility exercises as tolerated as well as some advanced lumbar stabilization exercises, providing they do not aggravate the area. The spinal musculature needs to be strengthened in preparation for return to activity.

### Muscle and Tendon Injuries

An ATC rarely sees a ruptured muscle at the lumbar spine, but mild and moderate strains are common. Characteristics of lumbar strain include pain to one side of the spine, spasm, and lack of movement. Also, with a muscle strain of the lumbar spine the athlete will often present with pain on the opposite side from the direction in which she bends. For example, if she bends to the left and the pain is on the right side of the spine, the muscle to the right of the spine may be strained. The pain associated with sprains is very localized, whereas pain caused by a muscle strain usually moves up and down the length of the muscle especially when the athlete tries to use the muscle while bending. Remember that the spine is like a mast on a ship, and the muscles are the guy wires. If the spine is bent to one side, the muscles on the side opposite will attempt to stabilize it. The ATC can initially apply ice to the injury, and gentle stretching using a knees-to-chest routine often speeds healing. Once pain is decreased, flexibility and strength can be restored to normal using strengthening and stretching routines. The ATC should observe the athlete for proper posture and lifting mechanics to avoid reinjury.

## Bone Injuries

Bone fractures are possible in the lumbar spine, especially with severe mechanisms of injury like compression—forcefully landing on the buttocks could cause a compression fracture. Fractures of the spine are hard to determine without an X ray. However, if an ATC knows the mechanism of injury and finds a great deal of back pain, muscle spasm, and tenderness when touching the vertebrae, a fracture must be suspected. If the ATC suspects a lumbar fracture, the athlete should be treated conservatively; that is, he should be put on a backboard with the help of appropriate emergency medical personnel and taken to the nearest hospital.

## Other Common Injuries

One of the most common injuries of the lumbar spine is a disk bulge (see figure 11.6). This condition is not common in younger athletes, but older athletes seem to be susceptible to it. Although some people call this a slipped disk, that is not an appropriate term. The disk is attached to the body of the vertebrae and rarely slips forward or backward. What actually happens with a disk bulge is that the jellylike nucleus pulposus at the center of the disk pushes through the rings of cartilage. For example, if you were to place the palms of your hands on the top and bottom of a jelly doughnut and squeeze, jelly would begin to ooze through the layers of dough. A similar thing happens when a disk is compressed. The nucleus pulposus begins to press

through the layers of cartilage around it and eventually can press against the very outer layer, causing it to bulge.

Disks rarely bulge toward the front of the spine for two reasons. First, the front of the spine is covered with a very thick ligament called the anterior longitudinal ligament, and second, most individuals have postures that flex the spine forward most of the time. Flexion of the spine tends to put more pressure on the front aspect of the disk, pushing the nucleus pulposus toward the posterior aspect. Most often disks bulge posteriorly to one side or another, which may put pressure on the nerve exiting the spinal cord at that level (see figure 11.6).

Disk bulges are quite aggravating and can be disabling. If the disk bulge is putting pressure on a nerve, numbness, tingling, and pain can occur down the leg. Another characteristic of this condition includes pain in the lower back that increases with sitting.

Treating an athlete with a disk bulge requires the ATC to understand the causes of this condition. Most often disk bulges are the result of poor posture and body mechanics that put the spine in a great deal of flexion over a long period of time. For example, a softball infielder who is not disciplined enough to maintain a spinal neutral posture may await a pitch with the spine flexed forward. If this same individual sits with a slouchy posture and uses poor lifting mechan-

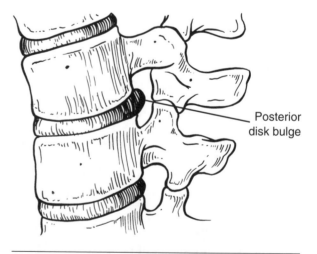

**Figure 11.6** A posterior disk bulge. As the spine is flexed, pressure is put on the anterior part of the disk, which encourages the nucleus pulposus to push through layers of the annulus fibrosus.

**Compressing the Spine**

Sitting creates more of a compressive load on the spine than standing.

ics as well, she may eventually put herself at risk of a disk bulge.

Under the direction of the team physician, an ATC will often treat a disk bulge by initially using active rest, as with a sprain. Also, correcting poor posture and helping the athlete move into spinal extension can be helpful. It is thought that if proper posture and body mechanics are used, the nucleus pulposus will not bulge quite as much, which will give the athlete some relief. The ATC will make certain that none of the exercises aggravates the leg pain or causes more numbness or tingling. As the athlete progresses, extension exercises, and sometimes traction (discussed in chapter 21), may help reduce the disk bulge. He should also be instructed about proper sitting, standing, and lifting postures to minimize pressure on the disk, and he should avoid prolonged sitting. Strengthening the spine with lumbar stabilization techniques is also helpful.

# Treating Cervical Spine Injuries and Conditions

As you might imagine, the types of injuries incurred at the cervical spine are similar to those at the lumbar spine. Keep in mind, however, that the cervical spine has more mobility than the lumbar spine, and thus, the treatments used to treat similar problems differ.

## Ligament Injuries

Despite having an excellent range of motion, the cervical spine is subject to ligament sprains when it is forcefully moved beyond its normal range. Cervical sprains are usually the result of hyperextension or hyperflexion of the neck. Take, for example, a football receiver who stops, turns toward the quarterback to catch the ball, and then gets tackled by a defender. When hit forcefully from behind, the receiver often suf-

fers a whiplash injury—in fact, many a receiver would say that it felt like he was hit by a car! The body is forced forward by the blow while the head moves backward, which places the cervical spine into extension and stretches the ligaments and muscles at the front of the neck. When his body stops—because he hits the ground or is tackled from the front—his head snaps forward, stretching out the posterior neck ligaments and muscles.

Cervical ligament sprains have symptoms of neck and arm pain. The athlete may even complain of pain between the scapulae. Because of the possibility of a spinal cord injury, any neck trauma should be thoroughly evaluated by the ATC. Provided there is no sign of nerve injury, she can treat the neck. Like many other ligament injuries, the neck needs to be treated with protection, rest, ice, and support. No compression with an elastic bandage should be applied to the neck, however, because this may slow blood flow to the brain. A neck brace can be used to help the athlete hold her head up. A follow-up examination from the team physician is a must to rule out any other conditions.

Further treatment for the cervical spine sprain includes strengthening exercises to regain stability, and full range of motion should be reestablished. Before the athlete is allowed to return to participation she must have the following:

- Full strength
- Full range of motion
- Full confidence
- No symptoms
- Physician clearance

## Muscle and Tendon Injuries

A cervical muscle strain can also occur from a whiplash injury by the mechanism previously described. Characteristics of cervical muscle strains include muscle spasm, restricted range of motion, weakness against resistance, pain, and tenderness of the muscle. An ATC should treat cervical strains much like the cervical ligament sprains. The criteria for returning an athlete to play are the same as for cervical sprains. Manual resistance works well for strengthening the neck. There is not a lot of exercise equipment designed specifically for the neck; an alternative is performing cervical stretches while a partner provides resistance with his hand.

## Bone Injuries

Bone injuries to the cervical spine include fractures and dislocations, which can produce devastating results including permanent disabilities and death. Fractures to the cervical spine are often the result of an axial load. This occurs when the head is lowered into flexion that straightens the cervical spine like a drinking straw and then having a force applied to the head. If you take a drinking straw and push on the end of it hard enough, it will eventually bend. A similar event occurs at the cervical spine—a vertebra fractures. A dislocation of the cervical vertebrae is often the result of a combination of excessive neck flexion and rotation.

Cervical spine fractures and dislocations have similar signs and symptoms. The athlete will often report pain around the cervical spine and weakness, numbness, and tingling down the arms. With a dislocation, there is often a visible deformity, but because of equipment or positioning, it is sometimes difficult to observe. Initial care for both injuries is identical. Emergency care procedures should be followed, and after ruling out life-threatening conditions, the neck should be immobilized and the athlete put on a backboard. If he is wearing a helmet and a cervical fracture or dislocation is suspected, the helmet should be left in place because attempting to remove it may cause excessive movement of the neck, which could lead to further damage. Appropriate emergency medical personnel should take the athlete to the nearest hospital facility.

## Other Common Injuries

The intervertebral disks and the nerves that exit the cervical spine are subject to other athletic-related injuries, including a condition known as brachial plexus syndrome.

### Disk Injuries

Disk injuries in the cervical spine are not nearly as common as those in the lumbar spine, but they can occur. An athlete with a cervical spine disk bulge often will report more neck pain with sitting and while flexing the neck forward than

with standing and walking. She may report discomfort down the back, between the shoulder blades. The treatment for disk bulges of the cervical spine includes improving the neck posture and then progressing to cervical extension exercises that do not aggravate the condition. Cervical traction can also be used by the ATC under the direction of the team physician to help reduce the disk bulge. Full neck mobility and strength should gradually be regained. As with suspected fractures, if an athlete presents with severe symptoms, such as numbness, tingling, and burning of the arm, he should be put on a spine board and referred to a hospital by an ATC. The ATC should consult the team physician regarding returning an athlete to participation following such a condition.

### Brachial Plexus Injuries

The brachial plexus is a network of nerves that exit the cervical spine and run a course through the shoulder and down the arm. An athlete who falls, runs into, or attempts to tackle another player can stretch the brachial plexus. Picture a linebacker tackling an opponent. As he makes the tackle, the shoulder is pressed downward and the neck is forced into a stretch in the opposite direction. This mechanism of injury often results in stretching the brachial plexus resulting in burning, tingling, numbness, and stinging sensations of the arm and shoulder (figure 11.7). In fact, this condition is often called

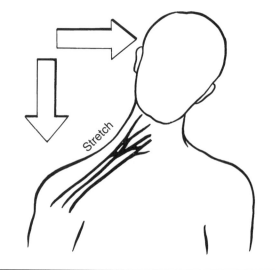

**Figure 11.7**  Stretching the brachial plexus causes burning, tingling, numbness, and stinging sensations of the arm and shoulder.

a "**burner**" or "**stinger.**" Depending upon the severity of the injury, the burner may last for a matter of seconds or minutes. More severe cases can last much longer, even weeks. Treatment often consists of neck strengthening exercises and range-of-motion/stretching of the area. A football player is usually fitted with a neck roll that limits lateral flexion. Before returning an athlete to play following a burner he must have the following:

- No symptoms
- Full strength
- Full range of motion of the neck and shoulder
- A problem-free neck and shoulder evaluation by the ATC and the team physician

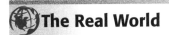
## The Real World

After school the athletic trainer was called to assist an injured female gymnast. She had been performing a back flip in the gym when she landed shoulders and neck first. She was lying face down, with her right arm under her body, and her head turned to the side.

The initial exam revealed point tenderness along her trapezius muscles and lower cervical spine. All neurological signs were fine. The athlete was laughing and wanted to get up. The athletic trainer felt extra caution was necessary based on how she fell. The emergency medical service was summoned. The young lady became upset, but the athletic trainer reassured her that this was the best option. The athletic trainer knows that appearances and an athlete's attitude do not always represent an accurate picture.

Several hours later, the injured girl's father called the athletic trainer to thank him for being so "cautious." The girl had suffered a fracture dislocation of C3, and fractures of C4 and C5. By insisting that she be backboarded and transported, the athletic trainer may have saved her from paralysis or death.

The athlete was placed in a special neck brace for three months. The fractures healed, but the C3 dislocation remained out of alignment. She had surgery to fuse the vertebrae. The young lady kept a positive attitude, was courageous, and had a wonderful smile throughout her ordeal. She is a definite inspiration to those with whom she made contact. And, although she was unable to return to participating in gymnastics, she is able to function normally in other aspects of her life. In fact, she even teaches gymnastics to younger athletes and has recently enrolled in a college athletic training curriculum.

Roger Kalisiak, ATC

## Summary

The spine is an articulated series of vertebrae that protect the spinal cord; numerous muscles attach to it. A neutral spine is stable and absorbs shock—it is promoted by proper posture. The spine may receive sprains and strains in the lumbar and cervical regions, but because of the spinal cord, nerve roots, and disks, other injuries to the spine may be more serious, even life threatening. After any injury in the spinal area an athlete must learn proper bending and lifting and perform muscle-strengthening exercises, to reduce the risk of further injury.

## Key Terms

Define the following terms found in this chapter:

| | | |
|---|---|---|
| annulus fibrosus | kyphosis | nucleus pulposus |
| burner or stinger | lordosis | sacrum |
| cervical | lumbar | scoliosis |
| forward head posture | neutral spine | thoracic |
| intervertebral disk | | |

## Questions for Review

1. List the spinal segments, and discuss which of the segments is most commonly injured and why. pp. 95-96, 98
2. Describe the different types of spinal injuries and how they occur. pp. 99-103
3. If an ATC were working with an athlete who reported burning sensations down the arm that lasted only about 15 seconds, what might have happened? pp. 102-103
4. Why is proper posture important, and why do you think it is hard for some people to use proper posture? p. 98

## Activities for Reinforcement

1. Check each other's posture—who has lordosis, kyphosis, rounded shoulders, or forward head?
2. Have an ATC demonstrate how to evaluate the lumbar and cervical spine.

## Above and Beyond

1. What types of spine injuries do you think are most common in football? Why? What types of spine injuries are most common in gymnastics? Why? What about sports like tennis and racquetball?
2. Select one or more of the following suggested readings and write a report on spine injuries.

    Gebhard, J.S., D.H. Donaldson, and C.W. Brown. 1994. Soft-tissue injuries of the cervical spine. *Orthopedic Review* May Suppl.: 9–17.

    Hopkins, T.J., and A.A. White. 1993. Rehabilitation of athletes following spine injury. *Clinical Sports Medicine* 12(3): 603–19.

    Hoppenfeld, S. 1976. *Physical examination of the spine and extremities.* Norwalk, CT: Appleton-Century-Crofts.

    Porterfield, J.A., and C. DeRosa. 1991. *Mechanical low back pain.* Philadelphia: Saunders.

    Stith, W.J. 1990. Exercise and the intervertebral disk. In *The Spine in sports,* ed. S.H. Hochschuler, 4. Philadelphia: Hanley and Belfus.

3. Write a mock back-strengthening program for one of your school teams. Keep in mind the level of conditioning required as well as the amount of training time that the team can devote to your program. Share your program with your ATC, and get some feedback. The resource below is one that may be used.

    Brittenham, D., and G. Brittenham. 1997. *Stronger abs and back.* Champaign, IL: Human Kinetics.

# Abdominal Injuries

## OBJECTIVES

Upon completing this chapter the student will be able to do the following:
- Understand the anatomy of the abdomen.
- Understand the implications of illness or injury related to a specific organ.
- Understand how to prevent injuries of the abdomen.
- Describe the care necessary to treat an injury within the abdomen.

Although abdominal organs are not generally protected in sporting activity by padding, abdominal injuries occur infrequently. A serious injury of the abdomen, however, may not become apparent for days. In this chapter we discuss function of the abdominal organs, injury prevention, and treatment.

## Anatomy of the Abdodmen

The abdominal cavity is bounded by the lumbar spine posteriorly, the diaphragm superiorly, the abdominal musculature anteriorly, and the pelvis inferiorly. For purposes of discussion, the abdominal cavity is divided into four quadrants by an imaginary horizontal line across the abdomen through the navel and an imaginary vertical line running from the sternum through the navel to the area between the legs (see figure 12.1). The upper right quadrant lies just below the ribs on the athlete's right side—it contains the liver, a portion of the pancreas, right kidney, gall bladder, large and small intestine. The upper left quadrant lies just below the ribs on the athlete's left side—it contains the stomach, a portion of the liver, a portion of the pancreas, left kidney, spleen, large and small intestine. The lower right quadrant contains the large and small intestine, appendix, a portion of the bladder, uterus and right ovary (in females) and prostate (in males). The lower left quadrant contains the large and small intestine, a portion of the bladder, uterus and left ovary (in females), and prostate (in males).

There are both solid and hollow organs in the abdomen. Injuries to the hollow organs such as the bladder, intestines, stomach, and appendix rarely cause rapid death. Moreover, the hollow organs tend to move and bend away if an athlete is hit in the abdomen. Hollow organs are basically tubes that assist in transporting substances from one organ to another and are connected to one another by sheetlike membranes. Solid

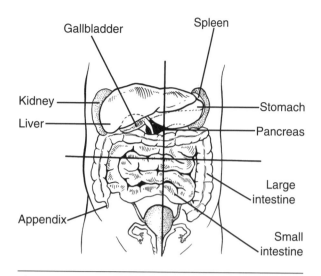

Gallbladder  Spleen
Kidney
Liver
Stomach
Pancreas
Large intestine
Appendix
Small intestine

**Figure 12.1**  The abdominal quadrants.

organs such as the liver, kidneys, and spleen aid in body chemistry and can cause rapid death if injured because they have a large blood supply.

Abdominal organs can be divided into three categories: digestive organs, urinary organs, and reproductive organs. The organs included in the digestive system are the stomach, liver, pancreas, large and small intestine, appendix, spleen, and gallbladder. The organs of the urinary system are the kidneys, ureters, and bladder. Organs of the female reproductive system include the ovaries and uterus. Organs in the male reproductive system are the prostate and seminal vesicles.

## Digestive Organs

The stomach secretes gastric juices that assist in breaking down food before it enters the intestines. The liver has several functions, including the detoxification of chemicals that the body perceives as poisons, such as alcohol. The liver also stores several vitamins, produces bile, and assists with food metabolism. The gall bladder is located at the liver and is a storage tank for **bile,** which is passed into the small intestine where it assists with the digestion of fat. The pancreas produces insulin and enzymes for digestion. The small intestine completes the digestive process of breaking down food; from here the products of digestion are absorbed into the circulatory system. The sequential contraction and relaxation of the intestinal muscles,

which is called peristalsis, pushes the food onward through the intestines. By the time it reaches the large intestine, the material that has not been digested or absorbed into the circulatory system is considered waste. In the large intestine water is absorbed, leaving a solid waste for excretion. The appendix is part of the large intestine and has no known function. The spleen, which is covered with a thin sheath, has numerous functions: it produces and destroys red blood cells, it assists in the destruction of harmful microorganisms, and it is a storage site for blood.

## Urinary Organs

The kidneys are responsible for maintaining the sensitive acid-base balance within the body. If the acid-base balance changes, the body systems begin to shut down, eventually resulting in death. The kidneys filter the blood and remove the waste products of metabolism to keep the acid-base relationship stable. If either kidney does not have adequate blood supply (whether by injury or illness) the kidney can secondarily cause hypertension from a chemical constriction of the body's blood vessels. The ureters are tubes attached to the kidneys that transport urine to the bladder, which is the holding tank for liquid waste products.

## Reproductive Organs

In females, the ovaries produce eggs for possible fertilization and the hormone estrogen. Estrogen is the chemical that stimulates the development of and maintains feminine characteristics. The uterus is the organ in which a fertilized egg develops. The lining of the uterus is released during a menstrual period if a fertilized egg is not present. In males, the seminal

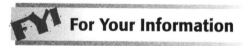

**For Your Information**

### Enzymes

An enzyme is a protein that allows a biochemical reaction to take place at normal body temperature but is itself not changed in the reaction.

vesicles and prostate gland are responsible for adding fluid and nutrients to seminal fluid.

## The Pelvis

The pelvis is a structure that provides a bony base and solid protection for some abdominal organs. The top edge of the pelvis is known as the iliac crest (see figure 1.2, a-b), which is the attachment point for the abdominal muscles. The pelvis of the female has a larger opening and is wider than in the male, to permit childbirth.

## Abdominal Muscles

Although the liver and spleen are slightly covered by the inferior-most portion of the ribs, protection of the abdominal organs is mainly provided by the abdominal musculature and fat. The primary muscles of the abdomen are the rectus abdominis and the obliques. The rectus abdominis, when well developed, gives the washboard-ripple effect to the abdomen. It attaches at the hipbones and extends to the lower ribs and sternum. The rectus abdominis is responsible for forward flexion or bending of the trunk. Each oblique attaches on the lateral aspect of the lower ribs on one side of the body and runs diagonally to the hipbone. The obliques help compress the abdomen—for example, if someone threatens to hit you and you tighten your muscles you are contracting the obliques. Refer to figures 1.2 and 1.3 for a review of these muscles and the bones to which they are attached.

# Preventing Abdominal Injuries

Preventing injuries of the abdominal organs is essential—abdominal trauma can quickly cause death. Sport rules that require protective equipment and limited contact during the event are designed to prevent abdominal injuries. Ice hockey goalies, for example, generally wear protective equipment for the abdomen and reproductive organs. Other players can protect themselves by tightening their abdominal muscles. So that a player can protect himself, most sports do not allow tackling or checking (physically moving an athlete) from behind. Boxing has a rule that says it is illegal to "hit below the belt." Prior to games all athletes should be reminded to empty their bladders because full bladders are more prone to rupture on impact than empty ones.

# Treating Abdominal Injuries and Conditions

Injuries within the abdominal cavity, especially to the hollow organs, are rare. The solid organs—the liver, spleen, and kidneys—can be injured, and internal bleeding may result. The athletic trainer should assess any athlete for injury who has received a blow to the abdominal area, especially if there is abdominal pain, signs of shock, muscle spasms, or blood in the urine.

## Rupture of the Spleen

A blow to the abdomen may injure the spleen. A spleen that is enlarged from an infection is more prone to a rupture—athletes recovering from illnesses, especially mononucleosis, should not be allowed to play without a physician's permission. Athletes with a spleen injury will experience abdominal pain and perhaps pain in the left shoulder, which is referred to as **Kehr's sign**. The left shoulder pain is caused by internal bleeding that puts pressure on the diaphragm, which presses on a nerve causing referred pain to the shoulder. The athlete will often indicate that he is nauseous, cramping, and weak, and he may pass out. Upon examination, the athletic trainer may note abdominal spasms, vomiting, rapid heart rate, decreased blood pressure, and shock. The athlete must be transported by EMS to a hospital immediately—an injured spleen is a medical emergency. A ruptured spleen can bleed severely, causing rapid blood loss and a drop in blood pressure.

## What Would You Do If...

In the locker room everyone is gathered around an athlete who is showing off a quarter-sized bulge near his navel. He pushes on the bulge and it disappears, but when he holds his breath and bears down the bulge reappears. Everyone laughs, and he continues showing off.

While I was working a summer basketball camp, one of the athletes was accidentally kneed in the abdomen. When we got to him, he complained of high pain levels in the lower abdomen off to the left side. We determined that he could move so we assisted in walking him to the sideline and finished our evaluation. He exhibited tenderness over the spleen with a positive Kehr's sign. The coach encouraged the athlete to "walk it off," but because I suspected a spleen injury—a Kehr's sign most often suggests a spleen injury—I overruled him. We removed the athlete to the training room where he began to show signs of shock. We thought his spleen must be ruptured, and we called for EMS immediately. While we waited, we monitored his vital signs and treated him for shock. He showed a decreasing level of consciousness and a significant drop in blood pressure. We recorded vital signs at five-minute intervals before EMS arrived, and that cut down on time of transfer from our care to theirs. He was taken to the local hospital and was later airlifted to a larger hospital. He did have a ruptured spleen, and he was rushed into surgery. The athlete recovered fully, and the next summer—he was back at the same camp.

Alex Embry, ATC, EMT

An athlete with less severe spleen injuries will be hospitalized overnight for observation. A ruptured spleen must be surgically removed. Athletes who have had their spleens removed are able to play sports after total recovery. The spleen can be protected from injury through the use of padding.

## Pancreas Injury

The pancreas lies just behind the stomach near the liver and the spinal column. It is prone to injury during deceleration—for example, when an athlete running with the ball hits a wall. The wall does not cause the injury but as the pancreas shifts forward when the rest of the body has stopped, it tears. The athlete will have pain in the middle of the abdomen to the back as well as nausea, vomiting, and signs of shock. The athlete should be referred to the hospital for additional examination—a ruptured pancreas must be surgically repaired.

A cross-country runner reports that she has blood in her urine. She does not remember being hit over her kidney.

## Kidney Injury

A direct blow over the kidney can cause a contusion, laceration, or rupture. The athlete will experience pain just under the posterior ribs to the side of the spine, and the pain may radiate to the bladder. Pain will increase with trunk extension and ease with knee or hip flexion. The athlete may feel nauseous and vomit. Urine may have visible blood, and the blood loss may cause the athlete to go into shock. Thus, the injury requires prompt emergency care and hospitalization. Generally, an athlete with a kidney injury is required to rest for several weeks before returning to competition. Possible complications are scarring of the kidney and hypertension.

## Hernias

A hernia is a lump of tissue, usually the intestine, that bulges through a weakness in the abdominal wall. The hernia can result from increased abdominal pressure, which may occur if the athlete holds his breath while weightlifting or going to the bathroom. The lump may go away when he lies down and bulge again when he stands up or exerts abdominal pressure. In males the intestine may go through the inguinal canal and stay in the scrotal sac. The athlete may or may not have pain. A hernia must be surgically repaired, although a strap, called a truss, can be used temporarily to apply pressure externally to keep the bulge inside the abdomen. A truss does not work for inguinal hernias and cannot be used by athletes who participate in contact sports or sports like weightlifting that require exerting internal abdominal pressure. If not treated, the bulge of tissue can get stuck in the abdominal wall or inguinal canal—this is called strangulation. Strangulation cuts off the blood supply to the tissue and eventually the tissue will die. If intestine tissue is involved, a bowel obstruction will result. The obstruction prevents the passage of waste material from the

## FYI For Your Information

### Inguinal Canal

The inguinal canal is a hole in the abdominal wall in the region of the groin.

body, causing pain and illness, and must be surgically repaired.

## Liver Contusions

A blow to the right upper abdomen can result in a contusion or rupture of the liver. The athlete will experience pain over the area that may radiate to the right shoulder. As the athlete loses blood she will go into shock, have a rapid weak pulse, and a drop in blood pressure. She must be referred to a physician immediately. Until he can rule it out, the athletic trainer should be suspicious of a liver contusion if the athlete receives any blow to the area. The athlete may die if the liver is ruptured and it goes untreated.

## Bladder Injuries

A rupture of the bladder will cause urine to leak into the surrounding area. The athlete may have painful urination, a contusion over the bladder, or blood in the urine. She should report any of these symptoms to the ATC. In severe cases of bladder injury athletes go into shock, causing rapid heart rate, decreased blood pressure, anxiety, and sweating. When the injury mechanism suggests a bladder injury, the athlete should be referred to a physician for immediate evaluation. The ATC should instruct the athlete to look for the signs and symptoms listed above and report any problems immediately.

## Side Stitch

A side stitch refers to pain in the upper abdominal region, just below the ribs. There are various theories about why this pain occurs—a lack of oxygen getting to the abdominal muscles, improper breathing technique, eating food just before exercising, air trapped in the abdominal organs, and muscle spasms—but generally the lesser fit tend to get more stitches. Athletes experiencing the pain of a stitch resolve it by stopping exercise or by pressing directly over the area. If an athlete believes the stitch is a result of eating, she should change her eating patterns. A muscle spasm stitch can be resolved by raising the arm on the same side as the pain overhead and leaning away from the painful area. Pain that does not resolve needs to be referred to a physician for further evaluation.

## Summary

Most of the organs in the abdominal region are involved in the digestive process and therefore are hollow. It is difficult to injure the hollow organs, but the solid organs of the abdomen can be seriously injured. The ATC must know where the organs of the abdomen are located to properly evaluate an abdominal injury. Some serious injuries will not be immediately evident because they have delayed signs and symptoms. Athletes with abdominal injuries require immediate EMS. The number of serious abdominal injuries in sports has been reduced by rules restricting body contact and by requiring the athletes to wear protective equipment.

## Key Terms

Define the following terms found in this chapter:

bile                    Kehr's sign

## Questions for Review

1. List the major organs of the abdomen and their functions. pp. 105-107
2. What measures can be taken to prevent abdominal injury? p. 107
3. What organs are easiest to injure? pp. 105, 107

## Activities for Reinforcement

1. Have an ATC demonstrate how to evaluate an athlete with a suspected abdominal injury.
2. Use a stethoscope and listen to the four abdominal quadrants.
3. If you could redesign the abdominal cavity, how could you provide more protection for solid organs?

## Above and Beyond

1. Using some of the references that follow, draw the external abdomen. Include in the drawing the abdominal organs' pain referral points.

   Eichelberger, M.R. 1981. Torso injuries in athletics. *The Physician and Sportsmedicine* 9(3): 87–92.

   Hahn, D. 1978. The ruptured spleen: Implications for the athletic trainer. *Athletic Training* 13(4): 190–91.

   McGuine, T. 1996. Recognizing abdominal injuries in high school athletes. *Sports Plus* Winter/Spring: 2–3.

# Throat and Thorax Injuries

## OBJECTIVES

Upon completing this chapter the student will be able to do the following:
- Understand the basic anatomy of the throat and thorax.
- Understand how to prevent injuries of the throat and thorax.
- Know the care necessary to treat an injury within the throat or thorax.
- Understand the implications of illness or injury related to a specific organ in the thorax.

The thorax is the part of the body between the neck and the abdomen—it contains the heart and lungs. Compromise of the organs and passageways in the throat and thorax is life threatening. Prompt care can save an athlete's life.

## Anatomy of the Throat

The throat contains the carotid arteries, jugular veins, larynx, trachea, and esophagus. Because these structures are so sensitive and vital to life, the ATC must understand their purpose and location (see figure 13.1).

The **esophagus** is the passageway for food going from the mouth to the stomach. It lies in front of the cervical vertebrae and behind the trachea and larynx. The **trachea** is made up of circular rings of cartilage; it is the main trunk of the system of tubes by which air passes to and from the lungs for the exchange of oxygen and carbon dioxide. The **larynx** is the modified upper part of the trachea and contains the vocal cords.

One **carotid artery** and one **jugular vein** pass on each side of the trachea. The carotid arteries carry oxygenated blood to the brain while the jugular veins carry unoxygenated blood away from the brain. Severing one of these vessels can cause death in a short time, so protection of the neck is vital in sports such as ice hockey and field hockey.

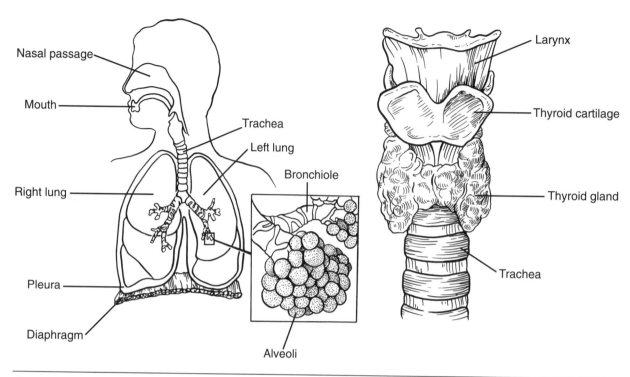

**Figure 13.1**   Anatomy of the throat and thorax.

## Anatomy of the Thorax

The bony structure of the thorax is made up of the thoracic vertebrae posteriorly, 12 ribs on each side, and the sternum anteriorly (see figure 1.2, a-b). These bones protect the sensitive organs in the thorax. The two lowest ribs do not attach to the sternum and are called floating ribs.

### Heart and Lungs

The heart is about the size of a fist and is responsible for pumping blood to all parts of the body. The blood carries nutrients and oxygen to cells and carbon dioxide and waste products away from cells. The heart is divided into four chambers: the upper chambers, the left and right **atrium**, and the lower chambers, the left and right **ventricles** (see figure 13.2). The ventricles are generally larger with thicker walls than the atria because they pump the blood throughout the body. Exercising the heart muscle makes it larger and more efficient at pumping. However, an enlarged heart can also be a sign of heart disease.

The heart pumps blood to the lungs and around the body. The right atrium fills with blood from a vein, which is carrying waste products and carbon dioxide. The right ventricle receives blood from the right atrium and pumps it to the lungs to get rid of carbon dioxide and pick up oxygen. The left atrium fills with the oxygenated blood from the lungs. The left ventricle, which is the largest chamber of the heart,

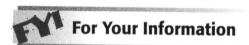

### For Your Information

#### Veins

Veins carry waste products and carbon dioxide back to the heart (except for the pulmonary vein, which carries oxygenated blood to the left atrium).

#### Arteries

Arteries carry nutrients and oxygenated blood away from the heart and throughout the body.

#### Oxygenated

Oxygen-rich. As blood passes through the lungs, it picks up oxygen and becomes oxygenated.

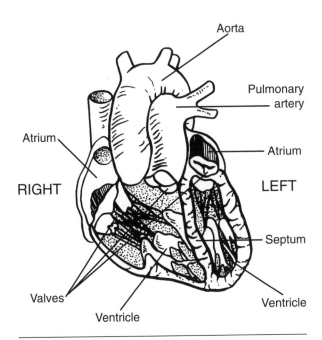

**Figure 13.2**   Interior of the heart.

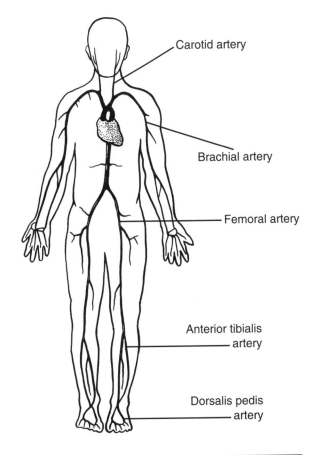

**Figure 13.3**   Major arteries.

receives the oxygenated blood from the left atrium and pumps it throughout the body. The main artery leaving the heart is known as the aorta. The aorta travels downward through the chest and abdomen—other large arteries branch off to the head (carotid arteries), arms (brachial arteries), and legs (femoral arteries) (see figure 13.3).

Two electrical nodes in the right atrium begin a contraction. A slight delay in impulses conducted from the nodes through the heart allows blood to be squeezed from one chamber to another. Injured or diseased electrical nodes will cause the heart to stop or to beat ineffectively.

The lungs, located on each side of the heart, function to exchange oxygen and carbon dioxide and to dissipate body heat. The trachea divides into two bronchi, the bronchi further subdivide into bronchioles, and each bronchiole ends in an alveolus, an air-containing cell of the lungs (see figure 13.1). It is in the **alveoli** that the exchange of oxygen and carbon dioxide occurs. There are three lobes in the right lung and two lobes in the left lung. Lung capacity is hampered primarily by smoking, pollution, and lung disease. The bronchi are filled with cilia, which are small hairlike projections that help remove foreign substances like dust and pollen. Coughing and sneezing help to keep the trachea and bronchi clear and remove **phlegm** and allergy-causing agents.

Lung function and breathing rate are controlled by carbon dioxide receptors. When receptors register the presence of too much carbon dioxide, inhalation occurs. Exercise increases cell metabolism and causes cells to need more oxygen and eliminate more carbon dioxide. This increased cellular need increases the number of breaths per minute. Over time, as the athlete exercises, the lungs' ability to exchange air effectively increases, and her breaths will become deeper and more forceful. Moreover, a conditioned athlete will return to a normal breathing rate more quickly after exercising than will an out-of-shape person.

A thin lubricated tissue called the pleura lines each half of the thorax and is folded back over the surface of the lung on the same side. The pleurae allow smooth movement of the lungs as they encounter the wall of ribs during inhalation and exhalation. There is a small space between the pleura and the lung.

## Diaphragm

The **diaphragm** muscle separates the thorax and the abdominal cavity. The diaphragm contracts and pulls down to assist in inhalation and moves upward to push air out of the lungs on exhalation (see figure 13.4). The diaphragm has three openings to allow passage of the esophagus (for food), the abdominal aorta (artery), and the inferior vena cava (vein).

# Preventing Throat and Thorax Injuries

Protective equipment and the rules in athletic contests are both designed to prevent injuries to the throat and thorax because these areas con-

tain organs that are vital to life. Thus, athletes wear throat protectors in softball, baseball, lacrosse, field hockey, and ice hockey. In field hockey, lacrosse, football, ice hockey, softball, and baseball, protective equipment—shoulder pads, chest protectors, and sternal pads—is provided for the thorax, especially for goalies. A safe distance between a playing surface edge and objects such as bleachers, fences, score tables, and spectators is 15 feet. Today we see that walls, tables, and fences are padded to prevent injury to athletes who may collide with these objects.

Many Little League softball and baseball players now are required to wear chest protectors when batting because of the danger of being struck in the chest with a ball. If a ball strikes the chest at exactly the instant before a heartbeat is initiated, it can cause the heart to beat irregularly or even stop, which could result in death.

When buying equipment that will protect an athlete in a potential life-and-death situation, buy the best equipment available. Make sure the equipment is certified and will do what it claims. When a baseball hits the chest of a Little Leaguer, the chest protector is supposed to absorb the force and reduce the impact to the heart. However, some of the chest protectors used by Little Leaguers are not certified and may actually increase the chance of irregular

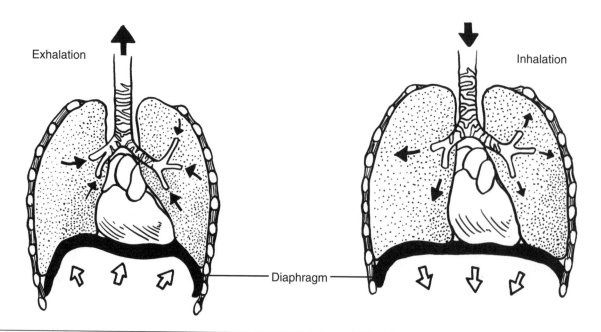

Exhalation

Inhalation

Diaphragm

**Figure 13.4** Breathing. The diaphragm moves upward during exhalation and downward during inhalation.

heart beat if a ball hits the chest, because they focus the impact over the heart.

# Treating Throat Injuries and Conditions

Throat injuries can be simple or devastating. Most of the injuries that occur to the throat are contusions caused by blows from sticks, feet, or arms. Contusions can be treated by applying ice. In any type of throat injury the general response by the athlete is coughing, spitting, difficulty breathing, and pain.

## Throat Lacerations

Lacerations that are not deep can be handled with direct pressure. Deep lacerations or those that affect a jugular vein or carotid artery are medical emergencies and require immediate treatment. Apply direct pressure over the site of the laceration and treat the athlete for shock. The vessels in the neck are large, and a massive amount of blood will be lost rapidly—the athletic trainer must respond quickly to save the athlete's life. To review procedures for treating hemorrhage, see page 35. A throat laceration could occur, for example, when one player's ice skate goes across another player's throat.

## Cartilage Fractures

A severe blow to the throat can result in a fracture of the circular cartilaginous rings of the trachea—this too can be life threatening. The athlete will have difficulty breathing, will gasp for air, spit up blood, complain of pain, have difficulty talking, and be very anxious. His skin may turn a bluish color due to lack of oxygen. The ATC must exercise caution when treating a cartilage fracture because the trauma also may

### ? What Would You Do If...

An athlete comes off the playing field right where you are standing. She is having trouble catching her breath. You ask her what happened and she says, "I just got the wind knocked out of me. I'll be fine in a minute." The minute passes, and she is still struggling to catch her breath.

have caused a fracture of the cervical spine. This is a medical emergency. The athletic trainer will place the athlete on a backboard for transport to the hospital and apply ice to the area to reduce swelling. Those treating the athlete must remain calm to keep the athlete calm; keep the airway free of blood; and make sure medical care is on the way.

# Specific Conditions and Treatment Considerations for the Thorax

The thorax, if not adequately protected, is vulnerable to blunt trauma that can result in fractures of the ribs or sternum. Moreover, severe trauma may cause a lung injury as well.

## Rib Fracture

A rib fracture is caused by direct impact or chest compression. On rare occasions, a sudden violent muscular contraction, such as throwing a baseball, will cause a rib stress fracture. Blows to the front or back of the ribs generally do not result in inward displacement of the fractured rib. Blows to the lateral aspect, however, are more likely to lead to inward penetration, causing complications such as internal bleeding or a punctured lung.

### The Real World

At an ice hockey game, a young man was trying to stop a shot on goal with a diving headfirst slide. The slap shot hit him square in the throat. It was immediately apparent that he was in life-threatening danger. The team physician and athletic trainer jumped onto the ice before play was stopped. They quickly assessed him: difficulty breathing, blue skin tone, inability to speak, and rapid swelling over the throat. They iced his throat and backboarded him. His breathing was constantly monitored, and the physician was ready to make an emergency airway. Paramedics arrived and took the young man to the hospital. He recovered—with a deeper voice and partial loss of use of his vocal cords. He now wears a throat protector, and he slides feetfirst to stop slap shots!

Lorin Cartwright, MS, ATC, EMT

An athlete with fractured ribs experiences pain and difficulty breathing. The pain increases with inhalation, and the athlete usually holds a hand over the injured area in an effort to support the ribs. The area may be deformed due to swelling. A key to determining if a rib is fractured or severely contused is to note whether the athlete experiences increased pain with inhalation but not exhalation. If she has pain during both inhalation and exhalation she more likely has a contusion of the rib.

Treatment for uncomplicated rib fractures involves applying ice and sending the athlete for X rays. The team physician will restrict the athlete's physical activity until inhalation is not painful. If he participates in a contact sport, all activity should be stopped for six weeks. Upon return to competition he should wear protective padding or equipment.

## Sternal Fractures

Sternal fractures occur due to direct impact. Impact to the sternum that causes a fracture can be expected to also cause internal injuries, so the heart and lungs may be involved. A suspected fracture of the sternum is treated by application of ice and referral to the hospital. If the sternum is only contused from the impact, the athlete could possibly return to activity with a special sternal pad.

## Pneumothorax

A **pneumothorax** is the presence of air in the pleural cavity, commonly known as a collapsed lung, which can occur either as a result of trauma or without trauma. A traumatic pneumothorax can occur from a rib puncturing the lung, a gunshot wound, or severe laceration. A nontraumatic pneumothorax occurs due to a weakness of the lung tissue. When a pneumothorax occurs, the injured lung moves toward the center of the chest, which puts pressure on the heart and the other lung. Because only one lung is functioning, the athlete will experience difficulty breathing and will gasp for air. As the athlete continues to breathe, air goes through the hole in the lung and into the chest cavity, which causes the collapsed lung to compress the heart and opposite lung even further.

### Spontaneous Pneumothorax

When there is an imperfection in the tissue of the lung, it can break and cause the lung to collapse—this is known as a spontaneous pneumothorax. There need not be any impact or illness associated with a spontaneous pneumothorax—the athlete in the past may have appeared healthy and had no previous signs of illness. The athlete will experience difficulty with breathing, chest pain, and possibly bluish color of the skin if breathing is poor.

The athlete should be placed so that the side with the injured lung is closest to the ground. The ATC will treat the athlete for shock and get her to a hospital. In general, a spontaneous pneumothorax will heal itself without surgical intervention.

### Tension Pneumothorax

An athlete with a pneumothorax may develop a more serious problem called a tension pneumothorax (see figure 13.5). As air leaks out of the collapsed lung and into the chest cavity it forces the lung to press against the other lung and the heart. As pressure builds up in the chest the trachea will move away from the side of the pneumothorax. If the trachea moves, the athlete will experience severe respiratory distress. As more air enters the chest cavity, more pressure builds up against the heart and uninjured lung. As the pressure mounts the heart will begin to labor as blood flow and breathing are impeded. Death can occur if the athlete is not treated rapidly. If the athlete has an external puncture wound, partially cover it leaving one side unsealed. Sealing the wound entirely will prevent the inner air from escaping, causing the tension pneumothorax to get worse.

With tension pneumothorax, the athlete will experience respiratory distress, absent breath sounds on the injured side, anxiety, and bluish skin color. Her pulse will be rapid and weak, and her blood pressure will drop. As the pneumothorax worsens, tracheal deviation and neck vein distention will occur as will bulging of the muscles between each of the ribs. The ATC will place the athlete so that the side with the injured lung is closest to the ground, treat her for shock, and get her to a hospital. This injury requires a physician to insert a chest tube to

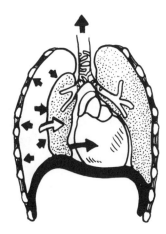

**Figure 13.5** The two most obvious signs of tension pneumothorax are tracheal shifting and a lack of breath sounds over the injured lung. If the ATC observes the trachea deviated to the side of the throat, she should suspect tracheal shifting.

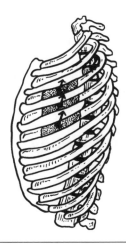

**Figure 13.6** When two or more ribs are broken in two places, it makes flail chest possible—the section of ribs that is broken moves inward toward the heart and lungs during inhalation and outward during exhalation.

allow air to escape and possible surgical intervention.

## Flail Chest

Flail chest occurs when several consecutive ribs are fractured in two or more places (see figure 13.6). This injury occurs from an impact directly to the ribs. The entire fractured portion moves in and out when the athlete breathes. However, the portion moves opposite to the normal breathing pattern. Normally, when an athlete inhales the chest expands and the ribs move outward, and on exhalation the chest moves inward. With a flail chest the fractured portion moves outward on exhalation and inward on inhalation. This movement creates extreme pain and difficulty breathing. Breathing will be painful and distressed, the athlete will be anxious, and skin tone will be bluish. The athlete should be checked for other internal injuries, especially lung contusions.

Treatment of a flail chest includes decreasing the movement of the fractured ribs. This can be accomplished by placing an object such as a sandbag or pillow over the fractured segment to keep it from moving. The athlete can be placed on his injured side as a way of controlling the movement of the flail chest; he should be treated for shock. This is a medical emergency and requires rapid advanced care.

## Pulmonary Contusions

A pulmonary contusion is a bruise of the lung due to impact—a baseball to the chest or a tackle could result in a pulmonary contusion. The contusion causes bleeding and swelling, which is an accumulation of fluid within the lung tissue. Unfortunately, the accumulated fluid keeps the lung from exchanging oxygen and carbon dioxide. The larger the contusion the more serious the injury. The athlete will have difficulty breathing and may have a bluish skin color. Application of ice may be helpful, but EMS must be called immediately.

## Hemothorax

A **hemothorax** is blood in the chest cavity. The bleeding can occur from an internal injury, like a ruptured lung or blood vessel. A hemothorax may also occur from an external wound that penetrates the chest, like a javelin into the chest.

A hemothorax is similar to a pneumothorax in that the blood puts pressure on the heart and lungs, which decreases their ability to function normally. As blood fills the chest cavity the athlete will have difficulty breathing, may turn blue from lack of oxygen, may become unconscious, will have a rapid weak pulse, sweat, and go into shock. Breath sounds may be absent on the side of the bleeding.

Bleeding into the chest cavity is serious and requires immediate care to prevent death. The ATC will call for immediate transport to the hospital and control bleeding as best she can. The athlete may require CPR if advanced help is delayed.

## Sucking Chest Wound

If the wall of the chest is punctured and air from the outside is drawn noisily into the cavity, this is known as a sucking chest wound (see figure 13.7). In this injury, the lung is not punctured. However, the air that is being sucked into the chest cavity applies pressure on the lungs and heart, causing distress for the athlete. The athlete will have difficulty breathing, and circulation may become impaired—he will have a bluish skin color. The athlete is best treated by sealing the wound with a cellophane wrap or a piece from a plastic bag. The EMS must be called immediately.

## Hyperventilation

**Hyperventilation** is quick deep breathing, more than 24 breaths per minute, which leads to abnormal loss of carbon dioxide from the blood. The athlete can become excited and begin hyperventilating, or she can have an underlying illness like diabetes. If she does not get her breathing under control, the athlete will experience lightheadedness, numbing of the fingers, toes, and lips, and loss of consciousness. As hyperventilation continues, muscular contractions occur in the limbs. To treat hyperventilation, the athletic trainer will talk calmly to the athlete and encourage her to control her breathing rate.

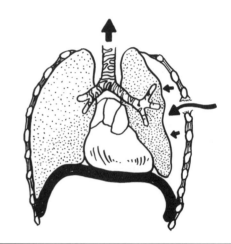

**Figure 13.7**  Sucking chest wound. When the chest is pierced, air can enter into the chest cavity directly from the outside, which causes the lung on the same side to compress. Breathing becomes difficult.

## Summary

Injuries to the throat and thorax can cause severe permanent damage or even death. The ATC must be able to evaluate injuries to the areas of the throat and thorax; prompt treatment is crucial in an athlete's survival. The history, signs, and symptoms will define the real injury. Most injuries to these areas are preventable if the athlete is wearing the proper equipment. Luckily, very few injuries occur in these areas, and when they do occur, most of them are not life threatening. For serious injuries, EMS is needed immediately.

## Key Terms

Define the following terms found in this chapter:

| | | |
|---|---|---|
| alveoli | hemothorax | phlegm |
| atrium | hyperventilation | pneumothorax |
| carotid artery | jugular vein | trachea |
| diaphragm | larynx | ventricle |
| esophagus | | |

## Questions for Review

1. Describe the normal breathing process. pp. 113-114
2. Describe the normal heart and circulation process. pp. 112-113
3. What types of throat and thorax injuries are life threatening? pp. 115-118
4. What are the common signs and symptoms of thorax injuries? pp. 116-118
5. How are the injuries to the thorax distinguished from each other? pp. 115-118
6. What are the common treatments for thorax injuries? pp. 116-118

## Activities for Reinforcement

1. Have a certified athletic trainer show the equipment that is available for different sports to prevent injuries of the throat and thorax.
2. Have a certified athletic trainer demonstrate how to evaluate throat and thorax injuries.
3. Use a stethoscope and listen to the heart and lungs.
4. Invite the local emergency medical service to demonstrate CPR and the electrical monitoring of the heart.

## Above and Beyond

1. Interview a cardiologist and write a report on sudden death syndrome.
2. Using a cow heart (local grocery store), label the parts of the heart. Give a classroom demonstration.

# Head Injuries

## OBJECTIVES

Upon completing this chapter the student will be able to do the following:
- Describe the anatomy of the head.
- Understand that head injuries can be prevented.
- Understand the urgency involved with caring for brain injuries.
- Describe the numerous types of head injuries.

When an athlete has a head injury, the ATC must act fast to lessen the chance of death and permanent injury. In this chapter we provide information to assist the student in understanding head injury and its prevention.

## Anatomy of the Head

The skull is comprised of 28 bones; it protects the brain. A suture line is the area where two bones in the skull come together. The single moveable bone in the skull is the mandible, or lower jaw. Figure 14.1 shows the major bones in the skull.

### The Brain

The brain is made of billions of cells—it weighs only about three pounds, but it requires 20 percent of the total body oxygen and 15 percent of the blood supply. Brain cells grow and develop until age 18. After that, brain cells can be destroyed but not reproduced. Depriving the brain of oxygen will cause unconsciousness, then death—pupils will dilate within 60 seconds. After four to six minutes without oxygen, biological brain death occurs, which means that large numbers of cells are dying.

The brain is divided into lobes, each named after the bony structure of the skull that covers it: occipital lobe, temporal lobe, parietal lobe, and frontal lobe (see figure 14.2). Each lobe is responsible for specific body functions. The brain attaches to the spinal cord at the brain stem via a crossover, so that the right side of the brain controls the left side of the body and vice versa. Preserving brain function is of utmost importance to an injured athlete—his quality of life, that is, his degree of recovery, depends upon how the brain injury is handled.

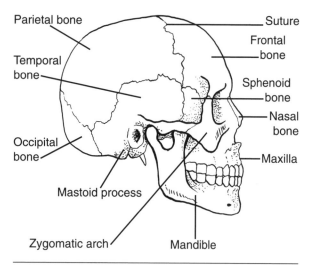

**Figure 14.1** Bones of the skull.

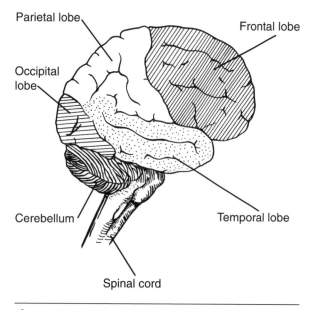

**Figure 14.2** Brain areas and function. The functions of the brain are based on location. Frontal lobe: voluntary muscle movement, emotion, eye movement; parietal lobe: sensation; occipital lobe: vision; temporal lobe: hearing, speech; cerebellum: equilibrium, muscle actions, and some reflexes.

**Cerebrospinal fluid** bathes the brain and spinal cord in chemicals for proper functioning, helps maintain regular pressure around the brain and spinal cord, and also protects the brain from impacts. The fluid is clear amber in color. In instances of severe head injury, cerebrospinal fluid may drain from an opening in the skull, the nose, or an ear, and it should be allowed to do so. Stopping the drainage will only increase the pressure within the skull and cause more brain damage.

## The Scalp

The scalp is the part of the skin that covers the skull—it contains a large number of blood vessels, muscles, and hair. Skin protects against infections; hair protects the skin from the sun and helps to keep dirt and sweat away from the eyes. The blood vessels are so numerous in the scalp that even a small laceration will bleed profusely. Cartoonists draw a large lump when a character is hit in the head. This can also happen to athletes; a blow to the head may cause the many blood vessels to break open and bleed under the skin, causing a lump, or hematoma.

The scalp has the ability to decrease the force of an impact to the skull due to the additional padding (however small) it provides and the increased elasticity created by the tension of the connective tissue between the scalp and the skull. It is believed that without the scalp the skull could be fractured with as little as 40 pounds of pressure. With the scalp, it may take 425 pounds of pressure before a fracture will occur. An athlete can sustain a serious head injury, however, without a break in the scalp, so the athletic trainer should not be fooled by a lack of bleeding.

## Preventing Head Injuries

Head injuries are prevented by helmets, mouth guards, rules, and common sense. A commonly forgotten piece of equipment in the battle to prevent head injuries is the mouth guard, which can prevent concussions as well as dental injuries. If an athlete is not wearing a mouth guard, an impact to the chin drives the mandible into the maxilla and causes the brain stem to twist slightly, resulting in loss of consciousness. A mouth guard provides spacing and shock absorption between the mandible and maxilla, so that the force of the impact will not be transmitted to the brain stem. For a mouth guard to be effective, however, the athlete must be wearing one, and it must be in good condition. A mouth guard that has been chewed up or cut off will not prevent the knockout impact.

Wearing a helmet and face mask is also important in preventing head injuries. In the early years of football the players did not wear helmets. Today, a properly fitted helmet helps protect a player's head from direct impacts. The helmet prevents head injuries, but not injuries of the face—thus the introduction of the face mask. With the head and face protected, the athlete began to use his helmet as a weapon to punish opposing players. Use of the head to make contact with another player is referred to as spearing. As spearing continued as a form of tackling, a progressive increase in the number of neck injuries resulting in permanent injury or death occurred—the advent of the helmet and face mask protected the head from direct impacts but resulted in other forms of injury. Spearing has since been deemed a penalty, an offense severe enough to get a player ejected from the game.

Athletes should be taught the proper skills so that injury can be prevented. Coaches and athletic trainers need to teach that the athlete cannot lead with the head when trying to stop an opponent; this is crucial in preventing head injuries. At the beginning of each season a film outlining sport safety should be shown. The athletic trainer should document attendance at this safety film—recording the date and an outline of the discussion should provide some legal protection if an athlete does sustain a serious head injury. The ATC should also document days when safety skills are taught at practice, and he should take attendance. He should explain the signs and symptoms of head injuries and the proper care of the helmet.

## Head Injury Mechanisms

Injury to the brain can be caused by impact or rotations of the head. The most common mechanism, however, is impact. The region most susceptible in the skull is the temporal region, because the bone is thinnest there. **Contrecoup** injuries occur when the head is moving and receives a blow. Upon impact, the brain "sloshes" to the side opposite the blow, where

it is stopped by the skull, and that is where the injury of the brain occurs. An athlete may complain of a headache opposite the impact—that is a contrecoup injury. Rotations of the head after an initial impact can cause the brain stem to stop functioning normally. The nerve receptors are overloaded with information to the brain. Brain overload causes unconsciousness. The unconscious state allows for a sorting of the impulses before the athlete returns to consciousness.

## Treating Head Injuries

Potentially life-threatening head injuries include skull fractures, concussions, and intracranial hematomas.

### Skull Fractures

Skull fractures occur when there is significant force against the head. There are several types of skull fractures: depressed, linear, compound, and penetrating. A depressed fracture pushes a portion of the skull inside toward the brain. There will be bleeding under the skin or even a laceration requiring bleeding control. A linear fracture goes across the skull. Although no bones are moved out of place, there are tears in the blood vessels on the inside of the skull. A compound fracture will result in a portion of the skull sticking through the scalp, with profuse bleeding. A penetrating fracture involves an object that has gone through the scalp, skull, and very likely the brain. A skull fracture will discolor the area behind the ear—a discoloration that is called a **battle sign**. Any skull fracture is significant and requires the immediate attention of a physician.

## ❓ What Would You Do If...

You have been instructed to walk an athlete with a first-degree concussion into the locker room. Another athlete insists you can cure a concussion by "cracking his neck." The athlete with the concussion says, "Yes, please make me better."

## Concussions

A **concussion** is the temporary impairment of brain function caused by impact to the head or by a rotation force. A rotation of the head during the impact will send a sudden massive number of impulses to the brain. The brain, not knowing what to do with all the impulses, is overwhelmed, and the athlete may be confused, dazed, or even lose consciousness. Other symptoms of a concussion include nausea, dizziness, headache, vomiting, difficulty speaking, ringing in the ears (**tinnitus**), loss of balance, unconsciousness, difficulty remembering things before or after the impact (**amnesia**), possible battle sign, and disorientation.

Although many different ways of grading the severity of concussions exist, they can be graded just like sprains and strains as mild, moderate, or severe. A mild, or first-degree, concussion, in which an athlete does not lose consciousness, should allow the athlete to recover quickly and should not cause any significant brain impairment, but the athlete may have problems remembering things. A moderate, or second-degree, concussion will cause the athlete to go unconscious for less than five minutes. He may also have other symptoms such as dizziness, confusion, and loss of coordination. If the athlete is unconscious for more than five minutes, he has sustained a severe, or third-degree, concussion. In the unconscious athlete there may be rapid eye movements that look like fluttering, and his pupils may be unequal in size. The pupil on the side of the head injury will be enlarged if the head injury is serious. The athlete may be in a coma, but he can hear what is being said, and it is important that someone talk to him while the athletic trainer is working. The ATC will detect increased blood pressure, decreased pulse rate, and signs of shock. A severe concussion can lead to death or paralysis. The

ATC must be cautious when dealing with a concussion because other injuries may have occurred during the impact. He should also consider the possibility of a neck injury and keep the athlete's head still.

When the athlete is being brought off the playing field it is not uncommon for other players trying to be supportive to hit the player on the head and say, "hang in there." They are unintentionally contributing to the concussion. Athletes must be instructed to keep hands off ahead of time, so that only the athletic trainer touches the injured athlete.

A concussion, with or without the loss of consciousness, should make the athletic trainer wonder about other injuries that may have occurred. It is best to backboard any athlete with a moderate or severe concussion.

An athlete who has suffered a concussion will need to be monitored and seen by a physician to determine when it is safe to reenter competition. In general, an athlete will not be allowed back into competition after the first concussion until there are no remaining symptoms. Specifically, the athlete will have no headache, nausea, dizziness, or amnesia and will have regained full coordination and normal blood pressure. After a second concussion within a year, the athlete must have at least one month free of all signs and symptoms before returning. A third concussion in one year puts the athlete out of competition for one year, starting the day of the third concussion. An athlete who has suffered a concussion should be told about the signs and symptoms of concussions and the implications of repeated impacts. An athlete who has suffered one concussion is four times more likely to suffer another.

## Intracranial Hematoma

An intracranial hematoma is severe bleeding within the brain caused by a blow to head, particularly over the temporal or parietal regions. The hematoma causes a significant increase in pressure on the brain, and rapid death can occur. Sometimes an athlete is thought to have a concussion and is allowed to go home. If he has a hematoma, he may die during the night. If an athlete is found in a coma, the chances of survival are only 40 percent. Survival depends on early examination by a physician and prompt surgical care. Physicians usually drill a hole in the skull, to allow drainage of the blood, and attempt to repair the bleeding vessel. If the athlete is not in a coma, the physician must give medication to put him into a coma. The comatose state helps keep the athlete calm and allows the brain to heal without movement.

Symptoms of a hematoma are headaches, nausea, vomiting, loss of consciousness, paralysis of extremities on the opposite side of the injury, and battle sign. If an athlete suffers any of the symptoms of a hematoma, EMS should be contacted for immediate care. The onset of some of these symptoms will be gradual, so the athlete needs to be continually monitored. With the first indication of a condition that is worsening, the athlete must be taken immediately to the hospital. An athlete with possible head injury should be monitored for at least 24 hours, and he must be awakened every couple of hours to check his status.

The signs of a hematoma are a rise in blood pressure with a drop in pulse rate. The pupil on the same side as the head injury will be enlarged. The athlete may have difficulty speaking, difficulty using the extremities on the side opposite the hematoma, stiffening of posture, rapid eye movements, unconsciousness or coma, and lack of coordination. Depending on the severity of the hematoma the athlete may

fully recover, or he may suffer permanent brain impairment or death.

## Postconcussion Syndrome

Postconcussion syndrome is the persistence of symptoms, which may include headache, ringing in the ears, dizziness, or confusion after a concussion. The athlete should be seen by a physician for a follow-up evaluation. Postconcussion syndrome does not usually last more than a week or two.

## Second Impact Syndrome

It is thought that damage from concussions and brain injury is cumulative in nature. Therefore, if an athlete is allowed to return to participation before the symptoms of his first concussion have completely subsided and he receives another blow to the head, he can quickly lose brain function and go into a coma. **Second impact syndrome** can occur when an athlete receives more than one concussion or blow to the head in a relatively short time period. Such trauma may disturb the brain's blood supply and present signs of a minor concussion followed quickly by a semi-comatose state. Athletes who have suffered brain injuries must not be allowed to return to participation until they are symptom free and have written permission from a doctor.

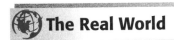

## The Real World

On Monday, September 20, 1993, at 2:35 P.M. our high school dismissed students. My student trainers and I went to work in the training room. It was a fairly busy fall Monday. My students were preparing athletes for football, soccer, and volleyball, while I was checking a few of the injured athletes. At approximately 2:50 P.M., the athletic director announced over the PA system that I was needed in the parking lot—there had been an accident. By the sound of his voice, I could tell we had a big problem.

I ran out of my training room at full speed. When I hit the doors just outside the athletic office, the athletic director met me, and we ran on together. The accident had occurred at the far end of the parking lot. I surveyed the scene as we approached. I saw a bunch of students standing around looking at something on the ground. On the right, next to a car, a female student—who appeared to be very upset—was talking with one of our teachers. I started asking questions as I made my way through the gathering of students. Someone said that a girl had fallen off the hood of the car while it was moving.

The next thing I saw took my breath. Lying on the ground was the student who had been in my office earlier in the day to arrange for a tutor. She was pale, sweaty, not breathing, and bleeding from her ears, nose, and mouth. I saw a patch of bloody hair on the pavement about 2 feet from us and 8–10 feet from the car. All I had to do was look at the athletic director and he got on his radio to his secretary to call an ambulance. I swung around to the young lady's head, and because I suspected both a head and neck injury, I stabilized her head and neck. I immediately opened her airway using the jaw thrust maneuver to open the airway with minimal head movement. When her airway opened she made a gurgling noise and a bloody froth bubbled from the corners of her mouth. As I continued to stabilize her head and neck, I asked a health teacher, who was at my side, to check the girl's pulse. Her pulse was faint, and her breathing was irregular. She was nonresponsive, and her face was covered with blood. An assistant principal was there with gloves and paper towels, and I had him gently clean her face so I could determine the major source of bleeding. I told the athletic director to keep bystanders back, and I sent the head custodian to the school entrance to direct the ambulance to us. All the time I was stabilizing the girl's head and neck and maintaining her airway, I was also trying to get a response from her. As we waited for the ambulance I realized that I did not have gloves on, but it was too late to worry about that. We seemed to wait forever. The girl started to choke, and we had to logroll her just as the ambulance made its way into the parking lot.

I continued to maintain the girl's head and neck while the paramedic checked her vitals. While he was doing this, she became combative. The paramedic got a collar on her, and I fought to maintain her head and neck stability while we put her on the backboard and then the stretcher. The paramedic asked me to ride in the ambulance to continue to maintain her head and neck. I held her head between my forearms while a second paramedic tried to get an IV going. In spite of her restraints it took several attempts; she was a lot stronger than I ever could have imagined. We were about a block from the hospital when she started to vomit and she aspirated. Now, clearing her airway became the most important priority. The paramedic yelled at me to grab the suction line as he turned it on. As he was suctioning the bloody vomit from her mouth, I was trying not to vomit on both of them.

We arrived at the emergency room; I was still maintaining her head and neck. They did a cross-table X ray, which was negative for cervical-spine fracture, and I was allowed to discontinue stabilization. I stayed with the girl in the ER until her parents got there. The doctor told me it was too early to tell how she would be. When I walked out of the ER, I met the athletic director waiting to give me a ride back to school. It was like coming back to the real world. I hadn't even thought about getting back to school or about practice.

The young lady spent two weeks in ICU being treated for a subdural hematoma. She later returned to school, showing few effects of the injury. I, however, have learned that my job extends far beyond the training room—and I always grab a pair of gloves on the way out the door.

Becky Clifton, ATC

# Summary

Although the brain is well protected by the skull, it is vulnerable to serious injury—the athlete may suffer intracranial bleeding, concussion, postconcussion syndrome, or second impact syndrome. If the brain lacks oxygen for any appreciable time, cellular death occurs. Typical signs and symptoms of a head injury include vomiting, unequal pupils, skull depression, increased blood pressure, and unconsciousness, any of which call for immediate EMS attention. It is imperative that an athlete who has suffered a head injury not have any signs or symptoms of the injury when he returns to participation, and he must have clearance from a physician.

# Key Terms

Define the following terms found in this chapter:

| | | |
|---|---|---|
| amnesia | concussion | second impact syndrome |
| battle sign | contrecoup | tinnitus |
| cerebrospinal fluid | | |

# Questions for Review

1. How can head injuries be prevented? pp. 122-123
2. What does an elevated blood pressure mean when there is a head injury? p. 124-125
3. What are the differences between first-, second-, and third-degree concussions? p. 124
4. What is the treatment for a second-degree concussion? p. 124
5. If the battle sign is present, what injury has occurred? p. 123
6. Why should an athlete be cleared by a physician before he returns to participation following a head injury? pp. 124-125

# Activities for Reinforcement

1. Have an ATC demonstrate how to evaluate an athlete with a head injury.
2. Identify the sports in your school and list the types of head injuries to which athletes in each sport are prone.
3. Have a coach bring a safety film on prevention of head injuries and show it to the class.
4. Make a list of reasons why athletes get head injuries.
5. Visit a head trauma or closed-brain injury center.

## Above and Beyond

The references listed at the end of this section may be used to complete any of the following projects:

1. Draw a side and front view of the brain. Label the parts of the brain, functions, and areas controlled.
2. Find other grading systems for concussions in the current literature.
3. Write a report on how long it takes to recover from a concussion.
4. Write a report on the physiological effects of concussions.

Guskiewicz, K., D. Perrin, and B. Gansneder. 1996. Effects of mild head injury on postural stability in athletes. *Journal of Athletic Training* 31(4): 300–306.

Hugenholtz, H., D.T. Stuss, L. Stethem, and M.T. Richard. 1988. How long does it take to recover from a mild concussion? *Neurosurgery* 22: 853–58.

Hugenholtz, H., and M.T. Richard. 1983. The on-site management of athletes with head injuries. *The Physician and Sportsmedicine* 11(6): 71–80.

Kuland, D.N. 1988. *The injured athlete.* 2d ed. Philadelphia: Lippincott.

McWhorter, J. M. 1990. Concussions and intracranial injuries in athletics. *Athletic Training* 25(2): 129–31.

Mueller, F.O., R.C. Cantu, and S.P. Van Camp. 1996. *Catastrophic injuries in high school and college sports.* Champaign, IL: Human Kinetics.

Nelson, W.J., J. Gieck, J. Jane, and P. Hawthorne. 1984. Athletic head injuries. *Athletic Training* 19(2): 95–102.

Putukian, M., and R. Echemendia. 1996. Managing successive minor head injuries. *The Physician and Sportsmedicine* 24(11): 25–38.

Torg, J., J. Vegso, B. Sennett, and M. Das. 1985. The national football head and neck injury registry. *Journal of the American Medical Association* 254(24): 3439–43.

Torg, J. 1991. *Athletic injuries to the head, neck, and face.* 2d ed. St. Louis: Mosby.

# Facial Injuries

Upon completing this chapter the student will be able to do the following:
- Describe the basic anatomy of the face.
- Describe how common facial injuries occur.
- Explain the common types of facial injuries and how to prevent them.
- Explain common steps of care for treating facial injuries.

Injuries of the face can lead to permanent disfigurement or visual impairment. The immediate action of the athletic trainer can lessen the chance of long-term problems. Protective equipment such as eye guards can also reduce the chance of permanent injury.

## Anatomy of the Facial Region

The face includes bones that are also a part of the skull, so the discussion in the previous chapter may clarify the anatomy that follows. There are 18 bones in the face (some are in pairs). Major bones include: the maxillae, mandible, and zygomatic bones (see figure 15.1). The maxillae are the two bones of the upper jaw and the mandible is the lower jaw. The nasal bones make up the bridge of the nose. The zygomatic bones are also known as the cheekbones. Within the structure of the sphenoid bone are the sinuses, which get stuffed up when a virus or infection invades the upper respiratory tract. The sinuses are located above and below the eyes (see figure 15.2). Some facial fractures may remain hidden because of bleeding into the sinuses rather than external bleeding.

### The Eye

The eye sits in a socket known as the orbital foramen, or orbit. Most of the eye is hidden inside the orbital foramen, which protects the eye on three sides and serves as an attachment point for the muscles that move the eye. Lack of eye movement can indicate either a head injury or serious eye injury (figure 15.3 shows the eye anatomy).

The eye itself is made up of the anterior and posterior chambers. The two chambers are filled with fluid, which gives the eye its rounded shape. An injury that causes the fluid to drain from the eye is likely to cause permanent damage, even blindness.

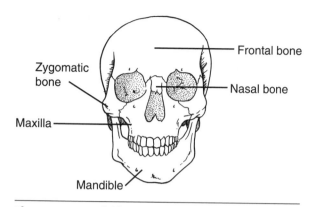

**Figure 15.1** Facial bones.

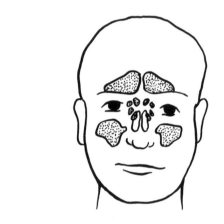

**Figure 15.2** Sinuses.

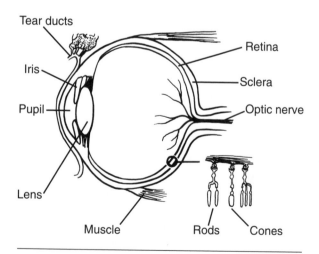

**Figure 15.3** Anatomy of the eye.

## ? What Would You Do If...

One of your friends shows you his ice hockey helmet, which has a crack in the back portion of the helmet. He has glued it back together. He says there is no rule that prevents him from playing in a game with his "newly repaired helmet."

The part of the eye you can observe has a white area and a clear center. The white outer covering of the eye is known as the sclera. A change of color of the sclera indicates that the athlete has a problem or an illness such as liver disease, lack of oxygen, or poisoning. The center clear portion of the covering of the eyeball is the cornea. The cornea protects other important structures from injury. It covers the iris and pupil and admits light to the interior. The cornea is made up of thousands of tiny cells that can be injured by wearing contact lenses too long or by something that scratches the eye. The iris is the contractile colored portion of the eye—its center-most portion is the pupil, which is the opening in the eye. Also located in the anterior portion of the eye is the lens. The conjunctiva is the lining of the inner surface of the eyelid and is continued over the forepart of the eyeball.

The pupil is the opening in the iris. The iris responds to light to change the size of the pupil. In bright light, the pupil will get smaller, thus limiting the amount of light entering the eye. In a dark room the pupil will get larger to allow all available light into the eye.

The lens focuses the light rays entering the eye on retina. There are times when a poke in the eye will dislodge the lens and an athlete's vision will be blurred or changed.

The main structures at the posterior aspect of the eye are the retina and the optic nerve. The retina lines the back of the eye and contains the rods and cones. Rods provide vision in black and white and cones provide color vision. The retina receives the image formed by the lens and converts it into chemical and nerve signals that the optic nerve sends to the brain, where vision occurs. Damage to the optic nerve can cause blindness. Injury to the optic nerve that has resulted in blindness will also prevent the pupil from functioning.

In the upper outside (that is, superior lateral) edge of each eye is a gland that makes tears. Tears wash diagonally across to the nose and drain into it through a duct. In the rims of each eyelid are small glands that secrete lubricating fluid allowing the eyelid to open and close smoothly.

Vision is measured by an arbitrary standard. Originally, the test consisted of reading letters on a chart from a distance of 20 feet. An athlete who could read the smallest letters was said to have 20/20 vision. Today's vision tests relate to that standard. An athlete who can see near objects more clearly than distant ones is nearsighted, and one who can see distant objects better than near ones is farsighted—these common visual problems are treated with corrective lenses or eye exercises.

## The Ear

The ear has three distinct areas: the external ear, the middle ear, and the inner ear (see figure 15.4). The external ear is comprised of the pinna, the ear canal, and the tympanic membrane. The pinna, which is the projecting portion of the external ear, is cartilage covered by skin; its purpose is to catch sound and funnel it into the auditory canal.

 **What Would You Do If...**

An athlete comes running into the training room. She is in tears, cannot see, and has pain in her eyes. She reveals that she is wearing a friend's contact lenses because she just wanted to try them out.

The auditory canal carries sound from the pinna to the tympanic membrane, or eardrum. Earwax, which is designed to keep dirt away from the sensitive eardrum, is found in the auditory canal. Too much wax in the ear prevents or delays the sound from reaching the middle ear.

## The Nose

Two small bones, called the nasal bones, attach to the frontal bone of the skull. About an inch in length, the nasal bones make up the bridge of the nose. The rest of the nose is cartilage.

Inside the nose is the septum, which is a cartilage piece that separates the left and right sides of the nose. Hairs inside the nose filter impurities from the air. The palate, which is the roof of the mouth, separates the mouth from the bottom of the nose.

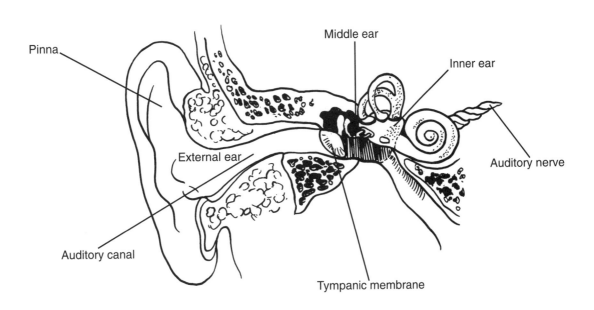

**Figure 15.4**  The ear.

Air that is inhaled through the nose is warmed, moisturized, and cleansed before reaching the lungs. In winter, breathing through the nose will decrease lung pain caused by inhaling cold air through the mouth. Athletes with asthma and upper respiratory infections should breathe moist air.

## The Mouth

The mouth is made up of the mandible (lower jaw), maxillae (upper jaw), temporomandibular joint, tongue, palate (roof of the mouth), and teeth.

The mandible attaches to the skull at the temporomandibular joint and is the only moveable bone in the face. The mandible moves when an athlete speaks or eats. The teeth give the face shape and are used to chew food; they are attached to both the mandible and the maxillae. An adult has 32 permanent teeth.

A tooth is composed of the crown, which is the visible portion above the gum line, and the root, which is below the gum line (see figure 15.5). The crown is capped with a thin layer of enamel, which protects against tooth decay. The root contains pulp and dentin. Dentin is the hard bony portion of the tooth. The pulp is the soft portion of the tooth containing the nerve and blood supply. The tooth's nerve is sensitive to pain, pressure, and temperature. The blood supply brings oxygen and food to the tooth to keep it alive. A live tooth is white in color, whereas a dead tooth is dark gray.

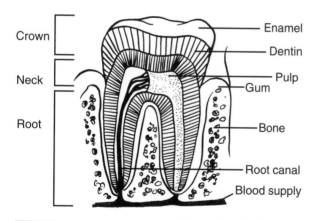

**Figure 15.5** Cross section of a tooth.

The teeth, tongue, and saliva work together to get food ready to be swallowed. The salivary glands under the tongue and in the back of the mouth provide saliva to begin digestion. The saliva makes it easier for the teeth to break food down and binds the food together before it is sent on to the stomach.

## Preventing Facial Injuries

Preventing facial injuries requires common sense. Athletes who fail to wear the proper equipment can easily become injured—a prime example is a catcher who does not wear a face mask when warming up a pitcher. There is equipment available in all sports to prevent facial injury: helmets, mouth guards, face masks, goggles, protective eyewear, and headgear. Athletes should take note: mouth guards are relatively inexpensive, but repairing injuries to the teeth and jaw is very expensive.

A properly fitted athletic face mask decreases the number of eye, nose, face, and mouth injuries. The face mask should be spaced a minimum of one inch from the nose, because if it is closer, an impact to the face mask can cause it to distort inward, resulting in a facial or nose injury. When selecting a face mask, make sure that no game equipment, such as a hockey puck or stick blade, can get through the openings in the mask and impact the face—if it can, the protective equipment must be changed.

Protective eyewear is crucial equipment in preventing blindness. All sports have the potential for eye injuries to occur—balls, sticks, elbows, and fingers are common items that injure eyes. Since an eye injury is unpredictable, it would be best if all athletes would wear eye protection designed for their sport. Eye guards—which are generally made of plastic frames and lenses, similar to glasses—or goggles should be worn if face masks are not worn. Athletes with fractures of the nasal bones, skull, or jaw should

### ❓ What Would You Do If...

You find the lost contact lens of a soccer player. It is covered with dirt and grass.

wear special padding, masks, or helmets to prevent additional injuries.

# Treating Eye Injuries

Eyes are precious, and it is better to send an athlete with any eye injury to a physician than have an athlete with permanent injury or loss of vision. The athletic trainer should be thinking about other injuries that may have occurred along with the eye injury—a head injury is a definite possibility that should be assessed.

Eyes move in coordination—even if an eye is injured, it will still have a tendency to move in cooperation with the noninjured eye. Thus, if an eye must be patched or shielded, the ATC should cover both eyes. This will reduce the movement of both eyes and thus reduce irritation of the injured eye.

## Corneal Abrasion or Laceration

An abrasion or laceration of the cornea is caused by being poked in the eye with a foreign object or by wearing contact lenses too long. An abrasion is superficial, whereas a laceration is deeper and more severe. The athlete will experience pain and have the sensation of something being lodged in the eye. She will have tears and sensitivity to bright light. If the injury is not treated, the eye may become infected or the athlete may have permanent vision problems. The physician treats her by patching the injured eye or eyes for 24 hours and applying antibiotic ointment. She will need help getting to the hospital because of limited vision. If wearing a contact lens too long caused the injury, a restriction will be placed on the athlete to keep this from recurring. She will prefer to use sunglasses while recovering. Corrective lenses may be necessary if the cornea becomes distorted. The athlete may have difficulty returning to competition for fear of re-injuring the eye, but using eye guards or goggles will help overcome this fear.

## Detached Retina

A blow to the eye, or even a hard sneeze, can cause the retina to detach. The athlete will experience pain, but the surest sign of a **detached retina** is that the athlete sees sparks, lights, and flashes that nobody else can see. The athlete may indicate that he is having difficulty seeing or that things look foggy. The athlete should be referred to a physician, who can do laser surgery to repair the detached retina. When the athlete returns to activity he must wear protective goggles to prevent reinjury. If a physician does not repair the damage promptly, blindness could result.

## Black Eye

A hard enough blow to the eye may cause a black eye. Like any contusion, a black eye is really caused by the bleeding and discoloration just under the skin. The athlete will not complain of any visual impairment, but there will be swelling and pain. If the athlete complains of any other difficulty, a referral to a physician is necessary. Ice application over a black eye is an accepted treatment.

## Foreign Bodies

A foreign body in the eye will cause tears, which attempt to wash it toward the nose. In some instances, tears will not clear the eye. In these cases rinsing with water from the nose outward can flush the particle out of the eye or over to one side where it can be removed.

If the object is stuck under the eyelid, the athletic trainer or athlete should lift the lid outward over the bottom lash. The bottom lash can brush the object out. If this process does not remove the object, it will be necessary to invert the upper eyelid. The inversion of the lid is accomplished by grasping the lid and pulling it outward; a cotton-tipped applicator is placed

---

### ? What Would You Do If...

A golfer comes into the training room assisted by several others. They tell you that someone yelled "fore," and she turned to look. The golf ball hit her in the eye. The athlete is in extreme pain and wants you to remove her contact lens. You can see several pieces of her contact lens sticking into her eye.

in the fold of the lid, and the lid is laid over the applicator. This will expose the underside of the lid so the object can be removed. If the inversion technique fails, the athlete should be referred to a physician for care. He must have both eyes patched to decrease eye movement and prevent scratching of the cornea.

## Embedded Object

An embedded object is one that is stuck in the eye; it may have been blown into the eye, or a blow from a ball may have shattered a contact lens. No matter how the object has gotten in the eye, the care the athlete receives will determine the quality of her vision in the future. The athlete will know the object is in the eye. She will reach for the eye and tearing will occur—she will experience pain, visual impairment, and anxiety.

The best treatment is to place an eye shield over both eyes and send the athlete for physician care. If the object, such as a pencil, is sticking out of the eye the ATC will stabilize it with bulky dressings—he will not remove the object. The physician will determine the severity of the injury, surgically remove the object, and stop any fluid release. The physician will prescribe antibiotics, and the eye will remain patched about a week. A vision test will be necessary to determine visual acuity. Eye guards and goggles will help the athlete protect the eye from re-injury.

## Subconjunctival Hemorrhage

Athletes who suffer from a terrible cough from an upper respiratory infection are prone to subconjunctival hemorrhage. The constant coughing may cause the small vessels in the eye to rupture, which turns the conjunctiva red. An athlete may also get poked in the conjunctiva or hit by a ball, which causes the same result.

Although the eye will look terribly painful, the athlete experiences minimal or no pain and no visual impairment. It is best to refer the athlete to a physician for an eye exam to be sure no other structures are injured. The treatment of this hemorrhage is to do nothing. The athlete is allowed to participate without restriction. Her biggest problem will be the funny looks she gets from others concerned about the appearance of her eye.

## Hemorrhage Into the Anterior Chamber (Hyphema)

A blow to the eye can cause bleeding within the eye. A **hyphema** is blood pooling in the anterior portion of the eye. When looking at the athlete the blood can be seen under the cornea. The athlete will complain of both the inability to see and of pain. He should have both eyes covered with a protective shield, but the ATC should not apply an ice pack. The physician needs to determine the severity of the injury. The athlete with a hyphema may suffer permanent damage, blindness, or develop cataracts.

## Blowout Fracture

A blow to the eye can force the eyeball backward into the socket. The thin bones beneath the eye absorb the sudden increase in pressure and fracture. This type of fracture is referred to as a blowout.

The athlete may experience double vision and may not be able to feel much pain as a result of the damage to surrounding nerve endings. The athlete may also experience numbing of the lip and upper jaw on the same side as the injury. The muscles of the eye often get caught in the fractured bones. Therefore, the ATC may notice that the athlete cannot control the injured eye—it will be looking in a different direction than the uninjured eye. The eye may appear to be sunken in the socket. There will be immediate swelling, and the conjunctiva will begin to discolor. The athlete may have a bloody nose on the same side as the injury, and the bleeding may fill the sinus, making it difficult to breathe. The eye may bulge when the athlete attempts to blow his nose.

The ATC should call 911 and help control any bleeding. The athlete should be monitored in case his condition worsens. A physician may have to surgically repair the fracture and release the muscles. The athlete may suffer permanent vision problems, including glaucoma and cataracts. He will remain out of competition for several months.

Boxers wear headgear to prevent such eye injuries. Although it is rarely seen, wrestlers, basketball players, and racquetball players should wear some form of eye protection to prevent a blowout.

## Fracture of the Orbital Roof

A blow to the eye or the area just above the eye can cause a fracture in the roof of the orbit. When this happens, the athlete will experience pain, a headache, signs and symptoms of a concussion, and a hematoma over the area.

The nose may bleed, and cerebrospinal fluid may drain from the nose. This injury requires immediate care by a physician. Most often hospitalization, for observation and care of the fracture, and rest will be required. The athlete will not be able to return to competition for about a year.

## Sinus Fracture

A sinus fracture can occur when there is a sharp blow to the face, for example, from a baseball taking a bad hop or a stick across the face. A headache, dizziness, and unsteadiness may occur. The athlete's nose may bleed on the same side as the injury. She will experience pain, but once the bleeding has stopped, the athletic trainer should do a quick assessment of the injury. The distinction in this fracture is that air will seep into the skin and tissues around the eye and nose. There will be a crackling sensation when the area is touched. The ATC should apply ice and refer her to a physician immediately. The physician will require special X rays to discover the exact location of the fracture.

A complication of this injury is a concussion, which could diminish the athlete's ability to give a history. In the case of a blow to the face, it is always prudent to recommend a physician's evaluation.

## Dislodged Contact Lens

Contact lenses come in two basic types: hard and soft. A hard contact lens covers the pupil of the eye, whereas a soft lens covers the entire cornea. A displaced hard contact lens feels like a rock in the eye. The athlete's vision will be impaired, and the displaced lens will irritate his eye. Usually the athlete knows where the lens is located in the eye because of the initial pain. When the eye is examined, the lens can be seen because of its color in contrast to the sclera. Some people believe that the lens can be lost behind the eye, but that is impossible. The lens will be in the eye—the ATC just has to keep looking. The hard lens can be moved back over the pupil, and usually the athlete will do it himself if the ATC provides a mirror. If he is unable to remove it, the ATC can remove it using a small suction-cup device that is placed over the lens. The athlete should then clean the lens before placing it back in his eye.

Soft lens displacement is less uncomfortable. The athlete will know the lens is out of place because she won't be able to see. A soft lens is more difficult to put back in place because it tends to curl up like a soggy cornflake. The athlete should wash her hands, then reach in and gently grab the lens. She must use caution, because roughly handling a soft lens will tear it. The lens should be cleaned with solution before being returned to the eye. Sometimes an athlete believes rinsing the lens by putting it in her mouth is acceptable. The practice of placing a hard or soft contact lens in your mouth is like dipping it in garbage before reinserting it. This practice must be discouraged!

## Eyelid Laceration

Think of an athlete who reaches out to grab the head of the opposing wrestler to gain control for a takedown. The opponent jerks his head away from the grasp but gets poked in the eye and experiences immediate eye pain. The eye is bleeding, and the athlete refuses to pull his hand away so the ATC can determine the extent of the injury. Once the athlete relaxes, the ATC can see that the eyelid is lacerated, maybe all the way through to the margin of the eyelash.

The immediate procedure is to control the bleeding with direct pressure. The ATC will question the athlete about his ability to see clearly, to determine the extent of other possible consequences of the poke. An eyelid laceration is similar to most lacerations except the tear duct may also be injured—permanent damage to the duct may result. Once the bleeding is controlled, the athlete must be referred to a physician to repair the lid.

A plastic surgeon should repair a laceration of the eyelid, to prevent scarring or permanent deformity of the lid. The ophthalmologist will want to check the eye for acuity and to insure that there are no other complications.

Athletes should keep their fingernails cut to prevent eyelid lacerations (this is a rule in wrestling). Goggles can also prevent this type of injury.

## Ruptured Globe

The globe—the eyeball itself—can be ruptured by any object small enough to enter the eye, such as a squash or racquet ball. Upon examination of the eye, the ATC will notice a lack of roundness of the globe and a hemorrhage of the eye. Associated injuries may include an eyelid laceration, blood in the front of the eye, the interior contents of the eye spilling out, or the pupil out of round (figure 15.6). Any sign that the globe has been ruptured requires that the ATC cover the eye with a protective eye shield that will not allow external pressure. The athlete must be taken to the emergency room immediately and referred to an ophthalmologist if his eyesight is going to be saved. He will not be able to return to competition for months.

# Treating Ear Injuries

The external ear helps to funnel sound to the inner ear. The inner ear plays a role in equilibrium. With its placement on the side of the head, the ear does not have a high incidence of injury. In high school athletics, earrings are barred from competition because of the potential for ear injury.

## Laceration of the Pinna

Ears stick out away from the head—enough that they may get in the way. Athletes should never wear earrings in practices or competitions because this increases the vulnerability of an already exposed body part. An earring can be caught by another athlete's finger, tearing the

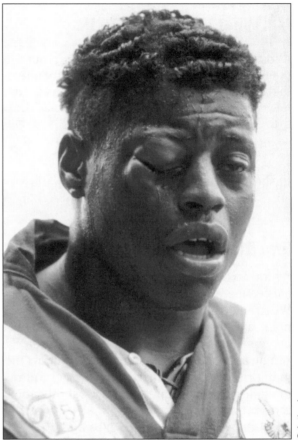

© Action Images

**Figure 15.6** Anytime there is excessive swelling, with possible leakage of fluid, a ruptured globe should be suspected. Both eyes must be patched and the athlete sent to the emergency room immediately.

ear lobe. Even in sports in which the ears are protected by a helmet, if the head is struck, earrings may be jammed against the wearer's head, causing serious discomfort if not injury. A laceration of the pinna is treated like any other wound—by controlling the bleeding with direct pressure, which can be applied on both sides for rapid control.

When a portion of the pinna is no longer attached, the missing piece must be found so that it might be reattached. The detached part should be wrapped in sterile gauze, put in a plastic bag, and placed in a container full of ice. (It is appropriate to place on ice as long as the ear is not directly touching the ice). In the case of a laceration, the athlete should be referred to a physician for stitches and a tetanus shot. The athlete can prevent lacerations and other wounds of the pinna by wearing proper protection and removing earrings.

## What Would You Do If...

A basketball player is chewing the end off his mouth guard. The mouth guard will still protect the front teeth.

## Cauliflower Ear (Hematoma Auris)

Wrestlers are the athletes who suffer the most from cauliflower ear. The wrestler involved usually is not wearing his headgear and gets hit hard in the ear, or his head is pushed hard into the wrestling mat. The pinna of the ear begins to bleed internally, causing swelling, redness, and pain. As the ear heals there is an excessive growth of reparative tissue, which distorts the pinna—someone thought it looked like a piece of cauliflower.

Treatment of cauliflower ear starts with ice and compression with moldable material, performed by the team physician. The team physician may lance, or drain, the ear to reduce the swelling and use steroid medication to keep the hemorrhage under control. In more complicated cases the physician may remove the tissue through surgery. Some athletes opt for plastic surgery to fix the ear if it is permanently distorted. Wearing headgear and applying petroleum jelly to reduce friction can prevent cauliflower ear.

## Otitis Externa (Swimmer's Ear)

Proper care of the ear requires that the ear and the canal be dried after swimming. There are times when a swimmer cannot remove water from his ear—he is hurrying to get home, or water is stuck in his ear. If water remains in the ear, an inflammation of the canal can occur, which is referred to as otitis externa, more commonly called **swimmer's ear**, for those most often affected.

The athlete will experience pain, itching, hearing loss, and possibly a smelly discharge from the ear. It will be easy to notice the discharge and the red swollen canal. If the infection is not controlled it can spread deeper into the canal. The athlete should be sent to a physician for ear drops and antibiotics.

Prevention of swimmer's ear can be as simple as drying the ear after swimming. Rubber or wax plugs can be used to lessen the flow of water into the ear. When using plugs, hearing is impaired, making it more difficult to hear some coaches. Some athletes prefer to use alcohol-based ear drops, which dry the ear canal.

## Foreign Bodies in the Ear

In athletics, foreign bodies in the ear are rare, but a bug or two has been known to take a look in an athlete's ear. The athlete will have the sensation that something is in the ear and may experience pain.

Probing the ear with a cotton-tipped applicator may just push the object further into the ear and should be avoided. The ATC could also rupture the eardrum while trying to get the object out. A physician can remove an object using mineral oil or special tweezers.

# Treating Nose Injuries

For some athletes the nose is always in the way. In boxing it is constantly being smashed by a fist. Wrestlers can find their noses rubbed into the mat and even used as a handy carrying handle by opponents. And basketball players' noses seem to be attracted to the elbows of opposing players. The nose is vital: it warms incoming air and acts as a filter to catch particles.

## Epistaxis (Nosebleed)

When an athlete goes up to head a soccer ball and it lands on her nose, that impact can cause an epistaxis. **Epistaxis** is the medical term for a bloody nose. An athlete may get a nosebleed from constantly blowing the nose during a cold. Those athletes taking special medications, as well as those having had a recent nosebleed, will be prone to epistaxis.

The nose will be bleeding from one or both nostrils and (if the nosebleed is from a blow) painful. The ATC will instruct the athlete to lean forward while pinching the nose (direct pressure). Applying ice to the nose and packing the nose with gauze that has been soaked with an astringent (medication that slows bleeding) are helpful. Leaning the head backward forces the blood into the throat, obstructs the airway, and should be avoided. The athlete should lean forward to allow blood to discharge from the nose and should spit out any blood draining into her throat—swallowing blood will cause vomiting. Discourage any attempt to blow the nose, as this will start the bleeding process again. If there is excessive (gushing like a faucet was turned on) bleeding from the nose, the athlete should be treated for shock and sent to the hospital for evaluation. The physician may cauterize the bleeding vessel (heat it up to close it off).

## Deviated Septum

The septum is the piece of cartilage that separates the left and right sides of the nose. A deviated septum has moved to one side causing decreased airflow through the nasal passageway. Any form of direct impact to the nose can cause a deviation.

The blow to the nose will have caused a nosebleed, so follow the instructions previously given regarding epistaxis before dealing with the deviation. Then wait a day or two to test the athlete for a deviated septum by blocking off one nostril and having the athlete force air out of the nose and then repeating the procedure on the other nostril. If one nostril forces more air through than the other does, the septum may be deviated. If the athlete has a deviated septum, the nose may also be broken. The athlete should be referred to a physician to determine if surgery is necessary. Many athletes who have deviated septa choose not to have surgery. Wearing a face mask will prevent further injury to the nose.

## Nasal Fractures

A direct blow to the nose can fracture one or both of the nasal bones. There will be a severe nosebleed, often like water running from a faucet. The ATC will treat the athlete by leaning him forward. Pinching the nose may not be possible. The ATC uses gauze to catch the blood as it comes out of the nose and applies ice. Gauze should not be forced into the nostril to slow bleeding.

The athlete may indicate that he heard a snap; he may have pain and difficulty breathing. The ATC should observe deformity (flat on one side) and swelling. He may feel crepitus and observe a deviated septum. The athlete should be referred to a physician for care. The physician may proceed with surgery to put the bones

back into place. Some athletes who opt to avoid surgery suffer from a permanently deformed nose. In the days after a nasal fracture the athlete will have black eyes from internal bleeding that pools underneath the orbits of the eyes.

# Treating Mouth Injuries

Although some people believe that losing teeth is no big deal since they can always get false teeth, they are wrong. False teeth are not nearly as good at biting and chewing as are real ones, making it difficult to maintain healthy nutrition. The athletic trainer should use caution when treating the mouth—some athletes may bite because of a seizure or as they are gagging.

## Fracture (Maxilla, Mandible)

Imagine getting hit in the face by a sharply hit baseball—this scenario is not uncommon in athletics. A direct blow to the jaw, either upper or lower, can result in a fracture. The athlete will experience pain that increases with movement. When the ATC observes the area of impact she will be able to see swelling. If the lower jaw has been fractured, she may be able to observe a space between teeth that was not there previously. The athlete will have discoloration under the tongue, and his teeth may not line up. Palpation will reveal crepitus, and the athlete will be cautious about moving the jaw. The ATC will make sure all the teeth are in place and that the airway is clear.

Ice should be applied to the area as tolerated by the athlete, who should be referred immediately to a physician for care. The physician will realign the jaw for proper closure and wire the mouth shut. The athlete will be eating through a straw for four to six weeks. Some athletes are allowed to return to activity as long as a special face mask protects the jaw.

Improper care or neglect of a jaw fracture can result in permanent deformity. The jaw may not be able to open wide enough to eat a hamburger, and the malalignment of the teeth can lead to further mouth problems.

## Temporomandibular Dislocation

A blow to the chin or a violent, forced opening of the mouth can cause a dislocation. The ath-

## 🌐 The Real World

I was covering a girls' soccer match. With two minutes left in the first half, the opposing team was inside the scoring circle. From where I was standing I could see a lot of bodies kicking and flailing around as our team was defending. Then our goalie was on the ground with the ball in her hands, and I knew something was wrong by the reaction of our players. The official summoned me onto the field. Our goalie had been kicked in the mouth, and there was blood everywhere. Unfortunately, she had not been wearing a mouth guard. She was conscious and spitting out blood. I did a head and neck evaluation and found no other problems. Upon examining her mouth I saw blood coming up from her gums in the molar region. She was able to move her mouth to talk, but her jaw was painful in the front. I packed sterile gauze between her gums and teeth all the way around her mandible. I had her put ice on the jaw where she had pain. Her father wanted to drive her to the emergency room because that was quicker than calling an ambulance. I felt she was stable enough and agreed he should take her. I gave her a pan to hold on her lap because she was still spitting blood.

The textbooks say to wrap a cravat with ice around the patient's jaw, if there is a suspected jaw fracture. However, in this case I chose not to follow that protocol. The athlete was spitting blood that would have gone into her stomach if I had strapped her jaw the way the books say. Blood is an irritant to the stomach, and chances are she would have starting vomiting, thus complicating matters. The emergency room physician said I did the right thing. The mandible was fractured in two places in the front of the jaw. On X ray it looked like a triangle had been cut into the mandible. This player's soccer season was over. However, she was back in goal next year, wearing a mouth guard.

Suzy Heinzman, ATC

lete will immediately grab and hold his mouth to keep it from moving. The jaw will lock itself in place by spasm of the local muscles. The athlete will be in extreme pain. His jaw will look deformed, locked open, or to one side. The athletic trainer can feel that the condyles are out of normal position. The ATC should never try to put the jaw back in place because the area around the jaw is filled with nerves and cartilage that can be permanently damaged. The team physician should relocate the jaw, which must be kept shut for several weeks. Some physicians wire the jaw shut to ensure this rest. Imagine trying to eat with a jaw that does not open.

## Tooth Dislocation

Direct impact to a tooth can knock it out of the jaw. The athlete will experience severe pain, bleeding, and swelling. The tooth will be dislodged and needs to be handled carefully. After putting on gloves, the ATC should pick up the tooth with a sterile gauze pad. It must be kept moist and should be placed in a designated saline tooth container or a glass of milk. The athlete must be seen by the team dentist so that the tooth can be put back in place, assuming it is not too severely injured to be reinserted. The ATC should treat the bleeding socket, placing a piece of sterile gauze where the tooth was located and having the athlete gently bite down to keep it in place with direct pressure.

## Fractured Tooth

Direct impact to the lower jaw or the teeth can result in a tooth fracture. The athlete will experience pain and have difficulty closing his mouth. A fracture can be seen if the tooth is examined closely. In some instances, a portion of the tooth will be gone. If a portion has broken off, it should be sent with the athlete to the dentist. Although the portion cannot be put back on, the dentist may find it helpful when reconstructing the tooth. The broken tooth may die and have to be removed.

## Summary

Any impact of the face could injure an eye, nose, ear, or jaw and could result in permanent disfigurement. Impairment of the organs of the face can be devastating to the injured athlete. Wearing the proper equipment, which is provided, easily prevents facial injuries. Facial injuries should be treated conservatively and evaluated by the team physician and team dentist.

## Key Terms

Define the following terms found in this chapter:

detached retina          epistaxis          hyphema          swimmer's ear

## Questions for Review

1. How do facial injuries occur? p. 132
2. How can facial injuries be prevented? pp. 132-133
3. If an athlete has epistaxis, what injuries may have occurred? pp. 137-138
4. What is the treatment for a fractured tooth? p. 139
5. What injury causes the athlete to see sparks? p. 133
6. Why are both eyes covered if one eye is injured? p. 133
7. What is the best head position for epistaxis? pp. 137-138
8. What does it mean to have 20/20 vision? p. 131
9. How can cauliflower ear be prevented? p. 137

## Activities for Reinforcement

1. Have an ATC demonstrate how to perform a face injury evaluation.
2. Ask the school nurse to do your hearing test.
3. Ask the school nurse to do your vision test.
4. Invite your local dentist or dental hygienist in to demonstrate proper brushing and flossing techniques.
5. Describe common eye injuries and how to care for them.
6. Invite an ophthalmologist to speak with the class.

## Above and Beyond

1. Collect brochures from your dentist's office and create a poster about the various types of dental injuries.
2. Write a report on a facial injury of your choice. Use the following materials for assistance.

   Hawkesford, J.E. 1994. *Maxillofacial and dental emergencies*. New York: Oxford University Press.

   Torg, J.S. ed. 1991. *Athletic injuries to the head, neck, and face*. 2d ed. St Louis: Mosby Year Book.

   Wolfe, S.A. 1993. *Facial fractures*. New York: Thieme Medical Publishers.

# Unit V

# Understanding Athletics-Related Injuries to the Upper Quarter

# Shoulder Injuries

The shoulder is an amazing structure with a great deal of movement capability. Many athletics-related injuries to the shoulder are the result of an overhead movement such as throwing a softball or serving a tennis ball.

## Anatomy of the Shoulder

The shoulder is a ball-and-socket joint like the hip but much more shallow. Therefore, it relies on muscular strength for its stability. Several bones link up at the shoulder, combining possibilities for movement across a wide range. The entire bony linkage of the shoulder is often referred to as the shoulder girdle.

### Bones

The shoulder has three basic bony components: the humerus, clavicle, and scapula (see figure 16.1). The head of the humerus, which is the bone of the upper arm, is round and smooth and fits into the glenoid fossa of the scapula. The humerus has a groove near the top, referred to as the bicipital groove, where the biceps tendon moves up and down during flexion and extension of the elbow.

The clavicle, or collarbone, articulates at the tip of the shoulder and at the sternum near the throat. The scapula, or shoulder blade, has two forward projections that are actually located on the anterior aspect of the shoulder: the acromion process and the coracoid process. The rotator cuff muscles attach to the scapula.

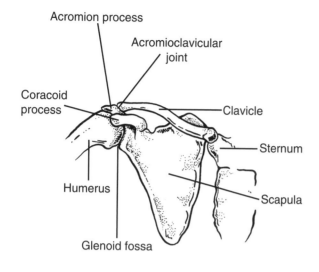

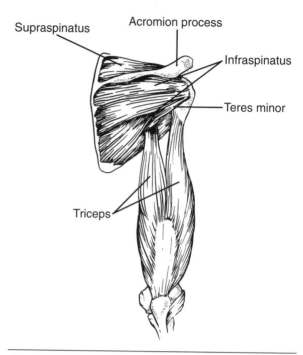

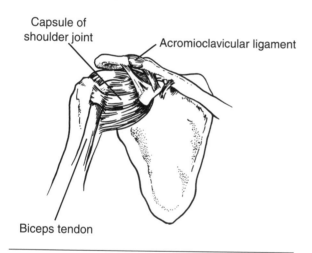

**Figure 16.1** Bones and ligaments of the shoulder.

**Figure 16.2** Rotator cuff muscles. The three posterior rotator cuff muscles are depicted. The subscapularis is found at the anterior aspect of the scapula and runs a course to the anterior aspect of the superior humerus.

## Muscles

The **rotator cuff** consists of four muscles: the subscapularis, infraspinatus, teres minor, and supraspinatus (see figure 16.2). These muscles are responsible for rotating the arm internally and externally, as well as abducting the shoulder. The rotator cuff muscles are easy to remember if you use the acronym **SITS** (**S**ubscapularis, **I**nfraspinatus, **T**eres minor, and **S**upraspinatus).

The deltoid muscle lies over the head of the humerus. It attaches to the acromion process and the lateral aspect of the humerus. The deltoid abducts, flexes, and extends the shoulder.

The muscles in the anterior portion of the shoulder are the pectoralis major and minor.

The pectoralis muscles attach at the sternum and to the anterior portion of the humerus.

The biceps muscle flexes the elbow. It attaches to the humerus and coracoid process on one end and to the radius on the other. The biceps tendon runs through the bicipital groove. This tendon is kept in the groove by a ligament. The triceps muscles opposes the biceps. They extend the forearm and shoulder. The triceps muscles attach to the posterior of the humeral head and the scapula. See figure 1.3b, page 9.

## Joints

The shoulder girdle is comprised of several joints but the most commonly injured ones include the acromioclavicular joint and the glenohumeral joint. The acromioclavicular joint is made up of the acromion process of the scapula and the distal end of the clavicle. The joint is held together by the acromioclavicular ligament. The glenohumeral joint is the articulation of the head of the humerus and the glenoid fossa, the saucerlike portion of the scapula. The glenoid fossa is very shallow, making the joint susceptible to injury. The end of the humerus is covered with a hard articular cartilage that moves against the glenoid fossa. A capsular ligament surrounds the entire glenohumeral joint from the scapula to the humerus, maintaining the scapula and humeral head in proper relationship and giving the joint stability. Muscles hold the scapula close to the thoracic ribs.

# Preventing Shoulder Injuries

The ATC or the athlete must know what kinds of injuries occur and how to prevent shoulder injuries. Shoulder injuries are often due to muscle weaknesses, postural problems, and the nature of the game itself.

## Addressing Muscular Weakness

"Out of sight, out of mind" applies to weight training. It means that athletes often lift weights only for those muscles they can see in the mirror ("mirror muscles"). As a result they experience weaknesses in the opposing muscles, most often the muscles on the posterior side.

Athletes who have rounded shoulders, tight pectoral muscles, or weak posterior shoulder muscles may predispose themselves to injury. The supraspinatus muscle, nerve, and blood vessel run through a very narrow space between the acromion process and the head of the humerus, and a narrowing of that space can cause one of those tissues to become pinched. The moral of the story is that when your mother tells you to stand up straight and stick your chest out, she is not only improving your posture, she is also preventing you from getting a shoulder injury. Mom always knows best.

When an athlete uses her arm continually in one way, such as in freestyle swimming or throwing, she is prone to injury. She needs to strengthen the muscles opposing the motion to prevent injury. A swimmer who swims 300 strokes freestyle must swim 300 strokes of backstroke to balance the strength of the muscles on both sides of the body. Athletes involved in throwing sports need to learn proper techniques. If an athlete does not throw with the body, she will be more prone to shoulder injury.

During the athletic physical examination, the physician must determine muscular weaknesses of an athlete so that they can be remedied with properly prescribed exercises. Some athletes have one shoulder that sits higher than the other

shoulder. Relaxation techniques and stretching can level the shoulders and prevent spasms.

## Using Protective Padding

Games that have a tremendous amount of shoulder impact allow the use of shoulder pads—the heavier the impact the thicker the padding. Ice hockey, football, and men's lacrosse are typical sports where shoulder pads are used.

# Treating Shoulder Injuries

Because the shoulder is often overworked due to throwing, striking, and catching, it is vulnerable to a variety of musculoskeletal injuries.

## Ligament Injuries

Several joints of the shoulder girdle are prone to sprains. The more common joints to be sprained include the acromioclavicular and glenohumeral.

### Acromioclavicular Ligament Sprain

A sprain of the acromioclavicular ligament is referred to as a **shoulder separation** (see figure 16.3), so as not to confuse it with a glenohumeral ligament sprain. Although these joints are in close proximity, they are not the same and involve different structures. The acromioclavicular joint can be injured by impact to the top of the shoulder or by falling on an outstretched arm. Falling on the elbow forces the humerus up and into the acromioclavicular joint. The athlete will indicate pain with movement whether it is a first-, second-, or third-degree sprain. The more serious sprains cause the clavicle to move superiorly. In a third-degree separation there will be a large abnormal bump caused by excessive upward displacement of the clavicle. The athlete is usually unable to move the arm and will hold it tight against the body. To treat a

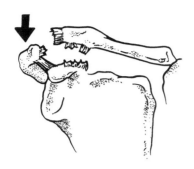

**Figure 16.3** A shoulder separation occurs at the acromioclavicular joint. It is a sprain of the acromioclavicular ligament.

## The Real World

After a Tuesday football practice, a player reported that he had some mild shoulder pain and thought he might have a problem. When the athlete removed his shirt, the end of his clavicle was pressing against his skin. The acromioclavicular ligament had been torn and no longer held the clavicle and the scapula together at the acromioclavicular joint. In fact, you could press the end down, but it would just shift upward again. We asked when he had injured it. He said that the previous Saturday he had fallen off a snowmobile and hurt it. He had normal strength and normal range of motion, and though an orthopedic surgeon suggested surgery, the athlete elected not to have surgery to screw the two bones together. We made him a custom pad to protect the acromioclavicular joint, and he was able to continue to participate. The orthopedic surgeon convinced the athlete to have surgery after the season ended to avoid arthritis and any future cosmetic problems (a bony prominence over the shoulder).

Anonymous

first-degree sprain, the ATC must use the PRICE method; a second- or third-degree sprain can be treated with PRICE initially, but the athlete must be referred to an orthopedist to rule out a fracture.

A physician can take two courses of action to treat a third-degree tear: surgery or harness. During surgery the acromioclavicular joint is wired or screwed together. A harness straps the clavicle downward in an attempt to hold the joint together long enough to allow the ligament to heal.

### Glenohumeral Ligament Sprain

The glenohumeral joint is especially vulnerable to sprains when it is placed in abduction and external rotation. If there is a third-degree sprain, a more serious problem, such as subluxation or dislocation, is likely. The athlete with a glenohumeral ligament sprain will have pain with motion. The athlete is treated by PRICE and is referred to a physician.

## Muscle and Tendon Injuries

Most shoulder muscle and tendon injuries are due to overuse. Athletes who throw, shoot, or repeat a swim stroke are prone to overuse injuries in the shoulder. Overuse injuries require rest, ice application, immobilization, and referrals to physicians for care. Common muscle and tendon injuries occur to the rotator cuff. Injury to the rotator cuff can also lead to impingement syndrome and bicipital tendon problems.

### Rotator Cuff Strain

A strain of the rotator cuff is categorized like other strains as a first-, second-, or third-degree strain. As noted in chapter 2, first-degree strains are indicated by pain with no loss of range of motion or stability. Second-degree strains will have pain with some loss in range of motion and stability. Third-degree strains will have pain with partial or complete loss of range and stability.

Strains of the rotator cuff occur from excessive motion beyond the normal range. Most often the supraspinatus muscle is injured. The athlete will have pain with motion and sometimes when the shoulder is not moving. The pain generally occurs with abduction of the shoulder. If the athlete is unable to abduct, a complete tear, or third-degree strain, is suspected. Strains due to repetitive movements can also result in crepitus and impingement syndrome. A complete tear must be surgically repaired, while a first- or second-degree tear can be treated initially with PRICE and then with gentle strengthening and flexibility exercises.

### Impingement Syndrome

An athlete develops an **impingement syndrome** from repetitive overhead types of movement. Freestyle swimmers, throwers, and tennis players are prone to impingement syndrome. The supraspinatus and biceps muscles run together through a space beneath the acromion process.

If the space narrows—from swelling, tendinitis, weak posterior muscle strength, or poor posture—the two muscles are impinged in the space. This creates pain and discomfort with overhead movements. Treatment of impingement syndrome includes modified activity, strengthening the posterior muscles of the shoulder, and improving flexibility of tight pectoral muscles.

### Bicipital Tendinitis

Bicipital tendinitis is common among athletes, like tennis players, who are constantly raising their arms above their heads. The repetitive nature of the movement will cause irritation of the tendon in the bicipital groove. The ATC may be able to palpate the tendon and feel crepitus. The athlete must stop the repetitive action causing the tendinitis. Pain is common, especially when repeating the motion that caused the tendinitis. Immobilization in a sling will make the athlete more comfortable. The team physician may prescribe ultrasound therapy and anti-inflammatory medication.

### Biceps Tendon Rupture

The biceps tendon can rupture in two instances: a direct blow or severe contractional forces. When the tendon ruptures, the athlete will be unable to flex the elbow. There will be a noticeable change in the appearance of the muscle as the tendon rolls up on itself—it will look like a golf ball under the skin. The arm must be iced and immobilized, and the athlete should be referred to a physician. The physician will surgically repair the tendon so that the muscle will be fully functional.

## Bone Injuries

As you might imagine, given the range of motion at the shoulder and amount of use it gets, a lot of stress is put on the bones. Epiphyses injuries must be considered, especially with younger athletes.

The shoulder is covered with heavy musculature and ligaments. The layers of tissue can make a fracture difficult to determine. Keen awareness of the mechanism of injury will tell the ATC when to suspect a fracture.

### Clavicular Fractures

The clavicle is most often fractured at its weakest point, the distal third. As you feel the clavicle, notice that it curves as it gets closer to the tip of the shoulder. An athlete can receive a direct blow or fall on the tip of the shoulder, which causes the fracture. The athlete will experience pain and hold the arm close to the body to prevent movement. Because the clavicle moves, arm movement must be restricted through the use of a sling. The use of ice to decrease swelling and pain is important. The team physician can set the clavicle in place using a harness. The fracture takes six weeks to heal.

### Humeral Fractures

Fractures of the humerus are not difficult to find if they are located midshaft, but the shoulder musculature can sometimes hide a fracture of the humeral head. A shoulder sprain can mimic a fracture, so added caution must be taken to insure proper assessment. The athlete will be unable to move the arm and will experience pain. He may report hearing or feeling a pop, and he will be holding the arm against the body. The easiest way to determine a humeral fracture is to palpate the circumference of the bone. If it is painful on all sides, it is likely a fracture. The ATC will refer the athlete to the team physician for immediate care. She will place the athlete in a splint from the shoulder to the fingertips. Checking the pulse before and after splinting is critical to determining the extent of the injury. If the pulse has decreased, the fracture has a serious complication. The nature of the fracture will determine how the athlete will be treated. In some instances a sling can be used and in others surgery and a long arm cast will be necessary. The humerus will take at least six weeks to heel.

### Epiphysis Injury

The growth plate in a young athlete's shoulder is susceptible to direct and indirect blows. A blow to the head of the humerus can cause an epiphyseal fracture. Falling on the elbow, driving the humerus into the glenoid fossa, can also cause an epiphyseal fracture. Epiphyseal fractures have the same signs and symptoms as humeral fractures: pain, inability to use the arm, desire to hold the arm still, and feeling a pop. Injuries to the epiphyses can cause permanent growth impairment. Application of ice, splinting, and a sling is the best course of action the ATC can take. The physician will decide the severity of the epiphyseal injury and determine the treatment. Some epiphyseal injuries require surgery to hold the head of the humerus to the shaft of the humerus. These cases are obviously more serious.

A teenage pitcher is prone to epiphyseal injury from excessive throwing. Because of this, pitchers should be limited in the number of games they are allowed to play as well as the number of pitches they throw. With this injury the athlete has pain around the circumference of the humerus. Pain will be exaggerated with flexion, as during the throwing motion. Caution must be exercised when dealing with this injury or else the loss in range of motion could be permanent. The team physician must see the athlete, and immobilization is essential.

### Avulsion Fractures

Avulsion fractures can occur in the shoulder. Avulsions may accompany a glenohumeral or acromioclavicular sprain. Recall that avulsion fractures are those in which a ligament or tendon pulls away a small portion of the bone as it is stressed during an injury. When the humerus is dislocating from the glenoid fossa, the capsular ligament is stressed and can sometimes pull on the scapula, resulting in an avulsion fracture. The athlete will experience pain associated with the dislocation and the avulsion fracture. It is difficult, if not impossible, for the ATC to know if an avulsion fracture exists. She must assume an avulsion fracture until an X ray reveals otherwise. Splinting and ice are appropriate care for sprain injuries.

### Glenohumeral Dislocations and Subluxations

"Glenohumeral dislocation" means that the head of the humerus is out of its socket (see figure 16.4). "Subluxation" means that the head of the humerus came out of its socket and then went back in. The cause for both injuries is the same—excessive abduction and external rotation, usually—but the results are completely different. A dislocation or a subluxation requires attention by the ATC and team physician.

A dislocation will sometimes cause the head of the humerus to tear the capsular ligament

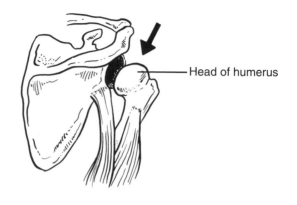

**Figure 16.4**  A shoulder dislocation occurs at the glenohumeral joint. The head of the humerus drops out of the socket, injuring the capsular ligament. The most common direction for a shoulder dislocation is anterior.

anteriorly. The instability of the capsular ligament allows the head of the humerus to shift forward, which is the most common type of shoulder dislocation. The athlete will experience pain and inability to use the shoulder. When the ATC looks at the dislocated shoulder he will see a deformity at the deltoid muscle. The shoulder will not be round but flat. The team physician must put a dislocation back into place. In the case of a subluxation the athlete may indicate that he felt the shoulder "go out of its socket but then pop back in." An X ray is necessary to determine the extent of the dislocation or the subluxation—there may be associated fractures, a tear of the cartilage of the glenoid fossa, or nerve or blood vessel injury.

An athlete may not indicate to the ATC that he has experienced a shoulder subluxation. Eventually, he will notice some changes as more subluxations occur. There can be permanent injury to the nerves, cartilage, and blood vessels. The athlete who has a dislocation or subluxation should strengthen the muscles of adduction and internal rotation. He may also wear a harness that restricts the movements of external rotation and abduction. An athlete who experiences recurrent subluxations or dislocations will require surgery to repair the capsular ligaments.

## Summary

There are many ligaments in the shoulder girdle. Consequently, it is vulnerable to sprains. The glenohumeral joint relies on the strength of the rotator cuff for stability, but a dislocation can occur, usually by forceful abduction and external rotation. The acromioclavicular joint can be sprained as well, which is called a shoulder separation. A rotator cuff strain can be extremely debilitating, and proper recovery is imperative before the athlete returns to competition. A strong rotator cuff and a well-conditioned shoulder will prevent many shoulder injuries.

## Key Terms

Define the following terms found in this chapter:

      impingement syndrome    rotator cuff    shoulder separation    SITS

## Questions for Review

1. Describe the rotator cuff. p. 144
2. Why do you think athletes like tennis players, pitchers, and swimmers, who perform many overhead motions, seem to have shoulder problems? p. 145
3. How can shoulder injuries be prevented? p. 145
4. Various sports require a lot from the shoulder. Make a list of sports and the types of shoulder injuries that will occur with each. pp. 145-148
5. What is meant by impingement syndrome? pp. 146-147

## Activities for Reinforcement

1. Have an ATC demonstrate how to assess a shoulder injury.
2. Interview several athletes who have had previous shoulder dislocations. Determine what position the arms were in when the injury occurred.
3. With a partner, name and point to each of the bones in the shoulder girdle.
4. With a partner, locate each joint included in the shoulder girdle.

## Above and Beyond

1. Write a brief one-page essay about the shoulder. Talk about redesigning the shoulder to make it less prone to the injuries listed in this chapter.
2. Read one of the following suggested readings:

    Heck, J., and J. Sparano. 1997. Shoulder instability. *Sports Medicine Update* 12(2): 4–7.

    Zairns, B.J., and W. Carson. 1985. *Injuries to the throwing arm.* Philadelphia: Saunders.

# Elbow Injuries

Upon completing this chapter the student will be able to do the following:
- Describe the basic anatomy of the arm and elbow.
- Explain common arm and elbow injuries that occur with athletic participation.
- Identify common signs and symptoms of arm and elbow injuries.
- Explain common treatment parameters performed by a certified athletic trainer for elbow injuries.

The elbow functions with any upper extremity movement. It is prone to muscle and tendon injuries because it is the site of many muscle attachments.

## Anatomy of the Elbow

The elbow is a hinge joint involving three major bones: the humerus, radius, and ulna (see figure 17.1). The radius and ulna are the bones between the elbow and wrist. Like the femur, the distal end of the humerus becomes wider, forming the medial and lateral epicondyles. The ulna is hooked to the end of the humerus and forms a tight joint. The radius is the bone on the thumb side of the forearm. It is not hooked to the humerus like the ulna; it rests against the humerus and is able to rotate, allowing the forearm to pronate and supinate.

### Ligaments

A ligament called the joint capsule surrounds the elbow. This gives some general stability to the elbow joint, but the elbow also relies on several major ligaments for stability, particularly the ulnar collateral, radial collateral, and the annular ligaments.

The ulnar collateral ligament helps to stabilize the inside, or medial, aspect of the elbow; the radial collateral ligament helps to stabilize the outside, or lateral, aspect. These ligaments are sometimes referred to as the medial and lateral collateral ligaments (figure 17.2).

The annular ligament helps to hold the radius and ulna together near the elbow joint. The radius and ulna are also supported by a structure known as the interosseus membrane. This tissue joins the radius and the ulna from the elbow to the wrist and keeps the two bones from separating.

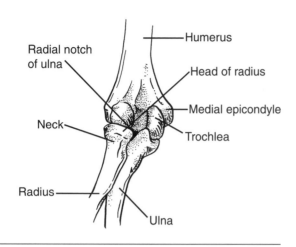

**Figure 17.1** Anterior view of elbow. The elbow is a tight joint, held together by many ligaments.

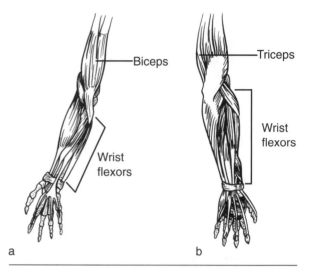

**Figure 17.3** *(a)* Anterior and *(b)* posterior view of elbow and wrist musculature. Many muscles make up the wrist flexors and extensors that attach to the medial and lateral epicondyles of the humerus.

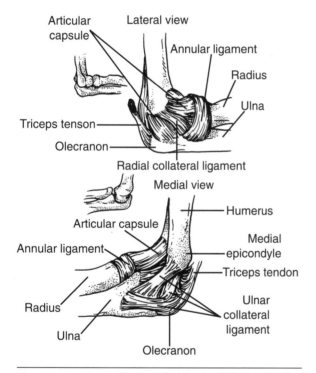

**Figure 17.2** Lateral and medial views of elbow. The ulna hooks on to the end of the humerus, while the radius rests against it. The **bursa** is a fluid-filled sac located between the olecranon and the skin.

## Muscles

As noted in chapter 16, the triceps muscle primarily performs elbow extension while the biceps accomplishes elbow flexion. The wrist flexors attach at the medial epicondyle of the humerus and then run a course toward the hand. The wrist extensors attach to the lateral epicondyle of the humerus (figure 17.3). These muscles help stabilize the elbow.

A number of nerves and blood vessels pass through the small spaces and grooves around the elbow en route to the lower arm. Therefore, any injury occurring at the elbow must be assessed to determine if any of these blood vessels or nerves have been damaged. Checking for a pulse and ascertaining if an athlete is able to feel her hand is a helpful procedure.

## Preventing Elbow Injuries

The elbow is not a frequently injured joint. Many of the injuries that ATCs see at the elbow joint are due to overuse. That is, the repetitive movements and stresses delivered to the wrist and elbow over a long period of time eventually break down the tissue, causing chronic inflammation and pain. This is especially true in racket sports such as tennis and racquetball where injuries to the lateral aspect of the elbow are most common. Many athletes pay a great deal of attention to strengthening the biceps and triceps muscles. Unfortunately, they fail to properly condition some of the smaller muscles such as the wrist flexors and extensors. Stretching and strengthening of these structures is recommended in order to prevent overuse injures. We describe some stretches in chapter 22.

It is imperative for the ATC to work with the coach to detect any improper techniques an athlete is using, because these can eventually lead to overuse injuries. Equipment is also a factor in the prevention of elbow injuries, especially in racket sports. For example, excessive stress on the elbow musculature can result from using a racket with a grip that is too small. The ATC and the coach can work together to identify these problems and prevent such injuries.

Many athletes who throw (such as baseball and softball players), should alter their activity and rest after long days of throwing. The rules limiting young pitchers' activity also help keep overuse problems of the elbow (and shoulder) to a minimum. ATCs at industrial sites have reduced overuse injuries by instituting job-rotation programs whereby workers do a variety of jobs rather than the same job, the same way, day after day.

# Treating Elbow Injuries and Conditions

The medial and lateral aspects of the elbow joint can suffer ligament sprains. Also, muscle and tendon injuries occur, because the elbow and wrist are involved with repetitive stress during athletics. Fractures of the elbow can be extremely serious.

## Ligament Injuries

Sprains of the elbow, like all sprains, are classified as mild, moderate, or severe. Moreover, any one of the elbow ligaments can be sprained, including the ulnar collateral ligament and the radial collateral ligament.

### Ulnar Collateral Ligament Sprain

The ulnar collateral ligaments seem to be more prone to sprains than the other ligaments of the elbow, especially for throwing athletes, due in part to the amount of stress placed on the inner aspect of the elbow. Every time an athlete throws a softball or baseball, or hits a tennis ball (forehand), the medial aspect of the elbow is stretched. Over time, this repetitive trauma may result in a ligament injury. This mechanism can also cause injury to the muscles that cross the

## ❓ What Would You Do If...

As a student assistant, you are walking by tennis practice and you notice one of the players rubbing the lateral aspect of her elbow. She is in obvious pain.

---

elbow joint. In addition, a direct blow may cause a disruption of the ulnar collateral ligament. Picture a wrestler supporting his weight on one arm as his opponent rolls into the lateral aspect of his elbow. This would cause a valgus stress (forcing the medial aspect of the joint to separate) and would put an excessive stress on the ulnar collateral ligament.

A sprain of this ligament will be characterized by medial elbow pain and swelling, especially if the ligament has been partially torn. When the ATC tests the elbow, joint laxity may also be present. Sprains need to be treated using PRICE—an elastic bandage works well for elbow swelling and support. A moderate or severe injury may need to be splinted, and the ATC will often refer these conditions to a physician for further diagnostic tests, specifically to rule out any fractures. The elbow should be observed for any ulnar nerve damage when the medial collateral ligament is injured. When rehabilitating injuries to the ulnar collateral ligaments, it is essential to strengthen the wrist flexor muscles because they cross the medial aspect of the elbow and help to provide stability to the joint. Exercises such as wrist curls and grip strengthening are helpful.

### Radial Collateral Ligament Sprains

Radial collateral ligament injuries to the elbow are rare. The characteristics of a radial collateral injury will be the same as for an ulnar collateral injury except that the pain, of course, is on the lateral aspect. Rehabilitation considerations for this ligament sprain include focusing on the wrist-extension musculature. These muscles cross the joint line at the lateral elbow and can provide dynamic stability to an elbow that has suffered a sprain of the lateral collateral ligament.

## Muscle and Tendon Injuries

Strains to the elbow musculature are most often caused by either excessive resistive forces or

## 🌐 The Real World

While pitching during a college baseball game, our school's pitcher heard a "pop." In obvious pain, he grabbed his elbow, fell off the pitcher's mound into the grass, and rolled around screaming that he had broken his elbow. With all that screaming, it was obvious the athlete was breathing and had a pulse. After calming him down, I determined that there were no obvious fractures around the elbow and that it would be okay for him to walk into the dugout for further examination. The athlete was very apprehensive about moving the elbow during examination because it was painful, and he continued to insist that his elbow was broken. He had extreme tenderness throughout the medial side of the elbow, especially just distal to the medial epicondyle. I took his distal pulse, checked capillary refill, and performed sensory tests. Grip strength was good, and the arm was neurovascularly normal. On valgus stress to the elbow, the athlete had a great deal of instability, which indicated an injury to the ulnar collateral fragment. We decided to ice the athlete's elbow, place him in a sling, and refer him to his family orthopedist. It turned out that he had a ulnar collateral ligament rupture that required reconstructive surgery and extensive rehabilitation. Although he never pitched again, he was able to play competitive baseball as a first baseman.

Greg Ehlers, MS, ATC

overuse. Elbow strains can occur to the elbow flexor and extensor musculature as well as the wrist flexor and extensor musculature. As with strains discussed in previous chapters, strains can be mild, moderate, or severe in nature. A complete strain or rupture of a muscular structure, such as the biceps, is usually evident by the deformity caused when the muscle balls up due to the elasticity of the muscle.

### Elbow Flexor Strain

Strains to the flexor muscles often are caused by a loaded movement that includes the elbow and shoulder together. The body's "two-joint muscles," that is, those muscles involved with creating movement at more that one joint, seem to be prone to strains. The biceps muscle is a perfect example of a two-joint muscle—it flexes the elbow joint and the shoulder joint. Minor elbow flexor strains will typically be character-

ized by discomfort at the anterior aspect of the elbow and minimal, if any, swelling. The athlete will also demonstrate some weakness and extra discomfort when elbow flexion is resisted. A moderate elbow flexor strain will have mild to moderate amounts of swelling and marked weakness when tested for strength. The initial treatment an ATC may give for an elbow flexor strain is PRICE, until the initial inflammation has subsided. The athlete can then perform mild stretching and strengthening exercises as indicated. A moderate strain can be treated in the same way, but the ATC must keep in mind that with more tissue damage, progress will often be slower. Complete muscle or tendon ruptures or suspected avulsion injuries should be referred to the team physician.

### Elbow Extensor Strain

Excessive resistance to the triceps muscle will often cause tissue damage to the elbow extensors. This can happen if the athlete falls and attempts to break the fall with an outstretched arm. The injury needs to be assessed carefully because, at the point of its attachment, the triceps tendon can often pull a bit of bone away from the ulna. The characteristics of extensor strains are the same as for a flexor injury, except of course the pain will be at the posterior aspect of the upper arm, and the athlete will often experience more pain when the ATC resists elbow extension. Treatment with PRICE is recommended, and after inflammation has subsided, the elbow extensor should be stretched mildly and strengthened as tolerated.

### Wrist Flexor Strains

Wrist flexor strains at the elbow often result in pain over the medial epicondyle of the humerus or the front of the forearm. These strains can result from excessive resistance during wrist flexion movements or, more commonly, from overuse. Initially this condition should be treated with PRICE and activity should be modified. Mild stretching can be performed by the athlete, and doing wrist curls and grip strengthening is helpful.

### Wrist Extensor Strains

Wrist extensor strains at the elbow frequently result in pain over the lateral epicondyle of the humerus. These strains can result from excessive resistance during wrist extension movements but more commonly come from overuse. Initially this condition should be treated with PRICE, and activity should be modified. The athlete can also perform mild stretching—doing reverse wrist curls can be helpful for this condition.

### Medial and Lateral Epicondylitis

As we have noted, the elbow is prone to overuse conditions that create chronic inflammation, which frequently occurs at the medial and lateral epicondyles of the humerus. These conditions are called medial epicondylitis and lateral epicondylitis, the latter being the more frequent type of chronic inflammatory injury.

As a result of poor mechanics and continual use over a long period, the wrist extensor tendons at the lateral epicondyle of the humerus can become chronically inflamed. Because racket sports are a common cause, this condition is also called **tennis elbow**. In the industrial setting, daily use of equipment like a hammer and any gripping and lifting activities can cause lateral elbow inflammation.

Lateral epicondylitis is characterized by pain over the lateral epicondyle of the humerus, and minimal swelling is sometimes present.

Initially, the ATC should treat the injury by attempting to reduce pain and inflammation. Therefore, the use of PRICE and a support, usually in the form of a tennis elbow strap that is wrapped around the elbow, is indicated. Limiting the amount of activity that aggravates the condition is also wise. Mild stretching of the extensor tendons is helpful, and muscle strength and endurance should be improved as tolerated. The athlete should gradually be allowed to participate in further activity. The ATC may reduce the number of repetitions performed by the athlete and may also suggest the use of a two-handed backhand in racket sports. The team physician may choose to use medication to help resolve the condition.

Although not as common as lateral epicondylitis, many athletes get medial epicondylitis, often as a result of repetitive throwing. This condition refers to inflammation of the wrist flexor tendons where they attach to the humerus. Some people refer to medial epicondylitis as Little League elbow. **Little League elbow** is also suggested to be a separation of the epiphysis at the medial aspect of the humerus in younger athletes (usually between ages 9–12) as a result of throwing.

Treatment for medial epicondylitis is similar to that of lateral epicondylitis—rest, ice application, and support. The athlete needs to decrease the amount of throwing and strengthen the wrist flexor muscles. The ATC will monitor either condition and perform a thorough evaluation because compression of the ulnar nerve is possible at the elbow joint, especially when a medial elbow injury has occurred. The ATC will refer the athlete to a physician if a fracture is suspected or if the athlete is complaining of numbness, tingling, or excessive pain.

## Bone Injuries

Bone fractures to the distal end of the humerus are not common in athletics. If they do occur, however, it is often due to very powerful mechanisms of injury, such as the hand being planted on the ground and someone forcing the arm into excessive side bending. Fractures between the condyles of the humerus are also rare in sports; but if direct impact is the mechanism of injury, and pain is located at the medial aspect of the elbow about two inches above the joint, a fracture should be suspected. If either type of fracture occurs, the ATC must consider this an absolute emergency because these fractures can result in compression on an artery or nerve.

### Epiphyseal and Avulsion Fractures

Epiphyseal and avulsion fractures are more common on the medial epicondyle or olecranon aspect of the elbow (the olecranon is the process of the ulna projecting behind the elbow joint). An epiphyseal injury should be suspected whenever an athlete presents with swelling, pain, and loss of movement. Remember that a growing athlete is more likely to injure the growth plate than suffer a bone fracture or ligament injury. Severe pain and deformity indicate an avulsion fracture. If either of these injuries is suspected by the ATC, she should refer the athlete to the team physician or primary care physician.

### Ulna Dislocation

The elbow is one of the most commonly dislocated joints in the body (see figure 17.4). As we mentioned previously, the ulna hooks onto the end of the humerus, making the elbow a fairly

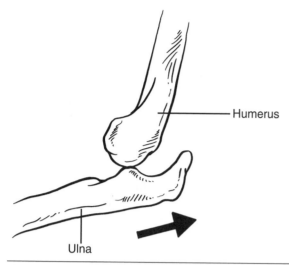

**Figure 17.4** Elbow dislocations typically occur in a posterior direction as depicted here.

tight joint. Therefore, it takes a very traumatic injury to dislocate the ulna from the humerus. Usually, a violent hyperextension injury or a severe blow to the lateral aspect of the elbow will dislodge the ulna from the humerus; most often it moves posteriorly. When a dislocation occurs, an obvious deformity will be noticed. The arm must be immediately splinted in the position it is found in, and the athlete must be seen in the emergency room by a physician so the dislocation can be re-placed.

## Other Common Injuries

An athlete will often fall on an outstretched arm or receive a blow that causes the elbow to be hyperextended. This particular mechanism can result in one of three problems: the athlete may

- sprain the ligaments at the anterior aspect of the elbow,
- strain the musculature at the anterior aspect of the elbow, or
- receive a painful bony compression if the olecranon process impacts the humerus.

This type of injury initially needs to be treated with PRICE. More severe conditions are referred to a physician. As the condition improves, range of motion should be reestablished and strength of the elbow flexor muscles should be improved. The athlete may need to wear an elbow hyperextension tape application upon initial return to play.

The elbow is a very bony joint with little natural padding. Contusions, therefore, are fairly common—they can typically be treated with PRICE. A variety of protective pads exist to offer further protection to the elbow.

If the olecranon process is contused, the olecranon bursa may become irritated. This causes a lot of fluid to build up at the "tip" of the elbow. While this is seldom a disabling condition, the fluid buildup can become the size of a golf ball. Compression wraps must be applied by the ATC, and if the condition persists, the team physician may want to drain the fluid from the area. In any event, the elbow needs to be adequately protected with padding to avoid any further contusions.

## Summary

The elbow is a hinge joint comprised of the humerus of the upper arm and the radius and ulna of the lower arm. The biceps and triceps muscles flex and extend the elbow, respectively. The wrist flexor and extensor muscles extend across the elbow and attach to the humerus. The elbow is also stabilized by the radial collateral ligament at the lateral aspect of the joint and the ulnar collateral ligament on the medial aspect of the joint. These ligaments are sometimes sprained in much the same way the medial and lateral collateral ligaments of the knee are sprained. The elbow is subject to some overuse injuries, such as tennis elbow.

## Key Terms

Define the following terms found in this chapter:

bursa            Little League elbow            tennis elbow

## Questions for Review

1. Describe the bony structures of the elbow and the motions that are produced by the muscles around the elbow. pp. 151-152
2. Describe tennis elbow. How should an ATC treat this condition? p. 155
3. Explain what types of injuries may occur if the elbow is hyperextended. p. 156
4. What mechanism would cause stretching or tearing of the ulnar collateral ligament? p. 153

## Activities for Reinforcement

1. Have an ATC demonstrate an elbow evaluation.

## Above and Beyond

Read one of the following suggested readings and write a report:

Andrews, J.R., and J.A. Whiteside. 1993. Common elbow problems in the athlete. *The Journal of Orthopaedic and Sports Physical Therapy* 17(6): 289–95.

Blackard, D. 1997. Management of an uncomplicated posterior elbow dislocation. *Journal of Athletic Training*. 32(1): 63–67.

Ellenbecker, T.S., and A.J. Mattalino. 1997. *The elbow in sport*. Champaign, IL: Human Kinetics.

Grana, W.A. 1985. Little League elbow: Prevention and treatment. *Sports Medicine Digest* 7(4): 1–3.

# Wrist and Hand Injuries

Upon completing this chapter the student will be able to do the following:
- Understand the basic anatomy of the wrist and hand.
- Explain various types of injuries that occur.
- Understand common mechanisms that cause injuries of the wrist and hand.
- Understand the signs and symptoms of the various types of fractures of the wrist and hand.

Catching a ball, holding a club, or grasping an opponent are essential tasks. An injury to a wrist and hand can be exceedingly limiting and demoralizing for an athlete. Recognizing the kind and the extent of injury will help determine the appropriate care and speed return to competition.

## Anatomy of the Wrist and Hand

The wrist and hand contain many bones, muscles, ligaments, nerves, and blood vessels. All are necessary for the total functioning of the hand—one of the most active body parts—and if any anatomical part is injured, it will decrease an athlete's functional ability.

### Bones and Joints

The wrist is the joint between the arm and the hand. It is made up of seven irregularly shaped carpal bones that articulate between the radius and ulna of the arm and the metacarpals of the hand to allow wrist movement (see figure 18.1). The scaphoid bone is of particular importance. It has a blood supply on only one end, and therefore has difficulty healing when it is fractured. When the fingers are spread, the scaphoid sits in a depression at the wrist that is referred to as the "anatomical snuffbox."

At the distal end, each of the five metacarpals joins with the proximal phalanx of one of the fingers. The metacarpals are numbered one through five, beginning at the thumb side of the hand. The fingers have a total of 14 phalanges.

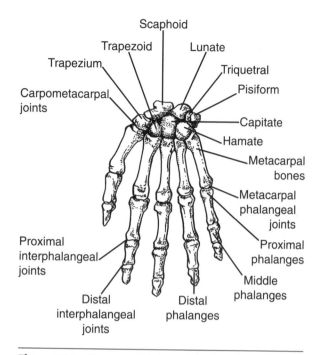

Scaphoid
Trapezoid
Lunate
Trapezium
Triquetral
Carpometacarpal joints
Pisiform
Capitate
Hamate
Metacarpal bones
Metacarpal phalangeal joints
Proximal interphalangeal joints
Proximal phalanges
Distal interphalangeal joints
Distal phalanges
Middle phalanges

**Figure 18.1** Bones and joints of the hand.

Joints in the hand are named for the bones that comprise them and whether they are distal or proximal. For example, the thumb has two joints: the metacarpal phalangeal joint and the interphalangeal joint. Each of the second through fifth fingers has a metacarpal phalangeal (MCP) joint, a proximal interphalangeal (PIP) joint, and a distal interphalangeal (DIP) joint.

## Muscles

The wrist and hand movements are controlled by many different muscles. There are extensor and flexor groups of muscles. The flexor muscle groups are found on the anterior surface of the forearm, and the extensor muscles are located on the posterior aspect of the forearm.

# Preventing Wrist and Hand Injuries

Commonly used protective equipment for the wrist and hand includes braces, tape, gloves, and padding. Wearing gloves or tape can protect the area from wounds of all types, and padding can prevent contusions of the dorsal hand. Many football players wear a thumb brace to protect against sprains. Athletic trainers can use plastic splints and braces to prevent injury for some-

one who may be susceptible. In some sports, however, rules prohibit the use of hard substances such as braces or allow the equipment only with a physician's note.

# Treating Wrist and Hand Injuries and Conditions

With a hand, one can manipulate objects and perform feats of astounding complexity. The slightest injury can change a movement or make it difficult for the athlete to participate in her sport.

## Ligament Injuries

Sprains, in many cases, are not serious and can be treated following PRICE. One common misconception about sprains is that they must be pulled back into place. This is not true! Sprains are injured ligaments. Pulling on an injured ligament can only cause more injury.

### Wrist Sprains

Wrist sprains commonly occur from overuse, falls, and forceful twisting motion. Which ligament is injured depends upon the stress. An excessive amount of ulnar deviation at the wrist, for example, will injure the ligament on the radial side due to too much tension or overstretching, and excessive radial deviation at the wrist will injure the ligament on the medial side. The athlete will experience pain, possibly decreased range of motion, decreased grip

## 🌐 The Real World

A male gymnast asked me to take a look at his hand. He said he had somehow cut his palm during a workout a couple of days earlier. He had cared for the injury himself but was unhappy that he was still having some problems. When I removed the bandages it became apparent why he was having a problem—he had used his mother's needle and black thread to stitch his own hand; luckily, it did not appear to be infected. I sent the student to his family physician, who removed the stitches, and placed him on antibiotics.

Lorin Cartwright, MS, ATC, EMT

strength, and some swelling. The athletic trainer will recommend PRICE. When the athlete returns to activity, taping for support may prevent further injury. Rehabilitation for wrist sprains focuses on reestablishing normal range of motion and strength.

### Dislocation of the Lunate

When an athlete falls upon his hand, it can be in flexion or extension at the time of impact. Either motion can result in a dislocation of a carpal bone, most commonly the lunate. This dislocation will cause deformity, pain, swelling, and decreased range of motion. The dislocation of any carpal bone should be splinted and referred to a physician. The physician must reduce the dislocation.

### Gamekeeper's Thumb

An injury to the medial collateral ligament of the thumb is referred to as **gamekeeper's thumb** (see figure 18.2). The term is an old one that was first used to describe the farmer who injured his medial collateral ligament when breaking the necks of birds intended for the cooking pot. This injury is also known as skier's thumb because the ski pole sometimes gets stuck and forces the thumb into abduction. In general, the ligament on the medial aspect of the thumb is injured when the thumb is forcefully abducted (e.g., a basketball being caught). The athlete will complain of pain over the joint, and the area may be swollen.

Treatment of the injury involves splinting the medial aspect of the thumb and icing. An X ray will be necessary to determine if an avulsion fracture is associated with the ligament tear.

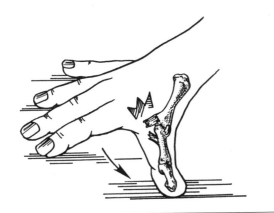

**Figure 18.2** Gamekeeper's thumb and mechanism. When the thumb is pulled away from the fingers, the medial collateral ligament can be ruptured.

**❓ What Would You Do If...**

A softball player slid headfirst into second base. Her index finger did not look "right." She had another player pull her finger, and she felt it pop.

### Interphalangeal Collateral Ligament Sprains

A collateral ligament is located on the side of each interphalangeal joint. The ligaments provide stability when the phalanges are stressed, but one can be sprained when a joint is stressed beyond normal—for example, if the finger is hit by a ball, if the athlete lands with fingers curled or extended, or if he accidentally catches a finger on an opponent's jersey. Injury to the collateral ligament is painful and disabling. The joint can swell and become discolored. The ATC will confer with the team physician to determine if an X ray is necessary to rule out a fracture. The application of ice will keep the swelling to a minimum; if the finger swells too much, the athlete will be unable to bend it. When he returns to competition, it is common to tape the injured finger to an uninjured neighbor (this is called buddy taping). Padding may be helpful in preventing additional injuries.

### Dislocation of the Interphalangeal Joint or the Metacarpal Phalangeal Joint

When a dislocation of the IP or MCP joint occurs, one bone usually moves dorsal and one volar. The team physician should relocate all dislocated fingers and thumbs because tiny tendons, nerves, and blood vessels course their way through joint spaces. If the relocation is done improperly, there can be permanent damage to that finger. In the case of a dislocation the ligament may tear, with possible fractures also occurring. We know of a softball player who dove for a ball and dislocated her finger. Her teammate, trying to be helpful, pulled on the finger, driving the splintered bone pieces into the tendon and severing it. Four pins and one surgery later the softball player has a straight finger that she will not let anyone touch.

## Muscle and Tendon Injuries

Any one of the numerous muscles of the wrist and hand can be strained. Repetitive stress and

## For Your Information

### Volar

Volar refers to the palm side of the hand.

### Dorsal

Dorsal refers to the back or posterior portion of the body in the anatomical position.

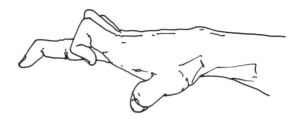

**Figure 18.3** An avulsion fracture of the distal phalanx of the fingers will result in a mallet finger. A mallet finger cannot be extended at the distal interphalangeal joint.

stretching will cause the muscles to strain. Pain, swelling, weakness, and inability to move are common signs and symptoms. The athletic trainer will use range of motion testing to determine which muscle has been affected. Analysis of the athlete's movements can help determine the cause when a repetitive stress is suspected. The athletic trainer will use the PRICE method and give exercises to strengthen a weak muscle to get the athlete ready for return to competition. Taping the muscle for additional support can also be helpful.

### Tendinitis

Tendinitis is defined as inflammation of the tendon. The cause of the inflammation can be overuse, stretching, or an impact. Because it is difficult to overcome, the ATC's goal is to prevent tendinitis by increasing strength and flexibility, by using padding, and by avoiding repetitive injuries.

The thumb is vulnerable to de Quervain's tendinitis, which affects the abductor pollicis longus and extensor pollicis brevis. Shot putters who hold the shot while the wrist is in radial deviation are prone to de Quervain's tendinitis. The athlete will have difficulty with abduction of the thumb, and he may experience swelling and crepitus. He needs to discontinue the repetitive movements. The PRICE method of care is appropriate in this case.

### Mallet Finger

Mallet finger (see figure 18.3) is the result of the fingertip receiving an impact. The impact causes the extensor tendon to be torn from the bone. The most distinguishing feature of this injury is that the fingertip is in flexion. The athlete cannot lift the tip of the finger to straighten the bone because the tendon is no longer attached. She will experience pain and some swelling.

The finger will be splinted into extension and referred to the team physician for care. The physician has two courses of action: treat it surgically or keep it splinted. The tendon can heal back to the bone if it is kept still and extended. If the tendon is retracted too far from its attachment, surgery will be required to reattach the tendon. In many instances an athlete will not consider this injury very important and fail to report it. This negligence will result in a permanent flexion of the distal interphalangeal joint.

### Jersey Finger

**Jersey finger** is very similar to mallet finger except that the flexor tendon tears from the fingertip. The athlete will not be able to flex the DIP joint of his finger. Injury occurs when the DIP joint is forcibly flexed, such as when the athlete is holding an opponent's jersey with a fist, and his finger is forced to extend, which tears the tendon. He will experience pain and swelling. Splinting and ice are good initial treatments to be given by the athletic trainer. The finger will require an X ray to determine the extent of the injury. A physician will decide if the athlete needs surgery.

## What Would You Do If...

A male gymnast was putting on his gymnastics pants. His hand slipped, and he noticed he could no longer lift the end of his finger. You explain this could be a mallet finger and should be seen by the ATC and team physician. The athlete refuses. You tell him that it could result in a permanent injury. The athlete responds by saying, "That's why we have insurance."

### Boutonniere Deformity

A boutonniere deformity occurs at the proximal interphalangeal joint of the fingers (see figure 18.4). A hard impact over the PIP joint can cause a tear in the joint capsule, which will allow the extensor tendons to fall laterally. When the tendons are in the lateral position, they contract and force flexion of the distal interphalangeal joint. The athlete will not be able to extend the

**Figure 18.4** Boutonniere deformity. If the sheath that holds the extensor tendon on top of the finger is torn, causing the tendons to slide to the sides of the finger, the PIP joint flexes and the DIP joint hyperextends.

PIP joint, and he will experience pain and swelling. The ATC will splint the finger and refer the athlete to a physician for treatment. In many instances the finger can be splinted, allowing the connective tissue that keeps the extensor tendons in place to heal. Otherwise surgical intervention is necessary.

## Bone Injuries

Any bone within the wrist and hand can fracture. Hands are used in all sports and are often put in harm's way. Direct impacts are the most common cause of the fractures. Swelling, pain, deformity, and disability are common with fractures. Two complications are associated with fractures: nonunion and death of the bone, which is also called **avascular necrosis** (death due to lack of blood flow). In the wrist, the scaphoid bone is the bone most often associated with nonunion and avascular necrosis. All fractures should be cared for by splinting and should be evaluated by a physician.

## Summary

The wrist and hand are involved in every athletic activity and thus are susceptible to numerous injuries, which can range from minor to permanently disabling. An athlete who is trying to be helpful can increase the severity of an injury, for example, by pulling on an injured finger. Because of the intricate structure of the wrist and hand, the signs and symptoms of many different injuries are identical. The athletic trainer, coach, or team physician should be the first one to provide care, to ensure the best possible outcome. The physician should evaluate most sprains to rule out fractures.

## Key Terms

Define the following terms found in this chapter:

avascular necrosis        gamekeeper's thumb        jersey finger

## Questions for Review

1. What bone is located beneath the anatomical snuffbox? p. 159
2. Describe the mechanism of injury for mallet finger. How should it be splinted? p. 162
3. Describe the mechanism of injury for gamekeeper's thumb. Why is it also known as skier's thumb? p. 161
4. How should jersey finger be splinted? p. 162
5. What are common methods used to care for the wrist, hand, and finger injuries? pp. 160-163

# Activities for Reinforcement

1. Find an anatomy text and review the location of the various carpal bones.
2. Have an ATC demonstrate how to perform a wrist and hand evaluation.

# Above and Beyond

1. Write a report on proper management of a specific hand injury.
2. Design a study guide for this chapter, using the following resources.

   Blauvelt, C.T., and F. Nelson. 1994. *A manual of orthopaedic terminology.* 5th ed. St. Louis: Mosby Year Book.

   Ellsasser, J., and A. Stein. 1980. Management of hand injuries in professional football team. *Athletic Training* 15(1): 34–37.

# Unit VI

# Preventing Athletics-Related Injuries

# Protective Taping and Wrapping

## OBJECTIVES

Upon completing this chapter the student will be able to do the following:
- Understand why tape and wraps are applied to the body.
- Develop an understanding of the type of tape available.
- Explain how to apply tape to the body by following the principles of tape handling, skin preparation, and taping techniques.
- Understand why and how elastic wraps are applied to the body for specific injuries.

Historically, taping and wrapping have been the hallmark of practice for ATCs. The techniques of selecting and applying protective tapes and wraps are skills that every ATC must have. Although we discuss these skills in relation to injury prevention, they are integral parts of athletic injury care as well. We consider these skills to be as much art as they are science.

## Principles of Taping Procedures

Protective tape is used to prevent injuries and to keep existing injuries from getting worse, but it must be applied only if its use is indicated. An ATC must understand the contraindications of applying tape, as well as the proper use of tape, which includes tape selection, tape handling, skin preparation, and taping techniques.

### Indications for Applying Tape

Tape may be applied for the following reasons:

- **Support and stability.** After a joint injury, ligaments may be overstretched and somewhat loose. Taping the joint can improve stability and give the athlete a feeling of security.

- **Immediate first aid.** Taping as first aid is usually to hold a bandage in place. Some tape procedures, such as the open basket weave that we will discuss, can provide some minimal compression to an injury if an elastic wrap is not available. In addition, applying tape to an area will reduce further movement.

• **To secure a pad or brace.** When treating an injury, an ATC often applies tape to secure a brace or pad in place. If the ATC needs to secure a foam pad to the skin to protect fresh bruises from another blow, he should cover it completely with tape; that is, the ATC will not be able to see the pad once he has taped it in place. Otherwise, it will dislodge itself and fall off the body. If an athlete is required to wear a brace on her knee, she may simply want tape applied over any straps so the brace does not loosen if she falls.

• **To prevent injury.** Tape is applied at specific joints to restrict certain motions. For example, the most common mechanism for ankle sprains is inversion. Therefore, tape is applied to the ankle to restrict that movement.

• **To restrict the angle of pull.** When tape is applied, it can be placed so that two bones are not allowed to move too far in a certain direction, thus limiting the range of motion. For example, if elbow extension is painful due to a biceps injury, tape can be applied to restrict the pulling on the biceps that occurs with elbow extension. When a muscle or tendon is strained, restricting the angle of pull can help reduce stress and prevent further injury.

• **Psychological assistance.** Although taping procedures are not intended to replace strong ligaments and muscles, they are sometimes used to give psychological assistance to athletes. Our experience suggests that occasionally an athlete will feel more confident knowing she is protected with a specific tape job.

Tape and wraps should not be used as a substitute for proper treatment. In fact, many ATCs do not tape or wrap an athlete unless he first takes the time to receive proper treatment.

## Proper Use of Tape

Proper use of tape goes beyond understanding application techniques and procedures—it includes tape selection, tape handling, skin preparation, and taping techniques.

### *Tape Selection*

There are four types of tape from which to choose: linen, elastic, hybrid, and moleskin (see

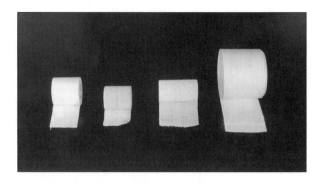

**Figure 19.1** Various types of tape include (from left to right) linen, elastic, hybrid, and moleskin.

figure 19.1). An ATC must understand the differences among the various tapes to select the best tape for the goals she has in mind.

1. **Linen tape** is the most common tape. It varies in width (from $\frac{1}{2}$ inch to 2 inches), but $1\frac{1}{2}$ inches is the size most frequently used, and it can be torn by hand. Many manufacturers produce linen tape, and the quality of the products differs. The higher-quality tape has more threads per square inch and comes off the spool evenly. An ATC must consider several factors when deciding what quality of tape to purchase. For example, if she tapes athletes quite often and frequently relies on taping procedures to prevent injury, purchase of a higher-quality tape is warranted. However, if a school has a small budget, then buying lots of high-quality tape may leave little money to purchase other supplies, and she may choose a lower quality of tape.

2. **Elastic tape,** like an elastic wrap, can return to its original length after being stretched. Elastic tape has extra adhesive on one side and usually has to be cut with scissors. It is used when material with a high strength is desired or when the tape ends need to pull toward one another. For example, if an athlete has a hyperextended elbow the ATC may not wish the elbow to move into full extension. He could apply elastic tape from the front of the forearm to the front of the upper arm. The tape (because it is attempting to go back to its original length) would pull the elbow into a slight amount of flexion and subsequently act to prevent hyperextension.

3. **Hybrid tape** is a combination of linen and elastic tape—it is a linen-based tape with some elastic qualities. Hybrid tape can often be torn by hand. Hybrid tape is often used to surround

strips of linen tape that have been applied to muscles and joints that must expand, contract, or bend. Covering the linen tape helps it stay in place. Hybrid tape is slightly more expensive per roll than a similar quality of linen tape.

4. **Moleskin** is a thick tape with a lot of adhesive on one side. It sticks well to the skin and is very strong. Thus, it is often used when added strength is needed. It is rather expensive compared to other types of tape but extremely useful when an athlete is returning to participation, for example, after an ankle sprain when a great deal of reinforcement is needed so he does not reinjure his ankle.

### Tape Handling

The smoothness and efficiency with which tape is applied depends upon how proficient the ATC is at tape handling, which involves proper tearing, proper winding, overlap, and contour.

Perhaps the hardest part of tape handling for beginners is tearing the tape. When tearing the tape, the tape roll is gripped in one hand and the strip of tape to be torn is held between the thumb and index finger of the other hand. A precise, quick movement must be used. The tape must not be pleated at the edge or the threads may not pull apart. Do not be discouraged if this is a difficult task. If at first you don't succeed, tear, tear again!

Proper winding refers to applying individual strips of tape rather than a continuous length of tape off the roll, which builds tension quickly and is likely to cut off circulation. For the times when tape is applied continuously around a joint, the ATC must be careful to apply the tape at a proper tension without cutting off the athlete's circulation. Some athletes may like tape to be applied tightly, but until the ATC becomes skilled at adjusting the right amount of tension, applying individual strips is most appropriate. A bluish color of the body part indicates a loss of circulation. She should ask the athlete if he can feel any tingling or if it feels as if his foot or hand is "falling asleep." The ATC should also check circulation by examining the capillary refill of the nail bed. That is, if she is taping the athlete's wrist, she should pinch his thumbnail to squeeze the blood from it. If circulation is adequate, when she stops pinching the nail bed should turn from white to pink in just a few seconds. She will do the same thing to a

toenail if she has applied tape to the foot or ankle.

Overlap refers to applying strips of tape so that one-half of the strip from one piece is covered by the next piece applied. If the ATC does not apply the tape using an overlap method, he runs the risk of gapping the tape and creating areas of friction and irritation.

The tape must be applied to follow the natural contour of the body area. The ATC will adapt the angle of application of the tape to the shape of the body area receiving the tape. He must be able to subtly alter the angle of application of the tape to get to the desired direction and subsequent support without affecting the body contour or disturbing the purpose of the procedure. If the ATC forces the tape into a change of direction too abruptly, he may create areas of high pressure or wrinkles, which can cause blisters, cuts, and even contusions, not to mention a very upset athlete.

### Skin Preparation

Prior to applying tape to the body, the skin must be washed and dried, and hair around the body part must be removed by shaving with either an electric hair clipper with a guard or a disposable razor. After the area is cleaned and shaved, a tape adhesive is applied. Tape adhesives come in spray cans or bottles and, once applied, they increase the stickiness of the skin, which allows the tape to be applied more securely.

When the tape adhesive has dried, a thin film of foamlike material is applied to the skin. This helps to prevent skin irritation (and helps prevent the tape from sticking to an athlete's hair if he has neglected to shave). Some body parts such as the front of the ankle and back of the heel are extremely sensitive because they rub against the shoe. Such areas are protected with thin foam pads to which the ATC applies a petroleum-based lubricant—the pads help to minimize friction and improve comfort. After the practice or game the athlete will remove the tape with special scissors or tape shears, which have a protective end so he will not cut himself. Finally, he should clean the area with soap and water while he is in the shower.

# Taping Techniques

If you were to ask 10 ATCs how to tape a body part, chances are you would get 10 different answers. Many different taping techniques can be applied to various body areas. We will explain and illustrate some basic procedures.

Many taping procedures have a common foundation; that is, they begin with anchor strips, which are simply single strips of tape placed around each end of the body part that will be taped. The anchor strips create borders within which to work. Once the anchor strips are in place, support strips are applied. Support strips may be overlapped to create a fan shape, they may be pulled from one side of a joint to another, or they may be swirled around a joint. Support strips are deliberately placed, depending upon the goals of the tape job. Closure strips, which are applied in the final step in most procedures, are placed over the support strips—they are vital to keeping the tape intact no matter how hard the athlete may practice or play. The ATC cannot be stingy with closure strips. When you see the illustrations you may wonder about the number of closure strips we've pictured for some of the procedures. We haven't gone crazy. When you're applying closure strips is not the time to try to save tape; you must be certain that your taping job won't fail when the athlete needs it most.

## Turf-Toe

The goal when taping for turf-toe is to restrict the extension movement of the great toe. We will first place anchor strips of linen tape around the foot and around the base of the great toe (see figure 19.2a). Then we place a minimum of three strips of 1-inch linen tape from the plantar aspect of the toe anchor strip to the plantar aspect of the arch on the anchor strip (see figure 19.2b). We apply closure strips over the loose ends to secure these strips in place (see figure 19.2c). Elastic tape may also be used for this procedure. In fact, elastic tape is especially useful around the foot because it allows the foot to expand during the weight-bearing portion of the stride without binding the foot.

## Longitudinal Arch

The purpose of the longitudinal arch procedure is to restrict the medial foot from flattening. We start with one to three anchor strips around the ball of the foot. We start the first strip of 1-inch linen tape at the medial side of the anchor and go back toward and around the heel to the starting point at the anchor (see figure 19.3a). We start the second strip at the lateral side of the anchor, take it around the heel, and then back to the starting point (see figure 19.3b). We overlap the strips until four to six strips have

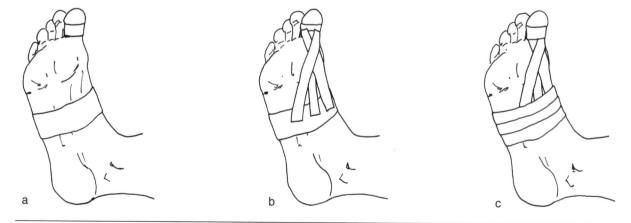

a    b    c

**Figure 19.2**  Turf-toe. *(a)* First apply anchors to foot and great toe, *(b)* apply three strips of linen tape on the bottom of the foot between the anchor strips, *(c)* cover the ends with closure strips.

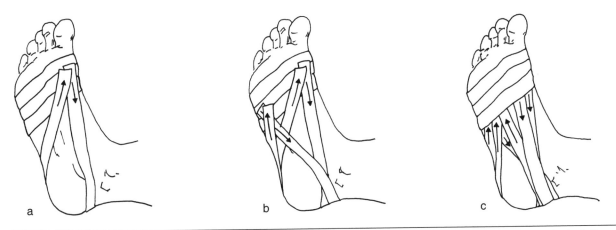

**Figure 19.3** Longitudinal arch. *(a)* When taping an arch, begin with an anchor strip. Place the first strip of 1-inch linen tape from the anchor, back toward the heel, and around to the other end of the strip at the anchor. *(b)* Overlap the strips until four to six strips have been placed. *(c)* Once the arch strips are situated, close the loose ends with closure strips.

been placed. We cover the loose ends with closure strips (see figure 19.3c). Many variations of this longitudinal arch taping procedure exist.

## Closed Basket Weave

The closed basket weave is used primarily to give support and help prevent inversion ankle sprains. We begin the closed basket weave with one anchor strip at the lower leg just below the bulky portion of the calf muscle and one at midfoot. With the anchors in place we begin placing alternate support strips, called stirrups and horseshoes, on the ankle. The first stirrup is applied to the anchor strip on the medial aspect of the leg, pulled down under the foot, and up to the anchor strip on the lateral aspect of the leg (see figure 19.4a). Once a stirrup is applied, we place a horseshoe strip at the distal aspect of the lower leg (around the ankle) from the lateral aspect to the medial aspect (see figure 19.4b). We apply these strips alternately, overlapping them, until a minimum of three stirrups and three horseshoes are applied (see figure 19.4c). Once this is completed, we apply a figure eight around the ankle. We start the figure eight at the outer anklebone (lateral malleolus) and guide the tape across the top of the ankle down to the medial aspect of the foot. The figure-eight strip will then come up the lateral side of the foot just in front of the lateral malleolus and run a course to the medial malleolus and then around to the back of the lower leg, stopping at the lateral

malleolus (see figure 19.4d). Once the figure-eight strip is in place, we apply two heel locks (one forward and one reverse). We start one heel lock strip just above the inside anklebone (medial malleolus) and angle it downward so that it crosses the outer aspect of the heel. Then the tape runs a course across the bottom of the foot and upward on the inside aspect angling toward the outer anklebone (lateral malleolus) where it stops (see figure 19.4e). We start the next heel lock just above the lateral malleolus and angle it downward so that it crosses the medial aspect of the heel, across the bottom of the foot, and upward on the lateral aspect angling toward the medial malleolus where it stops (see figure 19.4f). The heel locks can be done continuously once proficiency is developed with the angles and tape handling. After the heel locks are in place, we apply closure strips to cover all loose ends.

## Open Basket Weave

The open basket weave (see figure 19.5) is used with acute ankle sprains to help prevent swelling if an elastic wrap is not available. It is applied in the same manner as a closed basket weave, with a few exceptions. The idea is to leave a gap down the front of the tape job in case too much swelling occurs. Thus, we leave the anchor strips open on the front of the leg and on top of the foot rather than circling the leg and foot with them, and we do not perform the figure-eight procedure. We do the heel locks, making sure they do

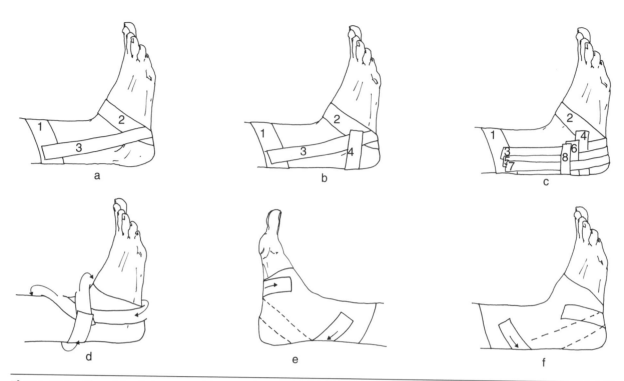

**Figure 19.4** Closed basket weave. *(a)* Once the anchors are in place (1 and 2), a stirrup is applied (3), *(b)* and a horseshoe strip is applied (4). *(c)* Stirrup and horseshoe strips are applied in alternating fashion (5-8), *(d)* followed by the figure-eight strip. *(e-f)* Heel locks are applied after the figure eight from above the ankle, wrapping under the heel.

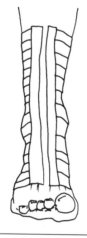

**Figure 19.5** An open basket weave is helpful for giving support to an ankle injury. The gap in the front of the tape job allows the ankle to swell.

not cross over the front of the ankle where a gap is to be left. The open gap allows for expansion of the ankle due to excessive swelling. This particular type of tape application is especially useful for an acute ankle sprain when an elastic wrap is not available and the ankle is expected to swell.

# Achilles Tendon Taping

Achilles tendon taping is performed to restrict the amount of dorsiflexion at the ankle. When a person dorsiflexes her foot, the Achilles tendon is stretched. Therefore, when applying an Achilles tendon tape procedure, we have the athlete lie on her stomach and point her injured foot into a few degrees of plantar flexion. Once the foot is in position, we apply anchor strips midcalf, about six inches from the malleoli, and at the ball of the foot. Place a fan shape of three strips of elastic tape from the top anchor to the bottom anchor. These strips should cross over the back of the heel (see figure 19.6a). Once the strips of elastic tape are positioned, place linen closure strips over several inches at the ends to secure them in place (see figure 19.6b).

# Shinsplints

The term shinsplints is sometimes used as a catchall for pain in the lower leg, because shinsplints—formally called medial tibial stress syndrome—can be extremely painful. Tape application can help reduce the pain. When an athlete

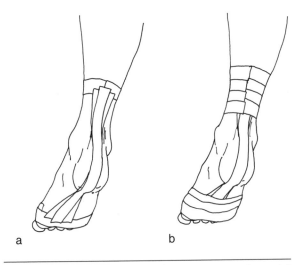

**Figure 19.6** An Achilles tendon tape procedure. *(a)* Place a fan shape of three strips of elastic tape from the top anchor to the bottom anchor, and *(b)* secure the strips with closure strips.

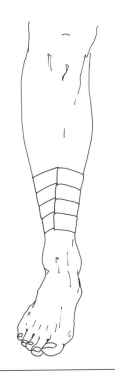

**Figure 19.7** Taping for shinsplints.

suffers from shinsplints, we place overlapping strips of tape around the lower leg from an inch above the ankle bones to the bottom of the calf. The strips should be applied one over the other from the Achilles tendon upward to the medial aspect of the lower leg (see figure 19.7). The small amount of compression that the tape pro-

vides can sometimes lessen the athlete's discomfort. This procedure should not be done if the athlete has compartment syndrome (see chapter 8), and the tape should be taken off if any symptoms get worse.

## Collateral Knee Ligament Sprains

Injuries to the medial or lateral ligament of the knee are taped in the same manner, on the appropriate side of the knee. Presented here will be a medial collateral ligament (MCL) tape procedure designed to reduce the amount of valgus movement, which opens up the medial joint line of the knee, subsequently stretching or tearing the medial collateral ligament (see chapter 9).

We begin taping the MCL by having the athlete stand, and we put a block of wood about two inches high under the heel of the leg we are going to tape. This places the knee into flexion. We place three or four anchor strips around midthigh and about two or three anchor strips around the lower leg. Once the anchors are positioned, we place a minimum of three 2-inch-wide strips of linen or elastic tape in the shape of a fan across the medial joint line of the knee (see figure 19.8a). We place closure strips over the ends of the tape at top and bottom to secure them (see figure 19.8b).

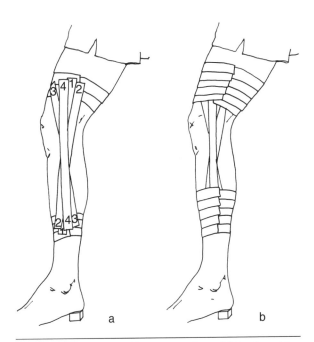

**Figure 19.8** Collateral knee procedure. *(a)* Anchor strips and fan placed across joint line; *(b)* closure strips for collateral ligament injury.

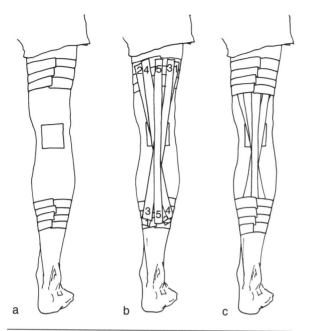

**Figure 19.9** Knee hyperextension procedure. *(a)* Knee hyperextension anchors and lubricated pad are applied; *(b)* five strips are placed in a fan shape; *(c)* enough closure strips are applied to make sure the tape remains in place. See figure 19.8 for block placement.

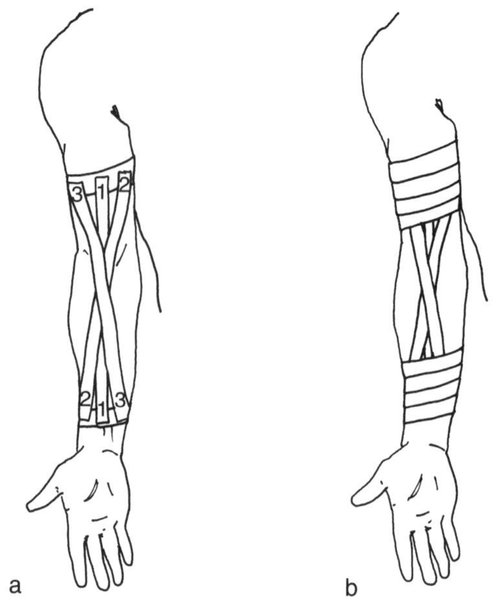

**Figure 19.10** Elbow hyperextension taping procedure. *(a)* Elbow hyperextension anchor strips with tape placed in a fan shape over them, and *(b)* finished with closure strips.

## Knee Hyperextension

Knee hyperextension mechanisms are responsible for injuring the anterior cruciate ligament. Taping a knee to prevent hyperextension also uses a fan technique. We begin by placing a block under the heel (figure 19.8) to put the knee into flexion, and we place a lubricated foam pad at the back of the knee. We position three to four anchor strips at midthigh and two to three at the lower leg (see figure 19.9a). A minimum of five strips are placed in a fan shape between the anchors across the back of the knee (see figure 19.9b). We finish by placing closure strips across all tape ends (figure 19.9c).

## Elbow Hyperextension

One of the most common mechanisms for elbow injuries is falling on an outstretched arm, which subsequently makes the elbow vulnerable to hyperextension injuries. The goal of taping for an elbow hyperextension injury is to limit extension. Before taping, we must first place the elbow in a slight amount of flexion. We place anchor strips at the top of the biceps of the upper arm and at mid- to lower forearm. Before applying the anchor strips, we make sure the athlete is making the biceps muscles tight. When the anchor strips are in position, we place three to five strips in a fan shape across the front of the elbow, running from anchor to anchor (see figure 19.10a). Elastic tape is preferred by ATCs for these strips, but linen tape is also acceptable. We apply closure strips over the anchors at the upper arm and forearm to cover all tape ends (see figure 19.10b).

## Wrist Hyperextension and Hyperflexion

Sprains and strains are very common injuries found at the wrist. Hyperflexion and hyperextension mechanisms cause most wrist sprains; therefore, our goal for wrist taping commonly is to prevent excessive flexion or extension. Because the majority of wrist injuries are due to hyperextension, we will show here a tape job to prevent it.

To prevent wrist hyperextension, we start by placing an anchor strip around the distal aspect of the forearm and another around the hand just above the knuckles. With the anchors in place,

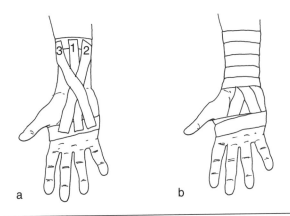

**Figure 19.11** Wrist hyperextension tape procedure. *(a)* Wrist hyperextension anchor strips and fan strips, and *(b)* closure strips.

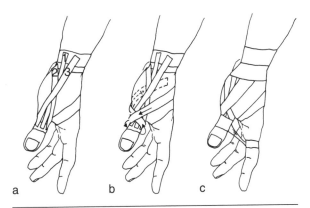

**Figure 19.12** Thumb hyperextension procedure. *(a)* Thumb hyperextension taping begins with anchors on wrist, hand, and thumb and strips of tape on dorsal aspect of thumb; *(b)* thumb taping complete with spica, and *(c)* check rein.

we position the wrist into slight flexion and place a minimum of three strips of linen tape in a fan shape across the palmar aspect of the wrist (see figure 19.11a). Closure strips are placed over the tape ends to secure them (see figure 19.11b).

## Thumb Hyperextension

We begin taping for a thumb hyperextension injury by placing anchors around the wrist, around the hand, and around the top of the thumb just above the nail. The thumb is then positioned into slight flexion and strips of 1-inch linen tape are applied over the back of the thumb in a fan shape between the anchors on the thumb and wrist (see figure 19.12a). Once these are in place, a tape wrap called a spica can be swirled around the joint. Begin at the palmar aspect of the wrist and guide the 1-inch tape toward the back aspect of the thumb, loop around the thumb, and then guide the tape toward the dorsal aspect of the wrist and tear the tape (see figure 19.12b). Repeat this spica

one more time and then apply closure strips around the wrist and through the hand to cover any and all tape ends. Also, to help keep the thumb stable, a **check rein** (see figure 19.12c) can be used to connect the index finger and the thumb.

## Finger Sprains

Finger sprains are commonly treated using "buddy taping"; that is, the sprained finger is moved toward an adjacent noninjured finger and either the first and second or third and fourth fingers are taped together. Tape is applied between the joints of the fingers; rarely is it applied across the joint itself (see figure 19.13)

## Elastic Wrapping Techniques

When an athlete suffers an injury, **elastic wraps** are often helpful for applying compression and support to the area. Elastic wraps come in various widths and lengths and are used for many musculoskeletal injuries, such as sprains and strains. Because the elastic wraps can be washed and reused, they are less expensive to use than tape. Like tape, elastic wraps come in a variety of sizes. Common widths include two, three, four, and six inches. Two- and three-inch elastic wraps are often used around the wrist or hand, four-inch wraps are commonly used around the foot or ankle, and six-inch elastic wraps are used around the thigh, hip, or shoulder.

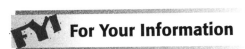
**For Your Information**

### Spica

A spica is a tape or wrap procedure applied to joints such as the thumb, shoulder, or hip. It is basically a figure eight applied to an area so that the tape or wrap encircles the joint and gives support.

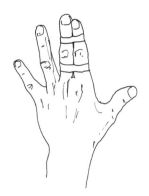

**Figure 19.13** Buddy taping for a finger sprain.

**Figure 19.14** Elastic wraps are applied to joints to prevent swelling.

## The Real World

I worked with an athlete who had once sprained his finger, and he liked to have his fingers buddy taped. He also felt that elastic tape was better for him than linen, so I would use elastic tape. On one occasion during practice, the athlete ran to the sideline and asked me to tape his fingers. He had a late class that day so he had not been taped before practice. I had some 1-inch wide elastic tape, and I began applying it to his hand, taping his fingers together. He was in a hurry to get back to practice and was practically dancing with impatience. He kept looking behind him to watch practice and his hand was moving all around. Although, I warned him several times to keep his hand still while I cut the tape, he continued to fidget. Sure enough, when I was cutting the tape he moved his hand toward the scissors, and I snipped the webbing of skin between his fingers. Although the wound was minor, I felt bad. The moral of the story is: precut the lengths of elastic tape before applying them to the body, unless you are in a controlled setting like the athletic training room.

Anonymous

## Ankle

When applying an elastic wrap, we make sure to leave the toes exposed so we can check circulation (see figure 19.14). We begin at the bottom of the foot close to the toes and wrap to above the ankle. We overlap the wrap by one-half of the width each time as we work up over the ankle, and we use a wrap with at least a four-inch width so that the finished wrap does not roll up on the edges and become too restrictive. We begin with moderate pressure, and as we apply the wrap toward and above the ankle, we decrease the amount of pressure. Always check the athlete's circulation after the wrap has been applied.

## Thigh

When wrapping the thigh for hamstring or quadriceps injuries, we use a double length, six-inch elastic wrap and begin just above the knee. We overlap the wrap as we apply it upward toward the hip. As we apply the wrap in a spiral around the leg, we use subtle upward and downward angles to contour the wrap appropriately. The finished product will look as though there are Xs up the front of the wrap. Secure the wrap in place with elastic tape (see figure 19.15).

## Adductor (Groin) Strains

We begin by having the athlete put on compression shorts, spandex shorts, or other shorts over which the wrap can be applied comfortably. When wrapping adductor strains, we place the hip in a slight amount of flexion and adduc-

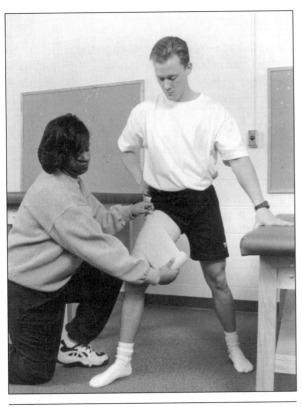

**Figure 19.15** Thigh wrap. Wrap the thigh from above the knee toward the hip.

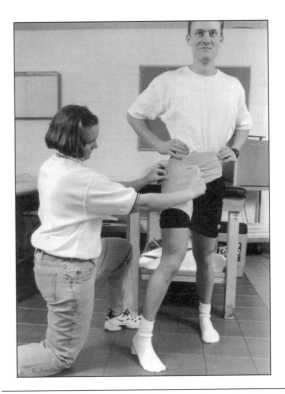

**Figure 19.16** Adductor strain wrap. Note the slightly flexed and adducted position of the thigh.

tion—we place a small block of wood under the heel or have him use a small step. We secure the wrap around the proximal thigh and then continue by moving the wrap around the waist above the iliac crest and then down around the upper thigh and repeat. We secure the wrap with elastic tape (see figure 19.16).

## Hip Flexor Strain

We begin by having the athlete put on compression shorts, spandex shorts, or other shorts over which the wrap can be applied comfortably. When wrapping hip flexor strains, we place the hip into flexion and slight adduction by using a small block or step under the heel. We secure the wrap around the proximal thigh and apply the wrap in a counterclockwise direction. We progress by moving the wrap around the waist above the iliac crest, down around the upper thigh, and repeat. We secure the wrap in place by taping over it with elastic tape (see figure 19.17).

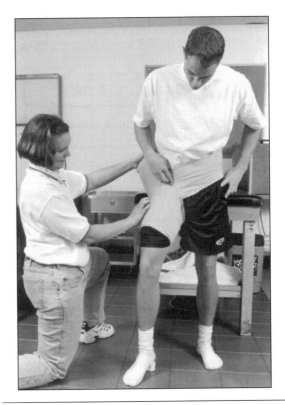

**Figure 19.17** Hip flexor strain wrap. Note the flexed position of the hip and leg.

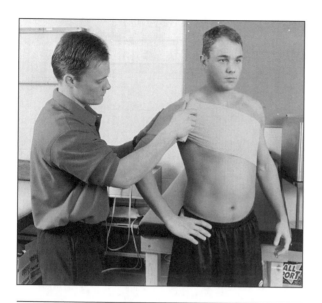

**Figure 19.18** Shoulder spica. Athlete's arm on hip with shoulder spica applied using an elastic wrap. This position puts the upper arm in an internally rotated position.

# Shoulder

Elastic wraps are often applied to the shoulder to restrict motion that causes shoulder dislocations (see figure 19.18). To begin, we have the athlete place the arm to be wrapped on his hip and his other arm straight out, like a teapot. We secure the wrap around the upper arm, applying the wrap in a clockwise direction. Once the wrap is secured to the upper arm, we pull the wrap from the posterior aspect of the shoulder around the front of the chest, under the opposite arm, and across the back to the shoulder. We loop the wrap around the upper arm (clockwise) and repeat. We secure the wrap in place by taping over it with elastic tape.

## Summary

Taping and wrapping have become essential skills for any ATC. Tape and wraps are commonly used for immediate injury care, such as to secure a dressing, pad, or ice in place, as well as for injury prevention. Proper tape application relies on understanding tape selection, tape handling, skin preparation, and taping techniques. Linen, elastic, and hybrid tape are used for different reasons. A variety of application techniques exist.

## Key Terms

Define the following terms found in this chapter:

| | | |
|---|---|---|
| check rein | elastic wraps | linen tape |
| elastic tape | hybrid tape | moleskin |

## Questions for Review

1. List the different reasons ATCs use tape and elastic wraps. pp. 167-168, 175
2. What are the different types of tape available, and what are the advantages of each? pp. 168-169
3. What do we mean by the term winding tension? Is it helpful or harmful? p. 169
4. Why should the tape be overlapped on a previous strip when applying it to the body? p. 169

# Activities for Reinforcement

1. Take a roll of tape home and practice tearing it effectively.
2. Under the supervision of an ATC, work with a partner and prepare the skin appropriately for being taped. Practice the various techniques included in this chapter.
3. Practice applying elastic wraps to your partner under the supervision of an ATC.
4. Have an ATC demonstrate alternative taping techniques and compare them to those in this text.
5. At the end of the year, have a tournament to identify the fastest and best quality tape job to an ankle.

# Above and Beyond

1. With a partner, practice taping continuous heel locks.
2. Read any of the suggested texts below and find alternative ways of taping and wrapping for the specific conditions found in this chapter.

Arnheim, D.D., and W.E. Prentice. 1997. *Principles of athletic training.* 9th ed. Madison, WI: Brown and Benchmark.

Kennedy, R. 1995. *Taping guide.* St. Louis: Mosby.

Wright, K.E., and W.R. Whitehill. 1991. *The comprehensive manual of taping and wrapping techniques.* Gardner, KS: Cramer Products.

# Protective Equipment Used in Athletics

## OBJECTIVES

Upon completing this chapter the student will be able to do the following:
- Explain the basic principles of protection.
- Describe general guidelines of protective equipment use.
- Explain what protective equipment is necessary for various sports.
- Describe proper equipment application.

Protective equipment is specialized equipment that has been designed to prevent the occurrence of an athletic injury. Every athlete should use equipment that provides protection to the body parts most often injured in his or her sport.

## Basic Principles of Protective Equipment

Each sport presents its own common injuries and thus requires specialized equipment to prevent them. Equipment is designed to dissipate forces away from the area it is protecting. It must be durable yet allow enough movement to enable the athlete to play the sport. The players should never use anything but certified equipment.

There are two primary agencies that test and certify athletic equipment. The National Operating Committee on Standards for Athletic Equipment (**NOCSAE**) sets the standards for football, baseball, and softball helmets. The Canadian Standards Association (**CSA**) sets the standards for eye guards and ice hockey helmets.

## Protective Equipment for the Head and Face

Equipment to protect the head and face falls into two categories: helmets and face masks. Unfortunately, it takes years to get athletes to accept new safety equipment.

Usually younger athletes follow the example of the professionals and use it if the pros do. Today, for example, there are helmets to protect soccer players who are making headers (to hit the ball with the head to make a pass or shot), but they are not used with any regularity by professional athletes, and thus they are relatively unknown among the younger players.

## Helmets

• **Football helmets.** In 1939 colleges began to require that players wear football helmets—until that time the head had been uncovered. Before helmets were invented football players let their hair grow long as a way of protecting their heads. Helmets have changed dramatically over the years—the first helmets were close-fitting leather caps. Today's helmet has a hard outer shell with either an air bladder or a fluid-filled cell liner, which is designed to disperse the force of impact over a wide area or away from the skull (see figure 20.1). Figure 20.2 illustrates proper helmet fit. Helmets should never be thrown or used to sit on. Sitting on or throwing a helmet can cause the shell to crack.

• **Ice hockey helmets.** Ice hockey helmets are manufactured by several different companies, but each one is tested and must meet the standard of the CSA. They do not, however, need to be retested annually. The interior of the helmet is made of foam that conforms to the helmet shell. A hockey helmet should fit snugly. If it is too loose it will not protect the head under

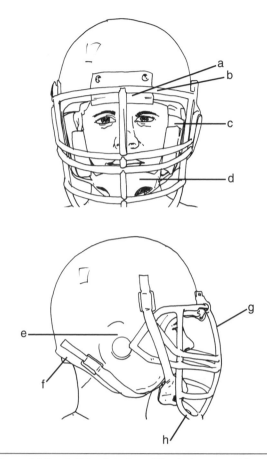

**Figure 20.2** *(a)* The interior of the helmet must be one finger-width above the eyebrow; *(b)* the forehead pad must fit snugly against the forehead; *(c)* cheek pads must fit snugly against the cheeks; *(d)* chin strap must be snug on the chin and square; *(e)* the ear hole must line up with the ear canal; *(f)* the neck pad must be snug to the head; *(g)* the face mask must be three finger-widths from the nose; and *(h)* the face mask must be lower than the chin.

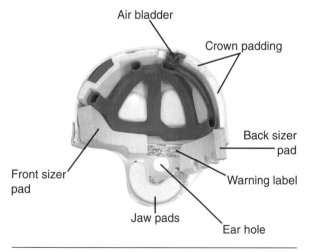

**Figure 20.1** Football helmet interior.
Photo courtesy of Schutt Sports.

significant impact. The last helmetless professional hockey player retired in 1997. Now all players in the National Hockey League wear helmets. Ice hockey helmets are also used in sports such as lacrosse and field hockey. Goalkeepers in many sports wear ice hockey helmets because they are lightweight, yet effective.

• **Batting helmets.** All batting helmets are required to have the NOCSAE inspection seal, but they need not be tested annually. Batting helmets for players from Little League through college are required to have earflaps on both sides (see figure 20.3). Professional baseball players are required to wear helmets, but earflaps are not required. However, most professionals wear a helmet with an earflap on the side

**Figure 20.3** Batting helmet and hockey helmet with full wire face mask, left to right.

closest to the pitcher when they are batting. The interior of the helmet is lined with hard foam, which distorts slightly on impact. Depending upon the type of league, there may be a requirement for a chin strap or even a face mask. Batting helmets with face masks are required for all fielders in Little League games.

## The Real World

I fit all freshmen, JV, and varsity football players' helmets for the season. As I was walking behind the quarterback on the sideline before the start of a game, I noticed a white cloth sticking out of the back of his helmet. Investigating further, I discovered that the player had stuffed a sock in place of the posterior pad. I asked him why he had altered his helmet. He replied, "I lost the other pad, and I know if the coach finds out he'll be upset and not play me." "Okay," I said, "Come here. Put your helmet on with the sock in place of the pad." I did all the usual stress tests, and the results convinced him that this was a bad idea. I took him to the helmet repair kit and found a new posterior pad. The coach never found out—it was our little secret.

Suzy Heinzman, ATC

## Face Guards

- **Football.** In football, the face mask is made either of rubber-covered metal or plastic. The face mask must be appropriate for the position the athlete will be playing. Quarterbacks and receivers wear face masks without a center bar, to help them see. Running backs and defensive backs wear face masks with center bars. Linemen, defensive ends, and linebackers wear extended masks with center bars to keep fingers away from their face and throat. Properly fitted, the face mask must be three finger-widths from the nose.

- **Hockey.** There are three types of face masks for hockey helmets: full wire, full plastic, and half plastic. The wire face mask has small, one-inch-square openings that prevent a puck or stick from entering (see figure 20.3). The full plastic face mask is clear, but sometimes the mask gets foggy during play. College-age and younger athletes are required to wear a full face mask, either wire or plastic. Referees and professional hockey players use the half mask.

- **Baseball.** A catcher wears a face mask that attaches to a protective helmet. The face mask has a padded interior surface that rests against the face, with elastic straps to hold it in place. It allows the catcher to see while protecting the face from errant balls.

You are walking behind a group of freshmen football players on the day of their first game. You notice that several of them are not wearing their hip pads.

## Other Protection for the Head and Face

• **Nose guards.** In recent years a clear face mask that is designed to protect an athlete's fractured nose has made an appearance. The nose guard fits against the face so that no pressure is applied to the nasal bones. If the athlete is hit on the nose, the pressure is borne by the areas of the face under the nose guard, rather than by the nose, and the force is dissipated. These nose guards are made of white or clear plastic. Most athletes prefer the clear plastic, because the white color is distracting and the athlete tends to notice it from the corner of his eye.

• **Mouth guards.** Mouth guards are worn to protect the teeth and the head from injury. They come in two types: custom and dip (see figure 20.4). A custom mouth guard is made by the athlete's dentist to fit her teeth. A dip mouth guard is purchased as a blank, placed in hot water for about 30 seconds, then put in the athlete's mouth to mold to her teeth. Mouth guards must fit over the molars so those teeth can be protected.

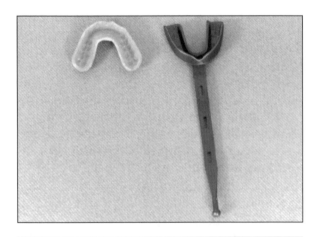

**Figure 20.4** A custom-made mouth guard and a dip mouth guard are shown from left to right.

• **Eye protection.** The Canadian Standards Association sets standards for eye guards. For example, sunglasses that are not certified by CSA may shatter—if a shard entered an athlete's eye it could cause blindness. A certified pair of sunglasses will not shatter upon impact. Athletes should not be fooled into believing that wearing any pair of glasses or sunglasses will automatically protect them from eye injuries. The glasses must be certified by the CSA.

• **Throat and neck protection.** Throat protectors are used in softball and baseball and by lacrosse and field hockey goalkeepers. The throat protector is attached to the face mask of a helmet by string, which allows the throat protectors to shift back and forth with the athlete's movement. The protectors work well as long as they are in place.

• **Neck rolls.** An athlete in ice hockey or football uses a neck roll, which is a pad that fits tightly around the neck and prevents excessive head motion. An athlete will often use a neck roll after he has suffered a neck or shoulder injury, like a burner—the neck roll restricts head movement and thus prevents stretching the nerve. Neck rolls are attached directly to shoulder pads.

• **Earplugs.** There are only two types of equipment for protection of the ear: earplugs, and helmets or headgear. Earplugs are used to prevent ear infections. They can be rubberized or wax, but wax provides better resistance because it molds itself into the curves of the ear.

• **Headgear.** Wrestlers and water polo players wear headgear that is made of a piece of aluminum covered by a quarter-inch of padding with earpieces to cover and protect the ears (see figure 20.5). The padded aluminum earpieces are held together by either cloth or straps. The straps need to be fastened tightly to hold the headgear in place.

## Protective Equipment for the Upper Body

Protective equipment for the upper body must allow the athlete to move yet absorb shock. Designers are challenged to make devices that can take impact when they are in a variety of positions. Most equipment is made of a hard

**Figure 20.5**  Wrestling headgear is designed to protect the athlete's ears.

exterior plastic shell with padding close to the body.

## Shoulder and Upper Arm Protection

Shoulder pads are the main protection for the shoulders in hockey, football, and lacrosse. All shoulder pads are designed in similar fashion— a plastic exterior with soft padding next to the skin.

Football shoulder pads are designed for the position the athlete plays (see figure 20.6). Regular shoulder pads cover the chest and shoul-

### ❓ What Would You Do If...

A lacrosse player has a laceration on the bridge of his nose. You notice blood on the inside of the front of the helmet. When you ask the athlete how the injury occurred, he says, "Some guy hit me and the helmet shifted downward." You tell him you would like to have the equipment manager look at the helmet. He says, "This happens every year. I just get stitches and that's it."

**Figure 20.6**  Football shoulder pads are designed not only to protect the shoulders but also to protect the sternum.

ders. A quarterback wears pads that are smaller and allow for more shoulder movement; a lineman's pads are larger and longer. The pads lace in the front and have straps that run from the back and lock in the front. The soft padding is covered with a sweat-resistant material.

Compared to football pads, ice hockey and lacrosse shoulder pads are made of very thin padding (see figure 20.7). They lace and have a hook-and-loop closure in the front so they are easily removed. These pads can be cleaned in a regular washing machine.

Shoulder lifts are thin (one-half inch) pieces of padding that are worn under shoulder pads. The lifts provide additional padding, and they are sometimes used after an injury. The lifts lace in the front and have underarm straps from back to front. Athletes who hit or who get hit the

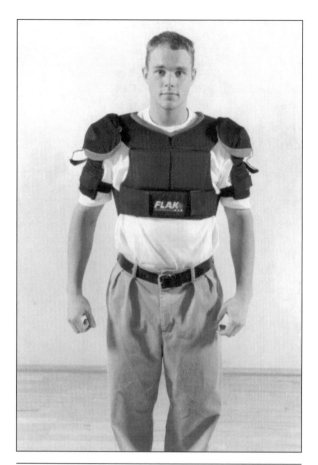

**Figure 20.7** Ice hockey pads are noticeably less bulky than football shoulder pads.

most, often wear lifts—quarterbacks, running backs, and linebackers.

A restrictive harness for the glenohumeral joint is worn when an athlete has had a dislocation or a subluxation of the shoulder joint. The harness is tightened to keep the arm from being lifted upward and abducted, since this is the position in which the shoulder is injured. The harness is made up of straps and laces, which can be adjusted to limit motion.

## Elbow, Wrist, and Hand Protection

Gloves are used by soccer and field hockey goalies, as well as by ice hockey, football, and lacrosse players. The glove style varies by sport. Soccer goalies wear a glove that has a tacky leather palm. A field hockey goalkeeper wears a leather glove that is padded on both sides for protection because he is not allowed to use a closed hand on the ball. Ice hockey goalies wear a different glove on each hand. One glove is a

large leather mitt that is strapped tightly about the hand and extends up to the middle of the forearm—it is used to catch a puck. The other hand wears a glove attached to a large pad called a blocker—it has a leather palm and a big chunk of padding over the top of the hand and fingers. A football lineman wears a fingerless glove with padding for the back of the hand, which is used during blocking. As an alternative to the glove, the lineman may wear a pad that can be pulled on over the back of the hand to protect it. Wide receivers use gloves made of neoprene—tacky and good for catching the ball—to protect the hands from cold and abrasions.

Elbow pads are worn most often by football and ice hockey players. Football players wear pull-on elbow pads—a soft pad enclosed inside elastic material. Hockey players wear pads with a plastic exterior that are fastened in place with a hook-and-loop closure. The newest hockey pads are made of thick, soft padding covered with sweat-resistant material. They are very protective. An elbow sleeve is made of either elastic or neoprene for warmth. The sleeve lacks padding so it does not offer protection from impact, but it is supportive and can prevent abrasions.

## Rib, Sternum, and Abdominal Protection

Football shoulder pads offer some chest protection but only for the upper-most ribs and the sternum. No other shoulder pads offer any chest protection. Specific equipment has been designed to protect the chest and abdomen in various sport activities. Chest protectors are actually designed to protect both the abdomen and the chest.

In field hockey, baseball, and women's lacrosse, players wear a standard chest protector that was designed specifically for baseball and softball. It is made of soft padding inside a

### ❓ What Would You Do If...

The best baseball player on your team slides into second base and "sprains" an ankle. You notice that there is not enough tape to apply a protective support. Thinking quickly, you remember that one of the benchsitters has an ankle brace.

durable cloth cover and uses elastic straps to hold it tightly against the body. Little League baseball players use a similar type of chest protector while they are batting. A word of caution—chest protectors are not safety rated. This means anyone can design a chest protector and claim that it works.

Football equipment manufacturers have designed a sternum protection pad that is not standard equipment, but which can be purchased if an athlete requires extra protection.

An ice hockey goalie wears a one-inch-thick chest protector to prevent puck impacts against his body. The protector is made of soft padding that covers the chest and abdominal areas. It is big and cumbersome and very effective in preventing injury as well as deadening the puck, something goalies like.

Athletes who have been, or are likely to be, injured and those who receive the most impacts, such as quarterbacks, running backs, and wide receivers in football, are equipped with rib protectors. Participants in impact sports such as men's lacrosse, football, and ice hockey are those most likely to be in need of such equipment.

## Low Back Protection

Back braces are designed to keep the athlete warm and to limit motion. Most of the back braces are made of neoprene or elastic and are fastened tightly in the front with a hook-and-loop closure. Back braces have small metal wires inside to provide a more stable brace.

# Protective Equipment for the Lower Body

Protection for the lower body must not hinder the athlete's movement. If you watch professional football, notice that many of the players do not wear all of the pads required by the rules. Players at the professional level are paid to play and be fast; they believe that lower body protective padding slows them down and may cost them their jobs.

## Thigh, Hip, and Tailbone Protection

Thigh pads are used in four sports: football, field hockey, women's lacrosse, and ice hockey. Thigh pads must be big enough to cover the

quadriceps musculature. They must fit properly, and the pants that cover them must be snug. Football and hockey pants are designed to hold the various pads tight against the bony areas they are designed to protect (see figure 20.8). Ice hockey pads go inside a pair of fitted shorts. These shorts hold thigh, hip, and lower

**Figure 20.8** Football pants are designed to hold a variety of pads in place to protect the thigh, iliac crest, and knee.

abdomen pads and are laced up in the front. Ice hockey pads are very effective. Field hockey and women's lacrosse goalkeepers wear ice hockey pads for protection.

Soccer goalkeepers wear shorts or long pants with hip pads in them. The padding is lightweight to allow maximum movement and provides limited protection.

Compression shorts were originally designed to hold football pads in place over the muscles, but they are now used to provide support and warmth to the muscles without padding. In baseball and softball a thin fiber pad that covers the hip is added to prevent sliding abrasions.

## Knee Protection

Repetitive bruises to the knee can limit an athlete's ability to play. Thus, knee pads were designed to cover the anterior aspect of the knee. The pads, which are made of foam and covered with an elastic material, are sewn into an elastic sleeve that is pulled on over the foot and up to the knee.

A variety of neoprene sleeves provide warmth and support, including patellar and shin sleeves, hinged sleeves, and sleeves with stays. A patellar brace has a horseshoe-shaped pad that fits around the patella to prevent it from slipping out of alignment.

A football player may wear a hinged knee brace—a metal or plastic bar with a hinge that protects the joint but allows flexion and extension of the knee. Some players, especially linemen and quarterbacks, think the brace prevents knee sprains. The braces are worn laterally, because most blows come from that side and stretch the medial ligament. Athletes claim that these braces slow them down, but the effect is insignificant. An athlete who has bowlegs or knock-knees should not wear this type of brace, because it tends to straighten the knee and cause soreness. Instead, he should have his knees taped, even though taping takes more time. Currently there is conflicting research on the effectiveness of wearing the brace, so the athlete's parents should decide if their son will use it.

## Lower Leg Protection

In some sports a shin guard and knee pad are combined into one protective pad, which is usually a hard outer plastic shell with a padded interior. A catcher in baseball or softball and an ice hockey player wear such protection. Straps hold the shin guard in place.

A catcher's shin guard has an extension that covers the ankle. In ice hockey, field hockey, and soccer the ankle is not covered, and it is vulnerable to injury from blows. For ice hockey, a special pad, which covers both malleoli and the front part of the ankle, is used only after a player has suffered a contusion of the anterior aspect of the ankle.

Field hockey and ice hockey goalkeepers wear goalie pads that cover the foot, shin, thigh, and knee. The thick padding is made of foam, cotton, and plastic and is covered with canvas or leather, with flaps around the sides of the legs and the feet. The pads are designed for protection and for deadening the ball upon impact. The pads come in different sizes based on the distance between the instep and the groin (the inseam) to insure proper fit. They are held in place with buckled straps. The goalie pads are very effective for preventing injury.

## Foot and Ankle Protection

In many sports athletes get their feet stepped on and injured. The top of the foot can swell so much that the athlete is unable to wear a shoe. The athletic trainer may have to design a special pad to protect the top of the foot when an injury occurs.

Heel cups are designed to prevent heel bruises. There are two types of cups: a rubberized padded cup and a rigid plastic cup. The rubberized cup has an elevated heel, which can compress downward so that the heel never actually makes contact with the interior of shoe. This type of heel cup is good for athletes who have been injured. A plastic heel cup fits snugly and does not allow the fat tissue to flatten, thus protecting the heel.

A heel pad is a soft cushion made of rubber, foam, or felt that is placed between the heel and the shoe. Heel pads are used to prevent bruises and to equalize an athlete's legs that are two different lengths. Unless a pad is being used to lengthen one leg, a pad should be used in each shoe.

Arch supports are soft foam, rubber, or leather pieces. The foot flattens during every step, and an arch support keeps the foot from flattening too much. Most athletic shoes have built-in arch supports. The athlete must be sure to purchase a shoe with an arch support that fits his foot.

## Ankle Braces

Ankle braces come in elastic, lace-up, and hinged versions. The elastic pull-on ankle brace provides support but only minimally—it does give the athlete an awareness of her ankle, thus possibly preventing an injury. The lace-up ankle brace is similar to a shoe without a toe. The brace is laced up tightly, especially over the ankle, to limit movement. Some lace-up braces have pockets in which to insert a plastic piece. The plastic pieces prevent inversion and eversion when they are inserted. In other lace-up braces, a figure-eight elastic strip can be pulled tight around the ankle to prevent inversion or eversion.

ATCs have become accustomed to designing special equipment to meet athletes' needs. In some cases foam and plastic pads provide needed protection, and other times taping and supportive wrapping will be the most effective. Padding and equipment are the first line of protection from impact.

## Summary

Equipment exists to protect an athlete from injury when she or he is participating in athletic activity. The athletes must be educated on the purpose and use of the equipment because, although no equipment will totally prevent injury, it can decrease the severity of injury. Properly fitted and certified equipment is essential—old or noncertified equipment should be discarded.

## Key Terms

Define the following terms found in this chapter:

CSA    NOCSAE

## Questions for Review

1. What are the basic principles of padding and equipment? p. 181
2. How does equipment vary by position on a team? pp. 182-188
3. What is the purpose of NOCSAE and CSA? p. 181
4. What types of equipment are available to prevent head and facial injuries? pp. 182-184
5. What equipment is recommended for arch pain? pp. 188-189

## Activities for Reinforcement

1. Assist the equipment manager in fitting football helmets and shoulder pads.
2. Have your ATC bring in a variety of equipment for the class to inspect.
3. Work with a team dentist who is making fitted mouth guards.
4. Try on a full set of pads and equipment for a sport you do not play. What does it feel like? What limitations does the equipment impose?
5. Ask the athletic trainer to make a list of common injuries, and design a new pad you think will prevent an injury.

## Above and Beyond

1. If you could change the rules of a game, speculate what kinds of padding and equipment might be needed or eliminated as a result.

2. Design a program to evaluate protective equipment for the head used by athletes in your school. The following materials may be used to assist in this project.

Anderson, M., and S. Hall. 1995. *Sports injury management.* Baltimore: Williams & Wilkins.

Arnheim, D.D., and W.E. Prentice. 1997. *Principles of athletic training.* 9th ed. Madison, WI: Brown and Benchmark.

Bike Athletic. 1989. *Winners wear Bike.* Knoxville, TN: Bike Athletic.

Doberstein, S.T. 1990. A procedure for fitting mouth-formed mouth guards. *Athletic Training* 25(3): 244–46.

Easterbrook, M. 1981. Eye protection for squash and racquetball. *The Physician and Sportsmedicine* 9(2): 79–82.

Kuland, D.N. 1988. *The injured athlete.* 2d ed. Philadelphia: Lippincott.

# Unit VII

# Rehabilitation and Reconditioning of Athletics-Related Injuries

# Concepts of Rehabilitation

# 21

## OBJECTIVES

Upon completing this chapter the student will be able to do the following:

- Describe the components of a SOAP note for medical documentation, and explain how it relates to the rehabilitation program.
- Identify the elements of physical function that should be included in a comprehensive therapeutic exercise program.
- Explain how to develop a therapeutic exercise program.
- Define, passive, active-assistive, and active range of motion.
- Compare muscular strength and endurance, and explain how to develop each.
- Compare and contrast therapeutic modalities, and explain the benefits of each.

ATCs understand that exercise is the most important aspect of a rehabilitation program. A logical and effective rehabilitation program, however, can only take shape after a logical and effective assessment of the problem. After assessment, the ATC needs to formulate a problem list, establish rehabilitation goals, develop a treatment plan, and continually reassess the athlete's progress.

## Assessing the Athlete and Documenting the Findings

Once an assessment is completed, a **SOAP note** will be written to document the findings. The SOAP note is a clean (no pun intended!), systematic way of documenting the assessment findings and recording an athlete's progress through a rehabilitation program. The acronym SOAP stands for **S**ubjective **O**bjective **A**ssessment and **P**lan. We discuss each of these kinds of information below, and you can see a sample SOAP note in figure 21.1.

- **Subjective.** Detailed information about the history of the injury and history of the athlete should be recorded as well as chief complaints, signs, and symptoms. This information will be referred to when the injury is followed up in the future.

# Athletic Injury/Accident Report

Athlete's name: Jane Doe          Today's date: 4-1-99          Injury date: 3-28-99
Body part injured: <u>Left ankle</u>          Sport: <u>Cross Country</u>
Was the injury due to athletic participation: _X_ Yes ___ No          Other: _____

## Subjective Information

Mechanism of injury: The athlete reports having stepped in a hole while running. She believes she turned her ankle inward. She also says she heard a popping sound.

Chief complaint: The athlete reports that her chief complaint is pain on the lateral aspect of the ankle, especially when trying to walk. She rates this pain as a 4 on a 0-10 scale with 10 being extreme pain.

Type of pain: She describes a dull pain that gets sharper when trying to put weight on her ankle.

Other: The athlete said she iced her ankle immediately and applied an elastic wrap to the area. The athlete saw her primary care physician on 3-29-99. An X ray was taken, and there are no fractures. She was told by her doctor that the injury is an ankle sprain. The physician recommended rehabilitation with the school's certified athletic trainer.

## Objective Information

Inspection (observation): A mild amount of swelling is visible on the lateral aspect of the ankle. There is also discoloration on the lateral aspect, just below the distal fibula.

Palpation: Upon palpation the athlete reported some tenderness around the distal fibula. No crepitus, warmth, or deformities were noted.

Range of motion and strength testing: Ankle range of motion is equal to that of her right ankle with plantar flexion, eversion, and inversion. Ankle dorsiflexion is limited, measuring 8 degrees of movement. Manual muscle testing was completed, and normal strength was found with plantar flexion and inversion. Eversion tested as Fair and dorsiflexion tested as Fair minus.

Neurological findings: Normal

Special stress tests: Anterior drawer test was negative for ligament laxity. Bump test was negative as well.

Functional tests: The athlete was only able to balance on her left foot for 10 seconds as compared to balancing on her right foot for 45 seconds. The athlete was able to walk slowly in a straight line but began to limp when asked to walk in a lazy S fashion. Therefore, functional testing was stopped.

## Assessment Information

Results of the assessment: The athlete's injury assessment reveals a possible grade one inversion ankle sprain with resulting weakness and swelling.

List of problems: 1) weakness of ankle musculature; 2) swelling; 3) trouble walking in functional pattern; 4) inability to balance equal to opposite leg; 5) lack of range of motion with dorsiflexion.

## Plan of Action

Initial treatment: Following the evaluation the athlete's ankle was Rested, Iced, Compressed with an elastic bandage, and Elevated for 20 minutes.

The athlete will be: ___ Referred to a physician ___ Referred to school nurse _X_ Treated by certified athletic trainer

Treatment will be _4_ days per week for _3_ week(s). Treatment will consist of: ice application, strengthening exercises, and functional activity as tolerated. The area is to be iced again after exercise program is completed. **Short term goals to be completed in 1.5 weeks:** 1) eliminate swelling; 2) attain strong dorsiflexion and eversion; 3) be able to walk lazy S and Z pattern; 4) be able to balance for 30 seconds; 5) be able to dorsiflex to 12 degrees; 6) decrease pain to a 2 rating. **Long term goals to be completed in 3 weeks:** 1) attain normal strength for all ankle movement; 2) be able to run a lazy S and Z pattern; 3) be able to balance on foot for 45 seconds; 4) have normal range of motion with dorsiflexion; and 5) have no pain.

Parents contacted: _X_ Yes ___ No. If yes give date: _4-1-99_. If no, give reason: _____

Signature of certified athletic trainer: *William A. Phiery*, MS, ATC _____

Attach all progress notes to this sheet.

**Figure 21.1** A sample SOAP note complete with problem list.

- **Objective.** The objective data are a record of test measurements. Here the ATC will state the information gained from inspection, palpation, and special tests.

- **Assessment.** In this portion of the SOAP note, the ATC will state the type and severity of the injury and list any problems associated with the injury. The statements should describe functional deficits resulting from the injury. The problems should be clearly and concisely identified. The ATC should keep in mind that the goals of treatment of the athlete are based on this list of problems.

Commonly identified problems include lack of range of motion, lack of strength, inability to perform certain functional movements, and pain with particular motions or activities. Developing a list of problems allows the ATC to determine what needs to be corrected so an athlete can return to participation as quickly and safely as possible. Once the ATC understands what needs to be corrected, a plan of action can be developed.

- **Plan of action.** Here the ATC will describe whether the athlete will be referred, treated, or monitored. Any rehabilitation procedures will be documented here, as well as the goals of the treatment.

Just as many of us have academic goals (getting an A+ in athletic training and sports medicine class) and career goals (becoming an ATC), an injured athlete must have rehabilitation goals. Therapeutic exercise goals must be both short and long term. That is, one set of activities should be those possible to achieve relatively soon, and another set should be those that will be achieved later in the program. The established goals should reflect the list of problems from the injury assessment, be objective, and

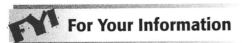

## For Your Information

### Therapeutic

The word therapeutic is used to describe something that has healing properties. In this case, a therapeutic exercise program means that the exercises themselves help heal the body.

have specific time frames. Moreover, the athlete should be involved with the goal setting, and her sport should also be considered. Certainly a competitive bowler's goals will be different from a football player's goals.

# Phases of Treatment

The extent of the injury and the phases of tissue healing should influence the selection of activities and goals to be included in the plan of action. Each program that is developed will follow a step-by-step **progression** that first attempts to control the initial response to the injury and then focuses on developing the elements of physical function. The elements of physical function (see figure 21.2) that should be addressed in a therapeutic exercise program are

1. mobility,
2. flexibility,
3. proprioception,
4. muscular strength,
5. muscular endurance,
6. muscular power,
7. cardiovascular endurance, and
8. sport-specific function.

These elements allow an athlete to be functional in her chosen sport.

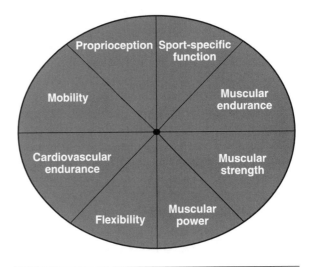

**Figure 21.2** The wheel of functional components necessary for normal physical function.

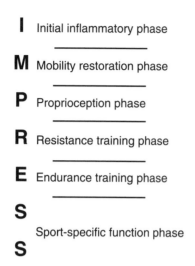

**I** Initial inflammatory phase

**M** Mobility restoration phase

**P** Proprioception phase

**R** Resistance training phase

**E** Endurance training phase

**S**
Sport-specific function phase
**S**

**Figure 21.3** IMPRESS program for organizing a rehabilitation program.

We think of the phases of treatment as the IMPRESS program (see figure 21.3): initial-injury phase (I), mobility restoration phase (M), proprioception phase (P), resistance training phase (R), endurance training phase (E), and sport-specific function phase (SS). An athlete should always try to maintain his cardiovascular endurance as much as possible during the program.

## Initial Injury Phase

In the initial phase of treatment, the ATC's primary goal is to control the amount of inflammation. Inflammation results from the body's response to an injury and is characterized by warmth, redness, swelling, and pain. Inflammation is the mechanism by which damaged tissue begins to get back to normal. While inflammation is necessary for tissue healing to occur, if the inflammation gets out of hand, chronic inflammation can result.

Controlling inflammation in the initial phase is accomplished by preventing further damage, reducing swelling, reducing pain, and reducing edema. As discussed in chapter 4, the critical treatment in this phase is PRICE. To review: the injured area must be **P**rotected, **R**ested, **I**ced, **C**ompressed, and **E**levated.

## Mobility Restoration Phase

Once inflammation is controlled—as characterized by decreased swelling, **edema** (a thick swelling caused by excessive protein), and pain, and

by improved comfort—joint mobility can be restored. This is done with therapeutic exercises that progress from passive range of motion to active-assistive range of motion to active range of motion. Once range of motion is back to normal, flexibility training can be started.

### Restoring Range of Motion

There are three phases to restoring normal range of motion:

1. **Passive.** When the ATC moves an athlete's body segment through the range of motion and the athlete simply relaxes and produces no muscle contractions, **passive range of motion** is being performed. Early pain-free passive range of motion to an injury has been shown to be beneficial for proper tissue healing. However, passive range of motion should not be done if it causes pain. In fact, most exercises should be done using pain as a guide—if the athlete complains of pain, the exercise should be stopped. Passive range of motion is most often used to keep the soft tissue structures from becoming too tight following an injury.

2. **Active-assistive.** When the ATC and the athlete move a body segment through the range of motion together, it is termed **active-assistive range of motion**. This would be done when an injured athlete is strong enough (and pain is no longer a problem) to produce a muscle contraction but not strong enough to move the joint through a full range of motion by herself. Active-assistive range of motion should also use pain as a guide.

3. **Active.** When an athlete can move a body segment through a full range of motion without any assistance, she is performing **active range of motion**. Active range of motion is necessary before strengthening of the joint can be started. Once active range of motion is established, flexibility training can begin.

### Establishing Flexibility

For an injured athlete, restoring mobility means getting his flexibility back to normal. It must be noted that range of motion and flexibility are not one and the same. **Flexibility** refers to the ability to move a joint through a full range of motion without restriction. Normal flexibility is needed for the body to function properly. In order to have normal range of motion, an athlete must have flexibility of the soft tissue structures around a joint including muscles, tendons, and skin. To develop flexibility, stretching exercises are often employed. These are covered in detail in the next chapter.

## Proprioception Phase

**Proprioception** is the body's ability to get information to the brain in response to a stimulus arising within the body; it also refers to the body's ability to sense the position of its limbs at any moment. For example, an athlete who has gone airborne and then lands on an opponent's foot may injure her ankle if her brain does not sense that she is landing on someone's shoe and not the floor. Without proper proprioception, the body may not get the right muscles to fire at the right time to protect a joint. Because an athlete may have deficient proprioception due to an injury, many ATCs believe that proprioception should be addressed in the early stages of a therapeutic exercise program, and thus many rehabilitation programs emphasize early proprioceptive training.

Proprioception training can be started early in a therapeutic exercise program by doing such things as balance or coordination exercises.

## Resistance Training Phase

Many programs exist that can be utilized to improve an athlete's strength, or ability to exert force against a resistance, following an injury.

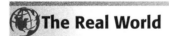

## The Real World

When I worked at a physical therapy clinic I helped to rehabilitate a patient who had just had minor knee surgery. His physician gave us orders to accelerate him through the program because the patient was getting married in three weeks and planned to snow ski in Lake Tahoe, Nevada. The athlete worked extremely hard and was very compliant. By the second week he had gained full range of motion and normal strength in his knee. His balance and proprioception continued to improve, and by the time he was ready to leave for his wedding, his knee was fully functional. It just goes to show you that when an athlete is motivated, he can accomplish anything.

Anonymous

## What Would You Do If...

You are assisting the ATC in the athletic training room, and an athlete who has been doing some extensive rehabilitation of her knee approaches you. She is disappointed that she is not allowed to return to practice because she has normal range of motion and normal strength.

When performing **resistance training**, not only will the muscles become stronger, but also other surrounding tissues such as the ligaments and bone will become stronger. Resistance training thus becomes a significant phase in the rehabilitation process. Resistance training can be done in a variety of ways including using free weights, resistive tubing, machines, and manual resistance. We will cover resistance training in detail in the next chapter.

## Endurance Phase

Besides establishing or maintaining cardiovascular endurance, muscular endurance must also be addressed. Not only do muscles need to be strong for athletic participation, they also need to have **endurance**, or the ability to perform movements over time. Cardiovascular endurance exercises should be performed as early as possible providing the injury is not aggravated. Developing muscle endurance with weight training often involves performing a high number of repetitions with a given movement and with a low amount of weight.

## Sport-Specific Function Phase

A therapeutic exercise program is not complete unless the athlete is fully prepared to meet the demands of his sport. At this phase of the therapeutic exercise program, the athlete performs functional activities and is slowly integrated back into practices. Thus, it is necessary that the ATC be fully aware of the requirements of the athlete's sport; the movement patterns involved; and the degree of strength, speed, power, and endurance needed for him to be successful.

The **sport-specific function** phase is marked by activities that mimic those the athlete will perform on the playing field or court. Athletes are required to run, jump, cut, and throw; they should generally progress from light functional exercises to heavy functional exercises and then to limited practice. Practices are often restricted, and the athlete can participate only if he has full range of motion, normal strength, normal flexibility, normal coordination, and normal cardiovascular endurance, as well as the consent of the team physician.

## Proper Progression

Although we have presented these phases of therapeutic exercises as a step-by-step process, in practice the progression is not quite so clear. Each athlete is different and progresses at a different pace. For example, some individuals may be able to begin light strengthening exercises prior to the establishment of full flexibility. The sports medicine team will work together with injured athletes to integrate them into practices prior to the establishment of full strength. Perhaps the most important thing for you to remember, as a future ATC, is to be as progressive as you can when rehabilitating an athlete, but never do anything that would cause harm.

## Therapeutic Modalities

Although the essential element of any rehabilitation program is exercise, many athletes cannot perform even minimally because their injuries become too painful or swollen. If the injured part is not used, however, the muscles may weaken and further complications may arise. To decrease pain and help with normal recovery, the ATC will use therapeutic modalities.

Therapeutic modalities include heat, cold, ultrasound, and electrical muscle stimulation. They can be categorized as (1) thermal, (2) mechanical, or (3) electrical. All therapeutic modalities must be used with extreme caution and, in many instances, only when prescribed by a physician.

### Thermal Elements

Thermal elements are those that transfer heat either into or out of body tissue. Thermal agents are used to make the tissue either colder or warmer. The indications and contraindications for thermal modalities can be found in table 21.1.

### Table 21.1 Indications and Contraindications for Thermal Modalities

| Type of modality | Indications | Contraindications |
|---|---|---|
| Heat | Chronic inflammatory conditions<br>Joint contracture<br>Tightened tissue<br>Chronic pain<br>Chronic muscle spasm | Acute injuries<br>Areas with sensory deficits<br>Areas with circulation deficits<br>Areas over tumors |
| Cold | Acute injuries<br>Pain<br>Swelling<br>In preparation for exercise<br>Muscle spasms<br>Inflammation | Cold-related allergies<br>Open wounds<br>Cardiovascular problems (heart disease)<br>Areas with circulation deficits<br>Areas with sensory deficits<br>Cold hypersensitivity<br>High blood pressure |

Data obtained from Pauls and Reed (1996), Starkey (1993), and Quillen and Underwood (1995).

## Heating Modalities

Heating modalities warm the body tissue to create a specific physiological response that helps the healing process. Heating modalities should only be used after the initial inflammatory response to injury is completed. Chronic (long-lasting) sprains and strains are common types of injuries treated with heat. Increasing the tissue temperature causes an increase in blood flow and an increase in tissue extensibility, which helps to increase range of motion, increases healing potential, and reduces swelling. Heating modalities should not be used on acute injuries, areas of poor or impaired circulation, or areas of impaired sensation.

One of the most commonly used heating modalities is a moist heat pack such as the hydrocollator pack (see figure 21.4). These canvas packs are filled with a gel that retains heat after being stored in hot water. The packs are to be placed on an athlete only after they are wrapped in several layers of towels or placed in a special premade cover, or they may cause burns.

## For Your Information

### Indications

Indications are reasons that a modality can be used on the body.

### Contraindications

Contraindications are reasons that a modality should not be used for treatment.

A warm **whirlpool** is also a common method of heating the tissue (see figure 21.5). Whirlpool application to an arm or leg can be performed for up to 20 minutes at a temperature range between 95 and 108 degrees Fahrenheit. The same contraindications apply for whirlpools as for hot packs. Furthermore, the whirlpool should not be turned on or off while the athlete is in the water, and the athlete receiving treatment should be in view at all times. He should not be placed in a whirlpool if the water turbulence irritates his injury, if he has any skin conditions or infected areas, or if he has a fever.

## Cooling Modalities

Cooling modalities cool the injured tissue, which constricts (narrows) blood vessels, decreases

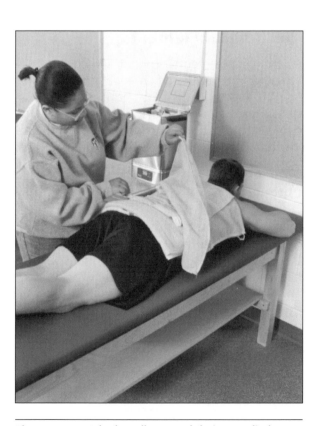

**Figure 21.4** A hydrocollator pack being applied to an athlete. Note the extra layers of towels used so the back will not get too hot.

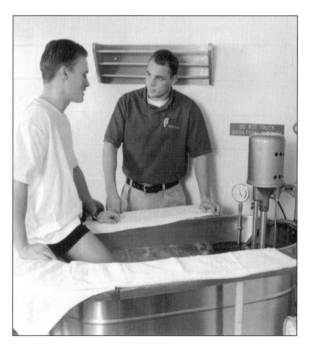

**Figure 21.5** Whirlpool application to the leg.

## ⚡ What Would You Do If...

An athlete who injured his ankle yesterday has just entered the training room. He gets a hot pack and places it on his ankle.

inflammation, decreases cell metabolism, decreases pain, and also decreases muscle spasm. Although cooling modalities are most commonly used to treat acute injures such as sprains and strains, they are also used during the rehabilitation process to decrease pain, thus allowing an injured athlete to perform exercises. **Cryotherapy** is the use of cold on the body to elicit specific physiological responses.

The most common cooling modality is the ice pack (see figure 21.6). Crushed or cubed ice in a plastic bag molds itself well around injured body

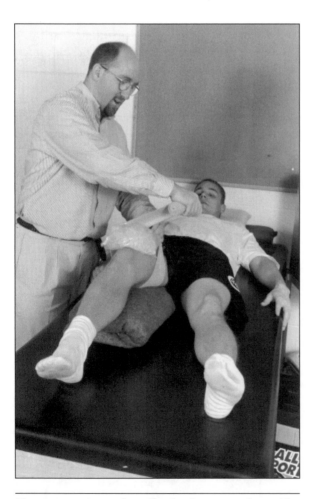

**Figure 21.6**   Ice pack application is commonly used for many athletics-related injuries.

parts and can be easily secured in place. Ice packs should not be applied too tightly with an elastic wrap, and although the risk of frostbite is low, the athlete should be checked periodically. Cold should not be applied over open wounds, to areas of numbness, to someone who is overly sensitive to cold, or to an athlete who has cardiac or respiratory problems. The ice pack is applied usually for about 20-30 minutes. When treating an acute injury, take the ice pack off after each 20-30 minute application and wait approximately 30-40 minutes before reapplying it.

Chemical cold packs are also popular because they can be stored in a freezer and reused. The ATC must be very careful, however, when utilizing chemical cold packs because they often get colder than 32 degrees Fahrenheit (0 degrees Celsius) and could cause tissue to freeze. When using such packs, he will be sure to place a barrier such as a towel between the pack and the skin surface. It is also helpful to check the skin several times during the application to make sure the athlete is not breaking out in a rash or developing blisters. Also, check to make sure the pack is not leaking—if it is, do not use it.

## Mechanical Elements

Mechanical elements produce a specific physiological effect with mechanical energy. They include ultrasound (acoustical energy), traction, massage, and intermittent compression devices. Indications and contraindications of mechanical elements can be found in table 21.2.

### Ultrasound

**Ultrasound** may be categorized as a thermal modality because it can produce a deep-heating effect, but it can also cause nonthermal reactions in the tissue. As sound waves pass through the tissue, heat is produced through a process known as conversion. If the sound waves are sporadic or intermittent, heat may not be produced. Ultrasound waves are extremely high frequency and cannot be heard by the human ear. Figure 21.7 shows ultrasound application.

Common ultrasound frequencies used in treating athletic injuries include the 1 megahertz (MHz) and the 3 MHz. These are much higher frequencies than we can produce with our voices. The frequency determines the depth of penetration of sound waves into the tissue, not the amount of intensity used on the machine. The

## Table 21.2  Indications and Contraindications for Mechanical Modalities

| Type of modality | Indications | Contraindications |
|---|---|---|
| Ultrasound | Inflammation<br>Acute injuries (nonthermal application)<br>Chronic injuries<br>Muscle strains<br>Ligament sprains<br>Bruises<br>Tightened soft tissue | Areas with circulation deficits<br>Areas with sensory deficits<br>Over tumors<br>Over growth plates in children<br>Over heart, eyes, nerve plexus<br>Acute injuries with continuous setting |
| Traction | Spinal disk protrusion<br>Degenerative disk disease<br>Degenerative joint disease<br>Soft tissue stiffness<br>Nerve root compression<br>Muscle spasm | Infection of the spine<br>Osteoporosis<br>Malignant tumors<br>Acute injuries<br>Pregnancy<br>Rheumatoid arthritis<br>Fractured vertebra<br>Spinal hypermobility |
| Massage | Promotion of relaxation<br>Muscle spasm<br>Pain<br>Soft tissue stiffness<br>When increased circulation is needed | Nonunion fracture sites<br>Over open wounds<br>Over dermatological conditions<br>Acute injuries<br>Over tumors |
| Intermittent compression | Postacute edema<br>Lymphedema | Acute injuries<br>When a fracture has not been ruled out<br>Peripheral vascular disorders<br>Compartment syndromes |

Because machines vary, manufacturer's guidelines should always be followed.
Data obtained from Pauls and Reed (1996), Starkey (1993), and Quillen and Underwood (1995).

1 MHz frequency penetrates deeper than the 3 MHz. Therefore, the 3 MHz may be better suited for injuries that are closer to the surface of the skin.

The effects of heating the tissue with ultrasound are the same as for a hot pack application. Ultrasound, however, has the capability of affecting deeper tissue than does a hot pack. In fact, it can penetrate up to 5 centimeters of tissue. In order to have the ultrasound create

heat, the machine must be set for a continuous emission—that is, sound waves need to be flowing 100 percent of the time. A pulsed setting interrupts the flow of sound waves and reduces the thermal effects.

When applying continuous ultrasound, the ATC must move the sound head slowly and continually. When pulsed ultrasound is applied, the sound head can be kept still. In either case, ultrasound must be applied using a coupling

**Figure 21.8** Indirect ultrasound application. Ultrasound can be applied under water. This is especially helpful when the body area being treated is bumpy and the sound head will not stay flat against the tissue.

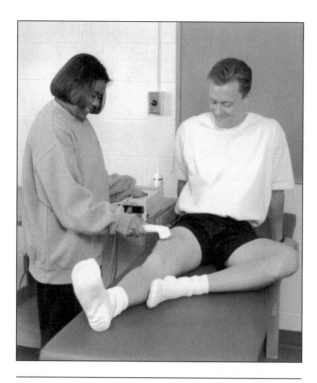

**Figure 21.7** An ultrasound treatment provides benefits, but it must be used carefully or it can damage tissue.

medium such as water or gel. When the sound head is applied on the body part through the coupling medium, direct ultrasound is being applied. Direct application should be used only if the area is smooth. Irregularly shaped areas such as the hand, ankle, and elbow may need to have ultrasound applied indirectly (see figure 21.8). Indirect ultrasound is usually applied underwater in a plastic tub. When applying ultrasound underwater, the sound head must be fully immersed, and it must be kept about 1/2–1 inch away from the tissue, but the ultrasound intensity must be increased. There are many contraindications for the use of ultrasound. Therefore, it should be used with caution when prescribed by a physician. Refer to table 21.2.

### Traction

**Traction** is a pulling force—here it refers to deliberately attempting to separate the joints of the body if they have been compressed together or if they have gotten stiff over a period of time. It is most commonly done to the vertebrae. Traction can be performed to both the cervical and lumbar spine and can be done either mechanically (with a machine) or manually (by the ATC). For example, if an ATC were given permis-

sion by a physician to perform cervical spine traction on an athlete, he would have the athlete lie on her back and he would place one hand under the back of her head, the other under her chin. The ATC would then gently pull on the neck to gradually separate the vertebrae. Such a technique would only be performed with extreme caution and only with a physician's permission.

Not only does traction separate bones that have been pushed too close together, it also causes minimal stretching of the ligaments and muscles in the area. It may also help the resolution of a disk protrusion, which we discussed earlier in chapter 11. It is thought that separating the vertebrae creates a suction force that can cause the protruded disk matter to move toward the center of the disk where it belongs. Additionally, separating the vertebrae opens up the space where the nerve roots exit the spinal cord (figure 21.9). By increasing this space, pressure can be removed from the nerve root, helping to decrease pain and facilitate healing.

As a precaution, patients should be monitored during their first treatment to assure that no complications arise, such as increased pain, discomfort, muscle spasm, numbness, or tingling. Also, it is important to perform traction in a quiet area where the patients can relax. The indications and contraindications for cervical and lumbar traction are summarized in table 21.2. A physician should check the athlete be-

**Intervertebral disk without traction**

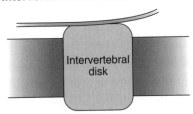

**Intervertebral disk with traction. Note how the nerve root is no longer touched by the disk.**

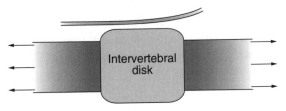

**Figure 21.9** The effects of spinal traction. Traction pulls the joints apart and is helpful for relieving pressure on nerve roots at the spinal cord. Traction must always be used cautiously and only if all contraindications have been ruled out.

fore he receives traction and again before he returns to participation.

### Massage

Another modality we have chosen to include in the mechanical elements is massage. **Massage** is the intentional and methodical kneading and stroking of the body's soft tissues. It is used to increase circulation, decrease muscle spasm, and relieve swelling. If the goal is to decrease swelling, however, you must be certain that the massage strokes move from below the injury site toward the heart. Several different types of massage strokes are effleurage, petrissage, vibration, percussion, and friction.

**Effleurage** consists of stroking the tissue with the palm of your hand in a smooth, rhythmical manner (see figure 21.10a). Effleurage is often

 **For Your Information**

### Nerve Root Impingement

A spinal nerve root impingement means that something, part of a disk or swelling for example, is putting pressure on the nerve where it exits the spinal cord.

done at the beginning and end of a massage session.

**Petrissage** is often described as a kneading of the tissue, in which the skin, muscle, and fascia are squeezed between the hands (see figure 21.10b).

A **vibration massage** is designed to cause the tissue to tremble or shake vigorously. Many ATCs choose to use a mechanical vibrator to achieve these effects. The vibration technique is usually done at joints to help improve mobility.

The **percussion massage,** or tapotement, uses a series of light chopping motions to the tissue. The ATC's hands should be relaxed while this stroke is performed. Physiological effects created by the percussion stroke include increased circulation and relaxation (see figure 21.10c).

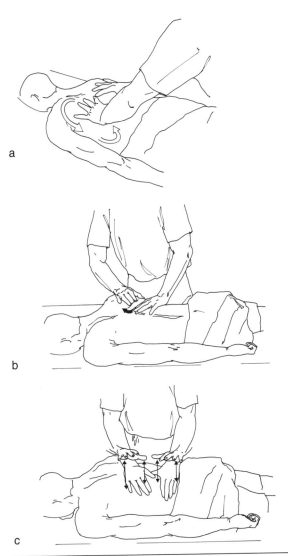

**Figure 21.10** Massage strokes. *(a)* Effleurage, *(b)* petrissage, and *(c)* percussion/tapotement massage strokes.

**Friction massage** requires enough pressure to affect the deep tissues. The deep penetration and pressure and movement of the finger, thumb, or elbow into the tissue have many benefits. For example, friction massage helps to break up scar tissue and relieve muscle spasms—it is an excellent procedure for individuals who have a thick scar from a deep cut. The indications and contraindications are summarized in table 21.2.

### Intermittent Compression

Like an elastic wrap, intermittent compression is useful for reducing swelling and edema following an injury (see figure 21.11). An **intermittent compression** device increases the pressure around the injury site and helps venous blood return from the injured extremity, which reduces the total amount of swelling.

Although this device is extremely useful for acute injuries, it should not be used until a fracture has been ruled out, nor should it be used on compartment syndromes of the lower extremity.

Treatment time varies from 20 minutes to an hour. The pressure selected should not exceed the athlete's diastolic blood pressure, and it should be comfortable. Therefore, the athlete's blood pressure must be taken before the treatment, and his comfort and tolerance of the device should be initially and periodically

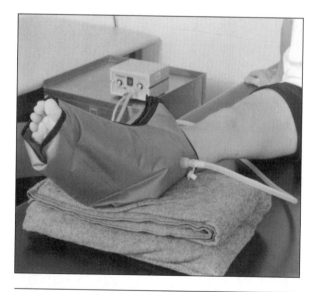

**Figure 21.11** Intermittent compression, combined with elevation, is helpful for removing swelling from an injured joint.

### For Your Information

**Diastolic Blood Pressure**
The diastolic blood pressure is the pressure in an artery while the heart is relaxed. It is the bottom number of a blood pressure reading.

---

checked. Generally, the treatment consists of alternating compression for 45 seconds with 15 seconds off. A stocking is usually used to cover the skin prior to application to reduce the chance of skin irritation.

## Electrical Elements

It may come as a shock to learn that electricity can be therapeutic. Many useful physiological changes occur when electricity is *safely* passed through tissue. Understanding these changes requires that we have a basic understanding of electricity. Again, we must warn of the dangers that can exist with the use of electrical modalities (see table 21.3). Such modalities should be used only by trained individuals and only after they are prescribed by a physician.

**Transcutaneous electrical stimulation** refers to the application of electrical current to the surface of the skin (see figure 21.12). There are several types of transcutaneous electrical stimulation including high-voltage electrical muscle stimulation, low-voltage electrical muscle stimulation, and transcutaneous electrical nerve stimulation. Passing electrical current over the body can create several different physiological effects, depending upon the type of current, the intensity, and the duration of the current. For example, high-voltage, pulsed, direct stimulation can cause a muscle contraction, which helps prevent a muscle from weakening when recovering from an injury. The muscle contractions can create a pumping action and help to get rid of unwanted swelling and edema. When electrical current is applied to the body at an intensity that can be felt but is insufficient to cause a muscle contraction, it is often helpful for reducing pain.

The majority of treatments to help reduce pain, however, use transcutaneous electrical

## Table 21.3  Indications and Contraindications for Electrical Modalities

| Indications | Contraindications |
| --- | --- |
| Pain | During pregnancy |
| Edema | When there is an unknown cause of pain |
| Prevent muscle weakness | Over infected sites |
| Reduce muscle spasm | Over heart, eyes, carotid sinus, upper airway, open wounds, or tumors |
| Reeducate muscle function | Pacemakers |
| Increase local circulation | Over some fracture sites |

Because machines vary, manufacturer's guidelines should always be followed.
Data obtained from Pauls and Reed (1996), Starkey (1993), and Quillen and Underwood (1995).

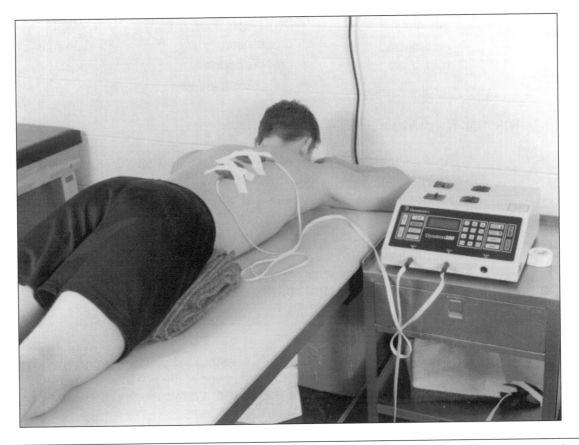

**Figure 21.12**  Electrical muscle stimulation is helpful for reducing spasm and pain and can also help prevent weakness.

nerve stimulation or TENS. Transcutaneous electrical stimulation is also used to reduce muscle spasms, to reeducate muscles that have not been capable of contracting on their own, and to increase blood flow. When the muscle is stimu-lated to contract, it does so without any help from the athlete, who just lies there on the table. While this sounds like a terrific thing, it will not make a person physically fit or help them lose weight.

## Summary

A SOAP note is used to document the findings of an injury assessment as well as to structure a plan of action for a rehabilitation program. In rehabilitation, we try to help an athlete regain normal function by regaining mobility, proprioception, strength, endurance, and sport-specific function. To aid the recovery process, ATCs will use therapeutic modalities such as heat, cold, ultrasound, electricity, and massage on the injury.

## Key Terms

Define the following terms found in this chapter:

| | | |
|---|---|---|
| active range of motion | intermittent compression | SOAP note |
| active-assistive range of motion | massage | sport-specific function |
| cryotherapy | passive range of motion (PROM) | traction |
| edema | percussion massage | transcutaneous electrical stimulation |
| effleurage | petrissage | ultrasound |
| endurance | progression | vibration massage |
| flexibility | proprioception | whirlpool |
| friction massage | resistance training | |

## Questions for Review

1. What are the elements of physical function that should be redeveloped during rehabilitation of an injured athlete? p. 195
2. When should an ATC use heat and when should she use cold? Is one more effective than the other? pp. 198-200
3. What are some of the physiological effects of ultrasound? When should it not be used? pp. 200-202
4. What are the components of a SOAP note and how are they helpful for designing a rehabilitation program? pp. 193-195

## Activities for Reinforcement

1. Have your instructor create injury scenarios for you and a partner. Take turns pretending to have an injury covered in one of the previous chapters while your partner fills out a SOAP note and develops a hypothetical therapeutic exercise program to get you back to playing a sport.
2. With a partner, select each of the modalities discussed in this chapter and think of the types of injuries in which the modality could be used by an ATC.
3. Invite an ATC to class to discuss the rehabilitation process.
4. Take a class field trip to a rehabilitation center.

## Above and Beyond

There are many texts and journals dedicated to rehabilitation. We have listed some below, or you can find different sources on your own.

Goldstein, T.S. 1995. *Functional rehabilitation in orthopaedics*. Gaithersburg, MD: Aspen.

Hopkins, T.J., and A.A. White. 1993. Rehabilitation of athletes following spine injury. *Clinical Sports Medicine* 12(3): 603–19.

Lephart, S.M., D.M. Pincivero, J.L. Giraldo, and F.H. Fu. 1997. The role of proprioception in the management and rehabilitation of athletic injuries. *The American Journal of Sports Medicine* 25(1): 130–37.

Prentice, W.E., ed. 1994. *Rehabilitation techniques in sports medicine*. 2d ed. St. Louis: Mosby.

# Reconditioning Programs

## OBJECTIVES

Upon completing this chapter the student will be able to do the following:
- Explain the principles of strength training.
- Identify the various ways to develop strength.
- Compare muscular strength and endurance and explain how to develop each.
- Discuss the principles behind developing cardiovascular fitness.
- Identify appropriate exercises for rehabilitating specific conditions of the upper quarter, lower quarter, and trunk region.

Reconditioning an athlete during rehabilitation is the same as conditioning in the sense that both programs utilize the same principles. The primary goal of reconditioning is to help the athlete get back to the preinjury level of fitness.

## Strength and Conditioning Principles

Injured athletes must get fit in order to successfully return to participation. Therefore, their physical conditioning must be addressed. As discussed with the IMPRESS program, this includes strength, muscular endurance, cardiovascular endurance, and flexibility. Primary principles for strength and conditioning include progressive resistive exercise, overload, and specificity.

### Progressive Resistive Exercise

When the goal is to develop an athlete's strength, **progressive resistive exercise (PRE)** is common—progressively increasing the load (i.e., weight or number of repetitions) both during the training session and over a period of time. By advancing the resistance training appropriately, further injury can be avoided and the body can adapt to the demands of the activity.

## Overload Principle

The **overload principle** means that for a muscle to gain strength or endurance it must be stressed beyond the demands of previous activity. For example, if an athlete bench-presses 50 pounds for 10 repetitions every other day for three weeks, she may not significantly improve her strength because she is not overloading the muscle. However, if she lifted 50 pounds for 10 repetitions one day and then lifted 55 pounds two days later, she probably stressed her muscles beyond the demands of the previous bench press.

Weight, however, is not the only factor we can increase. In fact, there are many variables that can be adjusted to provide an overload to the muscle—the frequency of the workouts, the intensity of the exercise, the length of the workout, and the type of exercise performed. The variable changed by the coach or ATC will depend upon the goal of the exercise. For example, if the athlete requires cardiovascular endurance for biking, the amount of time she spends biking during the workouts should be increased. If the goal is to develop muscular endurance, she will need to lift a lower amount of weight with a higher number of repetitions; if the goal is to develop strength, then she should use a higher amount of weight and fewer repetitions.

## Specificity of Training

**Specificity** means that the body systems will adapt to the specific demands placed upon them. For example, if an athlete wanted to become a better runner, his training should consist mostly of running. But if he wants to become a better hockey player, his training should consist mostly of hockey and ice skating activities. When an athlete does nothing more than lift weights, it is doubtful that his body will improve its cardiovascular function; likewise, if he only rides a bike, his upper body will probably not become stronger.

In the context of strength training, a muscle will get used to the specific activities required of it. Take the athlete who bench-presses 50 pounds for 10 repetitions every other day for four weeks.

While lifting this amount of weight for the first few days may have seemed difficult, she will find that it becomes easy by the fourth week. The muscle adapted to the specific exercise (bench press) and the demands placed upon it (50 pounds for 10 repetitions).

## Types of Movements

Muscles function in various ways. At times the muscles must contract simply to hold a joint still and not allow it to move. At other times, the muscle must contract to move a limb through a whole motion such as when a softball player throws a ball. There are three different types of muscle contractions: isotonic, isometric, and isokinetic. Regardless of which type of exercise an athlete performs, her goal is to overload her muscles to produce strength gains.

### Isotonics

**Isotonic contractions** occur when moving a joint through a range of motion with a fixed amount of resistance. Performing an exercise with a free weight is a perfect example. Isotonic resistance training involves movement at the joint, and the muscles shorten and lengthen against resistance. When a muscle shortens against resistance, it is termed a concentric contraction; when a muscle lengthens against resistance, it is termed an eccentric contraction. Adolescent athletes should refrain from doing only eccentric weight training as this places a great deal of stress on the muscles and tendons.

### Isometrics

When an **isometric contraction** is performed, there is no joint movement. Picture yourself pushing against a brick wall. While the muscles in your arms and chest contract, there is no joint motion produced. Because there is no motion at the joint, it is less likely to become irritated or cause pain. Therefore, isometrics are extremely useful in the early stages after an injury to prevent future weakness.

### Isokinetics

When an **isokinetic contraction** is performed, speed of movement is controlled. Isokinetics are typically performed using sophisticated

You are asked by the ATC to give a message to an athlete who should be working out at the weight room. When you enter the weight room, you notice that the athlete is alone, performing a bench press with a weight bar that has about 200 pounds on it.

equipment that controls the speed at which an athlete will work—no matter how much force he exerts against the machine, he will only make it move at a predetermined speed. (See the photo of an isokinetic machine in chapter 28, figure 28.2, page 276.) It is a lot like trying to pull a canoe paddle through the water—you can pull easy or hard, but its speed does not change.

# Muscular Development Programs

Although many resistance training programs exist, the premise of each is the same. The purpose of the program will be to overload the muscles in a specific manner using either isotonic, isokinetic, or isometric movements. However, most muscular development train-

ing programs use isotonic movements and free weights.

## Muscular Strength

**Muscular strength** is the ability to exert force against a resistance. Developing strength often leads to also developing muscular endurance and power. Generally, an athlete develops strength by using a heavy weight for a lower number of repetitions. To accomplish this, the athlete may find it helpful to use a constant set method; that is, using the same amount of weight for the same number of sets and repetitions, for example, 40 pounds performed in four sets of four repetitions.

The **pyramid method** uses multiple sets (three or more and sometimes up to five or six sets) in which the weight is increased or decreased with each set (see figure 22.1). The athlete may use an ascending pyramid method when she wants to build up to lifting the higher amount of weight with less chance of hurting herself. It is thought that using a descending pyramid technique works the muscle against a higher amount of weight earlier, when it is not as fatigued. Performing multiple sets, for example by doing both sides of a pyramid, often is thought to facilitate maximum strength gains. Provided that

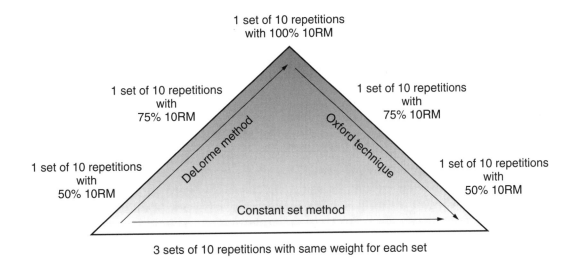

**Figure 22.1** Training programs. Pyramid training often involves the use of about five sets of a given exercise. When an athlete ascends the pyramid (increases the weight per set), he is using the DeLorme method. When an athlete descends the pyramid (decreases the weight per set), he is using the Oxford technique. If he follows the bottom of the pyramid (maintains the same weight per set), he is using the constant set method.

the muscle is overloaded, however, strength gains can be made regardless of the type of program the athlete follows.

The **DeLorme method** of progressive resistive exercise is an example of an ascending pyramid method. It requires that the athlete perform three sets in a progressive manner. Let's say that the maximum an athlete can military press for 10 repetitions is 200 pounds. In the DeLorme method, the 200 pounds is called the 10 repetition maximum weight, or 10RM, and the athlete does three sets of 10 repetitions at 50, 75, and 100 percent of 10RM. Thus, the athlete would perform the first set of 10 repetitions at 50 percent of 10RM or 100 pounds. This would be considered a warm-up. He would perform the second set at 150 pounds (75 percent of 10RM) for 10 repetitions. The third set would be performed at the maximum weight of 200 pounds, which is 100 percent of 10RM. DeLorme's program of three sets of 10 repetitions continues to be a very popular method of strength training today.

Another common method of training is sometimes referred to as the nautilus method of weight training—a person performs one set of an exercise to fatigue, or until she can no longer perform the exercise.

## Muscular Endurance

The ability of a muscle to perform repetitive movements for an extended period of time is referred to as **muscular endurance**. Activities that require a significant amount of muscular endurance include cross-country running, cross-country skiing, and many swimming events. An athlete can develop muscular endurance using the programs for building strength. However, using a lower amount of weight and performing a higher number of repetitions develops muscular endurance more efficiently.

Circuit training is a popular and effective method of developing muscular endurance as well as overall fitness. **Circuit training** is exercising at multiple stations (usually 8–20) that often target a full body workout (exercises to work all major muscle groups are selected). The athlete rotates from station to station either performing a given number of repetitions or exercising for a given period of time (30 seconds) at each station. It is wise to select stations that will target alternate body parts so the same muscles are not used at consecutive stations.

## Power

**Muscular power** refers to the ability to exert force quickly. Many programs that focus on developing power do so by using very heavy weights and a low number of repetitions—the movements, however, are performed quickly.

# Joint Flexibility

Stretching is performed to lengthen tissue that has been shortened due to lack of use, such as when an athlete is immobilized in a cast. Stretching should be performed if range of motion is limited because of soft tissue tightness around a joint. A stretch should not produce pain, and it should be comfortable for the athlete. Stretching should be done before and after heavy athletic activity, but it is necessary to perform a light warm-up (aerobic activity) before stretching—stretching a cold muscle might lead to injury.

There are two types of stretches. The first is **static stretching**—the muscle is isolated, stretched, and held in the stretch for approximately 30 seconds. The second is **ballistic stretching**. Ballistic stretching is when a specific muscle is isolated and quickly stretched and relaxed repetitively, as though the athlete is bouncing. This form of stretching is not recommended because it can often aggravate an existing injury or cause a different injury. Static stretching is the way to develop flexibility; it should be done three times in each exercise session, addressing each muscle.

# Exercises for Reconditioning Muscles

Because there are so many different exercises for various types of injuries, the ATC and the athlete need to decide which exercises to perform. While it is beyond the scope of this text to provide a comprehensive list of exercises, we will provide some information about basic exercises for reconditioning athletes following an injury and helping them develop general strength and mobility.

# Reconditioning Techniques for the Lower Quarter

When rehabilitating the lower quarter—besides improving strength—establishing proprioception is a major concern. Balancing activities such as working on wobble boards and stork standing are excellent exercises for regaining proprioception, even if the athlete can tolerate only partial weight bearing (see figure 22.2a). These exercises will address the entire lower quarter.

## The Foot, Ankle, and Lower Leg

Rehabilitation procedures of the foot, ankle, and lower leg, at the basic level, involve reestablishing flexibility and strength with active range of motion activities such as calf stretches (see figure 22.2b) spelling the ABC's with the foot while it is hanging off the end of a table. Strength in the area can be regained by using elastic bands while resistance is applied as the athlete inverts, everts, plantar flexes, and dorsiflexes his foot (see figure 22.2, c-f). If another person is not available, the bands can be made into loops and securely fastened around hooks mounted on the floor, wall, table leg, or the edge of the table. Exercises such as these are excellent for many ankle sprains and strains.

## The Knee, Hip, and Pelvis

To improve flexibility of the muscular structures around the knee, the athlete should perform static stretching of the involved muscle groups, specifically the quadriceps, groin, or hamstrings (see figure 22.3, a-c). These stretching exercises are especially helpful for improving decreased range of motion. Strengthening of the knee and hip musculature can be done initially by using the weight of the limb itself with straight leg raises and progressing to using resistive exercise tubing (see figure 22.3, d-g). Isotonic exercises with a knee/thigh machine

a       b       c

d       e       f

**Figure 22.2** *(a)* Balance activities and wobble boards are helpful for regaining normal proprioception. *(b)* Calf stretches. Ankle strength can be improved using resistive tubing while the athlete moves the ankle into *(c)* inversion, *(d)* eversion, *(e)* plantar flexion, and *(f)* dorsiflexion.

**Figure 22.3**   *(a)* Quadriceps, *(b)* groin, and *(c)* hamstring stretches. Straight leg raises, *(d-e)* performed while lying down and *(f-g)* against resistive tubing while standing, are helpful for regaining hip and knee strength. *(h-i)* In the later stages of rehabilitation, isotonic movement can be done with weight machines to develop quadriceps and hamstring strength. *(j, k)* Forward lunges and wall squats are a great functional way of strengthening the lower quarter.

can be done, as well as forward lunges and squats (see figure 22.3, h-k).

Beginning with straight leg raises helps to develop good basic strength for athletes who are weak. As soon as possible, however, the athlete should perform strengthening exercises

in a standing position (for example, with resistive tubing). As previously mentioned, to develop proprioception, a graded program of balancing can be performed. This may begin with a timed stork stand and progress to wobble board activity. An athlete can achieve knee and hip musculature endurance by swimming, biking, or running, provided these activities do not aggravate the injury. The ATC should always observe the athlete to make sure she is not favoring the knee during activity. Getting the athlete back into sport activity is done by having her do simple sport-specific change-of-direction exercises at a slow running speed and gradually increasing the speed of activity. For example, the athlete can run in a figure-eight pattern, between cones, or on the out-of-bounds lines on a basketball court. She will perform the exercises at slower speeds initially with less cutting and then progress to higher speeds and more cutting.

## Reconditioning Techniques for the Axial Region

Rehabilitation procedures of the spine must be done with extreme caution. In fact, people supporting a conservative approach to treating the spine argue that the athlete should progress only at a slow pace. The ATC must perform a thorough assessment before rehabilitation begins and reassess during the rehabilitation process. The athlete must be taught normal posture and how to treat his back before he can achieve a proper recovery. If he is rehabilitating the lumbar spine, the ATC will be concerned with reestablishing a balance between mobility, flexibility, and lumbar strength. Muscular endurance, cardiovascular endurance, and sport-specific function are also concerns. Flexibility of the muscular structures around the spine involves either flexion or extension movements, depending on the problem at hand. However, a good general flexibility exercise for athletes seeking to improve trunk flexibility is shown in figure 22.4a.

### Flexion Movements

Flexion movements of the spine are useful for athletes who have lordosis or muscle strains of the back extensor musculature. Flexion movements for regaining flexibility include simple single and double knee-to-chest exercises (see figure 22.4, b-c). If an athlete has a disk bulge of the lumbar spine, this type of movement should not be performed.

### Extension Movements

Extension movements of the spine are useful for athletes who have too little curvature in the lumbar spine or those who have disk bulges.

**Figure 22.4** *(a)* Trunk rotation stretch

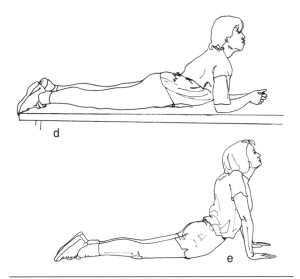

**Figure 22.4** *(b)* Single and *(c)* double knee-to-chest flexion exercises are helpful for stretching the lumbar region.

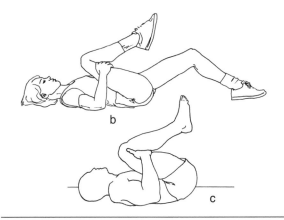

**Figure 22.4** *(d-e)* Extension movements of the spine are helpful exercises for disk bulges.

Extension movements for regaining flexibility and function include having the athlete lie on the stomach and push into trunk extension, first to the elbows and then progressing to using the hands for support (see figure 22.4, d-e).

### Lumbar Strength

To regain strength of the lumbar spine the athlete gets into a neutral spine position and then moves the extremities while this position is maintained. These lumbar strengthening exercises can be performed while the athlete is lying on the floor on the stomach or back, on hands and knees, lying on an exercise ball on the stomach or back, and even in a standing position (figure 22.4, f-g). Great care must be taken to begin with simple movements and progress to harder ones. The ATC must also constantly help the athlete maintain a neutral spine by giving him helpful feedback during activity. Remember too that abdominal strength is vital for a strong back. A simple abdominal curl can be used (figure 22.4h). The lat pull-down is a must in any conditioning program and an excellent exercise to help develop back strength (figure 22.4i).

### Cervical Region

Neck stretches will restore the mobility of the cervical region. The athlete can do a neck stretch as pictured in figure 22.5a. In a seated position, the athlete grabs her left wrist and pulls it to the outside of her right thigh while bending her head to the right; she grabs her right wrist and pulls it to the outside of left thigh while bending her head to the left. Simple neck range of motion activities can also be performed. To strengthen the neck, resistive tubing can be attached to the head and cervical movements can be resisted (see figure 22.5, b-c). We stress that any cervical stretching and exercise must be performed gently and gradually, otherwise further injury can result. Shoulder shrug exercises are also helpful to strengthen the trapezius muscle (see figure 22.5d).

## Reconditioning Techniques for the Upper Quarter

As with the lower quarter, when rehabilitating the upper quarter, getting the region stronger and reestablishing proprioception are major concerns. Balancing activities, such as using a ball for wall push-ups, help to reestablish proprioception of this area (see figure 22.6a).

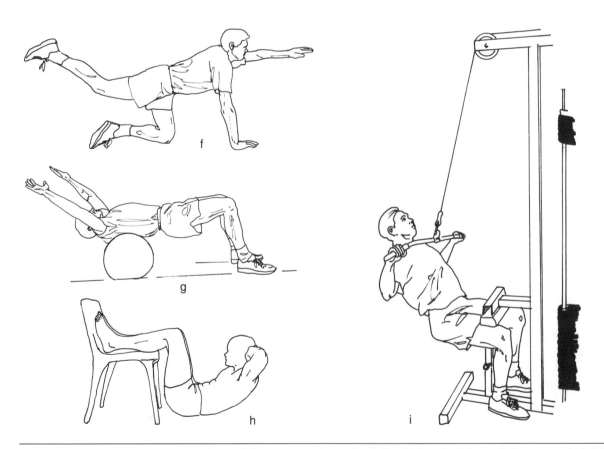

**Figure 22.4 (continued)** (f-g) Lumbar stabilization exercises, (h) abdominal curl, (i) lat pull-downs are helpful for general back strengthening.

**Figure 22.5**  *(a)* Lateral neck stretches; *(b-c)* resisted cervical movements with rubber tubing; *(d)* shoulder shrugs are helpful for strengthening the trapezius muscle.

### The Shoulder

Basic rehabilitation procedures of the shoulder involve reestablishing flexibility and strength. In order to accomplish this, active range of motion activities such as moving the arm into flexion, extension, abduction, and adduction can be performed, as well as stretches that will improve flexibility of the anterior and posterior aspects of the region (see figure 22.6, b-c). The athlete can learn wand exercises and wall walking with the fingers, which she can perform on her own. By gripping the wand with both hands as she performs the wand exercises, the injured shoulder is helped along by the good shoulder; as her fingers walk up the wall, they pull the arm up to work the injured shoulder. These exercises are helpful for athletes who need to work at home, but they will need some instructions about how to do so effectively (see figure 22.7, a-b and figure 22.8, a-b). Pendulum exercises

can also help improve mobility (see figure 22.9, a-b).

The athlete can regain strength of the area by moving the joint through the major motions while resistance is applied by using either free weights or elastic bands (see figure 22.10, a-b). Special attention should be given to the rotator cuff muscles. Internal and external rotation movements, as shown in figure 22.10, c-d, are especially helpful when recovering from rotator cuff injuries or impingement syndromes.

In the later stages of strengthening, bench press and military press may be performed with either dumbbells or with weights on a straight bar (see figure 22.10, e-f). These are excellent exercises to develop general shoulder strength and should be included in general conditioning programs. A spotter is necessary for each exercise at all times, regardless of the type of free weight equipment used.

**Figure 22.6** *(a)* Doing wall push-ups with a ball can help the athlete regain upper extremity proprioception. *(b)* Anterior and *(c)* posterior shoulder stretches.

**Figure 22.7** *(a-b)* Wand exercises are good exercises to have an athlete do on her own to help regain shoulder mobility.

**Figure 22.8** *(a-b)* Wall walking is another good exercise to have an athlete perform when the goal is to gain range of motion.

**Figure 22.9** *(a-b)* Pendulum exercises can be used soon after an injury to help restore mobility.

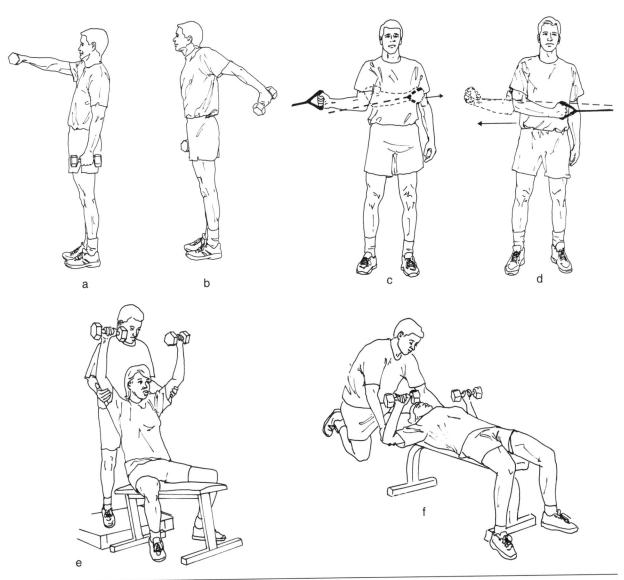

**Figure 22.10** Shoulder *(a)* flexion and *(b)* extension against resistance. *(c-d)* It is important to strengthen the internal and external rotators of the shoulder. *(e)* Military press and *(f)* bench press with free weights.

### The Elbow, Wrist, and Hand

At the basic level, the ATC is concerned with reestablishing elbow and wrist mobility, flexibility, and strength. Flexibility of the muscular structures around the elbow and wrist involves static stretching of the involved muscle groups (see figure 22.11a), specifically the extensor and flexor muscles. Strengthening of the elbow and wrist musculature can be done using handheld weights (see figure 22.11, b-d). To help the athlete bear weight on the limb, wall push-ups can be performed (see figure 22.11e). These are even helpful for some shoulder injuries. The biceps and triceps must not be neglected. They can be strengthened by performing triceps pull-downs and biceps curls (see figure 22.12, a-b) Hand injuries may also require that an athlete attempt to improve her grip strength by squeezing a racquetball or tennis ball, or she can squeeze hand clay between her fingers (see figure 22.12c). Elbow and wrist muscular endurance can be achieved by using a high number of repetitions while lifting weights, or by swimming, biking, or running, provided the injury is not aggravated. The ATC should always observe the athlete to make sure that she is not aggravating the elbow or wrist injury during activity. She can get back into sport activity by throwing, beginning with short distances and slow speeds and progressing to longer distances at higher speeds.

## Cardiovascular Conditioning

Just as proper resistance training taxes and overloads the musculoskeletal system and makes it stronger, properly administered aerobic training can enhance an athlete's **cardiovascular endurance** in preparation for returning to play.

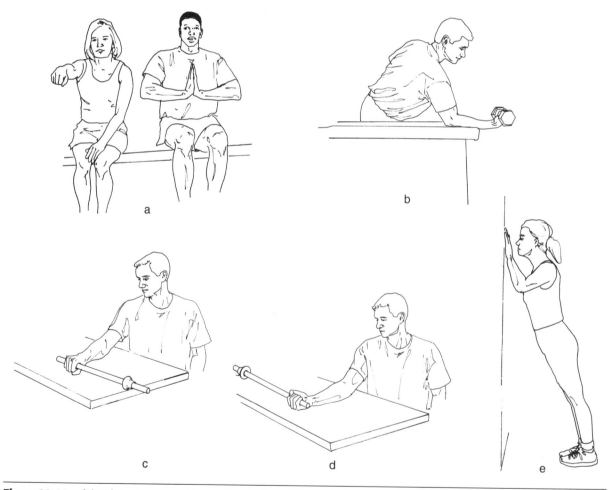

**Figure 22.11** *(a)* Wrist extensor and flexor stretch. *(b-d)* Wrist and elbow strengthening exercises. *(e)* Wall push-ups help an athlete begin to bear weight on the upper extremity.

**Figure 22.12** *(a)* Triceps pull-downs and *(b)* biceps curls are especially helpful for strengthening the upper arm. *(c)* Clay can be used to strengthen the fingers and hand.

The American College of Sports Medicine currently recommends training for three to five days a week in order to improve cardiovascular endurance. Training more than this can lead to overuse injuries, because some time must be taken to rest and recover throughout the week.

The intensity of the exercise should elevate the heart rate to between 60 and 90 percent of maximum heart rate. To determine maximum heart rate, subtract the athlete's age from 220. For example, let's determine the target heart rate for a 16-year-old cross-country runner. The formula determines her maximum heart rate: $220 - 16 = 204$. If she is new to running and just getting started, we may choose to start easy and increase the intensity as she gets in better shape. Therefore, if we begin training her at 60 percent of her maximal heart rate of 204 beats per minute, she must elevate her heart rate to about 122 beats per minute to get a training effect.

The duration, or amount of time, an athlete trains each session is another variable that can be controlled. To achieve maximum benefit, the exercise should be performed at the proper intensity for 15 to 60 minutes each session.

Generally, however, as the intensity increases, the duration decreases.

The type of exercise selected to improve, maintain, or reestablish cardiovascular endurance for the athlete depends upon several factors. Ideally, we would choose activities that are rhythmical, include large muscle groups, and can be performed continuously. However, the available equipment and the type of injury affect that decision. If an athlete has an injured ankle and is not yet allowed to perform much weight-bearing activity, he may need to perform an upper body aerobic exercise, and work on the upper body cycle machine, for example (see figure 22.13). Conversely, if he has an injured shoulder, he may need to limit upper extremity exercises, but he can ride an exercise bike.

## A Word on Safety

Safety during training should always be a chief concern. Don't let people using dumbbells act like dumbbells. Safety procedures must be established and faithfully followed.

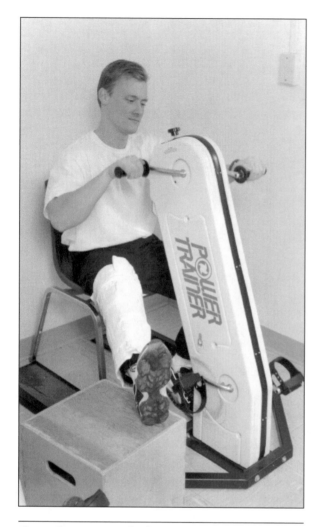

**Figure 22.13** Upper body exercises such as upper body cycling can help maintain cardiovascular fitness if an athlete has a lower extremity injury.

Whether an athlete is weight training or performing a cardiovascular workout, to prevent injury he needs a proper warm-up to prepare the body for the demands of the sport and a cool-down to help the body recover from the exercise more efficiently. The warm-up and cool-down should include some light cardiovascular work followed by stretching of each of the major muscle groups. Just how long the warm-up or cool-down should last is hotly debated among professionals, and its length is likely to vary from coach to coach and athlete to athlete. A

5 to 10 minute period of time for each, however, should be acceptable.

When weight training, an athlete should always train with a partner. The partner should know the exercise to be performed as well as the number of repetitions and be ready to lend assistance when needed. The athlete should not hold his breath while performing an exercise—he should exhale during concentric contractions and inhale during eccentric contractions. Any time a bar is used, the weights should always be secured with a collar. Proper exercise form should never be compromised just so a higher amount of weight can be lifted.

Proper weightlifting form has several components. The athlete should be stable—that is, when she is standing, lying, or sitting on a bench, she should maintain balance. She should be able to control the weight at all times—she should raise and lower the weight with a slow easy pace, usually raising the weight for two seconds and lowering it for four seconds. She should never cheat on her form just to be able to lift a weight.

When training for improved cardiovascular function, it is also a good idea to train with a partner. Training partners check on each other's water consumption and keep each other at an appropriate training level. Coaches and ATCs should always monitor the heat index to be sure the environment is safe for training.

## The Real World

A student of mine shared a video of a competitive power lifter's weight-training session. The athlete was performing a squat with about 550 pounds of weight on the bar. While he was squatting, his knee buckled and gave way. He collapsed to one side and lost control of the weight. Thankfully, his two spotters grabbed the bar, or he would have been badly hurt. Everyone watching the film got the message: Always train with a partner—or in some cases, two.

Bill Pitney, MS, ATC

## Summary

Progressive resistive exercise, overload, and specificity principles should always be followed by the ATC to insure that a reconditioning program is both safe and effective. A complete conditioning program will include aerobic activity for cardiovascular endurance that allows the athlete to reach the target heart rate. Stretching should be done statically to avoid injury in the warm-up, which should gradually raise the heart rate prior to the exercise program, and the cool-down, which should gradually lower the heart rate back to normal. Safety rules and guidelines must be implemented and followed to avoid any potential injury that may be involved with weight training and conditioning.

## Key Terms

Define the following terms found in this chapter:

ballistic stretching
cardiovascular endurance
circuit training
DeLorme method
isokinetic contraction
isometric contraction
isotonic contraction
muscular endurance

muscular power
muscular strength
overload principle
progressive resistive exercise (PRE)
pyramid method
specificity
static stretching

## Questions for Review

1. Explain the difference between strength, endurance, and power. How might an athlete develop each of these? pp. 211-212
2. What is the difference between isotonic, isometric, and isokinetic movements? pp. 210-211
3. If an athlete needs to become more flexible, what is the best way to stretch? p. 212

## Activities for Reinforcement

Find some alternative exercises that can be done for the upper quarter, lower quarter, and axial region.

## Above and Beyond

There are many texts related to strength and conditioning. We recommend the following as suggested reading:

Fahey, T.D. 1994. *Basic weight training for men and women.* 2d ed. Mountain-view, CA: Mayfield.

Fox, E.L., R.W. Bowers, and M.L. Foss. 1993. *The physiological basis for exercise and sport.* 5th ed. Madison, WI: Brown and Benchmark.

Glass, A.L. 1994. *Weight training.* Dubuque, IA: Kendall/Hunt.

Goldstein, T.S. 1995. *Functional rehabilitation in orthopaedics.* Gaithersburg, MD: Aspen.

Kisner, C., and L.A. Colby. 1990. *Therapeutic exercise.* 2d ed. Philadelphia: Davis.

Miller, D.K., and T.E. Allen. 1995. *Fitness: A lifetime commitment.* 5th ed. Boston: Allyn & Bacon.

Pearl, B. 1986. *Getting stronger.* Bolinas, CA: Shelter.

# Psychology and Athletic Training

## OBJECTIVES

Upon completing this chapter the student will be able to do the following:
- Have a broad understanding and appreciation for sport psychology.
- Understand relaxation and imagery techniques that are often used with athletes.
- Explain the athlete's perspective of an injury and the typical emotional reactions that he or she will display.
- Describe practical strategies to help an athlete better cope with an injury.

Athletes and ATCs are beginning to understand that physical considerations are not the only important factors in sport injury and rehabilitation. Psychological factors such as stress play a major role as well. Therefore, ATCs and athletes should learn the basics of sport psychology.

**Sport psychology** is the study of the effect of variables such as life stress, mood, and motivation on sport performance and sport-related injury. Generally, sport psychologists try to improve the mental well-being of athletes. They have many roles, including the following:

- Researching to better understand how these variables actually affect individuals
- Teaching coaches, athletes, and ATCs psychological techniques to improve performance
- Working directly with athletes in a clinical setting to help them deal with stress and improve sport performance

# Psychology and Athletics

Many ATCs become excellent at providing treatment and care to injured athletes. However, they also need to be aware that athletics-related injuries can often cause psychological problems, which inhibit not only performance but also proper recovery. Those ATCs who are the most successful have a clear understanding of the psychology of an athlete, injured or not.

## Anxious Athletes

As you might imagine, high school athletes must deal with many pressures. While few students could say they've never been stressed or anxious, in addition to the everyday stress of school and social life, athletes also must cope with the expectations of their peers, coaches, and parents regarding their sport performance. Because of this, many athletes become anxious prior to sport participation. Although ATCs are not sport psychologists, they spend a lot of time with the athletes and are in a good position to talk to them when necessary. The ATC must be able to counsel an athlete who is too anxious.

## Depression

**Depression** is the feeling of despair or hopelessness that causes behavior such as not wanting to be around other people, not being excited about things that might normally excite one, not taking the initiative to do things, and not talking very much to anyone. Many theories exist about what actually causes a person to become depressed: professionals think that depression is caused by biological (i.e., genetics), environmental (i.e., a traumatic childhood), or socio-

logical (i.e., a person loses a spot on a team) factors. Along with feelings of hopelessness, a depressed athlete may exhibit many other signs and symptoms including lack of appetite, nausea and indigestion, headaches, dizziness, and susceptibility to colds and other illnesses.

## Post-Traumatic Response

A **post-traumatic response** is a sustained emotional disorder that results from a very traumatic and stressful experience. For instance, a football player who was involved in a serious car accident in which a friend died might experience depression, problems with personal relationships, impaired concentration, or even attempt suicide.

Post-traumatic stress does not just happen to athletes—for example, an ATC, having dealt with a serious spinal cord injury to an athlete, may experience post-traumatic stress disorder. He may become fearful and be unable to work very well. He might also sleep a lot, refrain from eating, and avoid situations that are the same or similar to the one that caused the initial stress.

## Suicidal Tendencies

Because of the many pressures that come with being a student, the ATC at a high school should be concerned about suicide. A person who attempts suicide has usually experienced a stressful experience and is also suffering from depression. Warning signs of suicide include

- a change in an athlete's eating and sleeping patterns;
- statements indicating he wants to die;
- depression;
- anxiety;
- a recent loss, such as a death in the family, a broken relationship, or the loss of a job;
- a family history of suicide; and
- a lack of support from friends and family.

If a student suspects that a person may be suicidal, he should notify his school counselor and let him or her know that he is concerned about the individual.

If a student athlete has made a suicide attempt, the ATC should call 911. If the athlete has serious suicidal thoughts and is not thinking

## The Real World

I once worked with a football player who became so anxious prior to a game that he got physically sick before every game. He would have to leave the training room while he was being taped because he had to vomit. Once the game started, he was fine and actually played extremely well. This player was definitely a candidate for relaxation training.

Anonymous

clearly or if he is has some suicidal warning signs but denies being suicidal, he should see a counselor as soon as possible.

# Dealing With the Death of an Athlete

Despite all of the injury-prevention strategies and all of the measures taken by ATCs to ensure the safety of the athletes, there is an occasional instance when something goes terribly wrong. Although it may not happen on the court or on the field, the death of an athlete is a tragic event that leaves coaches, athletes, and parents with a devastating loss. An athlete who needs to talk about the loss of a teammate may confide in the ATC who holds a position of help and trust.

The ATC should understand that the athlete may express a great deal of anger during this time. The emotions that an athlete goes through when a peer dies are similar to those she will experience when she is injured.

# When an Athlete Is Injured

To understand the psychology of an injured athlete, we will examine the classic five-stage theory presented by Kubler-Ross in the late 1960s. These stages represent the emotional response that an athlete will have and how he may act after an injury or loss. The stages are (1) denial, (2) anger, (3) bargaining, (4) depression, and (5) acceptance. This theory has been widely referred to in much of the athletic-injury literature regarding psychological response. While many athletes will progress through these stages in sequence, it is important to keep in mind that everyone is different, and some may exhibit these stages out of order.

## Denial

When an athlete is first injured it is not uncommon for her to deny that there is a serious problem. Many athletes will tell themselves that things will soon be better. Unfortunately, when the athlete does not soon improve following a significant injury, she will feel very anxious. She may also be emotionally disorganized, and the ATC may hear her make unrealistic statements

such as "I will be fine, I'll be walking by tomorrow" when, in fact, that may not be the case.

## Anger

Another response an athlete will have is anger, especially when he realizes that the injury is real and potentially serious. He will often direct this anger at the nearest person, who, in many cases, is a student assistant or ATC. The athletic training staff, and any other members of the sports medicine team, must not take the anger personally. Each person must remember that this is not a personal attack but rather an emotional release. Listen to the athlete, and continue to respect him as an individual.

## Bargaining

Once an athlete's anger has diminished, she will begin to bargain with the ATC, coach, team physician, God, and even herself. She will attempt to make a deal with the ATC, such as "If I can play at least one quarter of the basketball game, I will do all of my exercises until my ankle is healed." When limits are set with the injured athlete, she may become depressed.

## Depression

The student assistant will be in a good position to see if the athlete is depressed. The depression phase brings with it a lack of motivation for the athlete and a feeling of hopelessness. This becomes a big challenge for the athletic training staff because athletes can often be noncompliant with their treatment, which is a concern of both sport psychologists and ATCs. The ATC needs to be supportive, motivational, and understanding to get the athlete to comply with the treatment plan. In addition, if the ATC takes the time to educate the athlete about the injury and to teach her why certain signs and symptoms exist, he can help her become more compliant with the rehabilitation program.

## Acceptance

When an injured athlete finally takes responsibility for her injury, she has come to the stage of acceptance. Accepting an injury means that the athlete has finally realized what it will take to get back to normal.

## ❓ What Would You Do If...

The ATC at your school has asked you to come up with some ideas to make the athletic training room bright and cheerful.

---

Many athletes become anxious when it comes time to return to participation. The ATC must see to it that the athlete in a rehabilitation program progresses gradually from simple to more complex exercises to build his confidence. Moreover, an ATC is wise to allow the athlete opportunities to be with his teammates so he can maintain contact and not feel isolated. In addition, a decisive therapeutic exercise program helps the athlete eliminate many fears of return.

# Practical Suggestions

There are some practical things the ATC can do in the athletic training room to help injured athletes cope with the injuries they have sustained—such things as modeling, maintaining a good physical environment, and encouraging relaxation.

## Modeling

Modeling means that an injured athlete has a successfully rehabilitated athlete with a similar injury to observe. The idea is that once he sees someone who is doing well with a similar injury, he may become less discouraged and more motivated to work at his rehabilitation program. The ATC and the student assistant should become positive, upbeat influences—another aspect of modeling. That is, they should be cheerful and helpful to the athletes. Nobody likes dealing with a slug! They should treat the athletes as they would want to be treated.

## Physical Environment

Imagine going into a doctor's office—when you walk through the door it is very dark and noisy, and it smells bad. Would you want to be there? Would you ever go back? Would you be comfortable performing exercises there? The same is true of the athletic training room. It is important to have a bright, clean, cheerful, and physically inviting atmosphere in which to treat athletes. In such an environment, the athletes may not feel that what they're doing is work; rather, it may be pleasant for them.

## Relaxation in Athletics

If you go to a high school track meet, take a look around at the athletes preparing for an event. You will see some of them listening to their headphones, others will be standing quietly with their eyes shut gently moving their bodies through various patterns, and others will be lying down taking deep breaths or stretching. Helping athletes relax has been recognized as a way to help them alleviate stress and cope with the demands of sport and sport injury. Several relaxation techniques that can be found in the literature include breathing techniques, meditation, imagery, music therapy, massage, and muscle relaxation. Among these techniques, we will discuss imagery and muscle relaxation.

### Imagery in Athletics

Imagery in the world of sport psychology is also known as visualization, mental training, and mental rehearsal, and several specific imagery techniques can be employed. Imagery is used in athletics to help reduce stress. An athlete pictures herself successfully completing a game, match, play, or event. Brian Seaward describes the mental imagery process as creating a motion picture. That is, the person doing the imaging is the writer, the actor, the producer, and the director all at once. She creates the scene, the athletic movement, and the outcome that can help her visualize success. Imagery can also be done in the athletic training room to aid in rehabilitation.

### Muscle Relaxation

Progressive muscle relaxation is one of the most common methods used to help athletes relax. This relaxation method originated in the early 1900s with a physician named Edmund Jacobson. Jacobson's routine consists of a series of muscle contractions and relaxations. The athlete assumes a comfortable position, probably lying down, and begins by contracting a muscle group (e.g., calves) at 100 percent effort for about 5 seconds and then relaxes them for a longer period of time, sometimes up to 45 seconds. Next, the athlete contracts the same muscles at 50 percent effort, followed by a rest period. Finally, he gently contracts the muscle group for 5 seconds and then rests. The athlete should select each main muscle group and work his way through his body, concentrating also on smooth rhythmical breathing.

## Summary

Athletes experience not only physical injuries but also psychological stresses that can be hard to manage. Sport psychologists can help athletes overcome many of the stresses they encounter with imagery and muscle relaxation techniques. Because ATCs get to know the athletes well and work with them everyday, they too can help the athletes overcome anxiety. However, the ATC must understand what an athlete will experience emotionally following an injury, as well as the warning signs of some mental problems.

## Key Terms

Define the following terms found in this chapter:

depression          post-traumatic response          sport psychology

## Questions for Review

1. State what is meant by sport psychology, and describe how sport psychologists might help an athlete who is experiencing anxiety. pp. 225, 226, 228
2. What is depression, and what are the warning signs you should look for if you think someone is depressed? p. 226
3. Explain an athlete's perspective of an injury and the typical emotional reactions that he will display. pp. 227-228
4. What are some of the warning signs that a student may be suicidal? p. 226

## Activities for Reinforcement

1. Discuss with your head ATC the various community agencies that an athlete could be referred to if she needed counseling.
2. Visit a suicide prevention hotline center.
3. Invite a sport psychologist to speak with the class.

## Above and Beyond

There is a great deal more to sport psychology than what is offered in this chapter. Below are some suggested readings for those who are interested in this topic:

Henderson, J., and W. Carroll. 1993. The athletic trainer's role in preventing sport injury and rehabilitating injured athletes: A psychological perspective. In *Psychological bases of sport injuries,* ed. D. Pargman, 15-31. Morgantown, WV: Fitness Information Technology.

Kerr, G., and H. Minden. 1988. Psychosocial factors related to the occurrence of athletic injuries. *Journal of Sports and Exercise Psychology* 10: 167–73.

Lavallee, L., and F. Flint. 1996. The relationship of stress, competitive anxiety, mood state, and social support to athletic injury. *Journal of Athletic Training* 31(4): 296–99.

Orlick, T. 1990. *In pursuit of excellence.* Champaign, IL: Human Kinetics.

Orlick, T. 1998. *Embracing your potential.* Champaign, IL: Human Kinetics.

Pargman, D. 1993. Sport injuries: An overview of psychological perspectives. In *Psychological bases of sport injuries*, ed. D. Pargman, 5-13. Morgantown, WV: Fitness Information Technology.

Seaward, B.L. 1994. *Managing stress.* Boston: Jones and Bartlett.

Wann, D.L. 1997. *Sport psychology.* Upper Saddle River, NJ: Prentice Hall.

# Unit VIII

# Other Athletic Conditions and Concerns

# Conditions and Illnesses

## OBJECTIVES

Upon completing this chapter the student will be able to do the following:
- Describe the conditions that cause illness.
- Understand how to prevent conditions and illness from occurring.
- Know that many of the signs and symptoms are similar among conditions.
- Describe various conditions that affect athletes.

An athlete may have a preexisting condition that can reduce her ability to perform normally. The ATC and team physician will attempt to discover all such conditions during the preparticipation physical. Knowing of a condition and preparing to care for it before a crisis occurs can make everyone more comfortable. Some conditions will require a limitation of activity. We will discuss conditions of the respiratory, gastrointestinal, neurological, and circulatory systems in this chapter.

## Conditions of the Respiratory Tract

Respiratory tract conditions generally affect the lungs. Any condition that reduces an athlete's ability to get air into her body will make it difficult to perform at a high level. The most common respiratory tract condition is asthma.

Bronchial **asthma** is a condition in which certain "triggers" may cause the sufferer's air passages (the bronchial tubes) to narrow, which obstructs breathing. The triggers vary from person to person but include allergies, emotional distress, exercise, or a body chemistry response. In some cases there may be a genetic component. An athlete with bronchial asthma describes it as running the 100-yard dash and then trying to catch her breath while breathing through a straw. Coughing that brings up no phlegm is common. The athlete will wheeze on exhalation and will be in obvious respiratory distress. Asthmatic athletes will have medication, often in the form of an inhaler, to open the air passage, the use of which should be permitted.

An asthma attack can be a very scary experience for the athlete and the athletic trainer. The athletic trainer needs to remain calm because exciting the athlete will only make the asthma more uncontrollable. He should ask the athlete to relax and breathe in through the nose and out through the mouth. By concentrating on his breathing pattern, the athlete can focus on something constructive. The athlete will be more comfortable sitting up than lying down. If he is not getting better, the ATC should call for an ambulance and get medical attention immediately. If the athlete stops breathing, the ATC should attempt to perform mouth-to-mouth resuscitation, but he may not be successful, because air cannot get to the lungs through the closed-off bronchial passages. An athlete who has had an asthma attack for the first time needs to be seen by a physician for evaluation.

Athletes who are known asthmatics are often required to give their inhalers to their coaches before practice. Athletes who fail to provide an inhaler that day are not allowed to practice. As a backup measure some athletic trainers carry the athlete's second inhaler. An athlete should not use another athlete's medication, because asthma medications vary. Each state and school district has rules about school personnel dispensing medication, so the ATC should check the rules before handling someone else's medication.

# Conditions of the Gastrointestinal Tract

The gastrointestinal tract includes the organs that are involved in processing food. We will discuss the stomach, appendix, and the large and small intestines.

## Appendicitis

An athlete with appendicitis will feel pain over the lower right quadrant of the abdomen. Diarrhea or constipation, nausea, vomiting, and a temperature increase, all within a couple hours, are common signs and symptoms. She will find that bringing the knees to the chest is the most comfortable position. The athlete needs to be referred to a physician for care because the appendix must often be surgically removed. She will be sidelined for at least four weeks. In severe cases the appendix can rupture and spread the infection throughout the abdominal cavity, which can result in death.

## Gastroenteritis (Food Poisoning)

Food poisoning is a common cause of diarrhea or an upset stomach. Recently, there have been many incidents of poisoning from foods (including fruits, meats, dairy products, and vegetables) contaminated with E. coli (Escherichia coli). Preventing food poisoning requires careful food handling and preparation—washing hands and utensils, cooking foods thoroughly, and bleaching countertops, dishrags, and cutting surfaces. An athlete with food poisoning will complain of abdominal pain, tiredness, vomiting, nausea, diarrhea, and possibly a high temperature. The athlete should be allowed to rest, drink plenty of fluids, and be referred to a physician.

## Indigestion

When an athlete eats a food that the body has difficulty digesting, we say he has indigestion. The stomach has a high acid content to break down food. When there are excessive acid levels, the acid may go up into the esophagus, causing a burning sensation called heartburn. The athlete may burp, have excessive gas, feel nauseous, and even vomit. He may experience pain about the heart, which mimics the sensations of a heart attack. Serious cases of indigestion will cause anxiety, sweating, pale skin, and nausea. Such cases must be referred to a physician. The athlete can avoid foods that cause indigestion and should also avoid overeating. A physician can recommend the use of over-the-counter medications to control the stomach acid. However, if used excessively, these medications may mask a more serious problem. If problems persist, a physician should be consulted to rule out a more serious condition such as ulcers.

## Diabetes

Diabetes occurs when the pancreas does not secrete insulin effectively or when the body is resistant to insulin. An athlete with untreated diabetes may lose weight, become unusually thirsty, urinate more often, get tired faster than usual, and have a high level of sugar in the blood stream. After a diabetic athlete eats, her blood sugar level rises. The pancreas releases insulin so the body can control the blood sugar. If the blood sugar level gets too high, it is called **hyperglycemia**; if it gets too low, it is called **hypoglycemia**. If a diabetic athlete who uses insulin forgets to eat, her blood sugar level may fall below normal, causing her to pass out (figure 24.1). Something similar may happen due to exercise. An exercising athlete requires energy from the blood stream (blood glycogen). If a diabetic athlete exercises excessively, she may use additional sugar for energy—if she also takes insulin, this situation can cause her blood sugar to be dangerously low. Many athletes can control their diabetes by eating foods that take time to digest, like meats and vegetables. Avoiding sugary foods and drinks will also help prevent a diabetic emergency.

## Diabetic Coma

A **diabetic coma** may occur when there is not enough insulin to control the amount of sugar in the blood. A diabetic coma may be preceded by an illness that alters the amount and availability of insulin. The coma comes on gradually with signs of vomiting and high temperature. The symptoms experienced by the athlete are thirst, abdominal pain, nausea, and confusion. The athlete approaching a coma will present labored breathing, sweet-smelling breath, and low blood pressure. A diabetic coma may be prevented by helping the athlete administer her insulin. Some athletes carry premade insulin shots, and if conscious they can inject themselves. Have an unconscious athlete rushed to a hospital emergency room.

## Insulin Shock

An athlete who needs injections of insulin to survive is known as insulin dependent. An insulin-dependent athlete usually takes insulin several times a day, especially near meals. Like all of us, an insulin-dependent athlete may not always eat regularly. If he takes insulin and then fails to eat, he may go into **insulin shock** because he has given himself medication to lower his blood sugar when it was not high. Insulin shock can also happen if he eats a food with a high sugar content that is absorbed rapidly, before the insulin has returned to the standard level.

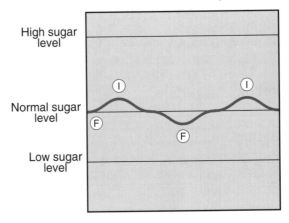

**a. Normal blood response**

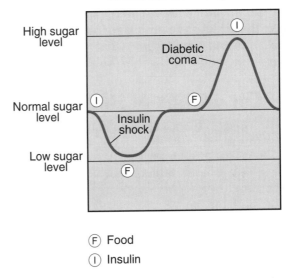

**b. Diabetic blood response**

Ⓕ Food
Ⓘ Insulin

**Figure 24.1**   Insulin response. *(a)* An athlete with normal blood sugar response: the athlete eats food, insulin is released, and the blood sugar level is brought back to normal. *(b)* Insulin shock occurs in a diabetic when the blood sugar is very low. The athlete may have taken insulin, but failed to eat enough or any food. A diabetic coma occurs when the blood sugar is very high. The athlete may have forgotten to take insulin just before or after eating.

When insulin shock occurs, the athlete will feel lightheaded and weak, and have ashen skin tone and rapid pulse. In many cases the athlete will appear to be intoxicated. The athletic trainer should give the conscious athlete juice or candy so the insulin will be temporarily counteracted—then the athlete should consume a meal to level off the insulin.

If the athlete is unconscious, liquid glucose (sugar) can be placed under the tongue. The

## 🎵 What Would You Do If...

A diabetic ice hockey player has forgotten to bring his juice box with him for a between-period snack. He tells you he can get along without a snack this time.

athletic trainer should never place hard candy or food into the mouth of an unconscious athlete—this action may cause an airway obstruction. Whenever a diabetic athlete is unconscious, the ATC should call the emergency medical system and get him to the nearest hospital. If the athletic trainer cannot remember the treatments for diabetic emergencies, he should give the athlete a sugar-based food—it will help the athlete in insulin shock, and it will not make a diabetic coma any worse (see table 24.1).

# Conditions of the Blood and Vascular System

If there is a problem with the blood, heart, or blood vessels, an athlete can become ill. The ATC should know about hypertension, hypotension, and anemia.

## Hypertension

**Hypertension** is defined as blood pressure above normal levels. (See chapter 5 for more information about blood pressure.) Generally if the blood pressure is taken on several different occasions and the systolic pressure is above 140 mm Hg at rest or the diastolic pressure is above 90 mm Hg at rest, hypertension is present. Hypertension has several causes, including poor diet; stress; overexercising; or severe vascular damage, such as constriction, or narrowing, of the blood vessels as a result of disease. Hypertension can also cause vascular damage. Athletes with high blood pressure may report frequent headaches. They should be referred to a physician to determine the severity of the disease and for treatment. Hypertension can usually be controlled with medication.

## Hypotension

**Hypotension** is abnormally low blood pressure. Some medications cause hypotension—an athlete taking these may pass out as blood pressure decreases. An athlete who has been bedridden may experience hypotension and may even pass out when she sits up or walks for the first time—her vascular system is no longer used to re-

| Table 24.1 Comparisons Between Diabetic Coma and Insulin Shock | |
|---|---|
| **Diabetic coma** | **Insulin shock** |
| Conscious but confused | Unconscious |
| No seizures | Seizures possible |
| Breath smells fruity | Breath smells normal |
| Low blood pressure | Normal blood pressure |
| Thirsty | Not thirsty |
| Rapid breathing | Normal breathing |
| Dry skin | Sweating |
| Possible fever | Normal body temperature |
| No body sensations | Tingling in hands and feet |
| Onset is gradual | Onset is rapid |
| Food intake normal | Food intake: little |
| No headache | Headache |
| Response to food: none | Response to food: quick |

sponding to changes in body position. After she moves around for a few days, the hypotension subsides. An athlete in shock or one who is losing blood will also experience hypotension. It is important to know the cause of hypotension so it can be treated properly. To get the athlete's blood pressure back to normal, she may have to be treated for shock, bleeding may need to be stopped, or her medication may have to be changed.

## Anemia

**Anemia** is the lack of red blood cells necessary to provide oxygen to the body tissues. Anemia occurs from loss of blood, lack of iron, improper functioning of cells, medication, or malfunction in the construction of cells. Anemia caused by surgery is corrected by blood transfusions. Menstrual anemia corrects itself in a couple of days.

### Iron-Deficiency Anemia

Red blood cells must have iron to carry oxygen. When iron is insufficient, the condition is known as iron-deficiency anemia. The athlete may not be eating enough iron-rich foods to meet the average body's needs. Or the athlete's body may have an unusually high need for iron. This condition can be resolved by eating liver, beef, oysters, and iron-enriched cereals. An athlete with iron-deficiency anemia will have pale skin, fatigue, dizziness, decreased capillary refill, and tiredness. The signs and symptoms are not unlike the characteristics of cross-country runners at the finish of a race. The best way to identify this type of anemia is for a blood test to be taken.

### Sickle-Cell Anemia

**Sickle-cell anemia** is a chronic inherited disease. Although it is often thought of as an illness of African-Americans, it also occurs in those of other races. People of eastern European descent are also at high risk for sickle-cell anemia.

The normal red blood cell is round and has a large surface area for carrying oxygen. The red blood cells of an athlete with sickle-cell anemia look like sickles or crescents, with points on each end (see figure 24.2). The sickling of the cells causes them to hook onto the sides of the blood vessels, producing a logjam of cells in the

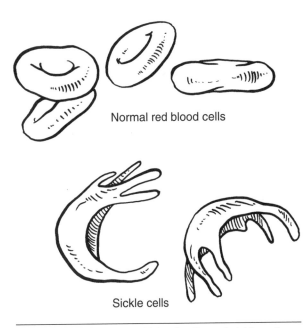

**Figure 24.2**   Normal red blood cells and sickle cells.

capillaries. Also, the sickle cell is not capable of carrying as much oxygen as a normal red blood cell. The result is that oxygen is not carried efficiently to all parts of the body. The athlete with sickle-cell anemia who is in crisis may have a blue skin tone, feel nauseated and weak, and have abdominal pain. Most often the athlete can be treated with high-flow oxygen from an oxygen tank. Therefore, some athletic trainers and team physicians will have oxygen tanks available for the athlete. However, if signs of shock or respiratory distress are evident, the athlete should be transported to the ER. Athletes with sickle-cell anemia have problems at high altitudes, and it may be best to restrict playing time or not allow the athlete to travel to these places. Preventing a sickle-cell crisis includes taking in fluids, avoiding high altitudes (above 4000 feet), warming up well, and avoiding short bursts of activity.

## Hemophilia

**Hemophilia** is a blood disorder that delays blood clotting with consequent difficulty in controlling hemorrhage even after minor injuries. Hemophilia is a sex-linked inherited blood condition, carried by females but occurring in males. An athlete with hemophilia may not be able to return to action after an injury, and the bleeding may continue to the point where a transfusion of

## ❓ What Would You Do If...

A good friend of yours is dying to tell you a secret, and you promise not to tell anyone. He is trying out for the football team and has told only you that he is a hemophiliac.

blood is necessary. An athlete can be taught to self-administer shots to improve clotting time. Hemophilia cannot be cured, but it can be controlled. An athlete with hemophilia should play noncontact sports to help avoid unnecessary bleeding episodes.

# Neurological Conditions

When the brain does not work properly, the entire body can malfunction. **Epilepsy** is the general term given to various disorders marked by disturbed electrical rhythms of the central nervous system.

The cause of epilepsy can be chemical, neurological (a brain defect), an infection, or trauma. A sign that an athlete has epilepsy can be a grand mal **seizure**—she may shake, drool, lose bladder control, or lose consciousness. The athlete who is about to have a grand mal seizure may hear a sound or see an aura, warning her to move to a safe area before the seizure begins. If her seizures are controlled by medication, exercising will not cause her to experience more problems. There is no reason to keep an athlete from participating because of epilepsy. Care for an athlete having a grand mal seizure includes moving items out of her way, loosening her clothing, padding her head, and allowing the seizure to end on its own. Because the tongue may fall back and block the airway, the athlete should be monitored for breath sounds. If an athlete experiences a first-time seizure the ATC should call EMS for immediate emergency care.

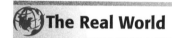

## The Real World

One afternoon, a student athlete rushed into the training room shouting that a student had seriously injured herself while running in the hall. I grabbed my bag and ran from one end of the school to the other. Upon reaching the injured girl, I found her lying face down and unconscious, with her glasses ajar. She was breathing and had a normal heartbeat. Saliva was dribbling from her mouth, but she had no visible wounds. No one could tell me what had happened, and no one knew her name. Furthermore, she was not wearing any identification or medical alert tags. Other athletic trainers who arrived on the scene performed a head-to-toe assessment of her and checked for a medical alert tag, while I held her head to keep her neck in alignment. Because she was unconscious, we immediately called 911. She was eventually backboarded and taken to the hospital without ever having regained consciousness. Had she accidentally run into the wall and knocked herself out because she wasn't watching where she was going? Did she have a previous condition that caused her to faint? We had no idea. The mystery was cleared up later when it was determined that she had experienced her first seizure.

Lorin Cartwright, MS, ATC, EMT

## Summary

Certain medical conditions affect an athlete's ability to participate in sport activities. The athletic trainer must be prepared to respond to emergencies, since an incorrect evaluation can result in serious consequences if the athlete has a condition like appendicitis, asthma, or diabetes. Regular physical exams can help find certain conditions early. Conditions that are not preventable, like asthma, diabetes, or epilepsy, may be controlled by medication and careful monitoring. The ATC should know if an athlete is in a high-risk category for certain conditions so she can assist the athlete in taking preventive measures such as selecting the proper sport, using protective equipment, making sure medication is available, and knowing first aid.

## Key Terms

Define the following terms found in this chapter:

| | | | |
|---|---|---|---|
| anemia | epilepsy | hypertension | insulin shock |
| asthma | hemophilia | hypoglycemia | seizure |
| diabetic coma | hyperglycemia | hypotension | sickle-cell anemia |

## Questions for Review

1. What is diabetes? How can it be treated? pp. 234-236
2. What does an ATC need to know to ensure safe athletic participation of asthmatics? p. 234
3. What is the treatment for hypertension? p. 236
4. What is the difference between anemia and sickle-cell anemia? p. 237
5. In which sports should a hemophiliac participate? p. 238
6. What is the care for an athlete who is suffering an epileptic grand mal seizure? p. 238

## Activities for Reinforcement

1. Make a list of common signs and symptoms discussed in this chapter and indicate the conditions with which they are associated.

2. Invite someone with asthma, diabetes, or another condition to class to talk about it.

3. Learn how to take someone's blood pressure.

## Above and Beyond

1. Make a poster about one of the conditions discussed in this chapter; include the causes, prevention, and treatment of the condition, and who is most likely to have it. Display the poster in the room.

2. Calculate the rate of diagnosis (by the day) of at least two conditions described within this chapter. Post the findings on a bulletin board. Some of the following textbooks may be helpful.

   Anderson, M., and S. Hall. 1995. *Sports injury management*. Baltimore: Williams & Wilkins.

   Bittings, L.A., C.A. Trowbridge, and L.E. Costello. 1997. A model for a policy on HIV/ AIDS and athletics. *Journal of Athletic Training* 3(4): 356–57.

   Eichner, E.R. 1987. Blood doping: Implications of recent research. *Sports Medicine Digest* 9(11): 4.

   Jimenez, C.C. 1997. Diabetes and exercise: The role of the athletic trainer. *Journal of Athletic Training* 32(4): 339–43.

   Kenna, K. 1983. The diabetic athlete. *Athletic Training* 18(2): 131–34.

   Nieman, D.C. 1997. Risk of upper respiratory tract infection in athletics: An epidemiologic and immunologic perspective. *Journal of Athletic Training* 32(4): 344–49.

   Thomas, C.L., ed. 1985. *Taber's cyclopedic medical dictionary*. 13th ed. Philadelphia: Davis.

   Weidner, T., and T. Sevier. 1996. Sport, exercise, and the common cold. *Journal of Athletic Training* 31(2): 154–59.

For a catalog listing free and low-cost government publications, write to the following address:

United States Government Printing Office
Superintendent of Documents
Public Documents Distribution Center
Pueblo, CO 81009

# Communicable Diseases

Upon completing this chapter the student will be able to do the following:
- Explain how contagious diseases affect athletic competition.
- Describe how to control and prevent contagious diseases.
- Describe the common signs and symptoms of contagious diseases.

Our environment contains microorganisms that can cause infectious diseases. The immune system helps defend the body from foreign cells and substances, but when the immune system is low or the invader is strong, the human body will become ill. Many of the illnesses can be transferred from one person to another through the air, by bodily contact, by using each other's personal items, or by unsanitary conditions. The student assistant and ATC will come in contact with illnesses on a day-to-day basis. To help prevent the spread of communicable diseases, the ATC (and the students) can keep vaccinations current, clean daily, avoid bodily fluids and sick athletes, use protective barriers, exercise properly, screen athletes during physical examinations, maintain healthy nutrition and hydration, and get enough sleep. In this chapter we discuss the various communicable diseases.

## Defending Against Microorganisms

**Microorganisms** are the microscopic and submicroscopic bacteria and viruses that are everywhere in the environment, including on and in everyone's body. If the microorganism is one the body has never encountered before, it may create an infection.

The infectious microorganisms that manage to get into the body are attacked by the lymphocytes of the **immune system**. Lymphocytes are specialized leukocytes, the white blood cells that look for invaders to attack.

When physicians draw blood it is easy to check the number of leukocytes. Elevated numbers of leukocytes may mean the body is fighting an infection. Low numbers of leukocytes are an indication that the body's immune system is deficient, and thus the athlete may be susceptible to infectious microorganisms.

Some microorganisms are effectively fought through the use of **vaccinations**—preparations of tiny amounts of the microorganism (sometimes live and sometimes dead) that are injected into the body. Once the microorganism has entered, the body begins to fight and build up immunity against it. Vaccinations against the following diseases exist: tetanus, measles, flu, hepatitis B, mumps, and polio. Viruses cause all of these diseases except tetanus, which is caused by bacteria.

# The Most Common Communicable Diseases

Medical science has done an outstanding job of increasing public awareness of communicable diseases. People are more careful than they used to be around others who appear to be ill. People with coughs and sneezes cover their mouths and wipe their noses. We can all do our part to prevent the spread of disease by getting vaccinations, washing hands, using sterile techniques, and staying at home when early signs and symptoms of illness appear. Sharing food, water, or clothing should be avoided. Daily cleaning of clothing, training tables, and doorknobs will reduce the possibility of infection through contact with these items. When the ATC notices an athlete with cold and flu symptoms—sneezing, itchy watery eyes, low-grade fever, runny nose, sore throat, headache, tiredness—or signs of a rash, the athlete should be referred immediately to a physician for care. Many of the early signs and symptoms of life-threatening illnesses mimic those of mild contagious illnesses. Neither the ATC nor the athlete should risk spreading a contagious disease among team- and classmates. There have been several outbreaks of rubeola among athletes when, unknowingly, an infected athlete was allowed to participate in a tournament—the illness can devastate every team attending. The physician should indicate when it is safe for the athlete to return.

# Viral Diseases

Many viral illnesses are considered "childhood diseases" because they once caused misery and even death for millions, primarily children. Though these diseases still thrive in many undeveloped countries, most of them have become rare in the developed world due to childhood vaccination programs. Yet, they are occasionally seen even in this country in either children or adults, and both ATCs and their assistants should be aware of them. Of the viral diseases listed below, only aseptic meningitis is not a childhood disease.

- **Mumps.** A virus causes mumps. The athlete will feel tired and have a headache. The most distinguishing feature of mumps is a swelling of the glands below and in front of the ear causing a fullness of the face and difficulty talking and swallowing. The swelling subsides in about a week. The athlete must be referred to a physician, who will recommend isolation, rest, fluids, aspirin, and soft foods. Prevention includes vaccination or avoiding those who do not feel well or who are known to have the mumps.

- **Chicken pox** is caused by a virus. It is characterized by a polka-dot body rash, a low-grade fever, tiredness, itching, and headache. The rash, if broken open, will leave small craterlike permanent scars. The athlete who gets this rash is able to spread it to others on the team through nose or mouth secretions and the fluids from broken blisters. She needs to be referred to a physician for treatment. After about one week, when the athlete has dried scabs, she will be able to return to school and competition. A vaccination against chicken pox is now available.

- **Measles (Rubeola).** There are two types of measles: rubeola and rubella (German measles). Viruses cause both. Rubeola causes cold symptoms, with a cough and high temperature in the early stages. As the disease progresses, the body becomes covered with a rash, including inside the mouth. The athlete will be tired, his eyes will be sensitive to bright light, and he will have a headache. The athletic trainer should refer the athlete to a physician for care—she will treat the symptoms. The prevention of rubeola is through vaccination.

- **Rubella (German measles)** causes a rash that starts at the head and covers the body within a day's time. The rash will stay for about three days, but the athlete remains contagious for about five. She is treated for pain or itching. Prevention of rubella is through vaccination.

- **Aseptic meningitis** is a viral inflammation of the coverings of the brain. The virus will cause the athlete to have flulike symptoms: headache, stiff neck, fever, and vision problems. The athlete, if healthy, can survive, and the virus runs its course in about two weeks. Outbreaks of the virus have caused several team members to be hospitalized, and some have even died from this virus.

Some athletic trainers tolerate two practices that can contribute to aseptic meningitis—they allow players to dip cups into water coolers, and they allow players to touch their lips to water bottles or cooler spigots. Prevention is simple—every player uses his own cup, no one dips a cup into the cooler, and no lips touch the water cooler spigot. Water coolers and bottles must be cleaned after each use with a bleach solution.

## Respiratory Conditions

The respiratory tract includes the nose, sinuses, trachea, bronchial tubes, and lungs, any of which can be affected by viruses or bacteria. Conditions of the respiratory tract include colds, sinusitis, pneumonia, influenza, asthma, and bronchitis.

- **Common cold (coryza).** The common cold is caused by a virus. The common signs and symptoms of a cold are sore throat, coughing, sneezing, runny nose, loss of voice, and tiredness. To prevent a cold you must maintain a good diet, wash your hands frequently, avoid others who have colds, avoid being in crowds, and avoid sharing cups. A viral illness can only

be treated symptomatically, which means to treat the signs and symptoms of the illness. An athlete with a sore throat or cough may use throat lozenges; a tissue should be used to cover a cough and dab a runny nose. An athlete who is tired should rest. A run-down athlete who does not treat his cold may become more susceptible to other illnesses to which he is exposed.

- **Influenza** is the medical name for the flu. An athlete with the flu will report a headache, nausea, vomiting, dizziness, tiredness, stomach upset, chills, and possibly fever. The flu is communicable and the sick athlete should stay away from her teammates. She is treated symptomatically and should get plenty of rest. Generally the team physician cannot do very much to comfort the athlete once she has the flu. There are some over-the-counter medications to decrease nausea, headache, and body aches. The athlete can avoid getting the flu by getting a flu shot and avoiding those who are ill.

- **Bronchitis.** Inflammation of the bronchial passages, called bronchitis, can be caused by an infection or an allergy. The athlete will have a fever, sore throat, tiredness, chills, a deep cough, and even wheezing. Bronchitis mimics colds, flu, and other respiratory conditions. It is best for the athletic trainer to refer to a physician the athlete who has persistent coughing and wheezing.

- **Laryngitis.** An inflammation of the larynx—not being able to talk—is called laryngitis. Laryngitis can be caused by an infection of the upper respiratory tract or from talking too much or too loudly. The athlete with laryngitis will have a sore throat and no voice. The infection may also involve the rest of the body, so he may have a fever. Drinking water will help humidify the throat and keep him more comfortable. He will need to refrain from talking until the infection subsides. The athlete should treat the symptoms, but if he has a fever, a physician's services should be sought.

## Skin Infections

The skin is a primary protector against disease—it keeps microorganisms from entering the body. Some microorganisms, however, directly infect the skin and then enter the body

## Table 25.1 Types of Skin Lesions

| Type | Characteristics |
|------|-----------------|
| Crusts | Dried accumulations of pus, often thought of as scabs. Often associated with impetigo and cold sores. |
| Pustules | Collections of pus from infection. Often associated with wounds, folliculitis, furuncle, and acne. |
| Ulcers | Open weeping wounds. Often associated with burns or trauma. |
| Vesicles | Collections of clear fluids under the skin. The vesicles may be singular or in bunches. The contagion is in the fluid, so breaking a vesicle causes the disease to spread. Some vesicles are of no consequence, like a blister. When vesicles break they are prone to infection. |

(see table 25.1). As a way of preventing the spread of skin infections, high school wrestling rules require that any wrestler with open sores be kept from wrestling. A physician's note indicating that the wrestler's rash is not communicable can permit participation, but the wrestling official can overrule the note.

### Herpes

Herpes simplex is a cold sore caused by a virus. The virus stays in the body, and when the immune system weakens, the cold sore appears. The athlete needs to make sure she is getting enough sleep, good nutrition, and exercise.

Signs of herpes simplex include a weeping open blister with a red base and a yellow crust, swollen glands, and possibly a fever. Herpes simplex is spread by skin-to-skin contact. In sports characterized by considerable contact, like wrestling and rugby, herpes simplex can spread rapidly.

Prevention involves showering after practice, covering all open wounds, excusing those with open wounds from practice, making sure that athletes do not share towels, toothbrushes, or clothes, and washing mats with a bleach/water solution or commercial product daily (be-

fore and after each use). Herpes runs its course in about two weeks. Three things will help a person who is subject to cold sores: eating properly (well-balanced meals), getting enough rest, and, most importantly, managing her stress level.

### Other Skin Infections

Some skin rashes occur as the result of an invader that attacks the whole body, like measles. In other cases the invader attacks a local area of the skin. Some skin areas become irritated by padding or athletic equipment, and the infection occurs. It is important for the athlete to recognize skin irritations early to prevent the spread to other athletes. A referral to a physician can keep a skin condition under control.

- **Molluscum contagiosum** is a skin condition caused by a virus that raises pink lumps in the area of contact. A physician removes the lumps surgically and applies a medication. They usually heal without scarring.

- **Impetigo** is a skin condition caused by a staphylococcus or streptococcus infection. There will be clusters of blisters that break open and get a crusted yellow exterior. The athlete will need antibiotics to stop the spread of impetigo. Washing playing surfaces and not sharing towels or clothing will help prevent or reduce the spread of impetigo.

- **Folliculitis** is an inflammation of a hair follicle. The athlete will need antibiotics to cure the infection, which is caused by bacteria, but he can participate with proper covering of the follicles. Wet hot packs can open the follicle,

 **For Your Information**

### Cold Sore

A cold sore is a group of blisters about or in the mouth caused by the herpes simplex virus.

## What Would You Do If...

While cleaning up after an athlete who was bleeding profusely, you notice a drop of blood on a recent abrasion on your forearm. You know the athlete and trust that she does not have any communicable diseases.

which may look like a pus-filled sore, and help reduce the infection more quickly. African Americans and athletes who wear protective equipment such as shoulder pads are more prone to folliculitis. These athletes should wear an additional layer of lightweight clothing to help decrease the pressure on the follicles.

• **Furuncle** is another name for a boil, which is a bacterial infection in a skin gland. The boil will be bright red with a hard central core that is painful to the touch. The furuncle will give the appearance of a large pimple, and the athlete may want to squeeze it. Instead, he should apply warm packs several times a day to draw the infection outward. The athletic trainer must use caution to prevent the bacteria from getting on the hot packs; a towel, which is assigned to the infected athlete and then sent to the wash daily, will be helpful. All parts of the body that have contact with protective equipment are prone to this infection—it needs to be treated by a physician.

## Blood-Borne Conditions

Two contagious blood-borne diseases are HIV and hepatitis B. These diseases are transmitted especially by contact with infected blood. Say a trainer treating an athlete's bleeding wound gets blood in a cut on her hand. Microorganisms in the blood can easily enter the cut. Needles or razors shared by more than one athlete may also transfer blood from one person to another. The best way to prevent transmittal is to place a barrier between the infected athlete and others. The universal precautions that were discussed earlier (see page 36) should be employed in these situations.

### HIV/AIDS

**HIV** (human immunodeficiency virus) is a disorder of the immune system that is acquired

### Hand Washing

1. If you are going to dry your hands on a paper towel, first unroll the towel from the dispenser without touching the paper towel.
2. Use the automatic liquid soap dispenser—if you do not have one, get one.
3. Use the large knobbed handles to turn the water on with your forearm.
4. Lather your hands and wrists, scrub hard under the fingernails and any jewelry.
5. Say your ABC's twice—this will be a long enough scrubbing time.
6. Rinse your hands.
7. Tear off the paper towel and dry your hands.
8. Using the wet paper towel, dispense another clean paper towel.
9. Throw out the used wet towel.
10. Turn off the water with the new paper towel.
11. Open the bathroom door with the same paper towel.
12. Discard the paper towel.

Proper hand washing can prevent the spread of germs.

through the transfer of bodily fluids: blood, semen, vaginal secretions, and breast milk can transfer the HIV to another person. Transmittal of the disease through saliva and tears is highly unlikely, as it takes about one gallon of saliva or tears to transfer enough of the HIV to give someone the disease.

Because an infected athlete's immune system is suppressed, the athletic trainer may notice that contusions or sores take longer to heal than normal. The athlete will lose weight, have a sore throat, and become tired. A series of blood tests over a six-month period will confirm HIV. The physician will prescribe medication to boost the athlete's immune system and reduce her susceptibility to infections. There has been dramatic progress in increasing the strength of the infected athlete's immune system.

The disease, AIDS (acquired immune deficiency syndrome), is caused by infection with HIV. The drug AZT inhibits replication of the HIV and is used to slow the progress of AIDS. The athlete will report fatigue, night sweating, sores

## What Would You Do If...

The athletic trainer evaluates an athlete and is puzzled by the signs and symptoms of a rash. You recognize the signs and symptoms as being similar to those of measles, which you had as a child.

that will not heal, coughing, and diarrhea. The disease is fatal, so the best thing to do is to prevent the illness—for the athletic trainer this means using the universal precautions outlined on page 36.

## Hepatitis B

Hepatitis B virus (**HBV**) causes an infection of the liver. The HBV tends to persist in the blood of the infected athlete and can be transmitted by contact with infected blood, including dried blood. Those who are infected with HBV have it for a lifetime and are more prone to cirrhosis (liver disease)—they may feel tired and nauseous and experience a lack of desire for food. Some infected individuals may be carriers of the disease, but are not themselves ill. The signs and symptoms of hepatitis B are not unlike those of a cold or flu. The athlete will have signs of jaundice—yellowing of the skin and sclera. He needs immediate medical attention to control the damage from hepatitis B. It is possible that he will have chronic problems and may even die.

The good news is that hepatitis B is totally preventable through a series of shots. Because athletic trainers and student assistants are in contact with blood on a regular basis, they should consider receiving the series of shots. Exposure to this condition, like HIV, can be limited by observing the universal precautions.

## The Real World

As a second-year athletic-training intern I ventured to New Zealand for a year of study abroad. I found a position working as a physio—a name often synonymous with an athletic trainer outside of the United States—for a men's semiprofessional rugby team.

At the first game I was getting an idea about the rules of the game from the equipment manager. At halftime I grabbed my kit to meet with the team. The equipment manager grabbed a bucket of water with a few sponges soaking in it. I worked my way around the team checking on all the wounded. I watched as a player removed a sponge and placed it on his sweaty head, wringing water on himself. He threw the sponge back in the bucket. Next, a player picked up a sponge, wiped some blood off his leg, then threw the sponge back in the bucket. Finally, a player rinsed his mouth guard in the bucket.

Being the outspoken American that I am, I asked the equipment manager, "Have you ever heard of blood-borne pathogens?" He responded, "Oh, we don't have those here."

After speaking to a few members of the sports medicine community, I learned that it was just taking more time to institute a commitment to hygiene in the rugby-playing community. My job as the team physio was to expedite the sanitation and hygiene process with my rugby club. The coach, manager, equipment manager, and I all got together to discuss changes that would be necessary to control disease. I left the team after the season knowing that their risk of disease and infection had, at the very least, been reduced.

Tracey Gropper, ATC

# Summary

Microorganisms may cause an illness when a person's immune system is low. It is the hope of all athletes and athletic trainers that those who are ill will stay at home to avoid infecting others. Maintaining a healthy lifestyle will keep the immune system high and keep the microorganisms at a distance. Avoiding contact with bodily fluids and using universal precautions will also prevent the transfer of some diseases.

Athletic competition will place athletes in close proximity to others and thus more at risk for contacting communicable diseases. Rules now force the removal from a game of an athlete who is bleeding, to protect other competitors. Signs and symptoms of many communicable diseases are the same. The only way to diagnose the offending microorganism is to be seen by a physician. Since athletes hide their illness and illnesses mimic one another, it is critical that the members of the athletic training team be up to date on their immunizations.

# Key Terms

Define the following terms found in this chapter:

| | | | |
|---|---|---|---|
| aseptic meningitis | folliculitis | impetigo | mumps |
| bronchitis | furuncle | influenza | rubella |
| chicken pox | HBV | laryngitis | rubeola |
| common cold (coryza) | HIV | microorganisms | vaccinations |
| | immune system | molluscum contagiosum | |

# Questions for Review

1. How can a student assistant protect herself from getting a communicable disease? p. 241
2. How are communicable diseases transmitted? pp. 241-246
3. What is the general treatment for communicable diseases? p. 242
4. How can communicable diseases be distinguished from one another? pp. 242-246
5. What sport rules were designed to prevent the spread of communicable disease? p. 244
6. Why does the athletic trainer recommend seeing a physician for communicable diseases that seem to be mild? p. 242

# Activities for Reinforcement

1. Investigate how vaccinations work.
2. Make a list of the signs and symptoms of each communicable disease.
3. Make a list of the ways to prevent each contagious disease.
4. Practice proper hand washing in public places.
5. Develop a presentation about the importance of hand washing and, with the direction of your ATC, present it to various groups such as elementary classes or boys and girls clubs.

## Above and Beyond

1. Volunteer your time at a walk-in clinic. What are the common forms of communicable diseases seen at this clinic? Investigate whether the communicable disease rate changes depending upon the clinic or the economic status of the community?

2. Design a plan for daily cleaning of the training room. What types of solutions and protective attire should be worn during the cleaning? Use some of the following textbooks to assist with your project.

Rees, A.M. 1997. *Consumer health USA.* Vol. 2. Phoenix: Oryx Press.

Rees, A.M. 1995. *Consumer health USA.* Phoenix: Oryx Press.

Thomas, C.L., ed. 1985. *Taber's cyclopedic medical dictionary.* 13th ed. Philadelphia: Davis.

U.S. Department of Health and Human Services. 1992. *Important information about hepatitis B, hepatitis B vaccine, and hepatitis B immune globulin.* Washington, DC: Government Printing Office.

Weidner, T., and T. Sevier. 1996. Sport, exercise, and the common cold. *Journal of Athletic Training* 31(2): 154–59.

# CHAPTER 26

# Common Drugs Used in Athletics

Drugs have long been thought capable of giving an athlete a competitive advantage. When certain drugs were found to give an advantage, the governing bodies of athletics banned their use. In this chapter we discuss a variety of drugs that enhance or are perceived to enhance athletic performance.

## What Is a Drug?

A **drug** is any substance other than food or water that changes the body's chemistry when it is either ingested or applied topically. Athletes use drugs for therapeutic purposes, performance improvement, and for recreational reasons.

## Therapeutic Drugs in Sport

**Therapeutic drugs** are those that have a medical purpose. They are often prescribed or recommended by the team physician. A therapeutic drug is used to treat a disease, an infection, a disorder such as diabetes, to relieve pain or swelling, and the like.

## Nonsteroid Anti-Inflammatory

**Nonsteroid anti-inflammatory drugs** are used to reduce the amount of tissue swelling after an injury—they include aspirin and ibuprofen. These are over-the-counter drugs, meaning they can be legally purchased without a prescription.

After an injury, aspirin can be used to reduce pain. Aspirin is a blood thinner and can cause more swelling in an area initially. An athlete who is anemic may want to avoid aspirin because of its blood-thinning ability; it will be counterproductive to resolving the anemia.

Ibuprofen will assist in the reduction of pain and swelling. Ibuprofen is commonly used for strains and sprains. In large amounts it often causes an upset stomach and, therefore, should be taken with food. Taking ibuprofen in large doses on a regular basis can cause liver and kidney damage.

## Local Steroids

A **local steroid** is applied to the skin or injected in a joint to reduce swelling and pain; it should not be confused with anabolic steroids. Local steroids are used mainly for allergies, skin disorders, or joint pain. The injected local steroids can cause tendons to be weakened. The team physician prescribes them and will also monitor their use.

## Beta-Adrenergic Drugs

**Beta-adrenergic drugs** are used by asthmatics to maintain the airway during an asthmatic attack by controlling the release of chemicals. These medications are available by prescription only and can be administered through injection, inhalation, or pill form. It is common to see athletes with inhalers. However, in some athletic competitions athletes are not allowed to use the inhaler during competition. Of course if the athlete needs the inhaler to save her life, she needs to use it regardless of the activity. The rules regarding use of medication change constantly. The athletic trainer should check the rules in each sport annually for clarification of which drugs are acceptable.

## Antibiotics

A physician prescribes antibiotics for bacterial infections. There are many antibiotics—the most

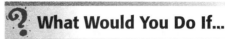

## What Would You Do If...

Before the start of every hockey game the players have a ritual of inhaling from ammonia capsules. They say it "makes us more aware of what's going on in the game."

famous are penicillin and its derivatives. The drug enters the blood stream and assists white blood cells. Using an antibiotic improperly, however, can cause bacteria to change and become resistant to the drug; thus the drug must be taken as prescribed and until it is gone so the infection will not flare up again. When bacteria become resistant to antibiotics the infection can take over.

## Recreational Drugs

Drugs that have no medical purpose are called **recreational drugs**. Many recreational drugs, like alcohol and smokeless tobacco, while legal for some age groups, are illegal for others. Other recreational drugs, such as cocaine, are illegal for everyone. Use of illegal drugs can present at least three major problems:

1. Negative side effects, ranging from lack of motivation to death

2. Unknown impurities in the drugs, which are a result of the lack of legal control over their manufacturing and sales, and which can have unexpected side effects, including death

3. Involvement with criminal elements which can result in both legal and personal problems

## Alcohol

Alcohol is produced by the process of fermentation, which is the breakdown by yeast of the carbohydrates in grains or fruits. Alcohol is consumed as beer, wine, and hard liquor.

The alcohol content in a can of beer, a glass of wine, and a shot of hard liquor—all of which are considered one drink—is roughly equivalent. The difference in the volume is the amount of water present with the alcohol—beer has the most water.

Alcohol causes the heart, breathing, and reaction time to slow—thus alcohol is a depressant. The slowing of bodily processes is not what an athlete needs during athletic competition. Imagine the runner who runs slower, loses balance, loses concentration, and forgets what he is doing. Alcohol also causes reaction time to slow, which makes it unsafe for the drinker to drive. The body treats alcohol as a poison—it is sent to the liver for detoxification. It takes about one hour and twenty minutes for the liver to detoxify one drink. If the body cannot remove the alcohol fast enough, the person will become intoxicated and perhaps vomit the poison from the body. If the drinking is rapid or continues, the person will lose consciousness, go into a coma, or die. Loss of consciousness occurs when the blood alcohol content is .40 percent, and death occurs shortly thereafter.

Those who use alcohol persistently and excessively are prone to liver disorders, nutrition problems, illness, brain disorders, stomach ulcers, and early death. Some studies have indicated that red wine used in moderation is helpful in the prevention of heart disease. However, before anyone decides to start drinking on the basis of those studies, he or she needs to give careful consideration to his or her overall health. No one should drink when harm could come to the person or someone else.

# Caffeine

Caffeine is a drug found in coffee, tea, and chocolate, and in some brands of aspirin, cold medications, weight-loss products, and soda pop. Caffeine is a stimulant, meaning it increases heart and breathing rates. It is also a diuretic, meaning it flushes fluids from the body. Recently, athletes in endurance events like marathons have used caffeine because they thought it would improve their endurance. However, you can't take bathroom breaks when you're running a marathon; thus most runners avoid its use.

The amount of caffeine present in different products varies. Some athletes may have difficulty sleeping after ingesting caffeine. An athlete with a headache may take an aspirin to help the pain without checking to see if it has caffeine and then lie awake all night. Athletes who become addicted to caffeine will have headaches, nausea, and tiredness when they go through withdrawal.

## Tobacco

Tobacco may be used in two forms: smoked and smokeless.

Tobacco is smoked in cigarettes, cigars, or pipes. It is well known that cigarette smoking is highly addictive. It lowers stamina, and its long-term side effects are negative. It greatly increases a person's chances of developing lung cancer, heart disease, emphysema and other breathing disorders, and blindness from macular degeneration. Some people are under the impression that cigar and pipe smoking are not as damaging, but this idea is incorrect.

Smokeless tobacco—snuff or chewing tobacco—is placed against the gums, and nicotine is absorbed into the bloodstream. Athletes use this form of tobacco because they have seen professional athletes use it, especially baseball players. Nicotine causes increased heart rate and breathing rate. All forms of smokeless tobacco contain cancer-causing substances.

Smokeless tobacco is regulated by the laws applying to all tobacco, so sale to a minor is illegal. High school and college association regulations state that smokeless tobacco is not to be used. In the professional ranks, use of smokeless tobacco is currently not regulated.

Those using smokeless tobacco can develop precancerous cells of the cheek, tongue, and gum within two years of use. These cells, called **leukoplakia,** develop so quickly because of the frequency with which the smokeless tobacco is held in the cheek. The precancerous cells are white and some have blisters. If a cancerous growth occurs, surgery may involve removal of the jaw and possibly the tongue. If the cancer

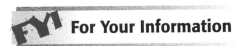

## For Your Information

### Emphysema

Emphysema is an incurable lung disease characterized by the inability to breathe deeply. It is progressive and will eventually destroy the sufferer's ability to take in enough oxygen to sustain life.

### Macular Degeneration

This eye condition causes loss of sight that begins in the center of the field of vision and grows toward the edges until complete blindness results. Sometimes, the loss of sight can be halted or slowed.

has spread throughout the body and the cancer warning signs are overlooked, the athlete may die. In addition, smokeless tobacco can cause serious dental complications—gum disease, bad breath, and cavities are more common among smokeless tobacco users than among others.

## Cocaine

Cocaine is a white powder that can be inhaled to give the user a feeling of euphoria, a feeling of well-being. The euphoric effects are short in duration. The more cocaine one uses, the more one requires to achieve euphoria. Athletes will be restless after use.

Side effects of cocaine use include death from heart problems, suppressed immune system, poor nutrition, loss of money, and cocaine bugs—the hallucination that insects are crawling under the athlete's skin. There are no benefits to be derived from the use of cocaine.

## DMSO

After research on animals showed that dimethyl sulfoxide, **DMSO**, decreased healing time and wound swelling, veterinarians began using DMSO as an anti-inflammatory agent. Athletes have considered using DMSO to speed their return to participation after an injury. The DMSO is absorbed quickly through the skin and leaves a garlic taste in the mouth. It has never been approved for human use, but athletes have found ways of obtaining DMSO. There are no human studies showing that DMSO actually works, and the long-term side effects are unknown.

## Performance-Enhancing Drugs

A performance-enhancing drug is one an athlete believes will make him play better. An athlete may choose to use alcohol to calm himself down before a game. Some athletes may use cocaine to get fired up. Other athletes choose steroids to increase muscle bulk. Regardless of the drug used to improve performance, its use is considered illegal, and most often it does not work and may cause death.

## Anabolic Steroids

**Anabolic steroids** are hormones like testosterone, the male hormone that is responsible for creating and maintaining male secondary sex characteristics. Physicians prescribe anabolic steroids to treat asthma, severe muscle injuries, and arthritis. Steroids have been used to combat the side effects of cancer, which may cause the whole body to atrophy. Athletes use anabolic steroids for the purpose of building muscle.

When athletes discovered that greater muscle mass could be obtained artificially, they began taking steroids to increase strength. Steroids are injected and ingested by a method called stacking. Stacking means the athlete uses a combination of pills and injections to try to avoid the side effects caused by taking a single high dose all at once. However, side effects cannot be avoided. A male using anabolic steroids will experience the following side effects: acne, decreased testicular output, heart problems, cancer, addiction, enlarged breast tissue, mental illness, hair loss, weakened ligaments, decreased growth, violent behavior ('roid rage), vascular problems, and impotence. In females who use anabolic steroids, side effects include deepening of the voice, addiction, stopping of the menstrual cycle, increased body and facial hair, and decreased body fat. These females are turning themselves into males without changing their anatomy.

Use of steroids is illegal in all competitions, including professional and Olympic competitions. Gold medals have been taken away from athletes who have used steroids. Asthmatics are allowed use of their inhalers, but drug-testing boards regulate the amount of steroids allowed.

## Blood Doping

An athlete participating in an endurance event can benefit from having extra oxygen-carrying blood cells, and the more red blood cells he has, the better his oxygen-carrying ability. On the basis of that theory, an athlete may have his blood drawn and stored while his body replaces the lost blood cells. He then has the stored blood reinjected just before the event so that he has more red blood cells than usual. However, placing additional blood into an athlete's system can result in shock.

## Drug Abuse

It is well known that people are living longer, partly because of the medications available to us. Unfortunately, with that idea comes the false notion that medications can solve any problem. Physicians are prescribing more medications, and recreational drugs are readily available. Some athletes choose to use drugs because they think their athletic performance will improve. Students pressure other students to use so they are not alone. Many students and athletes see professionals or their parents using drugs and copy that behavior. Athletes who use drugs may appear to enjoy themselves and seem more relaxed because the drugs reduce inhibitions. Ultimately, teenagers who believe in using drugs can develop long-term health problems. Remember there are more students and athletes who choose

 **What Would You Do If...**

The golf team has just won the state title. You are invited to a party at a local hotel. At the hotel the entire team is drinking and smoking cigars. Your ride home stumbles up to you and says it's time to go.

not to use drugs, and for more reasons, than those who chose to use.

## Drug Testing

There are few high schools that test for drugs, but drug testing is common in professional, international, and college settings. To test for illegal drugs, a urine sample is collected. After the competition the athlete who won is tested along with other competitors who are selected at random. To ensure that the sample is from the athlete, not someone else, the athlete must give the sample in a secured room while a drug-testing supervisor watches. The sample is sealed, signed by the athlete, and sent for testing to determine if the types of drugs used by the athlete are illegal. If a sample is found to have illegal substances, the results are given to the drug-testing governing board. The board determines the penalty for the illegal drug use. In some instances the penalty means the athlete will be banned for a period of competition, and in others it means the athlete will lose medals. Questions about drugs and their use in athletics can be answered through the United States Olympic Committee using the toll-free hotline at (800) 223-0393.

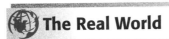 **The Real World**

I was working with a health-conscious athlete who made a habit of jumping from fad to fad looking for the most up-to-date methods for improving his fitness. He indicated that he had constant diarrhea but could not pinpoint a reason. I had him write down everything that he ate and all supplements that he took. I compared all the foods and supplements and found that he was overdosing on vitamin C. Once he stopped using large doses, his diarrhea went away. I recommended that he see a dietitian to help him develop a proper diet, but unfortunately, he did not heed my advice. He decided to simply try another new dietary fad.

*Anonymous*

## Summary

Athletes use drugs, which may be therapeutic or recreational, for a variety of reasons. Therapeutic drugs are used to assist an athlete returning from an injury or recovering from an illness or to prevent an illness from presenting itself during competition. Over-the-counter drugs can be purchased to treat illnesses such as headaches and colds. Recreational drugs have no real value—they are used during social occasions and for the feelings they create.

Some athletes believe that a drug will improve their performance only to find out the improvement is a myth. Caffeine, anabolic steroids, and oxygen are commonly used as performance-enhancing substances. Athletes who use performance-enhancing drugs may see an improvement in their performance, but the side effects and long-term problems outweigh any benefits. Is it worth the risks of using drugs?

The side effects of all drugs must be considered. The team physician should be consulted to determine proper use and dosage of a drug. Drugs can become habit forming. Addiction can be dealt with through various programs, depending upon the type of drug involved. Drug testing is commonplace among elite athletes. Olympic and international competitors are tested on a regular basis for banned drugs.

## Key Terms

Define the following terms found in this chapter:

| | |
|---|---|
| anabolic steroid | local steroid |
| beta-adrenergic drug | nonsteroid anti-inflammatory drug |
| DMSO | recreational drug |
| drug | therapeutic drug |
| leukoplakia | |

## Questions for Review

1. Define the difference between therapeutic and recreational drugs. pp. 249-250
2. What are the reasons that athletes use different drugs? pp. 249-253
3. What are the myths behind the use of recreational drugs in athletics versus the reality? pp. 250-253
4. Why is drug testing done? p. 253

## Activities for Reinforcement

1. Make a list of the types of helpful drugs and their common uses in athletics.
2. Write to the Olympic training center and get a copy of the list of banned drugs.
3. Visit a substance-abuse center and determine which drugs a substance abuser was most likely to have used initially.
4. Make a list of positive reasons why athletes choose not to use drugs.

## Above and Beyond

1. Attend a local meeting on substance abuse, and write a report describing various experiences people have had with drugs. Discuss why some people choose not to use drugs and why people have stopped using.
2. Interview a local dentist concerning the long-term effects of chewing tobacco use.
3. Obtain some brochures from the addresses below. Design your own brochure on one of the drugs discussed in this chapter.

For names, addresses, and phone numbers of health-oriented organizations, write to the following:

Association for the Advancement of Health Education
1900 Association Drive
Reston, VA 22091

To obtain a catalog listing free and low-cost government publications write to the following:

United States Government Printing Office
Superintendent of Documents
Public Documents Distribution Center
Pueblo, CO 81009

# Nutrition and Weight Control

## OBJECTIVES

Upon completing this chapter the student will be able to do the following:
- Understand the body's energy system.
- Understand the basic food groups.
- Understand the role that nutrition plays in a healthy body.
- Design a diet for an athlete.
- Understand that food myths are common with athletes.
- Identify and understand eating disorders.

The body's fuel is food and its energy system is known as **metabolism**. Food that can be broken down by the body for use consists essentially of carbohydrates, proteins, and fats. Other nutrients include vitamins, minerals, and water. The heat-producing, or energy-producing, value in food is measured in calories, and if the body does not require all of the metabolized calories for growth, maintenance, or heat, it stores them, yielding weight gain. If the number of calories brought in is less than what the body needs, the athlete will lose weight. When the body needs energy, it uses carbohydrates first, then fats, and finally protein or the body's muscles are used as fuel. People who are starving have lost muscle because the body needed it for fuel.

Metabolism is the sum of the chemical changes that take place as the body functions. The body's metabolism can change; the rate depends on activity level and sex. Males and teenagers normally have higher metabolisms, as do those who are exercising. An athlete's metabolism slows down as he gets older.

## Major Nutrients

**Nutrients** are those substances that the body uses in metabolism. The nutrients are carbohydrates, fats, proteins, water, vitamins, and minerals.

## Carbohydrates

Carbohydrates are the main fuel source for the body. The digestion of carbohydrates begins in the mouth when they are mixed with saliva secreted by the salivary glands. Nutritionists recommend that carbohydrates make up 40–50 percent of the daily diet and that athletes get about 60 percent of their calories from carbohydrates. See examples of carbohydrates below.

Fiber is the indigestible material found in foods high in carbohydrates. Fiber stimulates the intestines, so diets high in fiber reduce constipation and colon disease. A list of high-fiber carbohydrates is found below.

### Carbohydrates

| Simple | Complex |
| --- | --- |
| Honey | Breads |
| Candy/sweets | Potatoes |
| Fruits | Bagels |
| Soda pop | Cereals |
| Sports drinks | Beans |
| | Vegetables |
| | Nuts and seeds |
| | Pasta |

### Carbohydrates High in Fiber

| Beans | Vegetables | Nuts and seeds | Fruits |
| --- | --- | --- | --- |
| Lima | Peas | Almonds | Prunes |
| Kidney | Corn | Sunflower | Apples |
| | Broccoli | | Banana |
| | | | Coconut |

## Proteins

The basic components of protein are **amino acids**. The body uses amino acids to form new tissues and repair damaged tissues. Teenagers are growing and must make sure they are getting enough protein so that their growth is not slowed; they require more protein than adults do. Pro-tein is found in meat, beans, nuts, dairy products, fish, and eggs. Protein is the last source of energy used by the body. From 15 to 20 percent of an athlete's daily intake of food should be protein. A list of protein sources is found below.

Protein supplements are sold for those who may not get enough in their diet. Manufacturers of protein supplements advertise that their products build muscle. However, high amounts of protein in an athlete's diet can lead to higher fat (since protein-bearing foods usually have a lot of fat), loss of calcium from bones, and dehydration.

### Examples of Proteins

| High amount | Medium amount |
| --- | --- |
| Beef | Yogurt |
| Chicken | Milk |
| Fish | Beans |
| Turkey | Dried peas |
| Veal | Lentils |
| | Eggs |

## Fat

Fat is a necessary component of a healthy diet. For example, the female's reproductive system cannot function properly without a certain amount of fat, and her body cannot support a pregnancy if she doesn't have enough body fat. In addition to being a source of energy, fat helps cells function properly, it is required for the metabolism of some vitamins, and it helps to maintain normal body shape. Fats in food can be classified as saturated or unsaturated.

Saturated fats are found primarily in animal products such as meats, chicken skin, lard, milk, cheese, cream, and butter; some oils (e.g., coconut), and chocolate. Unsaturated fat is generally found in plant products such as soybeans, nuts, and oils (olive, canola, peanut). While fat can make food taste better, too much fat in the diet may contribute to an unhealthy lifestyle and lead to illness. Heart disease, high blood pressure, diabetes, some cancers, and obesity have all been linked to excessive fat intake—especially

## Examples of Fats

| Saturated fat | Unsaturated fat | High cholesterol |
|---|---|---|
| Meats | Fish | Brains |
| Chicken skin | Margarine | Kidneys |
| Lard | Oils (vegetable, olive, fish, and peanut) | Liver |
| Whole milk | | Egg yolk |
| Cheese | Nuts | Cheese |
| Some oils (coconut and palm) | | Lobster |
| Chocolate | | Dark turkey meat |
| Butter | | Butter |
| Processed cheese | | Pork |
| Ice cream | | Ice cream |
| Cream cheese | | Lamb |
| Cococa butter | | Veal |
| | | Cream |
| | | Salmon |
| | | Shrimp |

saturated fat. An athlete needs to review the amount and kinds of fat he is eating and determine if he can improve his diet.

**Cholesterol** is a fatlike substance produced within the body to perform essential cellular functions. Unfortunately, some cholesterol is not essential for life and is stored in the blood vessels. Cholesterol accumulation on a vessel wall can close off the vessel over time and lead to a heart attack.

The cholesterol levels in the body increase when more saturated fats are consumed. Many people avoid foods with cholesterol as a way of decreasing cholesterol in the blood vessels, so many food manufacturers label foods as cholesterol free. Cholesterol occurs in all products containing animal fat—it is found in egg yolks, milk, cream, cheese, butter, and all red meats.

## Vitamins

Vitamins are substances that help the body perform specific functions—they help regulate metabolic processes. Vitamins are found in all foods, so people with a balanced diet will get all of the vitamins they need on a daily basis. An athlete

### What Would You Do If...

The latest fad diet is eating a single food—cabbage. The athletes indicate that they can eat cabbage any way they want but nothing else is on the menu. They rave about how much weight they have lost and you begin to think, "maybe I should try this diet."

who eats improperly, however, will need to obtain vitamins through supplements to meet the daily needs for proper functioning of the body.

## Minerals

Minerals are inorganic chemical elements that are necessary for building bones and muscles, the conduction of nerve impulses, and normal metabolism and heart function. Minerals are found in all foods, and the athlete does not require a supplement unless her diet is not balanced. The incidence of some diseases has been reduced after scientists added minerals to commonly used products. For example, fluoride is added to water to prevent tooth decay, and calcium is added to orange juice to help bolster its intake for those who do not like dairy products.

## Water

Water is an essential component of the diet, and makes up about 57 percent of the total body weight. Water is necessary for proper body functioning. It is beneficial to the kidneys and excretion, chemical reactions throughout the body, sweating, blood flow, and lubrication of joints. Water comes from the faucet, in bottles, or in various products like soda pop, sport drinks, juice drinks, coffee, and tea. When an athlete is competing, the athletic trainer must remember that most athletes do not drink enough water to replace what they lose in sweat. An athlete's thirst level is a poor indicator of how much water is really needed to replace sweat.

An athlete should drink at least eight 8-ounce glasses of water a day. He should try to drink at least one liter of water for every thousand calories spent. Those who are trying to lose weight will find that drinking that much water will cleanse their system of waste products and also give them the feeling of being full.

Wrestlers are notorious for cutting weight to get into a particular weight class. Unfortunately, most often they cut the weight over a short period of time and the weight loss is just water loss. The restriction of water and the water weight loss will cause the wrestler to be fatigued and much less effective. Wrestlers who want to lose weight need to be supervised by a dietitian, and they must still drink eight glasses of water per day.

## Balanced Diet and Portions

A balanced diet is one in which the number of portions eaten daily will provide all of the nutrients necessary to remain healthy. A teenager's daily diet should include the following: six to eleven portions of bread, cereal, rice, and pasta; two to four portions of fruits; three to five servings of vegetables; two to three portions of meat, poultry, fish, beans, eggs, and nuts; three portions of milk, yogurt, and cheese; and fats, oils, and sweets are eaten rarely.

Foods in sauces generally contain fat. If an athlete is trying to watch his weight, then asking for the sauce or gravy on the side is best. He can then choose how much sauce to put on instead of letting someone else decide. No teenager should eat fewer than three portions from the milk group, two portions from the meat group, and four portions from the fruit, vegetables, and bread groups. Fast foods are less likely to contain necessary vitamins and are high in fat.

When choosing how much to eat, the size of the portion is of great importance. One meat portion is the size of a deck of cards. A slice of bread, half a bagel, or a tennis ball-sized muffin or serving of pasta is one portion of breads or carbohydrates. Half a cup of vegetables is considered a portion, no matter what kind of vegetable. Any whole fruit (apples, oranges) the size of a tennis ball is considered a portion. A portion of berries is one-half cup. One cup of milk is a portion. For ice cream and yogurt a portion is three-quarters of a cup. A portion of cheese is one-third the size of a deck of cards.

## Eating Disorders

Unfortunately, some athletes may participate in athletics to gain a thin "attractive" body. An

### What Would You Do If...

You are hauling a 10-gallon water cooler out to football practice. The head coach stops you, takes the lid of the cooler off, and pours in a container of creatine. You are shocked. The coach responds by saying, "If we are going to win a state title we need a little extra advantage." He insists that you bring him the water coolers every day.

athlete's excessive exercise may appear to be devotion to the sport, when in reality it is the first sign of an eating disorder that a coach may recognize.

All athletes should understand that the body has two types of fat: essential and storage. Essential fat is necessary for the body to function. The minimum essential fat for males is 7 percent and for females, 12 percent. Storage fat is excess fat—it's just hanging around with no purpose. If an athlete has "love handles" or a "beer belly' (which we hope is not from beer!) that he wants to get rid of—fine. But if a male athlete dips under 7 percent body fat, or if a female athlete goes below 12 percent body fat, those athletes are putting their health and their performance in danger.

Some athletes who are worried about how they look in a uniform may end up with an eating disorder as they try hard to make the proper weight or to look good. Sports such as swimming, cross-country, track, gymnastics, and wrestling are the sports in which eating disorders often appear. Officials who give scores based on a look, image, or smile push athletes in the wrong direction. Athletic associations and coaches could help by being more accepting of baggy shorts, shirts, or skirts—but do not count on that happening.

Athletes need to feel in control of something in their lives, even if it is only food. This desire for control can lead to overeating (and the development of obesity), **anorexia nervosa,** or **bulimia**. Anorexia nervosa and bulimia are most often thought of as eating disorders that occur chiefly in white females, but they are also common among males and athletes of color. Anorexia nervosa and bulimia have a death rate of 22 percent. The athletic trainer should check with the athlete's physician for a perspective on the athlete's ability to participate safely if he has an eating disorder.

## Anorexia Nervosa and Bulimia

Anorexia nervosa is characterized by a pattern of starvation and a fear of being fat. Bulimia is characterized by bouts of bingeing followed by self-induced vomiting. Both of these eating disorders are signs of deeper psychological problems, which must be addressed. An athletic trainer who recognizes an eating disorder must refer the athlete to a specialist on eating disorders for counseling. If the illness is severe, the athlete may need to be hospitalized.

## Signs and Symptoms of Anorexia Nervosa

1. Decrease in caloric intake
2. Excessive physical activity, which is compulsive
3. Obsession with being fat, constantly talking about being fat
4. A fear of being overweight, despite the appearance that there is no need to lose weight
5. Calorie counting and meal skipping
6. Severe mood swings
7. Weight is less than recommended on weight-height tables
8. Cardiac arrhythmia from lack of essential nutrients
9. Digestive problems—abdominal cramping, gas, constipation, or bloating
10. Skin problems and dry, brittle hair
11. Brittle bone disorder or stress fractures from lack of minerals in the system
12. Unnecessary weight loss of between 8 and 20 pounds (Bartimole 1995)
13. Abnormal blood chemistry
14. Fatigue and weakness
15. Having weight loss medications and laxatives
16. Inability to sleep

## Signs and Symptoms of Bulimia

1. Burns on the corners and interior of the mouth from stomach acid
2. Bingeing on massive amounts of food, usually sweets and junk foods, until overfull
3. Vomiting after eating
4. Leaving the room right after eating and going into the bathroom
5. Depression after eating large amounts of food
6. Vomiting, diuretics, laxatives, enemas, fasting, or high amounts of exercise after a bout of bingeing
7. Weight changes—gain, loss, or both
8. Feelings of lack of control when eating
9. Hiding of food, and eating when no one is around
10. Digestive problems—abdominal cramping, gas, constipation, or bloating
11. Facial problems—bags under the eyes, tearing, and red face
12. Cardiac arrhythmia from lack of essential nutrients
13. Loss of tooth enamel from stomach acid
14. Bingeing at least two times per week for a couple of months (Grandjean 1991)
15. Concern about body image
16. Having diet pills, enema bags, or syrup of ipecac
17. Swelling of the legs, face, and hands
18. Finger calluses on the back of the hand (Stephenson 1991)
19. Blood chemistry imbalances
20. Headaches
21. Red eyes

## Obesity

A male is considered to be obese if over 20 percent of his weight is fat; a female is considered obese if she has over 30 percent body fat. Obesity is associated with higher cholesterol levels, hypertension, kidney illness, joint problems, diabetes, lung diseases, cancers, heart disease, and early death. Obesity is usually

## The Real World

A couple of times a year the athletic training staff and student assistants go to dinner and see a movie together. On this occasion we went to the mall and had dinner at a fast-food restaurant. At the end of the meal, one of the girls excused herself and went to the rest room. Her meal had not been particularly large, nor was she. Upon her return we went to the movie, but I had a strange feeling about her use of the rest room. When the same thing happened again at another social event, I felt we had to do something. The assistant athletic trainer, who was also suspicious, decided to call her parents and told them that he was concerned about her behavior. The parents responded to the phone conversation by taking their daughter to a physician. She was diagnosed as bulimic and spent three months in an eating disorders clinic. She has asked me many times, "Who should I thank for saving my life?" I have never told her.

Lorin Cartwright, MS, ATC, EMT

## What Would You Do If...

In the locker room a swimmer accidentally drops her purse. All of the contents fall out onto the floor. You politely help her pick up her things. You notice she has some opened containers of laxatives and diet pills.

caused by a combination of factors: heredity, overeating, and lack of activity.

A tendency towards obesity can begin at birth because of genetic factors. Moreover, a child who is born to parents who are obese is likely to pick up their habits and also become obese. Overeating means that an athlete is ingesting more calories than the body is using—the additional calories are stored as fat in the body.

Many people are active in their teenage and college years. Once an athlete takes a job and starts a family, it becomes difficult to maintain the same level of physical activity. The lack of physical activity coupled with the same eating habits yields additional weight gain. Exercise must be a priority for athletes who have stopped playing sports so that they will not gain weight.

People are born with a certain number of fat cells. As an athlete continues to eat and gain stored fat, the fat cells increase in size until they can hold no more, then more fat cells are produced. Once a fat cell is produced it does not go away. A weight loss diet will cause the fat cells to shrink but not go away. People have undergone liposuction to have their fat cells sucked out, but remember, eating habits do not change be-

cause of liposuction. People can come home with a new-appearing body only to go back to their old eating habits and get their old body back.

Fat will be deposited in genetically predetermined areas. In other words, no one can control where the extra calories will be deposited, nor can we control where fat will be burned off with exercise. In females, fat is likely to be deposited in the hips, breasts, abdomen, and thighs. In males, it is likely to be deposited in the abdomen, chest, and thighs.

In some sports obesity is not an issue. Football requires several large players on the line. In wrestling the various weight classes will accommodate the obese wrestler. Shot putters, hammer throwers, and sumo wrestlers all tend to be large and sometimes obese.

## Athletic Nutrition

One of the most frequent questions to an athletic trainer is "what types of foods should an athlete eat to be the best?" The answer is very simple—eat a well-balanced meal suggested by the food pyramid. Balanced meals will provide all of the nutritional requirements to be healthy and perform well. When designing a program, the athletic trainer and dietitian need to know if the athlete wants to gain, lose, or maintain her weight.

The athletic trainer and dietitian can develop a diet that will insure all nutritional needs are met, based upon the nutritional and physical assessment of the athlete. An athlete trying to gain weight will be placed on a diet in which the number of calories eaten will exceed the energy expended. An athlete trying to lose weight will be placed on a diet that will supply fewer calories than the amount of energy expended. The athlete's weight loss should not exceed an average of two pounds a week. He should never increase room temperatures, sit in a hot tub or sauna, wear rubberized clothing, or work out in high temperatures with lots of clothes to lose weight. A strict exercise and weight-loss plan designed by the athletic trainer and the dietitian is the only plan to follow.

## Pregame Meals

Pregame meals should be high in carbohydrates and fluids. Carbohydrates are easier to digest than fats and proteins, and they can be converted into energy to be used immediately. The pregame meal should be eaten three to four hours prior to activity. Water is the best liquid to drink, and the athlete should be sure she is well hydrated about one hour before competition.

Athletes who are anxious about the upcoming competition may use high carbohydrate-loaded sport drinks. Sport drinks are digested quickly, which helps the anxious athlete avoid feelings of nausea.

When the athletic trainer and dietitian are considering recommending a pregame meal, they should remember the diversity of the team. Some of the athletes may have specific food preferences like Mexican, Arabic, Greek, or Latin foods. The athletic trainer has homework to do—he needs to analyze these diverse foods and determine what types are acceptable before the game. Another consideration is religious holidays for team members. An athlete may observe a holiday with fasting or by not eating meat. The athletic trainer and dietitian should be aware of this issue a week in advance to best prepare the athlete for the holiday diet. Vegetarians have special protein needs and should work with the athletic trainer and dietitian to make sure their food needs are met. The box lists different types of vegetarians.

Some good pregame foods include pasta, fruits, plain crackers, rice cakes, cereal, vegetarian foods, vegetarian tacos, potatoes, meatless lasagna, soup, rice, juice, bread, raisins, pancakes, and waffles. Besides eating foods high in carbohydrates, the athlete should eat familiar foods. A pregame meal is no time to experiment.

## Postgame Meals

Hopefully the team will do something to celebrate, and food can be there to replenish energy supplies. However, athletic trainers should

## Types of Vegetarians

**Semi-vegetarian:** Vegetable diet with occasional dairy and meats

**Lactoovo-vegetarian:** Vegetable diet with dairy and eggs

**Lacto-vegetarian:** Vegetable diet with dairy

**Vegan:** Vegetable diet

not use food as a reward—giving a team pizza, soda pop, and ice cream if they win—or punishment—driving the team straight home. Such actions can create an association between eating and pleasurable or miserable experiences that leads to overeating or not eating.

After the event athletes should eat complex carbohydrates, but some proteins, fats, and simple carbohydrates are also fine. Excessive eating should be avoided, and water replacement is necessary to compensate for sweating during competition. Several glasses of juice, water, or sport drinks are perfect choices.

## Meals During All-Day Events

Many athletic competitions take place over the course of a full day. The athlete may be asked to compete several times during the day, and a full-course sit-down meal is out of the question. So what should the athlete do to keep energy levels up? The answer is to eat small meals many times during the day. The meals should contain little protein and fat and a lot of complex carbohydrates and fluids (not soda pop). The amount of complex carbohydrates can be half a sandwich six times during the day. When the athlete eats is dependent upon when she must compete; she will provide time to allow the food to digest as much as possible. Good all-day-event foods are bagels (no cream cheese), English muffins, bananas, baked potatoes, soup, fruit, pasta, pancakes, sport drinks, yogurt, cereal, and vegetables.

## Carbohydrate Loading

Athletes who participate in endurance events (marathoners, bikers, triathletes, long distance swimmers) may benefit from a technique called carbohydrate loading. Carbohydrate loading means depleting carbohydrates for seven days and then ingesting large amounts of carbohydrates for three days before the event. The theory behind carbohydrate loading is that carbohydrate stores are used as energy during athletic competition. If the athlete has a lot of stored carbohydrate he is less likely run out of energy. Depleting before loading causes the body to store more carbohydrates than usual once carbohydrate consumption resumes. Remember that once carbohydrate stores are used up, the body begins to break down fat. Breaking down fat requires more energy than using the readily available carbohydrates, again draining energy away from athlete. So the greater the carbohydrate stores, the better off the athlete.

If an athlete is involved in an endurance activity, the athletic trainer and dietitian should design a program for carbohydrate loading. The athlete's diet will be changed ten days prior to competition; and three days before the event, 70 percent of what the athlete eats will be carbohydrates. During carbohydrate loading the athlete does not exercise for the three days prior to the event. Fats and protein foods are decreased as a part of carbohydrate loading.

# Popular Nutritional Supplements

There is always someone trying to sell something to make money. Companies hire famous professional athletes to hype their item. A good-looking person is used to hype a product while on a beach with a beautiful companion. The advertisement is designed to make the potential users believe if they use the product they, too, will be someplace warm with a beautiful companion. Some companies claim that certain nutritional items will help an athlete perform better, run faster, or have more energy. When you hear a promise but you don't see any independent research evidence to support the claim, keep your money in your pocket.

## Creatine

A popular nutritional supplement promoted on the market is creatine. This substance is found in the body in high levels right after exercise. Creatine is found in fish and in meats. An athlete would have to eat 15 pounds of meat per day to obtain the same amount of creatine recommended as a supplement. The advertisers claim that creatine is an energy source and it helps encourage muscle growth. Athletes who are strength training appear to have increased power for brief highly intense exercise, with creatine supplements. The long-term effects of its use are inconclusive; thus creatine should be avoided.

## Amino Acids

Amino acids are the building blocks of protein. Thus, people have thought that daily amino acid supplements (pills or powder) would make them stronger and faster and increase protein storage. The basis for these ideas was the notion that amino acids cause the release of growth hormone. Growth hormone does increase muscle mass, but amino acids do not cause growth hormone release. Amino acids are sold in fitness magazines with pictures of very muscular men and women holding the containers. Don't buy it. Amino acids supplements are very expensive, and the athlete's daily diet will provide all the necessary amino acids.

## Summary

An athlete's daily nutrition plays a critical role in his or her ability to give an optimal performance. Most athletes meet their daily requirements by eating proper-sized portions of a balanced diet. Some athletes consistently eat foods that are high in fat and cholesterol and low in fiber. This can lead to bad health consequences. As an athlete gets older her metabolism slows, and she must reduce the number of calories she consumes or she will gain weight.

Water intake and fluid replacement are key for athletic participation. The rule for fluid replacement is one liter for every thousand calories lost. The ATC and dietitian should decide on pregame and postgame meals based on the event and the athlete's needs, with consideration of the athlete's religion and cultural background. Athletes are constantly looking for an edge on their opponents. Fad diets and supplements are hyped as the greatest thing to improve performance. The athletes and the athletic trainer must research the supplement before anyone uses it.

## Key Terms

Define the following terms found in this chapter:

| | | |
|---|---|---|
| amino acids | bulimia | metabolism |
| anorexia nervosa | cholesterol | nutrients |

## Questions for Review

1. What are the basic nutrients? p. 257
2. What are the main food groups? p. 260
3. How much water does an athlete need during competition? p. 259
4. How can an athlete be sure he is drinking enough fluids? p. 259
5. How many servings are needed per day from each food group for males and females? p. 260
6. A pregame meal should consist of what types of foods? p. 263
7. If an athlete desires a postgame meal, what foods should be included? p. 263
8. How helpful are food supplements to athletic performance? p. 264

## Activities for Reinforcement

1. Design a pregame meal for fictitious swim and ice hockey teams.
2. Invite a specialist on eating disorders to class to further explain bulimia and anorexia nervosa.
3. Keep track of what you eat for one week and determine if you have any areas where you eat too much or too little. Make recommendations for improving your eating habits after talking with the athletic trainer and school dietitian.

## Above and Beyond

1. Observe your classmates' eating habits during lunch. What are the typical types of foods they eat, what categories are the foods in, and what foods are lacking in their diets?
2. Design a pregame meal for a fictitious insulin-dependent athlete.
3. Using the following textbooks and brochures and various ethnic recipe books, determine the common foods eaten by people with those backgrounds, and the fat, protein, vegetable, grain, and dairy in each.

Bartimole, J. 1995. The nutritional concerns of the female athlete. *NATA News* November, 4-5.

Clark, N. 1997. *Nancy Clark's sports nutrition guidebook.* 2d ed. Champaign, IL: Human Kinetics.

Clark, N. 1989. Good nutrition for older persons. *Sports Medicine Digest* 11(2): 6.

Coleman, E. 1984. Nutrition principles for the child athlete. *Sports Medicine Digest* 6(12): 6.

Grandjean, A.C. 1991. Eating disorders: The role of the athletic trainer. *The Journal of the National Athletic Trainer's Association* 26(2): 105–12.

Hegarty, V. 1988. *Decisions in nutrition.* St. Louis: Times Mirror/Mosby.

Katch, F.I., and W.D. McArdle. 1993. *Nutrition, weight control, and exercise.* Philadelphia: Lea & Febiger.

Miller, A.E. 1996. Creatine supplements in athletics. *Sports Medicine Update* 11(3): 12–16.

Peterson, M., and K. Peterson. 1988. *Eat to compete: A guide to sports nutrition.* Chicago: Year Book Medical.

Pfeiffer, R.P., and B.C. Mangus. 1995. *Concepts of athletic training.* Boston: Jones and Bartlett.

Sherman, M.W., and D.R. Lamb, eds. 1995. *International Journal of Sport Nutrition.* Vol. 5 Suppl. Champaign, IL: Human Kinetics.

Stephenson, J.N. 1991. Medical consequences and complication of anorexia nervosa and bulimia in female athletes. *The Journal of the National Athletic Trainers' Association* 26(2): 130–35.

Williams, M.H. 1989. *Beyond training: How athletes enhance performance legally and illegally.* Champaign, IL: Human Kinetics.

Williams, M.H. 1992. *Nutrition for fitness and sport.* 3d ed. Dubuque, IA: Brown.

Williams, M.H. 1993. *Nutritional supplements for strength trained athletes.* Gatorade Sports Science Exchange 6(6).

Food and Nutrition Information Center
National Agricultural Library ARS USDA
10301 Baltimore Avenue, Room 304
Beltsville, MD 20705-2351
*Resource lists*

General Mills Consumer Services
P.O. Box 1113
Minneapolis, MN 55440
*Fact sheets and recipes*

Giant Food Incorporated
Building 1 Department 597
Box 1804
Washington, DC 20013
*Brochures on food*

Consumer Response and Information Center
Kraft Foods Inc.
One Kraft Court
Glenview, IL 60025-5091
*Nutrition brochure series, recipes, and corresponding education sheets*

National Cattlemen's Beef Association
Fulfillment Center
2300 Windsor Court, Unit D
Addison, IL 60101
*Booklets and videos*

United States Department of Agriculture
USDA Agricultural Research Service
National Agricultural Service
Beltsville, MD 20705-2351
*Brochures and CD-ROM*

United States Government
Superintendent of Documents, Mail Stop SM
732 N Capitol NW
Washington, DC 20402-0003
*Books, cookbooks, brochures, CD-ROM*

# Unit IX

# Professional and Administrative Aspects of Athletic Training

# Athletic Training as a Profession

## OBJECTIVES

Upon completing this chapter the student will be able to do the following:

- Define athletic training.
- Describe the roles of the ATC.
- Describe the roles of other health care providers and the sports medicine team.
- List the requirements for becoming a competent ATC.
- Describe the job opportunities available to ATCs.

**Athletic training** is a profession dedicated to maintaining and improving the health and well-being of the physically active population and preventing athletics-related injuries and illnesses. While individuals have provided health care to injured athletes for centuries, it was not until 1991 that the American Medical Association formally recognized athletic training as an allied health care profession. The **National Athletic Trainers' Association (NATA)**, which is responsible for setting professional certification standards, was formed in 1950.

## Roles of the Athletic Trainer

NATA has established the various roles of the certified athletic trainer, which include the following:

- **Injury prevention.** Preventing athletic injuries includes preparticipation physical exams; proper strength and conditioning programs; proper equipment and equipment fitting; taping, bandaging, and bracing; and good nutrition.

- **Recognition, evaluation, and immediate care of athletic injuries.** When an athlete is injured, the ATC must be ready to respond. He must maintain first aid and cardiopulmonary resuscitation certification through such organizations as the **American Red Cross** and the **National Safety Council**. Moreover, the ATC must be able to recognize injuries and assess their severity so that he can know how to treat or whether he should refer an athlete to a physician.

• **Rehabilitation and reconditioning of athletic injuries.** After initial treatment, the ATC directs the athlete through exercises and treatments to help her return to normal function. This is called **rehabilitation**. **Reconditioning** is getting the athlete back into shape for athletic participation.

• **Health care administration.** ATCs are often responsible for managing state-of-the-art facilities, so they must have the administrative skills necessary for preparing work and purchase orders and scheduling staff. Injuries, treatments, and rehabilitation progress must be documented accurately.

• **Professional development and responsibility.** Technology is changing rapidly, and ATCs must continue their education to remain current with the latest health care developments—they attend seminars, read, write, and conduct research. ATCs must conduct themselves professionally and with integrity. No one likes receiving medical treatment from someone who is unprofessional.

A professional understands that she cannot accomplish everything by herself, so she works as part of a sports medicine team.

# Sports Medicine and the Sports Medicine Team

In this book, **sports medicine** refers to the care of the physically active population who have suffered an athletic injury or illness. The sports medicine profession includes ATCs, medical doctors, physical therapists, dentists, chiropractors, coaches, sport psychologists, strength and conditioning specialists, school nurses, sport nutritionists, and student assistants (see figure 28.1). A sports medicine team may include any or all of these individuals.

Like any team, the sports medicine team must work cooperatively. If a football running back runs wherever he wants with the ball, regardless of where the blockers are, his team will never win. The team must coordinate its plays if it is ever to be successful. This is how an effective sports medicine team works.

**Figure 28.1** The sports medicine team consists of central and peripheral members, each of whom has specific responsibilities and areas of expertise.

## The Central Team

Ideally, the central team comprises the injured athlete, his parents, the ATC, the team physician, and the coach. The central team works together to make initial decisions about injuries, illness, and even sport performance.

• **The athlete.** The athlete is the center of the team. He provides other members with vital information about the injury.

• **The athlete's parent or guardian.** Because the sports medicine team is concerned about making decisions in the athlete's best interest, both the athlete and his parent or guardian must be involved in the central team.

• **Team physician.** The team physician is the medical authority who oversees the sports medicine team effort. The physician examines the athlete for injuries and illnesses and performs tests such as X rays or blood tests to help determine an athlete's problem. The ATC acts under the direction of the team physician, who is typically an orthopedic specialist. **Orthopedists** deal primarily with injuries to the musculoskeletal system.

• **Certified athletic trainer.** The ATC communicates with the injured athlete, her parent or guardian, the team physician, and the coach. The ATC is on-site at a game or practice, and he often makes the initial injury assessment, provides emergency injury care, and provides follow-up treatment or referrals to other sports medicine team members as needed. Because of these multiple roles, the ATC is a critical link in the chain of professionals that comprises the sports medicine team.

- **The coach.** Because the coach has daily contact with the athletes, he may know them better than do the others on the sports medicine team. The coach often has close contact with the parents or guardians of the athletes as well. This allows him to play a vital role in communicating with the injured athlete and her parents. When an athlete is returning to competition following rehabilitation, the coach, in consultation with the ATC, can modify the training, exercises, and drills the athlete performs so she can safely progress to peak performance.

## The Peripheral Team

While the central sports medicine team work together to manage an athletic injury, they often rely on peripheral team members to provide specialized care or assistance.

- Many injured athletes have a **primary care physician**. Because this doctor has worked with the athlete before, the sports medicine team must include the primary care physician in their decisions. The primary care physician may refer the athlete to a specialist such as a podiatrist, allergist, urologist, gynecologist, cardiologist, neurologist, or pediatrician.

- A **podiatrist** examines and diagnoses problems below the knee and performs foot surgeries. He can prescribe corrective devices such as orthotics (shoe inserts).

- An **allergist** determines whether someone has an allergy, and if so, how to treat it. An **allergy** is an immune response, which can cause red swollen tissue or runny nose, to a substance that should normally be tolerated.

- A **urologist** treats problems of the urinary tract.

- A **gynecologist** deals with conditions and care of the reproductive system in women.

- A **cardiologist** treats heart disease and heart abnormalities.

- A **pediatrician** specializes in the medical treatment of children.

- A **dentist** may be involved if the athletic injury is to the facial area. The team dentist may also provide properly fitting mouth guards to prevent dental injuries.

- A **physical therapist** provides rehabilitation for bone and joint injuries, head injuries, and muscle injuries and imbalances so that individuals may return to normal physical function and active daily living.

- A **neurologist** is a physician who specializes in conditions of the nervous system and may examine an athlete who has suffered a head injury.

- A **student assistant** assists the ATC with many daily tasks. For example, a student assistant can enter treatment data into a computer program, tape athletes prior to practices and games (in some instances), help stock medical cabinets and bags, hydrate the athletes during practices in hot weather, and prepare for rehabilitation procedures (organizing weights, whirlpools, and equipment). Also, because they are often the same age as the athletes, student assistants can identify with the athletes and may develop strong bonds with them. This can be especially helpful because the athletes will feel comfortable enough to ask questions and clarify any information they have received. It is important to keep in mind that *student assistants can only function under the direct supervision of an ATC*.

### ❓ What Would You Do If...

An athlete was hit in the head during practice. He was evaluated by the ATC and the team physician. Each of these individuals wanted another opinion. The athlete complains to you, and says, "I don't understand why I have to see a neurologist. I have already been seen by our team physician."

- **A chiropractor** is a health professional who takes a holistic approach to patient care by focusing on spinal misalignments. Although chiropractors are not physicians, they may treat musculoskeletal disorders and restore normal function by manipulating bones, specifically at the spinal column.

- **The school nurse** is a health care professional trained to identify and care for illnesses and disorders. The school nurse is a valuable educational resource for the ATC and can help the athletic training team deliver safe, effective health care.

- **A registered dietitian** is a nutritional specialist who can help an athlete, and sometimes the entire athletic team, construct a proper diet based on the level of activity and dietary needs. He can also tailor meals for athletes who have specific problems, such as diabetes.

- **The equipment manager** purchases and maintains appropriate protective and supportive athletic equipment. This is a significant role because many athletic injuries can be prevented with proper equipment. Equipment managers stay current on the latest and best types of padding, headgear, and clothing that are available.

# Becoming a Certified Athletic Trainer

To become an ATC, an individual must earn a bachelor's degree from a college or university. Some schools offer a major in athletic training, but in others it is considered a minor or an area of specialization. This means that students must major in a different subject along with being enrolled in the athletic training curriculum. Just as in many other professions, an individual must be certified to be an ATC.

## Routes to Certification

There are at present two routes to becoming a certified athletic trainer—attending either an internship program or an approved program. An internship program requires 1,500 hours of hands-on experience. However, the internship route to certification will no longer be available after the year 2004. At that time, to be eligible to become an ATC, a student must graduate from an athletic training program approved by the Commission of Accreditation of Allied Health Education Programs (CAAHEP). Students enrolled in an undergraduate athletic training program are expected to receive a minimum of 800 hours of hands-on experience as well as specified courses related to athletic training. After graduation, the students must pass the NATA board of certification examination prior to practicing as an ATC. Many states have laws that require that the ATC also be recognized by the state. Failure to follow such guidelines could result in legal action, including arrest. The regulations for athletic training vary greatly from state to state. Three common forms of credentials include licensure, certification, and registration.

States that have **licensure** requirements generally specify who is allowed to practice athletic training and what duties they are allowed to perform. **Certification** insures that an individual has achieved basic knowledge and skill to practice athletic training, while **registration** requires an individual to register with the state prior to practicing athletic training.

## Required Areas of Study

When a student enters an athletic training curriculum program to become an ATC, she must study athletic injury evaluation, human anatomy, human physiology, exercise physiology, biomechanics, psychology, nutrition, pharmacology, physics, and organization and administration.

## 🌐 The Real World

Although I originally went to college to become a physical educator, I have always been interested in health care. Thus, I selected athletic training as a health profession because it deals with sports and because it is one of the few health professions where you are trained to prevent injuries, give immediate care to an injury, and rehabilitate an injury. We have the privilege of working with individuals from the moment they are injured until the moment they return to their sport. This is a claim that few health professions can make.

Bill Pitney, MS, ATC

- **Athletic injury evaluation** refers to understanding and identifying an athlete's readiness to participate in physical activity, identifying athletic injuries, and assessing progress during the rehabilitation of athletic injuries.

- **Human anatomy** refers to how the body is organized and to the study of bones, joints, muscles, organs, their structure and location. The ATC cannot recognize injuries unless she understands normal human anatomy.

- **Human physiology** refers to human bodily functions. The treatments rendered to athletes by ATCs must be based on sound physiological principles. For example, after an athlete is injured, the tissue will heal in several stages. The ATC must understand what is happening during each stage in order to prescribe exercises that won't reinjure the tissue.

- **Exercise physiology** examines how the body normally functions during activity. When an individual exercises, demands are placed on the body, and the body adapts to them. For example, an exercising person's heart and breathing rates will be higher than when that person is at rest. Understanding the changes that exercise causes in the body is essential for recognizing signs and symptoms of illness or injury.

- **Biomechanics** is also called **kinesiology,** which is the science of movement mechanics. ATCs are responsible for teaching athletes proper movements and exercises to recover from injuries. In addition, ATCs often apply tape and braces to prevent the athletes from performing certain movements in order to reduce the risk of injury. Such treatments cannot be effectively applied unless one first understands the normal biomechanics of the body.

- **Psychology** is the study of variables that affect human behavior. For athletes who have dedicated a tremendous amount of time to their sport, injuries are not only devastating physically but also emotionally. The ATC can use what he learns in psychology to understand an individual's behavior after an injury and to differentiate symptoms of an injury or illness from an emotional problem. Moreover, ATCs need to understand how to help athletes through the difficult task of rehabilitation after a serious injury. In addition, the ATC must know when and where to make referrals and how to develop alcohol and drug abuse prevention programs.

- **Nutrition** refers to the study of foods in relation to the metabolic needs of the body. Athletes have slightly different nutritional demands than people who do not exercise. ATCs must have a basic understanding of nutrition in order to give good advice and to refer athletes to proper specialists if advanced nutritional help is needed.

- **Pharmacology** refers to the study of drugs and drug interactions in the body. While ATCs cannot administer medications to athletes, they do need to have an understanding of both prescription and nonprescription medications. For example, when taking certain medications, an athlete should not be exposed to the sun; the ATC can recommend moving practice to a shaded area or see to it that the athlete is wearing appropriate clothing.

- **Physics** refers to the study of physical forces and their affects on objects. Knowledge of how physical forces affect the body and of the physics behind energy absorption, dissipation, and transmission may help the ATC select appropriate protective equipment.

- **Organization and administration** refer to the management aspects of athletic training and athletics. Many ATCs develop policies and procedures for operating various facilities. They also need to understand the legal issues that ATCs often face in athletics.

# Athletic Training Careers

ATCs have opportunities for employment in a variety of settings.

## Traditional Settings

Traditional employment includes teaching facilities, such as high schools, colleges, or universities, and professional or semiprofessional athletic teams.

- **Scholastic environments.** Considering the fact that many schools may have anywhere from 10 to 28 different sports, these settings can be very challenging. Some high schools have full-time ATCs, but many high school ATCs teach academic courses and receive a stipend (extra

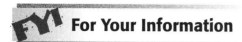

## For Your Information

### Starting Salary

According to Moss (1996), the average starting salary for a high school ATC/teacher position was $25,963 in 1994.

money) for providing athletic training after school. Most high school positions cover 10 months of the year; college athletic training positions range from nine- to 12-month contracts.

• **Professional teams.** While many students want to become an ATC with a professional sport team, this goal is difficult to achieve. Compared to colleges, high schools, and clinical settings, there are few positions in the professional ranks. Also, ATCs with pro teams often have a grueling travel schedule. The reward is the opportunity to work closely with elite athletes and coaches in an extremely competitive environment.

## Nontraditional Settings

Nontraditional settings for ATCs include clinics or rehabilitation centers, dual clinical/high school positions, corporate fitness centers, health clubs, and industrial settings.

• **Sports medicine clinic.** While most ATCs have diverse roles ranging from emergency care to health care administration, the clinical ATC tends to focus on rehabilitation. Many clinical ATCs enjoy the one-on-one relationships they build with patients during their rehabilitation programs.

• **Clinic and high school.** Many programs have combined the traditional and clinical settings and created new positions and job opportunities for ATCs. For example, it is not uncommon for a sports medicine center to have ATCs who work part of a day (usually the morning) in a clinic and then go to a local high school in the afternoon to cover practices and events.

• **Health clubs.** Many companies and health clubs have come to realize that ATCs are a

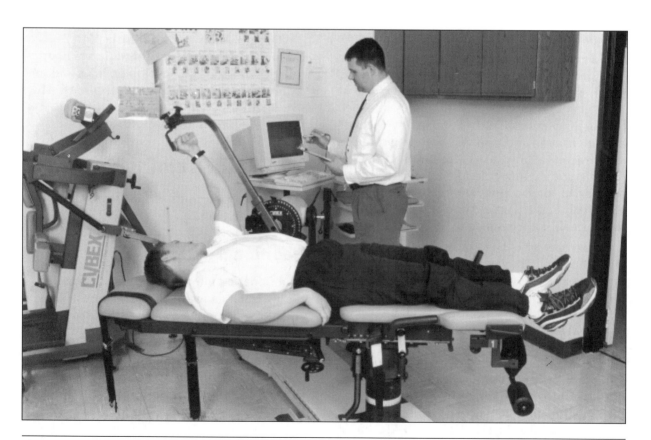

**Figure 28.2** Athletic trainers also work in nontraditional settings such as sports medicine clinics.

business asset. Not everyone who enters a health club or corporate fitness program is completely healthy. In fact, some may be under a physician's care for a particular injury and, therefore, may need an ATC to get them started on a safe fitness routine that will not aggravate the injury.

- **Industrial sites.** Businesses spend billions of dollars annually for health care. In an attempt to reduce health care costs, many companies are beginning to see the advantages of having a full-time ATC on staff to help prevent and treat work-site injuries. ATCs are often able to treat these injuries at the workplace, under the supervision of a physician, and decrease the work time lost to the "industrial athlete."

In the industrial setting, the supervisor takes the place of a coach, and the employee replaces an athlete.

- The peripheral team may add an ergonomics specialist to the other allied medical professionals. An **ergonomics specialist** measures, modifies, and adapts a work environment to prevent and treat musculoskeletal disorders. For example, rather than forcing workers to stand on a hard concrete floor and work at a bench that is so low they have to bend over for eight hours a day, executives may hire an ergonomics specialist to recommend changes in the physical environment that will reduce the wear and tear on the workers' bodies. Such modifications may be as simple as providing higher workbenches, special chairs, and cushioned floor mats.

- Some ATCs across the country have started their own businesses in a variety of areas that include physical fitness facilities, consulting firms, and creating and selling sports medicine equipment. ATCs will continue to expand their role and will have even greater opportunities as owners of health care facilities or businesses; the possibilities are endless.

## Summary

The ATC plays a vital role in providing health care to the physically active population. A successful ATC recognizes that the best health care is given through a team approach that draws on the strengths of a wide variety of professionals. ATCs provide health care in a variety of places including high schools, colleges, professional sports teams, sports medicine clinics, and industrial settings. To become an ATC, you must complete a bachelor's degree and have studied specific subjects including human anatomy and physiology, athletic injury assessment, and biomechanics.

## Key Terms

Define the following terms found in this chapter:

| | | |
|---|---|---|
| allergist | gynecologist | physical therapist |
| allergy | kinesiology | physics |
| American Red Cross | licensure | physiology |
| anatomy | National Athletic Trainers' | podiatrist |
| athletic training | Association (NATA) | primary care physician |
| biomechanics | National Safety Council | psychology |
| cardiologist | neurologist | reconditioning |
| certification | nutrition | registration |
| certified athletic trainer | organization and | rehabilitation |
| chiropractor | administration | school nurse |
| dentist | orthopedist | sports medicine |
| dietitian (registered) | pediatrician | student assistant |
| equipment manager | pharmacology | urologist |
| ergonomics specialist | | |

## Questions for Review

1. What is athletic training? p. 271

2. Name the members of the central sports medicine team, and describe their roles and responsibilities. When would members of the peripheral team become involved? Give an example. pp. 272-273

3. Describe the different ways in which an individual can become an ATC. Explain what you believe would be the advantages and disadvantages of each. p. 274

4. Consider the job opportunities available to ATCs. What personal attributes do you think would be necessary for success with each type of job? Justify your answer. pp. 275-277

## Activities for Reinforcement

1. Invite an ATC to come to class and discuss the setting in which she works.

2. Invite several ATCs who each work in a different setting to come to class and give a panel discussion.

3. Discuss which job opportunities in athletic training most interest you and why.

## Above and Beyond

1. Select one of the following suggested readings and write a review of the material:

   Gray, R.S. 1997. The role of the clinical athletic trainer. In *Clinical athletic training*, ed. J.J. Konin. Thorofare, NJ: Slack.

   Hunt, V.K. 1997. Fitness centers: Untapped job market for ATCs? *NATA News* October, 4-5, 20.

   Konin, J.J. 1997. The roles of allied health care providers. In *Clinical athletic training*, ed. J.J. Konin. Thorofare, NJ: Slack.

   Moss, C.L. 1996. 1994 Entry-level athletic training salaries. *Journal of Athletic Training* 31(1): 25–28.

   Rich, B.E. 1993. All physicians are not created equal: Understanding the educational background of the sports medicine physician. *Journal of Athletic Training* 28(2): 177–79.

   Straub, S.J. 1993. Working with adolescents in a high school setting. *Journal of Athletic Training* 28(1): 75–80.

2. For a list of accredited athletic training programs, visit the NATA web page at **http://www.nata.org**.

# CHAPTER 29

# Aspects of Administration and Professional Development

## OBJECTIVES

Upon completing this chapter the student will be able to do the following:

- Describe the concept of negligence, and explain ways to prevent being negligent.
- Understand the types of medical paper work and record keeping necessary for organizational and administrative purposes.
- Describe why insurance is necessary.
- Explain why preventing injuries is the best defense against legal liability.
- Describe the typical organization of a preparticipation physical exam.
- Understand the concept of professional practice in athletic training.
- State and describe the standards of professional practice in athletic training.
- Explain the importance of continuing education and the NATA requirements.
- Explain the elements of proper leadership.
- Describe characteristics that are helpful to being a future professional.

Apart from caring for and preventing athletic injuries, ATCs must also perform a variety of administrative duties. Moreover, they must be aware of various legal issues because these will greatly affect how they choose to administrate their athletic training program.

## Legal Issues

When athletes choose to participate in sports, they risk becoming injured or even permanently disabled. Because an ATC may be subject to legal liability due to athletes' injuries or illnesses, she must understand certain legal terminology.

# Negligence

**Negligence** is a legal wrong characterized by the failure to act as a reasonably prudent person would act in a similar situation. For example, if an ATC provides care below the standard of the law he may, in certain circumstances, be found negligent. To clarify this, picture an ATC who has noticed an extremely large hole on the field hockey field a couple of hours prior to game time. A reasonably prudent person would think this could cause an injury, and he would take reasonable action. For example, the ATC could contact appropriate personnel such as the grounds crew, athletic director, or maintenance to attempt to get the hole filled before game time, or he could place an orange cone in the hole to alert the players that there is a danger.

# Gross Negligence

**Gross negligence** has been described as a step beyond negligence. That is, an ATC fails to provide even a slight amount of care when needed. To distinguish negligence from gross negligence, let us look at an example. If we were to use basic first aid to care for a victim whose finger is bleeding severely, we would provide reasonable care for controlling bleeding by (1) applying direct pressure, (2) elevating the arm, (3)using a pressure bandage, when necessary, and (4) applying pressure at a pressure point. If the ATC who helped this individual only told her to elevate her arm and, after a long time, decided that perhaps he should put a dressing around the finger because it was still bleeding, he may be negligent. Gross negligence, remember, is a step beyond this. A grossly negligent ATC might fail even to provide instructions to the bleeding athlete. While an ATC (or a first aider) may not want to come into contact with someone's blood for fear of disease transmission, he can at least give instructions to the person so she can start giving care to herself and then seek additional resources to help.

# Assumption of Risk

Not warning athletes of the dangers and hazards involved in sports can leave the ATC open to charges of negligence. This is part of a concept called **assumption of risk**. An individual must fully understand that by participating in sports, she may be injured; that is, she "assumes the risk" of being injured after being fully warned of the dangers. Thus, an organization such as a high school must warn athletes and parents of the dangers that are common in the sports that they or their child will play. To make sure that athletes and parents understand the dangers, many programs require athletes to read and sign an assumption of risk form. See the bottom of this page for an example of a simple assumption of risk form. Many coaches and ATCs go even further and have the teams watch "injury" movies that explain the rules of the game and potential consequences of playing, such as injury or death. In addition, they use well-organized practice plans that document the day, time, and names of athletes who were given specific instructions about rules and technique.

---

**Assumption of Risk Form**

My son/daughter _____ (print name of athlete), and I,

_____ (print name of parent or guardian), have been warned about the dangers involved with sport participation and are aware that participating in athletics can result in severe injury or even death from a variety of circumstances, which include, but are not limited to, falls, collisions with other athletes or equipment, and/or weather conditions, while being involved in the sport of

_____. We, the undersigned, understand that athletic participation is inherently dangerous and understand and assume the risks involved.

Student athlete: _____ Date: _____

Parent or guardian: _____ Date: _____

## Informed Consent, or Permission to Treat

Before an ATC can perform any medical procedure, he must obtain the consent of the athlete (or a parent if the athlete is a minor). Failure to do so may make him liable for negligence. Therefore, the athlete or parent must be given enough information to make an intelligent decision about granting permission for care. Many schools have rules or laws addressing this particular issue. See page 282 for an example of a permission to treat (informed consent) form. This example also includes a medical data information card. In fact, many ATCs put the permission to treat and the medical information on different sides of an index card. If the information is organized in this manner, it is easy to transport in a file folder or medical bag. The hospital staff is often thankful to have this information as well.

## Proximate Cause

**Proximate cause** is described as a close connection between the way an ATC acted and the resulting injury to an athlete. Noticing that an action will lead to a certain end result and potentially or subsequently harm someone is a component of proximate cause. For example, suppose an ATC evaluates an athlete's injured neck and determines there is considerable weakness and a lack of movement when the athlete attempts to look up or down. Also, the athlete is in some pain. If the ATC were to allow the athlete to continue playing and this resulted in further injury and permanent neck damage, proximate cause could be shown. That is, the ATC's action (letting the athlete continue playing) may be directly linked to the further injury to the athlete (permanent neck damage).

Because ATCs utilize many products for the prevention and care of athletic injuries, they must be aware of the established guidelines for use of certain products. For example, the sports medicine team should only purchase football helmets approved by the National Operating Committee on Standards for Athletic Equipment (NOCSAE). Failure to do so may lead to injury or even death. We recommend that an ATC or an athletic program buy top-of-the-line products and look at available research to be sure that the product is of high quality.

## Avoiding Legal Problems

Several different authors in the athletic training literature have offered numerous suggestions for avoiding legal liability. These suggestions can be summarized as follows:

- **Have a written contract.** ATCs, coaches, and other pertinent personnel should have a detailed contract that provides a job description. Either in this contract or in a separate document, the relationship between the head ATC and any students or assistants should be explained. At the high school and college level, student assistants are under the direct supervision of an ATC. That is, anything that a student does in the athletic training room should be monitored. Students are able to observe and learn, which is a valuable experience. They can also assist the ATC with procedures if it is deemed appropriate by the ATC.

- **Use equipment that meets established safety standards.** Use equipment only for its intended purposes, and be sure it is properly fitted.

- **Require preparticipation physical examinations.** Preparticipation exams help identify existing conditions that may lead to injury. If these conditions can be identified, the injury can potentially be prevented, which limits any chance of liability.

- **Have all athletes and their parents or guardians sign an assumption of risk form.**

- **Maintain CPR and first aid certifications.** The ATC should practice these skills periodically.

- **Have a crisis plan.** The ATC must have an effective crisis plan in writing for all home and away contests. The crisis plan should explain all procedures to be carried out, and everyone involved should have a copy and know his or her role.

- **Document all injuries and procedures.** An ATC should not only detail all injuries that occur, but also all rehabilitation procedures, treatments, and follow-up care on the appropriate administrative forms.

- **Build trust.** Having an effective line of communication and good rapport within the athletic training team allows the ATC to build trust and respect with all individuals involved with an athletic injury.

## Permission to Treat

I, _____ (name of parent or guardian) give permission for

my child, _____ (name of athlete) to participate in

_____ (sport) during the _____ (year) athletic season. If my child is injured and emergency care is needed, I grant the school's qualified staff permission to provide emergency medical services. Should more advanced treatment be necessary, I give permission to qualified medical personnel to treat him/her with the necessary care with the understanding that every reasonable effort will be made to contact me.

Address: _____

Home phone: (    ) _____ Work phone: (    ) _____ Pager: (    ) _____ Cell phone: (    ) _____

Other emergency contact name: _____

Address: _____

Home phone: (    ) _____ Work phone: (    ) _____ Pager: (    ) _____ Cell phone: (    ) _____

### Student Athlete Medical Data Information

Social Security Number: _____ - _____ - _____          Sex: M ____  F ____

List any and all medical conditions (including allergies):

_____

_____

_____

_____

List any and all medications currently being taken by the athlete: _____

_____

_____

_____

Name of insurance company: _____

Address of insurance company: _____

Policy holder name (please print): _____

Policy number: _____ Group number: _____ Type: _____

I attest that the above medical information is accurate and agree to this permission to treat form.

Signature of parent or guardian: _____ Date: _____

Data obtained from Rankin and Ingersoll (1995), Roy and Irvin (1983), and Flegel (1992).

## The Real World

During an intercollegiate game, a goalie from a visiting soccer team received a blow to the head from one of his teammates while trying to scoop up a soccer ball. He was hit so hard that his skull was fractured. The host athletic trainer attended the athlete and called for EMS immediately. The athlete's condition was worsening even as he was being taken to the emergency room, and a helicopter was called because the athlete needed to be transferred to a trauma center in a different city. Unfortunately, the visiting team had no medical information about the athlete, nor any emergency contact information. Treatment, however, was initiated because the athlete was unconscious; permission to treat was implied. Because the athlete had recently "walked on" to the team, his full name was even a mystery—thankfully, a rare occurrence. It took many phone calls to the school before the athlete's name was determined and then more detective work to figure out how to reach his parents. The moral of the story is to always have appropriate medical information—complete with emergency contact numbers—with the team at all times.

Phil Voorhis, MSEd, ATC

- **Check for hazards.** Periodically examine athletic fields, courts, and equipment to identify potential hazards. If an ATC finds a hazard, he should have it removed and document his actions.
- **Stay educated.** ATCs have a responsibility to continue their education and stay current on the latest information in the allied medical field. An ATC must also understand his or her qualifications and know his or her limitations. Moreover, because state laws differ, it is important for ATCs to understand their state regulations.

## Preventing Athletic Injuries

Reducing the risk of legal liability includes practicing comprehensive injury prevention. A comprehensive injury prevention program includes education, rule enforcement, proper matching of participants, and elements of physical fitness. We will highlight some of the components involved in each of these elements of injury prevention.

- **Educating the athlete.** Education includes both teaching him about the dangers involved with sports and the proper technique of his particular sport. For example, the ATC and the coaching staff should educate a football player that his helmet is for protection and is not to be used as a weapon. When these educational sessions are completed, the coach should document which athletes were in attendance as a way to ensure that all athletes have been educated. Additionally, football players should be educated in proper technique several times a year. Failure to provide proper instruction is considered by many professionals to leave the ATC potentially liable for negligence.
- **Rule enforcement.** Many rules are designed to prevent injuries. Spearing, in football, for example, was banned in 1976. Enforcement of this rule is necessary to truly prevent an athlete from using his head as a weapon. Coaches must enforce these rules in practice settings as well, because most athletic injuries occur during practice.
- **Proper matching.** Participants should be matched according to several factors, especially in contact sports such as wrestling, boxing, football, field hockey, and hockey, to help reduce the risk of injury. These factors include weight, age, and skill level. For example, if a 132-pound wrestler were matched with a 232-pound wrestler during practice, the smaller individual would be at a definite disadvantage in terms of size. The larger opponent could easily use his weight to inflict injury.
- **Physical fitness.** Participants who are physically fit can reduce their risk of injury. Being physically fit means that the elements of muscular strength, flexibility, cardiovascular and muscular endurance, and body composition have been addressed through a comprehensive program.

## Administrative Issues and Documentation

It is essential that the sports medicine team document all the procedures they perform, to prevent lawsuits and for other reasons. For example, ATCs need to be able to compare current physical findings of an injured athlete to previous findings from a physical examination or injury report. Moreover, it may be essential to review past injury treatments in order to determine the best type of care to be given to an athlete.

## Administering Preparticipation Examinations

Preparticipation physical examinations are performed by a medical doctor to determine if an individual is able to participate in a sport without extra risk of injury or illness. Additionally, preparticipation physical examinations give baseline information from which to make comparisons if an injury or illness does arise. For example, if the ATC is examining an athlete who is complaining of dizziness and her blood pressure seems a little bit low, he can compare the value to the measurement recorded from a previous physical examination. The preparticipation physical examination should document an athlete's height and weight, blood pressure, and pulse. Also, the ears, nose, throat, heart, lungs, and abdomen, and flexibility, joint stability, and posture should be examined.

In many high schools, the ATC and the team physician will organize a large-scale physical examination for their athletes. These physical examinations will often include a set of stations, and the athletes will move from one station to the next until they have visited each station. The athletes, for example, could progress through the stations as follows:

1. registration
2. height, weight
3. blood pressure
4. flexibility and joint stability
5. posture
6. ear, nose, and throat
7. heart, lungs, and abdomen
8. check out with team physician in charge
9. post-registration

When the athlete first enters the exam area, he will register for the physical and receive his paperwork. He will fill out his name, address, and past medical history. He will then progress through the height, weight, and blood pressure stations. When the athlete arrives at the flexibility, joint stability, and posture screening station, an ATC at one of several substations will work with him individually to assess any past athletic injuries and to see if he has any joint problems, postural defects, or a lack of flexibility that may cause an injury. Usually, if a problem is found, the ATC will make a note of it for the team physician to check at the end. The athlete will then move to one of several physicians who will check his ears, nose, and throat. Next, the athlete will be examined by one of several physicians who will listen to his heart and lungs for any abnormalities. His abdomen is checked at this time as well. The team physician is the last doctor that the athlete will see. At this point, the team physician will recheck any noted conditions from the previous stations to determine whether the athlete can play. The athlete then progresses to the postregistration booth. It is here that he can pick up any information regarding the findings. For example, suppose an athlete was examined by an ATC and was found to have much less strength in one leg than in the other. Knowing that this lack of strength could create problems and increase the athlete's risk of injury, the athlete would be given an instruction sheet for a lower-body strengthening program to improve his condition.

## Medical Information Forms

The preparticipation physical examination is a good time for parents to fill out a medical information card along with the medical history. It is a good idea for an ATC to keep with her at all times an **informed consent** form (permission to treat), an athlete's insurance information, and medical information. It is impossible to remember every condition that each athlete has. Therefore, keeping a medical data information card for each athlete in the medical kit allows the ATC or coach to obtain crucial information at a moment's notice. For example, if a coach takes her tennis team to an away meet where one of her athletes is stung by a bee and suddenly begins to act ill, the coach can look at the medical data form and see if the athlete is allergic to bee stings. If any athlete needs advanced care at a hospital and the parent is not around, the medical data form can provide necessary information to give proper treatment. As previously mentioned, many high schools keep the permission to treat information and the medical information on the same card (refer to "Permission to Treat," page 282).

## Insurance Issues and How Insurance Works

In most organizations each athlete is required to have some type of medical insurance before he or she can participate in organized sports. Many athletic programs require that insurance forms be kept with the informed consent (permission to treat) forms that we discussed earlier. Why? Say that an athlete who is traveling with the team on the road gets injured. If the parents are not at the game, the injured athlete can still be treated at a local hospital because permission has been granted to treat and appropriate insurance information has been provided. Unfortunately, insurance coverage is becoming increasingly complicated—ask any ATC about the paperwork involved with insurance and watch her reaction. However, insurance is necessary because when an individual is injured medical costs can be substantial, and the medical insurance will offset the cost of medical care.

Medical insurance has been described as a written agreement between an insurance company and the individual who buys it. This agreement clarifies the terms of reimbursement for medical costs after an athlete has been treated. Many athletic programs will purchase supplemental insurance that covers the leftover costs not covered by the primary insurance. The insurance is usually for the injuries that occur as a result of athletic participation. Programs carry supplemental insurance so that an athlete's care is completely covered. Many athletic programs will also carry catastrophic insurance that is used for injuries that cause permanent disability, such as paralysis.

## Reports and Charts

We have already discussed why ATCs need to document their procedures. However, exactly which procedures must be documented is often

 **What Would You Do If...**

You are helping the team get ready for practice. You get to the football field and notice that there is a large hole in the ground of the practice area.

debated. The ATC should document any accident of which he is aware (even if it is not due to athletic participation), any treatment that an athlete receives, and the rehabilitation progress that an athlete makes. Many computer documentation or record-keeping systems are available to athletic trainers. These computer systems make it easy to document injury reports, rehabilitation progress, and referral forms.

### Accident and Injury Reports

Accident and injury reports should contain vital information including the athlete's name, the date of injury, the date of the report, the athlete's sport, the age of the athlete, and the body part that is injured. Additionally, the report must contain information about how the injury or accident occurred, note whether it is a new or previous injury, and include the ATC's inspection and assessment information and signature. The report should also contain the ATC's thoughts about the injury and record any treatment such as ice application, splinting, or medical referral. A sample injury report is shown on page 286.

### Treatment Logs

Any treatment an athlete receives must be documented (see "Daily Treatment Log," page 287). Such things as ice application, heat application, elastic wraps, stretching, and strengthening must all be logged on a specific form.

### Rehabilitation Charts

Once an athlete has been injured, her injury assessed, and a proper rehabilitation program designed and implemented, it is essential that the ATC document the athlete's progress (see "Treatment Progress Chart," page 288). The ATC must record the exact treatment received by the athlete, the date it was received, and note any problems or complaints, changes in treatments, the athlete's response to treatment, and re-evaluation data.

# Athletic Injury/Accident Report

Athlete's name: _____ Today's date: _____ Injury date: _____

Body part injured: L   R _____ Sport: _____

Was the injury due to athletic participation? _____ yes _____ no  Other: _____

## Subjective Information

Mechanism of injury: _____

_____

Chief complaint: _____

_____

Type of pain: _____

_____

Other: _____

_____

## Objective Information

Inspection (observation): _____

_____

Palpation: _____

_____

Range of motion and strength testing: _____

_____

_____

_____

Neurological findings: _____

_____

Special stress tests: _____

_____

Functional testing: _____

_____

## Assessment Information

Results of assessment: _____

_____

List of problems: _____

_____

## Plan of Action

Initial treatment: _____

The athlete will be: _____ referred to a physician _____ referred to school nurse _____ treated

Treatment will be: _____ days a week for _____ week(s). Treatment will consist of: _____

_____

_____

Parents contacted: _____ yes _____ no. If yes give date: _____. If no, give reason: _____

_____

Signature of certified athletic trainer: _____

Attach all progress notes to this sheet.

# DAILY TREATMENT LOG

| Date | Athlete's name (please print) | Sport (print) | ICE | HEAT | WHIRLPOOL | ULTRASOUND | MUSCLE STIM. | MASSAGE | EXERCISE | WOUND CARE | TAPE / WRAP | EVALUATION | ATC INITIALS |
|------|-------------------------------|---------------|-----|------|-----------|------------|--------------|---------|----------|------------|-------------|-------------|--------------|
| | | | | | | | | | | | | | |
| | | | | | | | | | | | | | |
| | | | | | | | | | | | | | |
| | | | | | | | | | | | | | |
| | | | | | | | | | | | | | |
| | | | | | | | | | | | | | |
| | | | | | | | | | | | | | |
| | | | | | | | | | | | | | |
| | | | | | | | | | | | | | |
| | | | | | | | | | | | | | |
| | | | | | | | | | | | | | |
| | | | | | | | | | | | | | |
| | | | | | | | | | | | | | |
| | | | | | | | | | | | | | |
| | | | | | | | | | | | | | |
| **Totals:** | | | | | | | | | | | | | |

Adapted, by permission, from Pioneer High School, Ann Arbor, MI.

# Treatment Progress Chart

page ___ of ___

Athlete's name: _____ Injury date: _____

Injury site: _____ Location:  left  right

Type of injury:  Sprain   Strain   Contusion   Other: _____

Sport: _____

Treatment date: _____ Treatment received: _____

_____

_____

Comments or notes: _____

_____

_____

_____

Status: _____ Certified athletic trainer: _____

Treatment date: _____ Treatment received: _____

_____

_____

Comments or notes: _____

_____

_____

Status: _____ Certified athletic trainer: _____

Treatment date: _____ Treatment received: _____

_____

_____

Comments or notes: _____

_____

_____

Status: _____ Certified athletic trainer: _____

Treatment date: _____ Treatment received: _____

_____

Comments or notes: _____

_____

_____

Status: _____ Certified athletic trainer: _____

# Professional Development

Professional development refers to the ongoing responsibility of improving one's skills and knowledge in order to deliver appropriate health care to injured athletes. The successful ATC will behave ethically, stay abreast of the latest medical issues and trends, display good communication skills, and be an effective leader.

## The Basis of Professional Practice

The ATC must treat people fairly, to the best of her ability, and do what is right. To help its members, the National Athletic Trainers' Association has developed standards of professional practice, which are summarized in the NATA code of ethics (NATA 1998). The principles of this code include the following:

> Principle 1: Members shall respect the rights, welfare, and dignity of all individuals.
>
> Principle 2: Members shall comply with the laws and regulations governing the practice of athletic training.
>
> Principle 3: Members shall accept responsibility for sound judgment.
>
> Principle 4: Members shall maintain and promote high standards in the provision of services.
>
> Principle 5: Members shall not engage in any form of conduct that constitutes a conflict of interest or that adversely reflects on the profession.

## Staying Educated

If medical professionals never learned how to use anything new or failed to utilize the most up-to-date technology an injured athlete would not get the best care. Therefore, once a person has the letters ATC after his name, he is required to continue his education on a regular basis. The NATA Board of Certification (NATABOC) requires that an individual complete 8.0 continuing education units (CEUs) every three years. One CEU is equivalent to 10 hours of course work. Therefore, ATCs need at least 80 hours of education every three years. The CEUs can be obtained in a variety of ways, such as attending educational workshops, writing and publishing, taking col-

## ❓ What Would You Do If...

While in the athletic training room, you notice that several athletes from the basketball team fail to write their names on the treatment log.

lege classes, and maintaining CPR certification (also a requirement—every three years an ATC must show proof of current CPR certification), just to name a few.

## Communication

Whether an individual works at a high school, college, or at a sports medicine clinic, she must have good communication skills. ATCs communicate daily with athletes, parents, physicians, coaches, and administrators at every level. A failure to send the right message can result in many anxious hours and negative consequences.

Jeff Konin, in a text titled *Clinical Athletic Training*, offers many practical suggestions to ATCs for enhancing communication skills. He suggests that as a listener, you should be attentive and open-minded. Establish good eye contact. Direct eye contact sends the message that a matter is important. Also, when you use direct eye contact, people often believe that you spent more time with them than you actually did. Pay attention to your gestures; they send messages that can be interpreted in unintended ways. For example, if a person crosses her arms, she can be thought of as closed, as though she is not really listening.

## Leadership

The profession of athletic training has progressed and flourished, undoubtedly because of the leadership of many of its members. Several principles and qualities of leadership are important for future ATCs—like you—to learn.

- **Integrity** refers to the ATC conducting herself in an ethical manner, such as following the standards of professional practice noted earlier.
- **Vision** refers to being able to anticipate the needs of the athletes. Asking questions, such as "how can we keep athletes from getting this type

of injury?" is helpful to begin looking forward with a vision.

- **Inspiration** refers to being able to persuade people that the vision you have is appropriate. For example, when an ATC rehabilitates an injured athlete, he inspires her to pursue the vision of normal function and return to participation.

- **Competence** refers to having the knowledge and skills necessary to perform effectively.

# The PREMIER Model for Becoming a Professional

The **PREMIER model** is an easy way of thinking about being a future professional. This model is based on our experience as professionals in athletic training. The acronym for this model can be found in figure 29.1.

- **Promote a professional image.** As a student assistant, you can project a professional

**P** Promote a professional image

**R** Remember your vision

**E** Engage in learning

**M** Maximize your strengths

**I** Innovate and create

**E** Enlist the help of others

**R** Reflect

**Figure 29.1** The PREMIER model gives helpful suggestions for developing yourself as a future professional.

image by the way you dress. An old saying states that "you don't get a second chance at a first impression." Although wearing shorts, tennis shoes, and T-shirts may be fine during practice or game coverage for warm-weather activities, it is imperative that the athletic training staff be distinguishable and professional looking in case someone needs to find you for help.

- **Remember your vision.** You must have a good understanding of your career goals and objectives and what type of person you are striving to become. Some people write down their vision statement so they can continually be reminded of their purpose and set proper personal goals.

- **Engage in learning.** It is important that as a student and future professional you take initiative to learn new things daily.

- **Maximize your strengths.** We all have limitations—if you dwell too much on them, you may not learn and do the things that can make you successful. Cultivate your strengths and ask yourself how they can support your personal vision.

- **Innovate and create.** Over the past 10 to 20 years, technology has constantly advanced. Today's problems cannot be solved with yesterday's solutions. As future professionals, it is important for you to develop new ideas. This will keep you excited about your work.

- **Enlist the help of others.** In the previous chapter you learned about the role of the ATC and the sports medicine team. The old saying that "there is no I in TEAM" is absolutely accurate. Be a team player.

- **Reflect.** When you become a professional, it will be essential—whether you are doing rehabilitation or performing a tape job on an ankle—that you think back on what you have done and consider the results. Get into the habit now of reflecting on your actions in the athletic training room to help you learn what you might do better in the future during a similar situation.

## Summary

ATCs must follow standards of professional practice as set forth by NATA. These standards guide the ATC in a quest to deliver professional health care. In order to maintain an acceptable level of knowledge, the ATC is required to participate in continuing education for 80 hours every three years. ATCs often find themselves in leadership roles and thus should conduct themselves with integrity, vision, inspiration, and competence. There are numerous administrative considerations for the ATC. Not only should proper documentation of injuries and treatments be a concern, but also the legal liability. An ATC should create an environment designed to prevent injury and should follow several steps toward preventing liability. One such step is to document the occurrence of all athletic and nonathletic injuries and illnesses, as well as the treatment or rehabilitation the athlete receives. Clear, concise medical documentation is imperative.

## Key Terms

Define the following terms found in this chapter:

| | | |
|---|---|---|
| assumption of risk | informed consent | PREMIER model |
| gross negligence | negligence | proximate cause |

## Questions for Review

1. Describe the different medical documentation forms that need to be utilized in an athletic training room. pp. 282-288
2. What are the various aspects of injury prevention covered in this chapter and how might they be useful for preventing injuries? p. 283
3. List each school sport and ways to prevent injuries involved with each. p. 283
4. Why does NATA have standards of professional practice? What could potentially happen if these are not followed? p. 289
5. What are the common qualities involved with leadership? Do you possess all of these? If not, think about how you might begin to improve yourself as a leader. pp. 289-290
6. What can a person do to improve his professional image? p. 290
7. Describe how insurance works and explain why it is necessary. p. 285

## Activities for Reinforcement

1. What are your strengths and how could you better maximize them?
2. Reflect on something you observed in the athletic training room this week. What do you think could have been done differently to improve the results?

3. Create different injury report forms, treatment logs, and medical information forms.
4. Volunteer to help with preparticipation examinations.

## Above and Beyond

1. Do a report on legal issues in sports.
2. Write a paper on what it means to be a leader.
3. Explore one or more of the suggested readings below:

   Amato, H.K., and M.J. Warner. 1996. Athletic trainers: Leaders in sports. *Athletic Therapy Today* 1(1): 30–32.

   Heinzman, S.E. 1991. Quality physicals that generate funds for the training room. *Journal of the National Athletic Trainers' Association* 26(1): 66–69.

   Koester, M.C. 1995. Refocusing the adolescent preparticipation physical evaluation toward preventive health care. *Journal of Athletic Training* 30(4): 352–60.

   Konin, J.J. 1997. The roles of allied health care providers. In *Clinical athletic training,* ed. J.J. Konin. Thorofare, NJ: Slack.

   Leverenz, L.J., and L.B. Helms. 1990. Suing athletic trainers: Part II. *Journal of the National Athletic Trainers Association* 25(3): 219–26.

   National Athletic Trainers' Association. 1998. *1998 Membership directory: NATA code of ethics.* Dallas: National Athletic Trainers' Association.

   Ray, R. 1994. *Management strategies in athletic training.* Champaign, IL: Human Kinetics.

# Glossary

**ABC's**: Airway, breathing, and circulation. These are the first three things to check after you have determined that a person is unresponsive.

**abduction:** Movement away from the midline of the body.

**acetabulum**: The bones that form the hip socket.

**Achilles tendon:** The structure that attaches the gastrocnemius muscle to the calcaneus bone of the foot.

**active range of motion (AROM):** The range through which the athlete can move his limb unassisted.

**active-assistive range of motion (AAROM):** The range of motion through which the athlete can move her limb with the help of the athletic trainer.

**adduction:** Movement toward the midline of the body.

**allergist:** A physician who specializes in determining the substances to which an individual is allergic and who treats such allergies.

**allergy:** A condition in which an individual has a low tolerance of such things as pollen, ragweed, dogs, cats, and sometimes specific foods. These often trigger an allergic reaction—typically a sudden runny nose; congestion; red, itchy eyes; and sneezing.

**alveoli**: The lung tissue where gas exchange of oxygen and carbon dioxide occurs.

**ambulatory:** Able to walk independently or with light support.

**American Red Cross:** A national organization that certifies individuals in first aid and cardiopulmonary resuscitation procedures. The American Red Cross also sponsors other services such as disaster relief for communities throughout the country and world.

**amino acid:** The basic component of protein.

**amnesia:** Loss of memory, due usually to a head injury.

**amphiarthrodial joint:** A joint of cartilage that links bones that don't move much, for example, where the ribs join the sternum.

**anabolic steroids:** A group of synthetic male hormones. Athletes use anabolic steroids to build muscle.

**anatomical position:** A standing posture with the arms at the side and the palms of the hands facing forward.

**anatomy:** The study of how the body is organized, concentrating on bones, joints, muscles, and organs, their kinds and their arrangements.

**anemia:** A condition in which there are fewer red blood cells than normal in the circulatory system. Anemia can be caused by bleeding.

**angina pectoris:** Pain commonly felt around the heart and chest cavity due to lack of oxygen to the heart muscle.

**annulus fibrosus:** The rings of tissue that surround the nucleus pulposus of an intervertebral disk.

**anorexia nervosa:** A serious eating disorder marked by a pathological fear of weight gain and a loss of appetite. The anorexic has a low body weight and low body fat but may exercise excessively and avoid eating.

**anterior:** Pertaining to the front of the body.

**anterior cruciate ligament (ACL):** A knee ligament that keeps the tibia from moving forward on the femur.

**apnea:** The temporary stopping of breathing.

**appendicular skeleton:** The bones of the extremities: the shoulders, arms, hands, legs, feet, and pelvis.

**arthroscopic surgery:** A type of surgery performed on a joint using only small puncture holes to insert instruments, including a camera, to observe and fix injured structures.

**articulate:** The coming together of two bones to form a joint.

**aseptic meningitis:** A viral inflammation of the coverings of the brain.

**assumption of risk:** When an individual fully understands that by participating in sports he or she may be injured.

**asthma:** A condition in which the air passages contract in response to an allergy. The contraction may close the air passage entirely.

**athletic training:** An allied medical profession that is dedicated to maintaining and improving the health and well-being of the physically active population and preventing athletics-related injuries and illnesses.

**atrium:** The upper chambers of the heart that receive blood from the veins and force it into the ventricles.

**avascular necrosis:** The death of body tissue from lack of blood.

**axial skeleton:** The bones of the body that comprise the spine, chest, and head.

**ball-and-socket joint:** A joint in which a rounded bone fits into a cuplike socket and swivels. Examples include the hip and shoulder joints. Also called "multiaxial joint."

**ballistic stretching:** A bouncing type of movement used to lengthen or stretch tissue.

**battle sign:** A discoloration behind the ear as a result of a skull fracture.

**beta-adrenergic drugs:** Drugs used to control the release of chemicals during an asthma attack by maintaining the airway.

**bile:** Bile is produced by the liver and stored in the gall bladder. Bile assists in the digestion of fat in the small intestine.

**biomechanics:** The study of movement of living creatures.

**body temperature:** The temperature at which bodily processes take place, normally 98.6 degrees Fahrenheit.

**breathing rate:** The number of breaths a person takes per minute. Normal breathing rate is 12 to 20 breaths per minute.

**bronchitis:** An inflammation of the bronchial passages, which can be caused by an infection or an allergy.

**bulimia:** An eating disorder characterized by bouts of bingeing and self-induced vomiting.

**burner:** A group of symptoms including burning, numbness, tingling, and pain down the arm that results from stretching a group of nerves called the brachial plexus. This condition is also known as a stinger.

**bursa:** A fluid-filled sac between a tendon and a bone that eases the friction of muscle movement.

**calcaneus:** The heel bone of the foot.

**callus:** A mass of connective tissue that forms at the site of a fracture and is converted into bone or a thickening of skin in response to repeated stress.

**Canadian Standards Association (CSA):** The committee that sets the standards for eye guards and ice hockey helmets.

**capillary refill:** The blood moving back into the end of a finger or toe after it has been pinched for a brief moment.

**capital femoral epiphysis:** The growth plate located between the head and the neck of the femur, which can be fractured, especially in young athletes.

**cardiac arrest:** When the heart stops beating.

**cardiologist:** A physician with specialized knowledge of the cardiovascular system.

**cardiovascular endurance:** The ability to sustain exercise over a long period of time.

**carotid artery:** One of two vessels that runs from the aorta through the neck and supplies the head with oxygenated blood.

**cerebrospinal fluid:** A liquid from the blood that maintains uniform pressure within the brain, bathes the brain in chemicals for proper functioning, and also protects the brain from impacts.

**certification:** An acknowledgement by an organization or certification board that states a person possesses specific skills and competencies.

**certified athletic trainer:** An individual who is concerned with the health and well-being of the physically active and athletic population. His or her credentials are ATC.

**cervical:** The seven vertebrae that comprise the uppermost region of the spine.

**check rein:** A taping procedure whereby a piece of tape is looped around the thumb and index finger in order to prevent the thumb from being forcefully abducted.

**chicken pox:** A childhood disease characterized by flu-like symptoms and a spotted rash.

**chiropractor:** Medical personnel who treat mainly musculoskeletal disorders and restore normal function by manipulating bones, specifically at the spinal column.

**cholesterol:** A fatlike substance produced within the body to perform essential cellular functions.

**chrondromalacia:** The softening or wearing away of the cartilage that lies on the back of the patella.

**circuit training:** A weight training method whereby a person rotates through a series of 8–20 different exercises. It is a full body workout that elevates the heart rate.

**circumduction:** The movement of a limb in a circular pattern. This occurs when a ball-and-socket joint (shoulder or hip) encompasses several directions with one motion.

**common cold (coryza):** A common virus characterized by runny nose, sneezing, and coughing.

**concussion:** A temporarily impaired brain function caused by jarring impact to the head or by a rotation force of the head.

**constrict:** To narrow an opening or a blood vessel.

**contrecoup:** An injury that occurs when the head is moving and hits an unyielding surface or object. Upon impact the brain is forced to the side opposite the blow.

**CPR:** Cardiopulmonary resuscitation, used when the heart stops. One CPR cycle for an adult is 15 compressions of the chest and 2 slow breaths.

**crisis plan:** The organized action that people should take if an emergency arises. It is also called an emergency plan.

**cryotherapy:** The use of cold on a body part during treatment or during rehabilitation.

**DeLorme method:** A weight-training regimen consisting of three sets of 10 repetitions performed at successively greater intensities.

**dentist:** A medical specialist who treats primarily teeth and gums.

**depression:** A feeling of hopelessness. Severe depression may need to be observed and treated by a physician, in which case it is referred to as clinical depression.

**detached retina:** When the retina of the eye is torn from its normal position. An athlete with a detached retina will have difficulty seeing and requires a physician's care.

**diabetic coma:** Occurs when there is not enough insulin to control the sugar in the blood.

**diaphragm:** The muscle located between the chest and the abdomen that contracts and relaxes to assist with breathing.

**diarthrodial joint:** A freely movable joint, such as the shoulder. This kind of joint has a joint capsule, a synovial membrane, cartilage, and ligaments.

**diastolic pressure:** The pressure in the arteries when the heart is resting. Normal diastolic pressure is 80 mm Hg.

**dietitian:** A specialist concerned with the dietary needs of individuals.

**dilate:** To widen an opening or a blood vessel.

**dimethyl sulfoxide (DMSO):** A veterinary medicine used to enhance tissue healing. Animal research found that DMSO decreased healing time and wound swelling.

**direct pressure:** External pressure applied to an open bleeding wound.

**dislocation:** An injury that disrupts the alignment of bones at a joint, resulting in obvious deformity.

**distal:** Away from the attachment of a limb.

**drug:** Any substance other than food or water that changes the body's chemistry when it is ingested or applied topically.

**dyspnea:** Difficult or labored breathing.

**edema:** Tissue swelling due to high levels of protein-based fluid.

**effleurage:** Massage, stroking the tissue with the palm of the hand in a smooth, rhythmical manner.

**elastic tape:** A flexible tape made of stretchy nylon fibers.

**elastic wraps:** Stretchy strips of cloth that come in varying widths. They are most commonly applied to the body to provide compression around a joint or injured area.

**endurance:** The ability to withstand fatigue and tolerate prolonged activity.

**epilepsy:** A disorder marked by disturbed electrical rhythms of the central nervous system.

**epiphysis (growth plate):** The area of the bone at which growth occurs.

**epistaxis:** A bloody nose.

**equipment manager:** The person responsible for assigning and fitting appropriate playing equipment to athletes.

**ergonomics specialist:** A person who measures, modifies, and adapts a work environment to prevent injuries.

**esophagus:** The passage at the back of the throat that carries food from the mouth to the stomach.

**eversion:** A movement that turns the sole of the foot outward, away from the midline of the body.

**extension:** An unbending movement around a joint to restore it to anatomical position. The anatomical position of the knee, for example, is straight.

**extrication:** The removal of an injured person from a dangerous situation in order to provide further care without causing more harm.

**failure point:** The amount of force required to cause a fracture.

**fibroblast:** A connective tissue cell that begins building fibers across an area of injury. Fibroblasts form the scar and take about six weeks to accomplish their task.

**fibrous joint:** A synarthrodial joint.

**flexibility:** The ability to move a joint through a full range of motion without restriction.

**flexion:** A bending movement around a joint in a limb away from its straightened position.

**folliculitis:** An inflammation of a follicle, especially of a hair follicle.

**forward head posture:** When the head is jutted forward so the athlete's ears are not lined up with her shoulders.

**fracture:** A break in a bone.

**friction massage:** Massage, using deep penetrating pressure into the tissue with movement of the finger, thumb, or elbow.

**frontal plane:** The plane that separates the body into front and back halves.

**furuncle:** An infection in a skin gland, forming a bright red lump that hurts when touched. It is also known as a boil.

**gamekeeper's thumb:** An injury to the medial collateral ligament of the thumb.

**gastrocnemius:** A large muscle at the back of the lower leg responsible for pointing the toes.

**girth:** The distance around a body part.

**gross negligence:** A step beyond negligence whereby a person fails to perform even a slight amount of care when needed.

**gynecologist:** A physician who specializes in the diagnosis and treatment of diseases of the reproductive system of women.

**hamstrings:** The name given collectively to the semimembranosus, semitendinosus, and biceps femoris muscles, which are responsible for flexing the knee and extending the hip.

**heart attack:** Occurs when the heart is injured by an insufficient blood supply due to a blockage of a vessel to the heart, a clot, stress over a period of time, or injury to the heart muscle itself.

**heart rate:** The number of times the heart beats in a minute, often measured in a superficial artery as the pulse. The normal pulse rate for a teenager is between 60 and 80 beats per minute.

**heat cramps:** A mild heat-related illness marked by sudden muscular contractions that will not release because the necessary minerals and water are not available.

**heat exhaustion:** A moderate heat-related illness caused by exercising in a hot humid environment. Effects are weakness, nausea, dizziness, and profuse sweating causing dehydration with excessive sodium loss through sweat.

**heat index:** The combined measurement of air temperature and humidity. It indicates how safe it is to participate in activities and the body's ability to dissipate heat on a particular day.

**heatstroke:** A severe heat-related illness caused by prolonged exposure to high temperature and humidity and marked by the shutdown of the hypothalamus, which causes body temperature to rise dangerously. Secondary causes of heatstroke include dehydration, excessive weight loss, obesity, alcoholism, cerebral palsy, and diabetes.

**hemiplegia:** The loss of sensation and muscular function on one side of the body that results from injury to or disease of the motor processes of the brain.

**hemophilia:** A hereditary blood disorder characterized by delayed clotting of the blood.

**hemothorax:** Blood in the chest cavity.

**hepatitis B virus (HBV):** A virus that tends to persist in the blood and causes an infection to the liver.

**hinge joint:** An articulation whereby the joint is able to move primarily in flexion and extension. An example of a hinge joint is the knee or elbow.

**history:** The portion of the assessment process consisting of understanding the injured athlete's chief complaint, determining exactly how the injury occurred, assessing functional problems that exist, noting signs and symptoms, and determining any preexisting medical conditions.

**HIT:** History, Inspection, and Testing.

**human immunodeficiency virus (HIV):** A virus known to cause acquired immune deficiency syndrome (AIDS), which affects the body's ability to fight off infection and disease.

**hyaline cartilage:** A thin layer of cartilage that covers the ends of a bone where it articulates with another bone.

**hybrid tape:** Tape made from both linen and elastic.

**hyperglycemia:** When the blood sugar level gets too high.

**hypertension:** Abnormally high blood pressure, especially arterial pressure.

**hyperthermia:** The excessive build up of heat within the body; an exceptionally high fever.

**hyperventilation:** Excessive rate and depth of breathing, 24 breaths or more per minute.

**hyphema:** An injury to the eye that causes blood to flow into the anterior chamber.

**hypoglycemia:** When the blood sugar level gets too low.

**hypotension:** Abnormally low blood pressure.

**hypothermia:** Subnormal body temperature from prolonged exposure to damp cold.

**immune system:** The internal defense mechanisms of the body.

**impetigo:** A skin disease that is characterized by itching and the development of yellow crustations.

**impingement syndrome:** A collection of symptoms caused by compression of either the biceps tendon or supraspinatus tendon below the acromion of the shoulder.

**influenza:** The medical name for the flu.

**informed consent:** When the parents give permission, after being informed of the possible dangers of participation in athletic activities, for medical staff to treat their son or daughter if he or she is injured.

**insulin shock:** A condition that results from having low blood sugar levels because the body has too much insulin.

**intermittent compression:** A device with a built-in sleeve that can be put on an athlete's swollen body part. The sleeve periodically fills with air and applies compression to the area.

**intervertebral disks:** Structures between the vertebrae that cushion them.

**inversion:** A movement that turns the sole of the foot inward, toward the midline of the body.

**isokinetic contraction:** The muscle applies a force against a machine that only allows it to move at a specific speed.

**isometric contraction:** A movement that causes the muscle to contract against resistance but does not change its length.

**isotonic contraction:** A movement that causes the muscle fibers to shorten and lengthen against resistance when lifting and lowering a weight.

**jersey finger:** An injury of the finger in which the flexor tendon tears from the fingertip.

**joint capsule:** A sac or sleevelike structure that covers a joint. The capsule has a synovial membrane containing synovial fluid to ease joint movement.

**Jones fracture:** A fracture occurring at the base of the fifth metatarsal bone.

**jugular vein:** One of two vessels that takes unoxygenated blood from the head to the heart.

**Kehr's sign:** Pain in the abdomen and the left shoulder that most often indicates injury to the spleen.

**kinesiology:** The study of human movement.

**kyphosis:** The excessive roundedness that can occur at the thoracic spine.

**laryngitis:** Inflammation of the larynx.

**larynx:** An enlarged tube at the top of the trachea made of cartilage and muscle. The voice is created by air passing through the vocal cords in the larynx.

**lateral:** Away from the midline of the body.

**lateral malleolus:** The most prominent aspect of the fibula located on the lateral aspect of the ankle.

**Legg-Calvé-Perthes disease:** A condition found in some young children characterized by a disruption of blood flow to the head of the femur, which causes the tissue at the head of the femur to die.

**leukocytes:** Infection-fighting white blood cells that go to site of an injury.

**leukoplakia:** Precancerous cells often found on the cheek, tongue, and gum of those using smokeless tobacco.

**licensure:** A state act that specifies who is allowed to practice athletic training and what duties they are allowed to perform.

**ligaments:** Tissues in the body that connect bone to bone.

**linen tape:** Tape made from cotton fibers.

**Little League elbow:** An injury to the medial aspect of the elbow in young throwing athletes, usually from overuse.

**local steroid:** A drug that is applied to the skin or injected in a joint to reduce swelling and pain; it should not be confused with anabolic steroids.

**lordosis:** Excessive curvature at the lumbar spine.

**lumbar:** The five vertebrae that comprise the low back, located just above the sacrum.

**massage:** Kneading and stroking of muscles and other soft tissue by the athletic trainer or massage therapist for therapeutic purposes.

**medial:** Toward the midline of the body.

**medial malleolus:** The end of the tibia on the medial side.

**meniscus:** A piece of cartilage within a joint, especially those pieces known as the medial and lateral menisci, which lie between the femur and the tibia.

**meniscectomy:** A surgical procedure whereby a meniscus is removed from a knee joint.

**metabolism:** The body's energy system.

**metatarsals:** The five longest bones of the foot.

**microorganism:** An organism of microscopic or submicroscopic size such as a virus or bacteria.

**moleskin:** A thick, soft, sticky tape. It cannot be torn by hand.

**molluscum contagiosum:** A skin condition caused by a virus. It is characterized by the formation of pink lumps.

**multiaxial joint:** A joint that has a large range of movement because it can move in a variety of planes.

**mumps:** A virus characterized by swelling around the jaw line.

**muscular endurance:** The ability of a muscle to perform repetitive movements for an extended period of time. It can be developed by using a high number of repetitions with a lighter weight.

**muscular power:** The ability to exert force quickly.

**muscular strength:** The ability to exert force against a resistance. It can be developed by using a low number of repetitions and a heavy weight.

**myositis ossificans:** The buildup of bone tissue in a muscle following an injury.

**National Athletic Trainers' Association (NATA):** The professional association that recognizes athletic trainers as its primary members and establishes codes of professional conduct.

**National Operating Committee on Standards for Athletic Equipment (NOCSAE):** A committee that sets the standards for football, baseball, and softball helmets.

**National Safety Council:** An organization that certifies individuals in first aid and cardiopulmonary resuscitation procedures.

**neck roll:** A form of protective padding that keeps the head within a safe range of motion.

**negligence:** A legal wrong characterized by the failure to act as a reasonably prudent person would act in a similar situation.

**neurologist:** A physician who specializes in neurological problems.

**neutral spine:** Normal cervical, thoracic, and lumbar curvature having neither too much flexion nor too much extension in a position that is comfortable for the athlete.

**nonsteroid anti-inflammatory drug:** A drug used to reduce the amount of tissue swelling after an injury.

**nonunion:** A fracture that does not heal and remains two pieces of bone when there was one before.

**nucleus pulposus:** The soft structure at the center of an intervertebral disk.

**nutrients:** Substances in food that the body uses in metabolism.

**nutrition:** The study of foods in relation to the metabolic needs of the body.

**organization and administration:** An aspect of athletic training that emphasizes issues related to management.

**orthopedist:** A physician who deals primarily with conditions and injuries of the musculoskeletal system.

**Osgood-Schlatter disorder:** A condition characterized by an irritation or loosening of the patellar tendon at its attachment at the top anterior aspect of the tibia, usually seen in younger athletes who perform a great deal of running and jumping.

**overload principle:** A strength and conditioning principle that in order for muscles to get stronger, they must be challenged to lift more than they are used to lifting.

**palpation:** Examination of an injured area by touch to determine the type of injury, for example, fracture, swelling, muscle ruptures, tendinitis, and pain.

**paralysis:** The inability to move.

**paraplegia:** The loss of sensation and muscular function in the lower extremities due to an injury of the spinal cord.

**partial airway obstruction:** When a portion of the airway is closed by an object in the throat.

**passive range of motion (PROM):** The extent to which an injured body part can be moved by the ATC without pain to or exertion from the athlete.

**pediatrician:** A specialist in the medical treatment of children.

**percussion :** Massage, using light chopping motions to the tissue.

**petrissage:** A massage stroke often described as a kneading of the tissue in which the skin, muscle, and fascia are squeezed between the hands.

**phagocytes:** Specialized white blood cells that clear the dead cells from the site of an injury.

**phalanges:** The small bones that make up our fingers and toes.

**pharmacology:** The study of drugs and the effects they have on the body.

**phlegm:** A thick mucous secreted in the respiratory passages due to allergy or infection, which the body expels by coughing.

**physical therapist:** An allied medical professional who specializes in rehabilitation of orthopedic and nonorthopedic conditions.

**physics:** The study of energy and matter.

**physiology:** The study of how cells and organ systems function.

**plantar surface:** The bottom of the foot.

**platelets:** Blood cells that carry blood-clotting materials.

**pneumothorax:** Having air in the chest cavity, commonly called a collapsed lung.

**podiatrist:** A specialist in foot disorders.

**post-traumatic response:** An emotional disorder resulting from a traumatic experience.

**posterior:** The back of the body.

**posterior cruciate ligament (PCL):** Prevents the tibia from moving posteriorly on the femur.

**PREMIER model:** A framework for thinking about being a professional: **P**romote a professional image. **R**emember your vision. **E**ngage in learning. **M**aximize your strengths. **I**nnovate and create. **E**nlist the help of others. **R**eflect on your actions.

**pressure point:** A place on the body where arteries, such as the brachial artery and the femoral artery, are easily accessed and pressure can be applied with your hand to slow the blood flow to a body part.

**PRICE:** An acronym for **P**rotection, **R**est, **I**ce, **C**ompression, and **E**levation of an injured body part that represents the initial steps of care for musculoskeletal injuries such as ligament sprains or muscle strains.

**primary assessment:** The aspect of assessment devoted to determining if an athlete has a clear airway, breathing, and circulation.

**primary care physician:** The physician an athlete must be referred to after he or she is injured.

**progression:** The advancement of an exercise or activity from simple to complex, slow speeds to fast speeds, and less aggressive activities to more aggressive activities.

**progressive resistive exercise (PRE):** The progression of the exercise is gradually harder from one set to the next and over a period of time.

**pronation:** A movement that turns the palm of the hand downward almost as if it were emptying a bowl of soup.

**proprioception:** The ability of the body to give information to the brain regarding the body's position, movements being performed, and forces acting on it.

**protraction:** Movement of the scapulas away from one another. The opposite of retraction.

**proximal:** Toward the attachment of the limb to the trunk.

**proximate cause:** A close connection between the act of a certified athletic trainer and resulting injury to an athlete.

**psychology:** The study of human mental processes such as behavior and personality.

**pulse points:** Areas where the artery lies close to the skin.

**pulse pressure:** The difference between the diastolic and systolic pressures.

**pulse rate:** The number of times the heart beats per minute, normally 60 to 80 per minute, taken at the wrist or neck.

**pyramid method:** A strength training regimen that involves multiple sets whereby the first set is low intensity, the second set is of moderate intensity, the third set is very intense, then the fourth set is back to moderate intensity, and the fifth set is of low intensity.

**quadriplegia:** The inability to move arms and legs.

**reconditioning:** Getting the athlete back into shape for athletic participation.

**recreational drug:** A drug that has no medical purpose.

**registration:** The step of contacting state authorities prior to acting in the capacity of an athletic trainer—required by law in some states.

**rehabilitation:** The process or means of getting a person back to his or her normal level of function following an injury or illness.

**resistance training:** An organized program to work the muscles, usually by lifting weights.

**retraction:** When the scapulas are moved, or pulled, together.

**rotation:** Occurs when a bony segment spins or turns on an axis.

**rotator cuff:** A group of muscles around the shoulder joint. The muscles of the rotator cuff are the supraspinatus, infraspinatus, teres minor, and subscapularis.

**rubella:** A form of measles often referred to as German measles. It is characterized by a rash and itching.

**rubeola:** A form of measles characterized by high fever, chills, rash (even inside the mouth), and coughing.

**sacrum:** The bottommost segment of the spine, which consists of bones that are fused together.

**sagittal plane:** A plane that divides the body into left and right halves.

**school nurse:** A licensed nurse that provides services to a school or school district.

**scoliosis:** Excessive side-to-side curvature of a spine.

**second impact syndrome:** A set of symptoms resulting from more than one concussion or blow to the head in a relatively short time period.

**seizure:** Uncontrollable shaking resulting from brain chemical imbalance or head injury.

**shinsplints:** A term for pain of the lower leg, often along the tibia.

**shoulder separation:** A sprain of the acromio-clavicular joint.

**sickle-cell anemia:** An inherited disease in which the red blood cells become shaped like sickles with points on each end, which causes the cells to hook onto the sides of the blood vessels creating a logjam of cells in a particular area. The result is that oxygen is not carried efficiently to all parts of the body.

**sign:** Observation that a rescuer can make of sweating, breath odors, temperature, blood pressure, breathing rate, heart rate, etc.

**SITS:** An acronym for the muscles of the rotator cuff: **s**upraspinatus, **i**nfraspinatus, **t**eres minor, and **s**ubscapularis.

**SOAP note:** Used to document the findings of an injury assessment using **s**ubjective, **o**bjective, **a**ssessment, and **p**lan of action components.

**specificity:** The principle that the type of activity a person performs in training is the type of activity he or she will get better at performing.

**sport psychology:** The study of variables such as life stress, mood, and motivation on sport performance and sport-related injury.

**sport-specific function:** Specific exercises and activities that are very much like the activities that the athlete will face upon return to participation.

**sports medicine:** A broad term that refers specifically to the care of the physically active who have suffered an athletics-related injury or illness.

**sports medicine team:** All of the individuals who may work with and care for an athlete at one point or another during his or her participation in athletics.

**sprain:** Injury to a ligament.

**standards of practice:** The way an athletic trainer is expected to act while doing his or her job.

**static stretching:** Holding a stretched muscle in one position for a short length of time.

**stinger:** A group of symptoms including burning, numbness, tingling, and pain down the arm that results from stretching a group of nerves called the brachial plexus. This condition is also known as a burner.

**strain:** Injury that occurs to a muscle or tendon.

**student assistant:** A student who volunteers to observe (and assist when deemed appropriate) a certified athletic trainer in order to learn more about the profession.

**supination:** A movement that turns the palm of the hand upward as if it were holding a bowl of soup.

**swimmer's ear:** An infection that results from water in the ear.

**symptom:** What the athlete feels but that cannot be seen, smelled, or heard, like pain, nausea, or anxiousness.

**synarthrodial joint:** A type of joint in which bones are held together by tough connective tissue making the joint essentially immovable.

**syncope:** Fainting due to lack of blood flow to the brain, for example, from standing up quickly.

**synovial membrane:** A tissue that completely surrounds diarthrodial joints and secretes a slippery fluid.

**systolic pressure:** The pressure in the arteries when the heart is beating. Normal systolic pressure is 120 mm Hg.

**talus:** One of the ankle bones located directly above the calcaneus.

**team physician:** The medical authority of the sports medicine team whose role is to work with the athletic trainer to oversee the entire sports medicine team effort.

**tendons:** Tissues in the body that connect a muscle to a bone.

**tendinitis:** Chronic inflammation of a tendon.

**tennis elbow:** Inflammation of the lateral epicondyle of the elbow, usually from overuse of the wrist extensor muscles.

**therapeutic drug:** A drug that has a medical purpose.

**thoracic:** Pertaining to the chest region of the body.

**tinnitus:** Ringing in the ears.

**total airway obstruction:** When an object blocks the airway, not allowing the athlete to speak, cough, or breathe.

**trachea:** A cartilage tube that allows passage of air from the larynx in the throat to the bronchial tube of the lungs.

**traction:** Pulling joints apart.

**transcutaneous electrical stimulation (TES):** The application of an electrical current to the surface of the skin that is designed to stimulate the region.

**transverse plane:** The plane that divides the body into top and bottom halves.

**triage:** The order in which you send injured patients to the hospital; the most seriously hurt go first.

**ultrasound:** A medical instrument that creates sound waves. Ultrasound can be used to create heat, break down tissues, or image soft tissues on a screen (used to determine the sex of an unborn baby, for example).

**universal choking sign:** A person who is chok-ing naturally grabs the throat with both hands, no matter what the person's nationality.

**universal precautions:** A set of procedures designed to prevent the spread of blood-borne diseases.

**urologist:** A physician who deals with problems of the urinary tract such as painful urination.

**vaccinations:** Injections of tiny amounts of viruses (sometimes live and sometimes dead) into the body to create an immunity to specific viruses.

**ventricle:** A chamber of the heart that receives blood from a corresponding atrium and from which blood is forced into the arteries.

**vibration massage:** A massage stroke designed to cause the tissue to tremble or shake vigorously.

**vital signs:** Observations made in the secondary assessment to determine the seriousness of an injury, including body temperature, skin color, breathing rate, heart rate, response to pain, pupillary reaction, ability to move, and capillary refill.

**whirlpool:** A tub of hot or cold water that is swirled around by jets of air.

**X rays:** Electromagnetic waves used to make a picture to aid in diagnosing injuries to bones and joints.

# Resources Used for This Book

Amato, H.K., and M.J. Warner. 1996. Athletic trainers: Leaders in sports. *Athletic therapy today* 1(1): 30–32.

American Academy of Orthopedic Surgeons. 1987. *Emergency care and transportation of the sick and injured.* 4th ed. Chicago: The Academy.

American Academy of Orthopedic Surgeons. 1991. *Athletic training and sports medicine.* 2d ed. Park Ridge, IL: American Academy of Orthopedic Surgeons.

American National Red Cross. 1973. *Advanced first aid and emergency care. Instructor's manual.* Garden City, NY: Doubleday.

American National Red Cross. 1987. *American Red Cross: Adult CPR.* [U.S.A.]: American National Red Cross.

American Red Cross. 1988. *American Red Cross standard first aid: workbook.* [U.S.A.]: American Red Cross.

American Red Cross. 1993. *Community first aid & safety.* St. Louis: Mosby-Lifeline.

Anderson, M.K., and S.J. Hall. 1995. *Sports injury management.* Baltimore: Williams & Wilkins.

Andrews, J.R., and J.A. Whiteside. 1993. Common elbow problems in the athlete. *The Journal of Orthopaedic and Sports Physical Therapy* 17(6): 289–95.

Anthony, C.P., and N.J. Kolthoff. 1975. *Textbook of anatomy and physiology.* St. Louis: Mosby.

Anthony, C.P., and G.A. Thibodeau. 1983. *Textbook of anatomy and physiology.* St. Louis: Mosby.

Arnheim, D.D. 1989. *Modern principles of athletic training.* 7th ed. St. Louis: Times Mirror/Mosby.

Arnheim, D.D., and W.E. Prentice. 1997. *Principles of athletic training.* 9th ed. Madison, WI: Brown and Benchmark.

Bachman, D., ed. 1981. *Football head/neck injuries & helmetry.* Ridell.

Bergeron, J.D., and H.W. Greene. 1989. *Coaches guide to sport injuries.* Champaign, IL: Human Kinetics.

Blauvelt, C.T., and F. Nelson. 1994. *A manual of orthopaedic terminology.* 5th ed. St. Louis: Mosby Year Book.

Booher, J.M., and G.A. Thibodeau. 1985. *Athletic injury assessment.* St. Louis: Times Mirror/Mosby.

Booher, J.M., and G.A. Thibodeau. 1989. *Athletic injury assessment.* 2d ed. St. Louis: Times Mirror/Mosby.

Boyd, J. 1997. *Research update: The PCL deficient knee.* Paper presented at the Great Lakes Athletic Trainers Association Annual Meeting and Symposium, Minneapolis, MN, March 13.

Bunton, E.E., W.A. Pitney, A.W. Kane, and T.A. Cappaert. 1993. The role of limb torque, muscle action, and proprioception during closed kinetic chain rehabilitation of the lower extremity. *Journal of Athletic Training* 28(1): 10–20.

Campbell, J.E. 1988. *BTLS: Basic prehospital trauma care.* Englewood Cliffs, NJ: Prentice Hall.

Casterline, M., S. Osowski, and G. Ulrich. 1996. Femoral stress fractures. *Journal of Athletic Training* 31(1): 53–56.

Chisholm, M.M. 1993. Anxiety. In *Mental health: Psychiatric nursing,* 3d ed., eds. R.P. Rawlins, S.R. Williams, and C.K. Beck. St. Louis: Mosby Year Book.

Coleman, E. 1984. Nutrition principles for the child athlete. *Sports Medicine Digest* 6(12): 6.

Crenshaw, D.A. 1990. *Bereavement.* New York: Continuum.

Dartmouth University. 1997. *A guide to suicide prevention.* Hanover, NH: Dartmouth University. Available: http://www.dartmouth.edu/community/chd/suicide_p.html [April 14, 1997].

Drowatzky, J.N., and C.W. Armstrong. 1984. *Physical education: Career perspectives and professional foundations.* Englewood Cliffs, NJ: Prentice Hall.

Dunlop, R.S. 1978. *Helping the bereaved.* Bowie, MD: Charles Press.

Easterbrook, M. 1981. Eye protection for squash and racquetball. *The Physician and Sportsmedicine* 9(2): 79–82.

Eichelberger, M.R. 1981. Torso injuries in athletics. *The Physician and Sportsmedicine* 9(3): 87–92.

Eichner, E. 1989. Sickle–cell trait and exercise–related death. *Sports Medicine Digest* 11(2): 4.

Ellenbecker, T.S., and A.J. Mattalino. 1997. *The elbow in sport.* Champaign, IL: Human Kinetics.

Fahey, T.D. 1994. *Basic weight training for men and women.* 2d ed. Mountainview, CA: Mayfield.

Field, L.D., and D.W. Altchek. 1995. Elbow injuries. *Clinical Sports Medicine* 14(1): 59–78.

Flegel, M.J. 1992. *Sport first aid.* Champaign, IL: Human Kinetics.

Fox, E.L., R.W. Bowers, and M.L. Foss. 1993. *The physiological basis for exercise and sport.* 5th ed. Madison, WI: Brown and Benchmark.

Gebhard, J.S., D.H. Donaldson, and C.W. Brown. 1994. Soft-tissue injuries of the cervical spine. *Orthopedic Review.* May Suppl.: 9–17.

Gerberich, S.S., J.D. Priest, J. Boen, C.P. Straub, and R.E. Maxwell. 1983. Concussion incidence and severity in secondary school varsity football players. *American Journal of Public Health* 73: 1370–375.

Glass, A.L. 1994. *Weight training.* Dubuque, IA: Kendall/Hunt.

Goldstein, T.S. 1995. *Functional rehabilitation in orthopaedics.* Gaithersburg, MD: Aspen.

Graham, L.S. 1985. Ten ways to dodge the malpractice bullet. *Journal of the National Athletic Trainers' Association* 20(2): 117–19.

Gray, R.S. 1997. The role of the clinical athletic trainer. In *Clinical athletic training*, ed. J.J. Konin. Thorofare, NJ: Slack.

Guten, G.N. 1991. *Play healthy, stay healthy.* Champaign, IL: Leisure Press.

Hartley, A. 1991. *Practical joint assessment.* St. Louis: Mosby Year Book.

Heck, J.F., M.P. Weis, J.M. Garland, and C.R. Weis. 1994. Minimizing liability risks of head and neck injuries in football. *Journal of Athletic Training* 29(2): 128–39.

Hegarty, V. 1988. *Decisions in nutrition.* St. Louis: Times Mirror/Mosby.

Heinzman, S.E. 1991. Quality physicals that generate funds for the training room. *Journal of the National Athletic Trainers' Association* 26(1): 66–69.

Henderson, J., and W. Carroll. 1993. The athletic trainer's role in preventing sport injury and rehabilitating injured athletes: A psychological perspective. In *Psychological bases of sport injuries*, ed. D. Pargman. Morgantown, WV: Fitness Information Technology.

Houglum, P.A. 1992. Soft tissue healing and its impact on rehabilitation *Journal of Sport Rehabilitation* 1: 19–23.

Hunt, V.K. 1997. Fitness centers: Untapped job market for ATCs? *NATA News* October, 4–5, 20.

Johnson, B.C., and L.A. Klabunde. 1995. The elusive slipped capital femoral epiphysis. *Journal of Athletic Training* 30(2): 124–27.

Katch, F.I., and W.D. McArdle. 1993. *Nutrition, weight control, and exercise.* Philadelphia: Lea & Febiger.

Kendall, P.F., E.K. McCreary, and P.G. Provance. 1993. *Muscles, testing and function.* 4th ed. Baltimore: Williams & Wilkins.

Kenna, K. 1983. The diabetic athlete. *Athletic Training* 18(2): 131–34.

Kennedy, R. 1995. *Taping guide.* St. Louis: Mosby.

Khoo, D., W. Carmichaels, and R.J. Spinner. 1996. Ulnar nerve entrapment. *Orthopedic Clinics of North America* 27(2): 317–38.

Kisner, C., and L.A. Colby. 1990. *Therapeutic exercise.* 2d ed. Philadelphia: Davis.

Knight, K.L. 1995. *Cryotherapy in sport injury management.* Champaign, IL: Human Kinetics.

Knight, K.L. 1996. Interview by the author in June in Orlando, FL.

Koester, M.C. 1995. Refocusing the adolescent preparticipation physical evaluation toward preventive health care. *Journal of Athletic Training* 30(4): 352–60.

Konin, J.J. 1997. The roles of allied health care providers. In *Clinical athletic training*, ed. J.J. Konin. Thorofare, NJ: Slack.

———. 1997. Communication skills in clinical athletic training. In *Clinical athletic training*, ed. J.J. Konin. Thorofare, NJ: Slack.

Kubler-Ross, E. 1969. *On death and dying.* New York: Macmillan.

Kuland, D.N. 1988. *The injured athlete.* 2d ed. Philadelphia: Lippincott.

Larson, J.P. 1993. Massage as a modality in trauma and sports medicine. *Trauma* 35(4): 81–94.

Lavallee, L., and F. Flint. 1996. The relationship of stress, competitive anxiety, mood state, and social support to athletic injury. *Journal of Athletic Training* 31(4): 296–99.

Lephart, S.M., D.M. Pincivero, J.L. Giraldo, and F.H. Fu. 1997. The role of proprioception in the management and rehabilitation of athletic injuries. *The American Journal of Sports Medicine* 25(1): 130–37.

Leverenz, L.J., and L.B. Helms. 1990. Suing athletic trainers: Part II. *Journal of the National Athletic Trainers Association* 25(3): 219–26.

Magee, D.J. 1987. *Orthopedic physical assessment.* Philadelphia: Saunders.

McCulloch, J.M., L.C. Kloth, and J.A. Feedar. 1995. *Wound healing: Alternatives in management.* 2d ed. Philadelphia: Davis.

Miller, A.E. 1996. Creatine supplements in athletics. *Sports Medicine Update* 11(3): 12–16.

Moss, C.L. 1996. 1994 Entry-level athletic training salaries. *Journal of Athletic Training* 31(1): 25–28.

Mottram, D.R. 1988. *Drugs in sport*. Champaign, IL: Human Kinetics.

Mueller, F.O., R.C. Cantu, and S.P. Van Camp. 1996. *Catastrophic injuries in high school and college sports*. Vol. 8. Sport Science Monograph Series. Champaign, IL: Human Kinetics.

National Athletic Trainers' Association. 1998. *1998 Membership directory: NATA code of ethics*. Dallas: National Athletic Trainers' Association.

Ollivierre, C.O., R.P. Nirschl, and F.A. Peltrone. 1995. Resection and repair for medial tennis elbow. *American Journal of Sports Medicine* 23(2): 214–21.

Pargman, D. 1993. Sport injuries: An overview of psychological perspectives. In *Psychological bases of sport injuries*, ed. D. Pargman. Morgantown, WV: Fitness Information Technology.

Paris, S.V. 1990. The spine and swimming. In *The spine in sports*, ed. S.H. Hochschuler, 121. Philadelphia: Hanley and Belfus.

Pauls, J.A., and K.L. Reed. 1996. *Quick reference to physical therapy*. Gaithersburg, MD: Aspen.

Peterson, M., and K. Peterson. 1988. *Eat to compete: A guide to sports nutrition*. Chicago: Year Book Medical.

Pfeiffer, R.P., and B.C. Mangus. 1995. *Concepts of athletic training*. Boston: Jones and Bartlett.

Porterfield, J.A., and C. DeRosa. 1991. *Mechanical low back pain*. Philadelphia: Saunders.

Prentice, W.E., ed. 1994. *Rehabilitation techniques in sports medicine*. 2d ed. St. Louis: Mosby.

Quillen, W.S., and F.B. Underwood. 1995. *Laboratory manual to accompany therapeutic modalities in sports medicine*. 3d ed. St. Louis: Mosby.

Rankin, J.M., and C. Ingersoll. 1995. *Athletic training management*. St. Louis: Mosby.

Rawlins, R.P. 1993. Hope-Hopelessness. In *Mental health: Psychiatric nursing*, 3d ed. Eds. R.P. Rawlins, S.R. Williams, and C.K. Beck. St. Louis: Mosby Year Book.

Ray, R. 1994. *Management strategies in athletic training*. Champaign, IL: Human Kinetics.

Rees, A.M. 1997. *Consumer health USA*. Vol. 2. Phoenix: Oryx Press.

Roy, S., and R. Irvin. 1983. *Sports medicine: prevention, evaluation, management, and rehabilitation*. Englewood Cliffs, NJ: Prentice-Hall.

Saunders, H.D., and R. Saunders. 1993. *Evaluation, treatment and prevention of musculoskeletal disorders*. 3d ed. Vol. 1. Bloomington, MN: Educational Opportunities.

Schwartz, G., P. Safar, J. Stone, P. Storey, and D. Wagner, eds. 1978. *Principles and practice of emergency medicine*. Philadelphia: Saunders.

Seaward, B.L. 1997. *Managing stress*. 2d ed. Boston: Jones and Bartlett.

Seeley, R.R., T.D. Stephens, and P. Tate. 1992. *Anatomy and physiology*. 2d ed. St. Louis: Mosby Year Book.

Sluijs, E.A. 1991. Checklist to assess patient education in physical therapy practice: Development and reliability. *Physical Therapy* 71(4): 561–69.

Solari, A. 1997. Interview by the author on February 10 in Ann Arbor, MI.

———. 1998. Interview by the author on January 14 in Ann Arbor, MI.

Starkey, C. 1993. *Therapeutic modalities for athletic trainers*. Philadelphia: Davis.

Starkey, C., and J. Ryan. 1996. *Evaluation of orthopedic and athletic injuries*. Philadelphia: Davis.

Steele, M.K. 1996. *Sideline help*. Champaign, IL: Human Kinetics.

Steinmuller, P., and L.N. Montana. November 1996. *Disordered eating impairs athletic performance*. NET Program.

Stith, W.J. 1990. Exercise and the intervertebral disk. In *The spine in sports*, ed. S.H. Hochschuler, 4. Philadelphia: Hanley and Belfus.

Stone, J.A., N.B. Partin, J.S. Lueken, K.E. Timm, and E.J. Ryan. 1994. Upper extremity proprioceptive training. *Journal of Athletic Training* 29(1): 15–18.

Straub, S.J. 1993. Working with adolescents in a high school setting. *Journal of Athletic Training* 28(1): 75–80.

Templin, J.M. 1992. *Anatomy and physiology laboratory manual*. 2d ed. St. Louis: Mosby Year Book.

Thomas, C.L., ed. 1985. *Taber's cyclopedic medical dictionary*. 13th ed. Philadelphia: Davis.

Tomberlin, J.P., and H.D. Saunders. 1994. *Evaluation, treatment and prevention of musculoskeletal disorders*. 3d ed. Vol. 2. Chaska, MN: The Saunders Group.

Torg, J. ed. 1991. *Athletic injuries to the head, neck, and face*. 2d ed. St. Louis: Mosby Year Book.

U.S. Department of Health and Human Services. 1992. *Important information about hepatitis B, hepatitis B vaccine, and hepatitis B immune globulin*. Washington, DC: Government Printing Office.

Vaccaro, P. 1987. Thoracic and vascular injuries in athletes. *Athletic Training* 22(4): 290–94.

Waman, D., and M. Khelifa. 1996. Psychological issues in sport injury rehabilitation: Current knowledge and practice. *Journal of Athletic Training* 31(3): 257–61.

Wann, D.L. 1997. *Sport psychology*. Upper Saddle River, NJ: Prentice Hall.

Weidner, T., and T. Sevier. 1996. Sport, exercise, and the common cold. *Journal of Athletic Training* 31(2): 154–59.

Williams, M.H. 1992. Alcohol and sport performance. *Gatorade Sports Science Exchange* 4(40).

Williams, M. 1989. *Beyond training: How athletes enhance performance legally and illegally*. Champaign, IL: Human Kinetics.

Williams, M.H. 1992. *Nutrition for fitness and sport*. 3d ed. Dubuque, IA: Brown.

Wright, K.E., and W.R. Whitehill. 1991. *The comprehensive manual of taping and wrapping techniques*. Gardner, KS: Cramer Products.

# Index

*Note:* Page numbers in italics refer to the figure or table on that page.

## A

AAROM. *See* active-assistive range of motion
ABC's 30, 31, 293
abdominal anatomy 105-107
abdominal curl 216, *216*
abdominal injuries 105-110
    preventing 107
    treating 107-109
abdominal muscles 107
abdominal protection 186-187
abdominal quadrants 105, *106*
abduction 7, *10,* 293
ability to move 43
abrasion or laceration, corneal 133
acceptance 227-228
access to injured athlete 25-26
accident and injury reports 27, 285, *286*
acetabulum 87, *88,* 293
Achilles tendinitis 75
Achilles tendon *73,* 75, 293
    rupture 5
    taping 172, *173*
ACL. *See* anterior cruciate ligament
acquired immune deficiency syndrome.
        *See* AIDS
acromioclavicular ligament sprain 145-146
acromion process 143, *144*
active-assistive range of motion (AAROM)
        196, 293
active range of motion (AROM) 196, 293
adduction 7, *10,* 293
adductor (groin) strain wrap 176-177, *177*
administrative aspects 275, 279-292
AIDS 245-246
airway 31
airway obstruction 32-33
    partial 33, 299
    total 33, 302
alcohol 250-251
all-day events 263
Allen, T.E. 224
allergists 273, 293
allergy 273, 293
Altchek, D.W. 304
aluminum splint *48*
alveoli *112,* 113, 293
Amato, H.K. 292, 303
ambulance
    calling for 24
    sideline signal for *26*
ambulatory (term) 293
ambulatory movement of athletes 64-65
American Academy of Orthopedic
        Surgeons 32, 303
American College of Sports Medicine 221
American National Red Cross 303
American Red Cross *25,* 28, 30, 32, 38, 49,
        50, 271, 293, 303
amino acids 258, 264, 293
amnesia 124, 293
amphiarthrodial joints 7, 293
amputation *14*
anabolic steroids 252-253, 293
anaphylactic shock

characteristics of *47*
    treating *48*
anaphylaxis 32
anatomical planes 3, *4*
anatomical position 3-12
    anterior 4, 294
    definition of 293
    distal 4, 296
    lateral 4, 298
    medial 4, 298
    posterior 4, 300
    proximal 4, 300
    terms of 4
"anatomical snuffbox" 159
anatomy 1-20, 275, 293
    of abdomen 105-107
    bony 5, *5, 6*
    of ear 131, *131*
    of elbow 151-152, *152*
    of eye 129-131, *130*
    of facial region 129-132
    of foot, ankle, and lower leg 71-73
    of head 121-122
    of hip, pelvis, and thigh 87, *88*
    of knee 79-80
    of mouth 132
    muscular 6, *8, 9. See also* muscles
    of elbow 152
    of nose 131-132
    of shoulder 143-145
    of spine 95-97, *96*
    of thorax *112,* 112-114
    of throat 111, *112*
    of wrist and hand 159-160
Anderson, M. 78, 190, 240
Anderson, M.K. 32, 303
Andrews, J.R. 157, 303
anemia 237
    definition of 293
    iron-deficiency 237
    sickle-cell 237, *237,* 301
anger 227
angina pectoris 34, 293
angle of pull, restricting 168
ankle *72*
    anatomy of 71-73
    bone injuries of 75-76
    bones of 71-72
    dislocation of 74-75
    elastic wrapping 176, *176*
    injuries to 71-78
        preventing 73-74
        treating 74-77
    ligaments of 73
    muscle and tendon injuries of 75
    muscles of 73
    reconditioning techniques for 213, *213*
    sprain 74
    strength of, improving 213, *213*
ankle braces 189
annular ligament 151, *152*
annulus fibrosus 96, *96,* 293
anorexia nervosa 260, 261
    definition of 294
    signs and symptoms of *261*

anterior chamber, hemorrhage into
        (hyphema) 134
anterior compartment syndrome 76-77
anterior cruciate ligament (ACL) 80, *80,* 294
    injuries to 82
Anthony, C.P. 12, 78, 303
antibiotics 250
anxious athletes 226
apnea 41, 294
appendicitis 234
appendicular skeleton 5, 294
arches of foot *72,* 72-73
arch sprain 74
arm lock 65, *66*
Armstrong, C.W. 303
Arnheim, D.D. 20, 78, 179, 190, 303
AROM. *See* active range of motion
arteries 112
    major 113, *113*
arthroscopic surgery 84, 294
articulate (term) 294
articulation 16
aseptic meningitis 243, 294
assessment 193-195
    emergency 29-30
    HIT technique 39-45, *40*
    person in charge of 23
    primary 30-31, 300
    secondary 30
Association for the Advancement of Health
        Education 255
assumption of risk 280, 294
assumption of risk forms *280,* 281
asthma 32
    bronchial 233
    definition of 294
ATC. *See* certified athletic trainer
athlete(s) 272. *See also* injured athlete(s)
    anxious 226
    death of 227
athlete education 283
athletic conditions 231-267
athletic injuries. *See* injuries
Athletic Injury/Accident Report *194, 286*
athletic nutrition 262-264
athletics
    drugs used in 249-255
    imagery in 228
    protective equipment used in 181-190
    psychology and 226-227
    relaxation in 228-229
athletics-related injuries. *See* injuries
athletic trainer, certified 272-273, 295
athletic trainers
    certification 274-275
    nontraditional settings for *276,* 276-
        277
    roles of 271-272, xi
    starting salary 276
    traditional settings for 275-276
athletic training 271. *See also* training
    careers in 275-277
    definition of 294
    as health profession 274
    as profession 271-278

professional and administrative aspects of 269-292
psychology and 225-230
atrium 112, *113,* 294
avascular necrosis 163, 294
avulsion fractures *16,* 148
of elbow 155
avulsions of hip, pelvis, and thigh 89
axial region
athletics-related injuries to 93-140
reconditioning techniques for 215-216
axial skeleton 5, 294
axis 9

**B**
Bachman, D. 303
backboarding 62-63
indications for 62
procedure for 62-63
backboards 47
sideline signal for *26*
"back school" 98
balance activities *213*
balanced diet 260
balancing activities 216, *218*
ball-and-socket joints 7, 294
ballistic stretching 212, 294
bandage 35
bargaining 227
Bartimole, J. 265
baseball, face masks for 183
basket weave
closed 171, *172*
open 171-172, *172*
batting helmets 182-183, *183*
battle sign 123, 294
Beck, J.L. 86
bench press 217, *219*
beta-adrenergic drugs 250, 294
biceps curls 220, *221*
biceps femoris 80, *81*
biceps tendon rupture 147
bicipital tendinitis 147
Bike Athletic 190
bile 106, 294
biomechanics 275, 294
bites and stings 56-57, *57*
Bittings, L.A. 240
Blackard, D. 157
black eye 133
bladder injuries 109
Blauvelt, C.T. 164, 303
bleeding
control of 35
external 35
blood-borne conditions 245-246
blood doping 253
blood pressure 32, 41-42
diastolic 204
measurement of 41-42, *42*
blood system, conditions of 236-238
blowout fracture *17,* 134-135
board splints *48*
body temperature 42, 294
body tissues 4-6
Boen, J. 304
bone fractures
acute inflammation of 18
healing 18
healing stages 18
remodeling 18
repair 18
bone injuries 15-18
of cervical spine 102
of elbow 155
of foot, ankle, and lower leg 75-76
of hip, pelvis, and thigh 89-90
of knee 83-84
of lumbar spine 100
of shoulder 147-148

types of 15-16
of wrist and hand 163
bones 5-6
facial 129, *130*
of foot, ankle, and lower leg 71-72, *72*
functions of 5-6
of knee 79, *80*
of shoulder 143, *144*
of skull 121, *122*
in spine 95-96
of wrist and hand 159-160, *160*
bone scan 76
bony anatomy 5, *5, 6*
Booher, J.M. 86, 303
boutonniere deformity 163, *163*
Bowers, R.W. 224, 304
Boyd, J. 303
braces
ankle 189
knee 81, *81*
securing 168
brachial artery 113, *113*
brachial plexus
injuries of 102-103
stretching *102,* 102-103
brain 121-122, *122*
breathing 31, *114*
mouth-to-mouth 32
breathing emergencies 31-33
breathing rate 40-41, 294
breath sounds 41
Brittenham, D. 104
Brittenham, G. 104
bronchial asthma 233
bronchiole *112*
bronchitis 243, 294
Brown, C.W. 104, 304
"buddy taping" 175, *176*
bulimia 260, 261, 294
in real world 262
signs and symptoms of *261*
Bunton, E.E. 303
"burner" *102,* 102-103, 294
return to play after 103
bursa 156, 294

**C**
caffeine 251-252
calcaneus 72, *72, 73,* 294
calf stretches 213, *213*
callus 18, 294
Campbell, J.E. *25,* 303
Canadian Standards Association (CSA) 181, 294
Cantu, R.C. 128, 305
capillary refill *42,* 42-43, 294
capital femoral epiphysis 89, 294
Cappaert, T.A. 303
carbohydrate loading 263-264
carbohydrates 258, *258*
cardiac arrest 34, 294
cardiogenic shock
characteristics of *47*
treating *48*
cardiopulmonary emergencies 33-34
cardiopulmonary resuscitation 34, *34,* 295
certification 281
cardiovascular conditioning 220-221
cardiovascular endurance 220, 294
careers 275-277
Carmichaels, W. 304
carotid artery 111, 113, *113,* 295
Carroll, W. 229, 304
Carson, W. 149
cartilage 6, 18
hyaline *7,* 297
of knee 79-80
cartilage fractures, tracheal 115
Cartwright, Lorin 90, 115, 160, 238, 262
Casterline, M. 91, 303

cauliflower ear (hematoma auris) 137
cerebrospinal fluid 122, 295
certification
athletic trainer 274-275
required areas of study 274
routes to 274
CPR and first aid 281
definition of 295
certified athletic trainer 272-273, 295. *See also*
athletic trainers
cervical movements, resisted 216, *217*
cervical region, reconditioning techniques for 216
cervical spine 95, *96*
disk injuries of 102
injuries of 101-103
requirements for return to participation
after 101
sideline signal for *26*
protection for 184
charts 285
check rein 175, *175,* 295
chicken pox 242, 295
chiropractors 274, 295
Chisholm, M.M. 303
choking, universal sign for *33, 33,* 302
cholesterol 259, 295
chondromalacia 83, 295
circuit training 212, 295
circulation 31
circumduction 7, 9, *10,* 295
Clark, N. 265, 266
clavicle 143, *144*
clavicular fractures 147
Clement, J. 86
Clifton, Becky 125-126
clinic 276
closed basket weave 171, *172*
clothing
adjusting 53-54
removal of uniforms 62
coach 273
cocaine 252
code of ethics 289
Colby, L.A. 224, 304
cold-related problems 54-55
preventing 55
cold sores 244
cold therapy
indications and contraindications for *198*
modalities 199-200
Coleman, E. 266, 303
collateral knee ligament sprains 173, *173*
color, skin 42
coma, diabetic 235, *236,* 295
comminuted fracture *17*
common cold (coryza) 243, 295
communicable diseases 241-248
precautions against 35-37
transmission of 35-37
communication 289. *See also* signs and
signals
notifying parents or guardians 26
press relations 27
competence 290
compression, intermittent 204, *204,* 297
indications and contraindications for *201*
compression fracture *16*
concussions 124, 295
conditioning. *See also* reconditioning
cardiovascular 220-221
principles of 209-210
connective tissue 7
conscious athletes 31
consent, informed 281
constant set method *211*
constriction 295
pupillary 43
Consumer Response and Information Center 267
contact lens, dislodged 135

contraction
isokinetic 210-211, 298
isometric 210, 298
isotonic 210, 298
contracts, written 281
contraindications 199
contrecoup injuries *14,* 123, 295
contusion *14,* 77
liver 109
pulmonary 117
cooling modalities 199-200
indications and contraindications for *198*
coracoid process 143, *144*
corneal abrasion or laceration 133
corticosteroids 15
coryza. *See* common cold
Costello, L.E. 240
counseling 27
CPR. *See* cardiopulmonary resuscitation
cramps, heat 52, 297
creatine 264
creation 290
Crenshaw, D.A. 303
crepitus 44
crisis plan 23-27, 281
adaptability for different facilities 27
assisting team members through 27
definition of 295
summary 28
cross-country running 27
crowd control 24
crusts *244*
cryotherapy 200, 295
CSA. *See* Canadian Standards Association
cyanosis 47
cystic fibrosis 41

**D**

Daily Treatment Log *287*
Dartmouth University 303
Das, M. 128
Davidson, R. 86
death of athlete 227
deformity 18
DeLorme method *211,* 212, 295
denial 227
dentist 273, 295
depressed fracture *17*
depression 226, 227, 295
DeRosa, C. 104, 305
detached retina 133, 295
deviated septum 138
diabetes 234-236
diabetic coma 235, *236,* 295
diabetic illness 31
diabetics 19
diaphragm 32, *112,* 114, 295
diarthrodial joints 7, 295
diastolic blood pressure 41, 204, 295
diet, balanced 260
dietitians 295
registered 274
digestive organs 106
dilation, pupillary 43, *43*
dimethyl sulfoxide (DMSO) 252, 295
directional terminology 7, *10*
direct pressure 295
diseases
communicable 35-37, 241-248
viral 242-243
disks, intervertebral *96,* 96-97, 297
cervical, injuries of 102
dislocation 16, 296
of ankle 74-75
of elbow 155-156, *156*
glenohumeral 148, *148*
of hip 89-90, *90*
of interphalangeal joint or metacarpal
phalangeal joint 161

of lunate 161
of patella 83-84
temporomandibular 138-139
of tooth 139
of ulna 155-156
dislodged contact lens 135
distal interphalangeal joints 160, *160*
distal tibia and fibula, epiphyseal injury of 76
DMSO. *See* dimethyl sulfoxide
Doberstein, S.T. 190
doctors. *See* physicians
documentation 283-285
accident report forms 27
of findings 193-195
of injuries and procedures 281
reports and charts 285
SOAP notes 193-195, *194,* 301
Donaldson, D.H. 104, 304
dorsal (term) 162
Drowatzky, J.N. 303
drug abuse 253
drugs 249-255, 296
beta-adrenergic 250, 294
nonsteroidal anti-inflammatory 250, 299
performance-enhancing 252-253
recreational 250-252, 300
therapeutic 249-250, 302
drug testing 253
Dunlop, R.S. 303
dyspnea 41, 296

**E**

ear 131, *131*
cauliflower (hematoma auris) 137
foreign bodies in 137
injuries to 136-137
earplugs 184
Easterbrook, M. 190, 304
eating disorders 260-262
Echemendia, R. 128
edema 196, 296
education 283, 290
for athletes 283
professional 289
effleurage 203, *203,* 296
Ehlers, Greg 154
Eichelberger, M.R. 110, 304
Eichner, E. 304
Eichner, E.R. 240
elastic tape 168, *168,* 296
precut 176
elastic wrapping
adductor (groin) strain *177*
ankle 176, *176*
hip flexor strain 177, *177*
shoulder 178, *178*
techniques for 175-178
thigh 176, *177*
elastic wraps 175, *176,* 296
elbow
anatomy of 151-152, *152*
dislocations of 155-156, *156*
hyperextension of 174, *174*
injuries to 151-157
preventing 152-153
treating 153
muscular anatomy of 152, *152*
protection for 186
reconditioning techniques for 220, *220, 221*
strengthening exercises for 220, *220*
elbow extensor strain 154
elbow flexor strain 154
electrical elements 204-205
indications and contraindications for *205*
electrical stimulation, transcutaneous 204,
*205,* 302
elevate 35
Ellenbecker, T.S. 157, 304
Ellsasser, J. 164

embedded objects, in eye 134
Embry, Alex 108
emergencies
breathing 31-33
cardiopulmonary 33-34
movement in 62, *63*
phone numbers for 23-24
procedures and assessment for 29-30
supplies for 26
emergency medical response team
assisting members through crisis plan 27
obstacles to 27
emergency medical system (911), signs and
symptoms that require 32
emergency services
access to injured athlete 25-26
directing to injured athlete 26
Emergency Telephone Contacts 24, *25*
emphysema 251
employment
nontraditional settings for *276,* 276-277
traditional settings for 275-276
endurance 197, 296
cardiovascular 220, 294
muscular 212, 298
treatment phase 197
environment
heat loss and 52-53
physical 228
scholastic 275-276
environmental injuries 51-58
enzymes 106
epicondylitis, medial and lateral 155
epilepsy 238, 296
epiphyseal fractures *17*
of elbow 155
of hip, pelvis, and thigh 89
epiphyseal injury 147-148
of distal tibia and fibula 76
epiphysis (growth plate) 6, 296
capital femoral 294
epistaxis (nosebleed) 137-138, 296
equipment 24
adjusting 53-54
protective 181-190
removal of 59-62
safety standards for 281
equipment manager 274, 296
ergonomics specialist 277, 296
esophagus 111, 296
ethics, NATA code of 289
evacuation of facilities 27
evaluation of injuries 271
eversion 7, 8, *10,* 296
exercise(s)
isotonic 213-214, *214*
lumbar stabilization 216, *216*
pendulum 217, *219*
progressive resistive 209-210, 300
for reconditioning muscles 212-220
upper body 221, *222*
wand 217, *218*
exercise physiology 275
exercise programs 195, *195*
exhaustion, heat 52, 297
extension 7, *10,* 296
of spine 215, *215*
extrication 59-68, 296
eye
anatomy of 129-131, *130*
black 133
embedded object in 134
foreign bodies in 133-134
injuries to 133-136
protection for 184
eyelid laceration 135-136

**F**

face, protective equipment for 181-184

face guards 183
face mask removal 59-60, *60*
facial anatomy 129-132
facial bones 129, *130*
facial injuries 129-140
    preventing 132-133
facilities
    crisis plan for 27
    evacuation of 27
Fahey, T.D. 223, 304
failure point 16, 296
false movement 44
fat(s) 258-259, *259*
Feedar, J.A. 305
femoral artery 113, *113*
femoral epiphysis, capital 294
femur 79, *80*
femur fractures 89
fiber, carbohydrates high in *258*
fibroblasts 15, 296
fibrous joints 7, 296
Field, L.D. 304
fifth metatarsal avulsion fracture 75, *76*
finger splints *48*
finger sprains, buddy taping for 175, *176*
fire ant stings 57
first aid 29-38
    certification 281
    crisis plan 23-27, 28, 281, 295
    for environmental injuries 51-58
    immediate 167-168
    person in charge 23
    secondary procedures 39-50
flail chest 117, *117*
Flegel, M.J. 50, *282*, 304
flexibility 196, 296
    establishing 196-197
    joint 212
flexion 7, *10*, 296
flexion movements, of spine 215, *215*
Flint, F. 230, 304
folliculitis 244-245, 296
Food and Nutrition Information Center 266
food poisoning. *See* gastroenteritis
foot
    anatomy of 71-73, *72*
    arches of *72*, 72-73
    bone injuries of 75-76
    bones of 71-72, *72*
    injuries to 71-78
        preventing 73-74
        treating 74-77
    joints of 71-72
    ligaments of 73, *73*
    muscle and tendon injuries of 75
    muscles of 73
    plantar surface of 72
    protection for 188-189
    reconditioning techniques for 213, *213*
    stress fractures of 76
football
    face guards 183
    face mask removal 60, *60*
    head posture for 64
    helmets 182, *182*
        removal of 61, *61*
    pants 187, *187*
    shoulder pads 184, *185*
forearm extensors *9*
forearm flexors *8*
foreign bodies
    in ear 137
    in eye 133-134
forward head posture 98, 296
forward lunges 214, *214*
Foss, M.L. 224, 304
Fox, E.L. 224, 304
fractured tooth 139
fractures 16, 296

assessing and managing 47-48
avulsion *16*, 148
    of elbow 155
    fifth metatarsal 298
    fifth metatarsal (Jones) 75
blowout *17*, 134-135
bone, healing 18
cartilage, tracheal 115
clavicular 147
comminuted *17*
compression *16*
depressed *17*
epiphyseal *17*
    of elbow 155
of femur 89
greenstick *17*
growth plate, of hip, pelvis, and thigh 89
humeral 147
Jones 75, 298
longitudinal *16*
of mouth (maxilla, mandible) 138, 139
nasal 138
nonunion 18
oblique *17*
of orbital roof 135
patellar 83
pathological *17*
rib 115-116
of sinus 135
of skull 123
spiral *16*
sternal 116
stress *16*
    of hip, pelvis, and thigh 89
    of lower leg and foot 76
transverse *17*
types of *16-17*
friction massage 204, 296
frontal bone *122*, 129, *130*
frontal lobe 121, *122*
frontal plane 3, *4*, 296
frostbite 55
Fu, F.H. 207, 304
furuncle 245, 296

**G**
gallbladder *106*
gamekeeper's thumb 161, *161*, 296
Gansneder, B. 128
Garland, J.M. 304
gastrocnemius 73, *73*, 296
gastroenteritis (food poisoning) 234
gastrointestinal tract conditions 234
Gebhard, J.S. 104, 304
General Mills Consumer Services 266
Gerberich, S.S. 304
German measles. *See* rubella
Giant Food Incorporated 266
Gieck, J. 128
Giraldo, J.L. 207, 304
girth 4-5, 296
Glass, A.L. 224, 304
glenohumeral dislocations and subluxations 148, *148*
glenohumeral ligament sprain 146
glenoid fossa 143, *144*
globe, ruptured 136, *136*
glove removal 36
Goldstein, T.S. 207, 224, 304
Graham, L.S. 304
Grana, W.A. 157
Grandjean, A.C. 266
Gray, J.J. 86
Gray, R.S. 278
great toe sprain 74
greenstick fracture *17*
groin strain wrap. *See* adductor strain wrap
groin stretches 213, *214*
Gropper, Tracey 246

gross negligence 280, 296
growth plate. *See* epiphysis
guardians. *See* parents or guardians
Guskiewicz, K. 128
Guten, G.N. 304
gymnastics, cervical spine injuries in 103
gynecologists 273, 296

**H**
Hahn, D. 110
Hall, S. 78, 190, 240
Hall, S.J. 32, 303
hamstring muscles 80, *81*, 88, 296
hamstring stretches 213, *214*
hand
    anatomy of 159-160
    bones and joints of 159-160, *160*
    injuries to 159-164
    preventing 160
    treating 160-163
    muscles of 160
    protection for 186
hand washing 245
Hartley, A. 86, 304
Hawkesford, J.E. 140
Hawthorne, P. 128
hazards, checking for 283
HBV. *See* hepatitis B virus
head
    anatomy of 121-122
    protective equipment for 181-184
headgear 184, *185*
head injuries 121-128
    mechanisms of 123
    preventing 122-123
    treating 123-125
head posture 64
    forward 296
healing
    bone fracture 18
    soft tissue
        stages of 15
        time 15
health care administration 272
health clubs 276
heart 112-114
    interior of 112, *113*
    listening to 44
heart attack 33-34, 296
heart rate 40, 296
heat cramps 52, 297
heat exhaustion 52, 297
heat index 53, 297
    training standards *53*
heat loss 52-53
heat-related illness
    preventing 53-54
    preventive measures for 54
    types of 52
heat-related problems 51-54
heatstroke 52, 297
heat therapy
    indications and contraindications for *198*
    modalities 199
Heck, J. 149
Heck, J.F. 304
Hegarty, V. 266, 304
Heinzman, S.E. 292, 304
Heinzman, Suzy 139, 183
helmet removal 61, *61, 62*
helmets 182-183
    batting 182-183, *183*
    football 182, *182*
    hockey 183, *183*
    ice hockey 182
    in real world 183
Helms, L.B. 292, 304
hematoma
    intracranial 124-125
    subdural 125-126

hematoma auris. *See* cauliflower ear
hemiplegia 43, 297
hemophilia 237-238, 297
hemorrhage 34-35
    into anterior chamber (hyphema) 134
    subconjunctival 134
hemorrhagic or hypovolemic shock
    characteristics of *47*
    treating *48*
hemothorax 117-118, 297
Henderson, J. 229, 304
hepatitis B 246
hepatitis B virus (HBV) 297
hernias 108-109
herpes 244
high school 276
hinge joints 7, 297
hip
    anatomy of 87, *88*
    bone injuries of 89-90
    dislocations of 89-90, *90*
    injuries to 87-91
        preventing 88
        treating 88-90
    ligament injuries of 88
    muscle and tendon injuries of 88-89
    muscles of 87, *88*
    protection for 187-188
    reconditioning techniques for 213-215, *214*
hip and thigh muscle contusions 90
hip flexor strain wrap 177, *177*
history 39-44, 297
History, Inspection, and Testing. *See* HIT
history of injury, questions for 40
HIT (History, Inspection, and Testing) 39-45, *40*
HIV. *See* human immunodeficiency virus
hockey helmets 183, *183*
Hopkins, T.J. 104, 207
Hoppenfeld, S. 104
Houghlum, P.A. 304
Hugenholtz, H. 128
human immunodeficiency virus (HIV) 245-246, 297
humeral fractures 147
humerus 143, *144*, 151, *152*
Hunt, V.K. 278, 304
hyaline cartilage 7, 297
hybrid tape *168*, 168-169, 297
hydrocollator pack 199, *199*
hygiene 246
    hand washing *245*
hyperextension
    elbow 174, *174*
    knee *173*, 174, *174*
    thumb 175, *175*
    wrist 174-175, *175*
hyperflexion, wrist 174-175, *175*
hyperglycemia 235, 297
hypertension 236, 297
hyperthermia 51, 297
hyperventilation 32, 118, 297
hyphema 134, 297
hypoglycemia 235, 297
hypotension 236-237, 297
hypothermia 55, 297
hypovolemic shock
    characteristics of *47*
    treating *48*

**I**

ice hockey
    helmets 182
    shoulder pads 185, *186*
    throat injuries in 115
ice pack 200, *200*
illnesses 233-240
    heat-related 52
    summary 239
imagery 228
immediate care of injuries 271

immune system 241, 297
impetigo 244, 297
impingement syndrome 146-147, 297
IMPRESS program 196, *196*
incision *14*
indications 199
indigestion 234
industrial sites 277
infections, skin 243-245
inflammation, acute 15
influenza 243, 297
informed consent 281, 297
informed consent forms 284
infraspinatus 144, *144*
Ingersoll, C. *282*, 305
inguinal canal 109
injured athlete(s) 227-228
    access to 25-26
    assessing 193-195
    directing emergency services to 26
    lifting and moving 62-67, *63*
        from field of play 24-25
        proper procedures for 98, *99*
    notifying parents of 26
    practical suggestions for helping 228-229
    removal of equipment from 59-62
    "triage area" for 26
injuries
    to axial region 93-140
    of bladder 109
    bone 15-18
        of cervical spine 102
        of elbow 155
        of foot, ankle, and lower leg 75-76
        of knee 83-84
        of lumbar spine 100
        of shoulder 147-148
        of wrist and hand 163
    of brachial plexus 102-103
    of cervical spine 101-103
    cold-related 55
    disk 102
    documentation of 281
    of ear 136-137
    of elbow 151-157
    emotional response after 227
    environmental 51-58
    epiphyseal 147-148
        of distal tibia and fibula 76
    evaluation of 271, 275
    of eye 133-136
    facial 129-140
    of foot, ankle, and lower leg 71-78
    of head 121-128
    of hip, pelvis, and thigh 87-91
    history of 40
    immediate care of 271
    initial 196
    of kidney 108
    of knee 79-86
    life-threatening 30
    ligament
        of cervical spine 101
        of elbow 153
        of foot, ankle, and lower leg 74-75
        of hip, pelvis, and thigh 88
        of knee 82-83
        of lumbar spine 99
        of shoulder 145-146
        of wrist and hand 160-161
    of lower leg 71-78
    to lower quarter 69-91
    of lumbar spine 99-101
    meniscal 84
    of mouth 138
    muscle and tendon
        of cervical spine 101-102
        of elbow 153-154
        of foot, ankle, and lower leg 75

    of knee 83
    of lumbar spine 99-100
    of shoulder 146-147
    of wrist and hand 161-163
    of neck, sideline signal for *26*
    of nose 137-138
    of pancreas 108
    person in charge of assessment of 23
    preventing 165-190, 271, 283
    recognition, evaluation, and immediate
        care of 271
    rehabilitation and reconditioning of 191-
        230, 272
    of shoulder 143-149
    soft tissue 13-15, *14*
    spinal 95-104
    of throat and thorax 111-119
    tissue 13-20
    to upper quarter 141-164
    of wrist and hand 159-164
innovation 290
insect bites and stings 56-57, *57*
inspection 44
inspiration 290
insulin response 235, *235*
insulin shock 235-236, *236*, 297
insurance 285
integrity 289
intermittent compression 204, *204*, 297
    indications and contraindications for *201*
interphalangeal collateral ligament sprains
    161
interphalangeal joint 160
    dislocation of 161
intervertebral disks *96*, 96-97, 297
    cervical, injuries of 102
intracranial hematoma 124-125
inversion 7, 8, *10*, 297
iron-deficiency anemia 237
Irvin, R. *282*, 305
isokinetics 210-211, 298
isometrics 210, 298
isotonics 210, 298
    exercises 213-214, *214*

**J**

Jane, J. 128
jersey finger 162, 298
jerseys, removal of 60
Jimenez, C.C. 240
Johnson, B.C. 91, 304
joint capsule 7, 151, *152*, 298
joints
    amphiarthrodial 7
    ball-and-socket 7, 294
    classification of 7
    diarthrodial 7, 295
    fibrous 7
    flexibility of 212
    of foot, ankle, and lower leg 71-72
    of hand *160*
    hinge 7, 297
    multiaxial 7
    of shoulder *144*, 144-145
    synarthrodial 7
    of wrist and hand 159-160
Jones fracture 75, *76*, 298
jugular vein 111, 298

**K**

Kane, A.W. 303
Katch, F.I. 266, 304
Kehr's sign 107, 108, 298
Kendall, P.F. *46*, 50, 304
Kenna, K. 240, 304
Kennedy, R. 179, 304
Kerr, G. 230
Khelifa, M. 305
Khoo, D. 304
kidney injury 108

kinesiology 275, 298
Kisner, C. 224, 304
Klabunde, L.A. 91, 304
Kleiner, D.M. 68
Kloth, L.C. 20, 305
knee
    anatomy of 79-80
    bone injuries of 83-84
    bones of 79, 80
    cartilage of 79-80
    hyperextension 173, 174, 174
    injuries to 79-86
    preventing 81
    treating 82-84
    ligaments of 80, 80
    muscle and tendon injuries of 83
    muscles of 80
    protection for 188
    reconditioning techniques for 213-215, 214
knee braces 81, 81
Knight, K.L. 304
Knowx, K.E. 68
Koester, M.C. 292, 304
Kolthoff, N.J. 78, 303
Konin, Jeff 289
Konin, J.J. 46, 278, 292, 304
Kubler-Ross, E. 304
Kuland, D.N. 128, 190, 304
kyphosis 98, 298

**L**
laceration 14
    corneal 133
    of eyelid 135-136
    of pinna 136
    of throat 115
lactoovo-vegetarians 263
lacto-vegetarians 263
Lamb, D.R. 266
large intestine 106
Larson, J.P. 304
laryngitis 243, 298
larynx 111, 112, 298
lateral collateral ligament 80, 80
lateral collateral ligament injuries 83
lateral epicondylitis 155
lateral malleolus 72, 72, 298
lateral neck stretches 216, 217
lat pull-downs 216, 216
Lavallee, L. 230, 304
leadership 289-290
learning. See education
leg. See lower leg
legal issues 279-281
    avoiding problems 281-283
Legg-Calvé-Perthes disease 90, 298
leg raises, straight 213, 214
Lephart, S.M. 207, 304
leukocytes 15, 298
leukoplakia 251, 298
Leverenz, L.J. 292, 304
licensure 274, 298
life-threatening injuries 30
lifting and moving athletes 62-67, 63
    from field of play 24-25
    proper procedures for 98, 99
ligament injuries
    of cervical spine 101
    of elbow 153
    of foot, ankle, and lower leg 74-75
    of hip, pelvis, and thigh 88
    of knee 82-83
    of lumbar spine 99
    of shoulder 145-146
    of wrist and hand 160-161
ligaments 6, 298
    of elbow 151
    of foot, ankle, and lower leg 73, 73
    of knee 80, 80
    of shoulder 144

light, pupil response to 43, 43
lightning 56
linen tape 168, 168, 298
listening 44
Little League 114
Little League elbow 155, 298
liver contusions 109
local steroids 250, 298
location, medical terms of 3-4
longitudinal arch 72, 72, 170-171, 171
longitudinal fracture 16
lordosis 98, 298
low back protection 187
lower body, protective equipment for 187-189
lower leg
    anatomy of 71-73, 72
    bone injuries of 75-76
    bones of 71-72
    injuries of 71-78
        preventing 73-74
        treating 74-77
    ligaments of 73
    muscle and tendon injuries of 75
    muscles of 73, 73
    protection for 188
    reconditioning techniques for 213, 213
    stress fractures of 76
lower quarter
    athletics-related injuries to 69-91
    reconditioning techniques for 213, 213-215
Lueken, J.S. 305
lumbar (term) 298
lumbar spine 95, 96
    injuries and conditions of 99-101
lumbar stabilization exercises 216, 216
lumbar strength 216
lunate, dislocation of 161
lungs 112, 112-114

**M**
macular degeneration 251
Magee, D.J. 46, 304
mallet finger 162, 162
mandible 121, 122, 129, 130
    fracture of 138, 139
Mangus, B.C. 266, 305
manual muscle testing (MMT) 45
    strength-grading system 46
Marti, Steve 35
massage 203-204, 298
    friction 204, 296
    indications and contraindications for 201
    percussion 203, 203
    strokes 203, 203
    vibration 203, 302
mass casualty, available personnel for 26-27
mastoid process 122
matching 283
Mattalino, A.J. 157, 304
maxilla 122, 129, 130
    fracture of 138
Maxwell, R.E. 304
McConkey, J. 86
McCreary, E.K. 46, 50, 304
McCulloch, J.M. 20, 305
McGuine, T. 110
McKenzie, D. 86
McWhorter, J.M. 128
meals
    during all-day events 263
    portions 260
    postgame 263
    pregame 263
measles (rubeola) 242, 300
measles, German. See rubella
mechanical elements 200-204
    indications and contraindications for 201
medial collateral ligament 80, 80

medial collateral ligament sprains
    mild 82
    moderate 82
    severe 82
    treating 82-83
medial epicondylitis 155
medial malleolus 72, 72, 298
medial tibial stress syndrome 76
medical conditions 233-240
    blood-borne 245-246
    of blood system 236-238
    of gastrointestinal tract 234
    neurological 238
    respiratory 243
    of respiratory tract 233-234
    of vascular system 236-238
medical information
    appropriate and complete 283
    forms 284-285
medical terms
    directional 7, 10
    of location 3-4
meningitis, aseptic 243, 294
meniscectomy 84, 298
menisci (meniscus) 79, 298
    injuries to 84
metabolic shock
    characteristics of 47
    treating 48
metabolism 257, 298
metacarpal bones 159, 160
metacarpal phalangeal joints 160, 160
    dislocation of 161
metatarsal arch 72, 72
metatarsal bones 72, 298
microorganisms 241, 298
    defending against 241-242
military press 217, 219
Miller, A.E. 266, 305
Miller, D.K. 224
Minden, H. 230
minerals 259
"mirror muscles" 145
MMT. See manual muscle testing
mobility restoration 196-197
modeling 228
moleskin 168, 169, 298
molluscum contagiosum 244, 298
money 23-24
Montana, L.N. 305
Moss, C.L. 276, 278, 305
motion. See range of motion
Mottram, D.R. 305
mouth 112, 132
    fracture of 138
    injuries to 138
mouth guards 184, 184
mouth-to-mouth breathing 32
movement 7-9
    ability to move 43
    ambulatory 64-65
    directional terms for 7, 10
    false 44
    after splinting 47
    types of 210-211
moving athletes 62-67, 63
    in emergency 62, 63
    from field of play 24-25
    methods for 65-67
Mueller, F.O. 128, 305
multiaxial joints 7, 298
mumps 242, 298
muscle injuries
    of cervical spine 101-102
    contusions, of hip and thigh 90
    of elbow 153-154
    of foot, ankle, and lower leg 75
    of hip, pelvis, and thigh 88-89
    of knee 83

muscle injuries (cont.)
of lumbar spine 99-100
of shoulder 146-147
tears 77
of wrist and hand 161-163
muscle relaxation 228-229
muscles 6, 8, 9
abdominal 107
of elbow 152, 152
of foot, ankle, and lower leg 73, 73
of hip 87, 88
of knee 80
reconditioning exercises for 212-220
rotator cuff 144, 144
of shoulder 144
of spine 97
"two-joint muscles" 154
of wrist and hand 160
muscle testing, manual 45
strength-grading system 46
muscular development programs 211-212
muscular endurance 212, 298
muscular power 212, 298
muscular strength 211-212, 299
muscular weakness 145
myositis ossificans 90, 299

**N**

nasal bone 122, 129, 130
nasal fractures 138
NATA. See National Athletic Trainers'
Association
National Athletic Trainers' Association (NATA)
271, 292, 299, 305
Board of Certification (NATABOC) 289
code of ethics 289
web page 278
National Cattlemen's Beef Association 267
National Operating Committee on Standards
for Athletic Equipment (NOCSAE) 181, 299
National Safety Council 271, 299
neck. See also cervical spine
injury to, sideline signal for 26
protection for 184
neck rolls 184, 299
removal of 60-61
neck stretches, lateral 216, 217
necrosis, avascular 163, 294
negligence 280
definition of 299
gross 280, 296
Nelson, F. 164, 303
Nelson, W.J. 128
nerve root impingement 293
neurological conditions 238
neurological shock
characteristics of 47
treating 48
neurological testing 45
neurologist 273, 299
neutral spine 95, 299
Nieman, D.C. 240
911. See emergency medical system
Nirschl, R.P. 305
NOCSAE. See National Operating Committee
on Standards for Athletic Equipment
nonsteroidal anti-inflammatory drugs 250, 299
nonunion fractures 18, 299
nose 131-132
injuries to 137-138
nosebleed. See epistaxis
nose guards 184
notifying parents or guardians 26
nucleus pulposus 96, 96, 299
nutrients 257, 299
major 257-260
nutrition 257-267, 275, 299
athletic 262-264
summary 264-265
nutritional supplements 264

**O**

obesity 261-262
objective information 195
oblique fracture 17
obliques 8, 97, 107
obstruction, airway 32-33
partial 33, 299
total 33, 302
occipital lobe 121, 122
Ollivierre, C.O. 305
one-person carry 65, 66
open basket weave 171-172, 172
orbital roof fracture 135
organization and administration 275, 299
Orlick, T. 230
orthopedists 272, 299
Osgood-Schlatter disorder 84, 299
Osowski, S. 91, 303
osteogenesis 18
osteoporosis 18
otitis externa (swimmer's ear) 137, 301
overload principle 210, 299
Oxford technique 211
oxygenation 112

**P**

padding
protective 145
removal of 62
securing 168
pain, response to 43-44
palpation 44, 299
order of 44
pancreas injury 108
paralysis 43, 299
paraplegia 43, 299
parents or guardians 272
notifying 26
Pargman, D. 230, 305
parietal lobe 121, 122
Paris, S.V. 305
partial airway obstruction 33, 299
participation
preparticipation physical examinations
281, 284
proper matching and 283
return to play
after burner 103
requirements for 101
Partin, N.B. 305
passive range of motion (PROM) 196, 299
patella 79, 80, 81
dislocation of 83-84
fracture of 83
patellar femoral syndrome 83
patella tendon rupture 83
pathological fracture 17
Pauls, J.A. 198, 201, 205, 305
pay phones 23-24
PCL. See posterior cruciate ligament
Pearl, B. 224
pediatrician 273, 299
Peltrone, F.A. 305
pelvis 107
anatomy of 87, 88
bone injuries of 89-90
injuries to 87-91
treating 88-90
ligament injuries of 88
muscle and tendon injuries of 88-89
reconditioning techniques for 213-215, 214
pendulum exercises 217, 219
percussion/tapotement massage 203, 203, 299
performance-enhancing drugs 252-253
permission to treat 281, 282
Perrin, D. 128
personnel available for mass casualty 26-27
Peterson, K. 266, 305
Peterson, M. 266, 305

petrissage 203, 203, 299
Pfeiffer, R.P. 266, 305
phagocytes 15, 299
phalanges 71, 72, 159, 160, 299
pharmacology 275, 299. See also drugs
phlegm 113, 299
physical environment 228
physical examinations, preparticipation 281,
284
physical fitness 283
physical function, components of 195, 195
physical therapist 273, 299
physicians
primary care 273, 300
sideline signal for 26
team 18, 272, 301
physics 275, 299
physiology 275, 299
basics of 1-20
exercise 275
human 275
Pincivero, D.M. 207, 304
pinna, laceration of 136
Pioneer High School 287
Pitney, Bill 43, 222, 274
Pitney, Lisa V. 83
Pitney, W.A. 303
plan of action 195
plantar surface 299
platelets 15, 299
pneumonia 41
pneumothorax 116, 300
spontaneous 116
tension 116-117, 117
podiatrists 273, 300
Porterfield, J.A. 104, 305
portions 260
postconcussion syndrome 125
posterior cruciate ligament (PCL) injuries 80,
80, 82, 300
posterior disk bulge 100, 100
post-traumatic response 226, 300
posture 97-98
abnormal 98
forward head 98, 296
head 64
normal 97, 97-98
power, muscular 212, 298
PRE. See progressive resistive exercise
precautions
necessary 36
rationale for 35-36
universal 36, 302
PREMIER model 290, 290, 300
Prentice, W.E. 179, 190, 207, 303, 305
preparticipation physical examinations 281
administering 284
example stations for 284
press relations 27
pressure, direct 35
pressure point 35, 300
preventing injuries 165-190, 271, 283
PRICE method 48, 300
Priest, J.D. 304
primary assessment 30-31, 300
order of 30
primary care physician 273, 300
Pritchett, J. 86
professional aspects 269-292
professional development 272, 289-290
aspects of 279-292
PREMIER model for 290, 290, 300
summary 291
professional education 289
professional image 290
professional practice 290
professional responsibility 272
professional teams 276
progression 195, 198, 300

progressive resistive exercise (PRE) 209-210, 300
PROM. *See* passive range of motion
pronation 7, 8, *10,* 300
proprioception 197, 300
protective equipment 181-190
    basic principles of 181
    for elbow, wrist, and hand 186
    for eye 184
    for foot and ankle 188-189
    for head and face 181-184, 184
    for knee 188
    for low back 187
    for lower body 187-189
    for lower leg 188
    for rib, sternum, and abdominal 186-187
    for shoulder and upper arm 185-186
    for thigh, hip, and tailbone 187-188
    for throat and neck 184
    for upper body 184-187
protective padding 145
protective taping and wrapping 167-179
proteins 258, *258*
protraction 7, 8, *10,* 300
Provance, P.G. *46, 50,* 304
proximal (term) 300
proximal interphalangeal joints 160, *160*
proximal phalanges 159, *160*
proximate cause 281, 300
psychogenic shock
    characteristics of *47*
    treating *48*
psychological assistance 168
psychology 275, 300
    and athletics 226-227
    and athletic training 225-230
    sport 225, 301
pulmonary contusions 117
pulse points 40, 300
pulse pressure 41, 300
pulse rate 40, 300
puncture *14*
pupil response 43, *43*
pustules *244*
Putukian, M. 128
pyramid method *211,* 211-212, 300

**Q**
quadriceps muscles 80, *81*
quadriceps stretches 213, *214*
quadriplegia 43, 300
questions for history of injury 40
Quillen, W.S. *198, 201, 205,* 305

**R**
radial collateral ligament 151, *152*
radial collateral ligament sprains 153
radius 151, *152*
range of motion (ROM)
    active 196, 293
    active-assistive 196, 293
    passive 196, 299
    restoring 196
    testing 44-45
Rankin, J.M. *282,* 305
Rawlins, R.P. 305
Ray, R. *292,* 305
reconditioning 191-230, 272, 300
reconditioning exercises 212-220
reconditioning programs 209-224
reconditioning techniques
    for axial region 215-216
    for elbow, wrist, and hand 220
    for foot, ankle, and lower leg 213, *213*
    for knee, hip, and pelvis 213-215, *214*
    for lower quarter *213,* 213-215
    for shoulder 217
    for upper quarter 216-220
recreational drugs 250-252, 300
rectus abdominis *8,* 97

rectus femoris 80, *81*
Reed, K.L. *198, 201, 205,* 305
Rees, A.M. 248, 305
reflection 290
registered dietitians 274
registration 274, 300
rehabilitation 191-230, 272
    concepts of 193-207
    definition of 300
    in real world 197
    summary 206
rehabilitation charts 285, *288*
rehabilitation program 196, *196*
relaxation 228-229
remodeling 15
repair 15
reports and charts 285
reproductive organs 106-107
resistance training 197, 300
resisted cervical movements 216, *217*
resistive exercise, progressive 209-210, 300
respiratory arrest 31
respiratory conditions 243
respiratory shock
    characteristics of *47*
    treating *48*
respiratory tract conditions 233-234
responsiveness 30-31
retina, detached 133, 295
retraction 7, 8, *10,* 300
return to play
    after burner 103
    requirements for 101
ribs
    fractures of 115-116
    protection for 186-187
Rich, B.E. 278
Richard, M.T. 128
risk, assumption of 280
Robinson, John 19
ROM. *See* range of motion
rotation 7, 9, *10,* 300
rotator cuff 300
rotator cuff muscles 144, *144*
rotator cuff strain 146
Roy, S. *282,* 305
rubella (German measles) 243, 300
rubeola 242, 300
rule enforcement 283
running, cross-country 27
rupture
    of biceps tendon 147
    of globe 136, *136*
    of patella tendon 83
    of spleen 107-108
    of ulnar collateral fragment 154
Ryan, E.J. 305
Ryan, J. *46,* 305

**S**
sacrum 95, *96,* 300
Safar, P. 305
safety 221-222
    checking for hazards 283
    standards for equipment 281
sagittal plane 3, *4,* 301
salary, starting 276
Saunders, H.D. 305
Saunders, R. 305
scalp 122
scaphoid bone 159, *160*
scapula 143, *144*
scholastic environments 275-276
school nurse 274, 301
Schwartz, G. 305
scoliosis 98, 301
scoop stretcher 67, *67*
Seaward, B.L. 230, 305
secondary assessment 30

secondary procedures 39-50
    PRICE method 48, 300
second impact syndrome 125, 301
Seeley, R.R. 12, 305
seizures 238, 301
semimembranosus 80, *81*
semitendinosus 80, *81*
semi-vegetarians *263*
Sennett, B. 128
septic shock
    characteristics of *47*
    treating *48*
septum, deviated 138
sesamoids 72, *72*
Sevier, T. 240, 248, 306
Sherman, M.W. 266
shinsplints 76, 301
    taping for 172-173, *173*
shock 41, 45-46
    anaphylactic *47, 48*
    cardiogenic *47, 48*
    hemorrhagic or hypovolemic *47, 48*
    insulin 235-236, *236,* 297
    metabolic *47, 48*
    neurologic *48*
    neurological *47*
    psychogenic *47, 48*
    recognizing 45-46
    respiratory *47, 48*
    septic *47, 48*
    signs of 46
    treating 46-47, *48*
    types of *47*
short boarding 63-64, *65*
    procedure for 64
shoulder
    anatomy of 143-145
    bones and ligaments of *144*
    injuries to 143-149
        preventing 145
        treating 145-148
    joints of 144-145
    muscles of 144
    protection for 185-186
    reconditioning techniques for 217, *219*
    separation of 145-146, *146,* 301
shoulder pads
    football 184, *185*
    ice hockey 185, *186*
    removal of 60, *60*
shoulder shrugs 216, *217*
shoulder spica 178, *178*
shoulder stretches 217, *218*
sickle-cell anemia 237, *237,* 301
sideline signals 24, *26*
side stitch 109
signs and signals 30, 301
    sideline signals 24, *26*
    universal choking sign 33, *33,* 302
sinuses 129, *130*
sinus fracture 135
SITS (Subscapularis, Infraspinatus, Teres minor, and Supraspinatus) 144, *144,* 301
skeleton
    appendicular 5, 294
    axial 5, 294
skin 4-5
    preparation for tape 169-170
skin closure 15
skin color 42
skin infections 243-245
skin lesions *244*
skull
    bones of 121, *122*
    fractures of 123
Sluijs, E.A. 305
"sneezers" 36
SOAP (Subjective Objective Assessment and Plan) notes 193-195, *194,* 301

soft tissue injuries 13-15, *14*
   acute inflammatory 15
   healing stages 15
   healing time 15
   remodeling 15
   repair 15
Solari, A. 305
soleus *9, 73*
Sparano, J. 149
specificity 301
spica 175
spinal injuries 95-104
   preventing 98-99
spinal traction 202, *203*
spinal vertebra, extra 10
spine
   anatomy of 95-97, *96*
   bones in 95-96
   cervical 95, *96*
      injuries and conditions of 101-103
   compressing 101
   extension movements of 215, *215*
   flexion movements of 215, *215*
   lumbar 95, *96*
      injuries and conditions of 99-101
   muscles of 97
   neutral 95, 299
   thoracic 95, *96*
Spinner, R.J. 304
spiral fracture *16*
spleen, rupture of 107-108
splinting, moving after 47
splints
   aluminum *48*
   board *48*
   finger *48*
   sideline signal for *26*
   types of 47, *48*
   vacuum *48*
spontaneous pneumothorax 116
sport psychologists 225
sport psychology 225, 301
sports. *See also* athletics
   therapeutic drugs in 249-250
sports medicine 272-274, 301
sports medicine clinic 276, *276*
sports medicine team 23, *272*, 272-274, 301
   central 272-273
   members of 272-273, 273-274
   participation in 290
   peripheral 273-274
   questions to answer 23-27
sport-specific function 197-198, 301
sprains 13. *See also* injuries
   acromioclavicular ligament 145-146
   ankle 74
   arch 74
   cervical spine 101
   collateral knee ligament 173, *173*
   definition of 301
   glenohumeral ligament 146
   great toe 74
   interphalangeal collateral ligament 161
   medial collateral ligament 82-83
   radial collateral ligament 153
   ulnar collateral ligament 153
   wrist 160-161
stability 167
standards
   heat index training *53*
   of practice 301
Starkey, C. *46, 198, 201, 205*, 305
starting salary 276
statements from witnesses 27
static stretching 212, 301
Steele, M.K. 305
Steele, V. 50
Stein, A. 164
Steinmuller, P. 305

Stephens, T.D. 12, 305
Stephenson, J.N. 266
sternal fractures 116
sternum protection 186-187
steroids
   anabolic 252-253, 293
   local 250, 298
Stethem, L. 128
"stinger" *102*, 102-103, 301
stings 56-57, *57*
stitches 160
Stith, W.J. 104, 305
Stone, J. 305
Stone, J.A. 305
Storey, P. 305
straight leg raises 213, *214*
strains 13, 301. *See also* injuries; sprains
   adductor (groin) 176-177
   elbow extensor 154
   elbow flexor 154
   hip flexor 177, *177*
   rotator cuff 146
   wrist extensor 154-155
   wrist flexor 154
Straub, C.P. 304
Straub, S.J. 278, 305
strength(s)
   lumbar 216
   maximizing 290
   muscular 211-212, 299
   principles of 209-210
strength testing 45, *46*
strength training
   exercises for wrist and elbow 220, *220*
   pyramid method *211*, 211-212, 300
stress fractures
   of hip, pelvis, and thigh 89
   of lower leg and foot 76
stretcher 65-66
   scoop 67, *67*
stretches and stretching
   ballistic 212, 294
   calf 213, *213*
   groin 213, *214*
   hamstring 213, *214*
   lateral neck 216, *217*
   quadriceps 213, *214*
   shoulder 217, *218*
   static 212, 301
   trunk rotation 215, *215*
   types of 212
   wrist extensor and flexor 220, *220*
student assistants 273, 301
Stuss, D.T. 128
subconjunctival hemorrhage 134
subdural hematoma 125-126
subjective information 193
subluxations, glenohumeral 148
subscapularis 144, *144*
sucking chest wound 118, *118*
suicide 226-227
   warning signs of 226
supination 7, 8, *10*, 301
supplies 24
   emergency 26
support 167
supraspinatus 144, *144*
surgery, arthroscopic 84, 294
suture 121, *122*
swimmer's ear 137, 301
symptoms 30, 301
synarthrodial joints 7, 301
syncope 34, 301
synovial membrane 7, 301
systolic pressure 41, 301

**T**
tailbone protection 187-188
talus 72, *72*, 301

tape
   elastic 168, *168*, 296
   handling 169
   hybrid *168*, 168-169, 297
   linen 168, *168*, 298
   proper use of 168-170
   selection of 168-169
   types of *168*, 168-169
taping
   Achilles tendon 172, *173*
   "buddy taping" 175, *176*
   closed basket weave 171, *172*
   collateral knee 173, *173*
   elbow hyperextension 174, *174*
   finger sprains 175, *176*
   indications for 167-168
   knee hyperextension *173*, 174, *174*
   longitudinal arch 170-171, *171*
   open basket weave 171-172, *172*
   principles of 167-170
   protective 167-179
   for shinsplints 172-173, *173*
   skin preparation for 169-170
   techniques for 170-175
   thumb hyperextension 175, *175*
   turf-toe 170, *170*
   wrist hyperextension and hyperflexion 174-175, *175*
tapotement massage 203, *203*
Tate, P. 12, 305
Taunton, D. 86
team physician 18, 272, 301
telephone calls
   for ambulance 24
   emergency phone numbers 23-24
   emergency telephone contacts 25
   money for pay phone 23-24
temperature, body 42, 294
Templin, J.M. 12, 305
temporal lobe 121, *122*
temporomandibular dislocation 138-139
tendinitis 162, 301
   Achilles 75
   bicipital 147
tendon injuries
   of cervical spine 101-102
   of elbow 153-154
   of foot, ankle, and lower leg 75
   of hip, pelvis, and thigh 88-89
   of knee 83
   of shoulder 146-147
   of wrist and hand 161-163
tendons 6, 301
tennis elbow 155, 301
tension pneumothorax 116-117
   signs of *117*
teres minor 144, *144*
terminology
   directional 7, *10*
   of location 3-4
TES. *See* transcutaneous electrical stimulation
testing 44
   manual muscle 45
   neurological 45
   range of motion 44-45
   strength 45
therapeutic (term) 195
therapeutic drugs 249-250, 302
therapeutic modalities 198-205
   categorization of 198
thermal elements 198-200
   indications and contraindications for *198*
Thibodeau, G.A. 12, 86, 303
thigh
   anatomy of 87
   bone injuries of 89-90
   injuries to 87-91
      treating 88-90
   ligament injuries of 88

muscle and tendon injuries of 88-89
  protection for 187-188
thigh muscle contusions 90
thigh wrap 176, *177*
Thomas, C.L. 240, 248, 305
thoracic spine 95, *96*
thorax
  anatomy of *112*, 112-114
  injuries to 111-119
    preventing 114-115
    treatment considerations for 115-118
throat
  anatomy of 111, *112*
  injuries to 111-119
    in ice hockey 115
    preventing 114-115
    treating 115
  lacerations of 115
  protection for 184
thumb hyperextension 175, *175*
thunder and lightning 56
  helpful hints for sudden storms 56
Timm, K.E. 305
tinnitus 124, 302
tissue injury 13-20. *See also* injuries
tobacco 251
toes
  great toe sprain 74
  turf-toe 170, *170*
Tomberlin, J.P. 305
tooth 132, *132*
  dislocation of 139
  fractured 139
Torg, J.S. 128, 140, 305
tornadoes 56
total airway obstruction 33, 302
trachea 111, *112*, 302
traction 202-203, 302
  indications and contraindications for *201*
  spinal 202, *203*
training
  athletic 294
    as profession 271-278
    professional and administrative aspects
      of 269-292
    psychology and 225-230
  circuit 212, 295
  constant set method *211*
  DeLorme method *211*, 212
  heat index standards *53*
  Oxford technique *211*
  pyramid method *211*, 211-212, *300*
  resistance 197, *300*
  specificity of 210
  weight 222
training kit, sideline signal for *26*
transcutaneous electrical stimulation (TES)
  204, *205*, 302
transporting athletes 62-67, *63*
  from field of play 24-25
  methods for 65-67
  proper procedures for lifting 98, *99*
transverse arch 72, *72*
transverse plane 3, *4*, 302
trauma, post-traumatic response 226, *300*
treatment
  endurance phase 197
  initial injury phase 196
  mobility restoration phase 196-197
  phases of 195-198
  proprioception phase 197

resistance training phase 197
  sport-specific function phase 197-198
treatment logs 285, *287*
triage 26, 302
"triage area" 26
triceps 152, *152*
triceps pull-downs 220, *221*
Trowbridge, C.A. 240
trunk rotation stretch 215, *215*
trust 281
turf-toe 170, *170*
"two-joint muscles" 154
two-person carry 65, *66*

**U**
ulcers *244*
ulna 151, *152*
  dislocation of 155-156
ulnar collateral fragment rupture 154
ulnar collateral ligament 151, *152*
ulnar collateral ligament sprain 153
Ulrich, G. 91, 303
ultrasound 200-202, *202*, 302
  indications and contraindications for *201*
  indirect 202, *202*
unconscious athletes 30
Underwood, F.B. *198, 201, 205,* 305
uniforms, removal of 62
United States Department of Agriculture 267
United States Government Printing Office 240,
  255, 267
United States Olympic Committee 253
universal choking sign 33, *33*, 302
universal precautions 36, 302
  rules for 36
upper arm protection 185-186
upper body exercises 221, *222*
upper body protection 184-187
upper quarter
  athletics-related injuries to 141-164
  reconditioning techniques for 216-220
upper trapezius 97
urinary organs 106
urologists 273, 302
U.S. Department of Health and Human
  Services 248, 305

**V**
Vaccaro, P. 305
vaccinations 242, 302
vacuum splint *48*
Van Camp, S.P. 128, 305
vascular system, conditions of 236-238
vastus intermedius 80, *81*
vastus lateralis 80, *81*
vastus medialis 80, *81*
vegans *263*
vegetarians *263*
Vegso, J. 128
veins 112
ventricles 112, *113,* 302
vertebra(e) 95-96, *96*
  body 96, *96*
    spinous process 96, *96*
    transverse process 96, *96*
vesicles *244*
vibration massage 203, 302
viral diseases 242-243
vision 289-290, *290*
vital signs 40, 302
vitamin C overdose 253
vitamins 259

volar (term) 162
Voorhis, Phil 57, 77, 283

**W**
Wagner, D. 305
walking
  ambulatory movement of athletes 64-65
  wall walking 217, *218*
wall push-ups 220, *220*
  with ball 216, *218*
wall squats 214, *214*
wall walking 217, *218*
Waman, D. 305
wand exercises 217, *218*
Wann, D.L. 230, 306
Warner, M.J. 292, 303
water 259-260
weather
  helpful hints for sudden storms 56
  severe 56
Weidner, T. 240, 248, 306
weight control 257-267
weight training 222
Weis, C.R. 304
Weis, M.P. 304
whirlpool 199, *199,* 302
White, A.A. 104, 207
White, J. 50
Whitehill, W.R. 179, 306
Whiteside, J.A. 157, 303
Wildermuth, B.P. 86
Williams, M. 306
Williams, M.H. 266, 306
witnesses, statements from 27
wobble boards *213*
Wolfe, S.A. 140
wound healing
  in diabetics 19
  stages of 15
  time 15
wounds, sucking chest 118, *118*
wrapping
  elastic 175-178
  protective 167-179
wraps, elastic 175, *176*, 296
wrestling headgear 184, *185*
Wright, K.E. 179, 306
wrist
  anatomy of 159-160
  bones and joints of 159-160
  hyperextension and hyperflexion of 174-
    175, *175*
  injuries to 159-164
    preventing 160
    treating 160-163
  muscles of *152*, 160
  protection for 186
  sprains 160-161
  strengthening exercises for 220, *220*
wrist extensor strains 154-155
wrist extensor stretch 220, *220*
wrist flexors 152, *152*
wrist flexor strains 154
wrist flexor stretch 220, *220*
written contracts 281

**X**
X rays 302

**Z**
Zairns, B.J. 149
zygomatic bone 129, *130*

# About the Authors

**Lorin Cartwright**, MS, ATC, EMT, is assistant principal and athletic director at Pioneer High School in Ann Arbor, Michigan. As a teacher and the school's head athletic trainer for 14 years, she has extensive experience with all aspects of student athletic trainer instruction.

She won the Most Distinguished Athletic Trainer Award from the Michigan Athletic Trainers Society in 1998 and the National Service Award from the National Athletic Trainers' Association in 1997.

Cartwright is the author of the best-selling book *Preparing for the Athletic Trainers' Certification Exam*. She was the first woman and first high school athletic trainer to serve as the president of the Great Lakes Athletic Trainers' Association.

Cartwright earned a bachelor's degree in physical education from Grand Valley State College in 1979 and a master's degree in Education from the University of Michigan in 1981.

**William Pitney**, MS, ATC, is an athletic training instructor at Northern Illinois University. He has been a certified athletic trainer since 1988 and has experience in clinical, high school, and college settings. He has been an athletic training instructor since 1994.

Pitney serves as a consultant for the Northern Illinois Student Athletic Training Association. He has been published in the Journal of Athletic Training and has twice been named the first runner-up for best clinical article.

Pitney earned a bachelor's degree in physical education with a specialization in athletic training from Indiana State University in 1988 and a master's degree in physical education from Eastern Michigan University in 1992.